PERSECUTION

PERSECUTION

How Liberals Are Waging War Against Christianity

DAVID LIMBAUGH

Cataloging-in-Publication Data on file with the Library of Congress.

ISBN 0-89526-111-1

Published in the United States by
Regnery Publishing, Inc.
An Eagle Publishing Company
One Massachusetts Avenue, NW
Washington, DC 20001

Visit us at www.regnery.com

Distributed to the trade by
National Book Network
4720-A Boston Way
Lanham, MD 20706
Printed on acid-free paper
Manufactured in the United States of America

10 9 8 7 6 5 4 3

Books are available in quantity for promotional or premium use. Write to Director of Special Sales, Regnery Publishing, Inc., One Massachusetts Avenue, NW, Washington, DC 20001, for information on discounts and terms, or call (202) 216-0600.

To my son, Scott Armstrong Limbaugh

I WANT TO THANK REGNERY PUBLISHING for its confidence in and support of this project. I am grateful to my principal editor, Rick Pearcey, for excellent suggestions throughout. He was a pleasure to work with, extremely diligent and responsive, and the final product was much improved by his efforts. Harry Crocker was also extraordinarily helpful in the editing process, as always, and helped to tighten the language in the earlier chapters in particular. Harry was a believer in this book from the beginning and was of invaluable assistance, from the initial outline to the final product. Thanks also to Rowena Itchon for valuable research assistance. I also want to thank Trish Bozell for her magical touches in the closing phases. During the final weeks, Paula Decker proofread and edited masterfully and patiently, and graciously endured my endless last-minute changes right down to the deadline.

I want to thank Greg Mueller and his Creative Response Concepts for their support and assistance. And I thank Brannon Howse with Worldview Weekend for providing me background materials and helping to put me in touch with various other people and resources. I also want to thank Liberty Counsel's Mathew Staver and the Rutherford Institute's John Whitehead for helping to clarify important points about various cases their fine organizations worked on for the cause of religious liberty. I also appreciate Wallbuilders and David Barton for providing me with materials. I thank Karen England of

Capitol Resource Institute for assistance in clarifying certain troublesome California legislation. My thanks to Greg Hoadley of the Center for Reclaiming America for helping me sort through some of that legislation as well and for helping to introduce me to Dr. D. James Kennedy. Jerry Newcombe was also helpful in introducing me to Dr. Kennedy and in providing certain background materials on America's Christian origin. I am appreciative of my friend Randy Black's sharp eye for current examples of discrimination and for forwarding me news stories as he encountered them.

I am very grateful for the participation of some of America's most influential Christians in the final chapter of this book: Dr. James Dobson, Dr. Michael Novak, Dr. Marvin Olasky, Dr. Ravi Zacharias, Nancy Pearcey, and Dr. D. James Kennedy. It is an honor to have their thoughts within the covers of my book. I am also very grateful to some of their assistants for helping to facilitate these interviews: Mary Anne Bunker for Dr. Kennedy, Ron Reno for Dr. Dobson, Michael Leaser for Dr. Novak, and my friend Danielle DuRant for helping with the Dr. Zacharias interview and for a host of other things.

Special thanks to my good friend Sean Hannity for listening and for his support and ideas throughout the project.

I remain grateful to Ann Coulter for her invaluable advice when I was writing my first book, *Absolute Power.* That advice proved just as helpful for this book and will guide me through any books I do in the future. I also want to thank the following friends for their support and guidance during the project: Mark Levin, Phyllis Schlafly, Michelle Malkin, and Emily Costello.

And, I want to thank my friends Pastor Ron Watts, Associate Pastor Rob Mehner, and Dr. Steve Johnson for spiritual nourishment and mentorship.

As always, I thank my brother, Rush, for his inspiration and support on this and all other projects I pursue.

Finally, book projects demand a grueling work schedule, and most of all I am indebted to my wife, Lisa, and the kids for their perennial encouragement, support, and patience.

Contents

Introduction

THIS BOOK CHRONICLES discrimination against Christians in American society. While tolerance is touted as the highest virtue in our popular culture, Christians are often subjected to scorn and ridicule and denied their religious freedoms. In no way does this book mean to imply that other groups are not subjected to discrimination or to deny the seriousness of that discrimination. The difference, however, is that it seems that when other groups (or individuals from those groups) experience discrimination or mistreatment the popular culture properly decries it. But when it comes to anti-Christian discrimination, the culture's attitude seems to be, "Yes, please do shut up those Bible-thumping idiots!"

Anti-Christian discrimination occurs in a variety of contexts throughout our culture, from the public sector to the private sector, in the mainstream media and in Hollywood, in the public education system and in our universities. Often the discrimination comes from activist judges misinterpreting the law (the hostility to Christian religious freedom infects our judiciary as much as anywhere else); other times it comes from entities misapplying the law. It also comes from what we call "political correctness." The discrimination mostly stems from a hostility to Christianity and from rampant disinformation in our society about what the Constitution actually requires in terms of the so-called "separation of church and state."

Though there is a significant body of law safeguarding religious liberties, the law is not always followed—even when the courts interpret it correctly (in accordance with the framers' original intent). Now, it is also true that though the courts, including the Supreme Court, have often ruled directly against the obvious original intent of the Constitution, I can't always say their rulings are unconstitutional. Why? Because the law *is what the highest court says it is*. Even if it's wrong, the court is the final arbiter. What I can say is that these rulings *ought* to be seen by the Court as unconstitutional. This highlights why the appointment of Supreme Court justices and other appellate judges who hold to the original intent of the Constitution is so vital to the preservation of our liberties. When we cast our ballots for politicians, we should think about that.

Anti-Christian discrimination in our society is getting more blatant and more widespread every day. The cultural assumptions of our society influence changes in the law, and the culture is moving against the public expression of Christian belief. The famous prayer case we discuss later, *Engel v. Vitale* (1962), could not have occurred at any other time in our history. And since 1962, the wedge of secularism against the public expression of Christianity has been driven much, much farther.

The fundamental issue, as mentioned earlier, is that people freely throw around phrases, such as the "separation of church and state," without understanding their true meaning, especially under the Constitution as originally written. So let's establish a few basic facts.

First, we must recognize that the framers believed that religious freedom was of paramount importance; it was a primary reason for emigration to America. Religious freedom was so important to them that they sought to guaranty it by the placement of two separate clauses in the very first amendment to the Constitution. The First Amendment begins with the two clauses back to back: "Congress shall make no law respecting an establishment of religion, or prohibiting the free exercise thereof..." The first clause is known as "The Establishment Clause" and the second, the "Free Exercise Clause."

You'll note there is no language in either—or anywhere else in the Constitution—mandating a wall of separation between church and state. That phrase, as we'll see in Chapter One, comes from a letter of Thomas Jefferson, several years after the Constitution and Bill of Rights were well in place. Moreover, the phrase has been taken out of context, distorting what Jefferson meant. Nevertheless, those advocating a strict separation (often referred to in this book as "separationists"), point to the "Establishment Clause" as evidence the framers intended a strict separation.

But it's important to understand that both clauses, the Establishment Clause and the Free Exercise Clause, were adopted by the framers for the explicit purpose of *promoting*, not suppressing religious freedom. That may be obvious with the Free Exercise Clause—its literal language says as much—but people tend to overlook it with the Establishment Clause. The purpose of the Establishment Clause was to prevent the *federal* government from establishing a particular denominational religion that would serve to inhibit our religious freedoms; it was not intended to keep Christianity out of the public square. Yet today the Establishment Clause is routinely used to suppress people's free exercise rights of religion in our schools and in public life.

Of course, one of the problems of applying original intent analysis to these issues is that the relationship between government and education today is radically different from how it was at the time of the nation's founding.

In the first place, the Establishment Clause only restricted the federal government, not the states. Its language makes that quite clear, "Congress shall make no law..." At the time of the ratification of the First Amendment, many states in fact had state-established religions. There is no better evidence—besides its plain language—that the Establishment Clause was never intended to prevent state governments from establishing their own religions. Again, the language of the clause is instructive. "Congress shall make no law *respecting* an establishment of religion." That clearly meant that the federal government was precluded from establishing a national religion, but also that the federal government was precluded from interfering with the right of individual states to do as they pleased *respecting* the establishment of their own religions. Later, of course, the Fourteenth Amendment was ratified and the Supreme Court, in a series of abhorrent decisions we will discuss later, ruled that the First Amendment Establishment Clause was applicable to the states through incorporation in the Due Process Clause of the Fourteenth Amendment.

While there is no question that these decisions were gross examples of judicial activism and that the Fourteenth Amendment was never intended to constitute a federal restriction on the state's right to establish a religion, these precedents are now the law of the land. Worse, though, is that as government has grown, so too have its restrictions on the free exercise of religion.

The courts say that public schools, because they are partially funded by federal money (First Amendment) and because they are predominantly funded by state money (Fourteenth Amendment) cannot engage in activities that are deemed an endorsement of a religion. Just the slightest nod to a religion will be enough to trigger an Establishment Clause violation. As we'll see, many schools and courts take this to absurd extremes, and to get to these absurd extremes they have had to torture the original intent of the Constitution.

Indeed, we should remember that when the Constitution was written, Christian religious instruction was the primary purpose of education. To the extent that we can imagine public schools being endorsed by the founders, we can be certain that they would not have objected to religious instruction, but would have insisted on it. If the founders could have anticipated that our schools would become a government near-monopoly and that the Establishment Clause would be stretched beyond recognition to prohibit Christian instruction, I think it's safe to say they would have opposed public education altogether.

We all know the framers were among the wisest men in history. Ignoring their original intent for the First Amendment of the Constitution, as we shall see, has already had alarming consequences for our precious freedoms. And unless we do something about it, it's going to get worse, seriously worse.

part I

The War in Our Public Schools

Discrimination against Christians and the suppression of Christian religious expression pervade our society, and its perpetrators are legion. This survey begins by examining our country's education system, for two reasons. First, modern misinterpretations of the First Amendment's Establishment Clause—"Congress shall make no law respecting an establishment of religion"—are often rooted in *Everson v. Board of Education*,[1] a 1947 Supreme Court case dealing with public funds and education. Second, because education plays such an important role in shaping children's values and worldviews, it greatly influences the character and future of our society. Today's social engineers recognize this, which is why they have tried to convert our public school classrooms into laboratories for social transformation.

The anti-Christian tenor of these social engineers after World War II and especially since the 1960s represents a dramatic change in American history. Most Americans would probably be shocked to discover the dominant influence of Christianity in America's colonial culture and schools, where the Bible was routinely used as a textbook.

Before some of you panic, be assured that this book does not advocate a return to a Christian-oriented education in our public schools, though it does encourage educational freedom. The federal education bureaucracy should relax its chokehold on our education system, including its opposition to the school choice and home-schooling movements. But we must understand that when virtually every vestige of Christianity, including its associated values, is meticulously removed from public schools, something has to replace that void. And it has. While the education establishment vigorously opposes the dissemination in schools of any value or belief that can be remotely traced to the Bible, it affirmatively endorses other values that many Christians find repugnant. Public schools are replete with values-laden curricula, from sex education and sexual orientation instruction to notions of self-esteem and death education.

Ideally, the schools should strive for neutrality on matters of religion—at least in expressing a preference for one over the other. But, in reality, our children are often being inculcated with values and attitudes that conflict with or are hostile to Christianity.

There has been a systematic sweeping away of all things Christian from our public schools, combined with a sweeping in of secularism. Chapters One and Two chronicle the elimination of Christian ideas, symbols, activities, and expressions from our public schools. Chapters Three and Four document how educators are not remaining neutral, but are embracing secularism. Chapter Five discusses the anti-Christian and pro-secular biases in American universities.

chapter one

Christianity Out, Part 1

CHRISTIAN EXPRESSION IS TREATED as profanity and worse in many public schools and certain federal courts across the nation. In May 1995, Samuel B. Kent, U.S. District judge for the Southern District of Texas, decreed that any student uttering the word "Jesus" would be arrested and incarcerated for six months. Lest you think this was some month-late April Fools' joke, the judge expressly avowed his earnestness in his official order. His ruling stated, in part:

> And make no mistake, the court is going to have a United States marshal in attendance at the graduation. If any student offends this court, that student will be summarily arrested and will face up to six months incarceration in the Galveston County Jail for contempt of court. Anyone who thinks I'm kidding about this order better think again .... Anyone who violates these orders, no kidding, is going to wish that he or she had died as a child when this court gets through with it.[2]

In fairness, Judge Kent also prohibited references to other deities. "The prayer," he said, "must not refer to a specific deity by name, whether it be Jesus, Buddha, Mohammad, the Great God Sheba or anyone else." But let's not fool ourselves. These kinds of cases almost always involve Christian expression, as this one did. In this case, the school district had allowed students to read overtly Christian prayers.[3] So while the court's language was nominally directed toward prayers of all religions, in reality it was targeted solely at Christian prayer, because it was the only kind at issue.

Don't think the judge's threat of criminal liability was an isolated aberration. A few years ago, Connecticut law enforcement officials threatened to arrest a man for corrupting the morals of a minor if they could prove he passed out religious tracts to a student.[4] Even without threats of prosecution, school officials often bear down forcefully on young Christians. For example, a Vermont kindergartner was forbidden to tell his classmates that God is not dead, because such talk "was not allowed at school."[5] School administration officials at a Kentucky public school told a student he was not permitted to pray or even mention God at school.[6] A teacher in an elementary school in Florida overheard two of her students talking about their faith in Jesus and rebuked them, not for talking in class, but for talking about Christ in class. In no uncertain terms, she ordered them not to discuss Jesus at school.[7]

Teachers are also sometimes targets of their school's religious discrimination. A school in Edison, New Jersey, reportedly rebuked a substitute teacher for leaving religious literature in the faculty lounge because of its potentially offensive content. Yet the school had allowed other teachers to leave literature trashing the "religious right."[8] A teacher in Los Angeles posted his objection to the school's celebration of Gay and Lesbian Pride Month on the school bulletin board. Other teachers were routinely permitted to post items on the bulletin board without incident, but this teacher's post was removed.[9]

Another teacher was singled out in a Denver elementary school, where the principal removed his Bible from the library and also made him remove his personal Bible from his desk, where he kept it to read during silent time. School officials didn't want that book in the students' sight, so they prohibited the teacher from reading it and made him hide it during the school day, even though he never read from it to his students.[10] In Ohio, thanks to the National Education Association (NEA), teachers who requested that their mandatory union dues be paid to a charity rather than the union's politically liberal causes were annually subjected to an invasive questionnaire. "For years the NEA has issued this particular scheme to intimidate and harass teachers of faith who dare to challenge their radical agenda," said Stefan Gleason, vice president of the National Right to Work Legal Defense Foundation. But this case had a happy ending when the Equal Employment Opportunity Commission, in response to a religious discrimination suit, ordered the NEA to curtail this practice.[11] The NEA and state teachers' unions use this scheme in other states. But when challenged, they usually meet the same fate. That's what happened recently in California. To avoid a religious discrimination action, California Teachers Association officials reluctantly consented to redirect an Arcadia elementary school teacher's monthly union dues to charity because the union's political and social causes were incompatible with her religious beliefs.[12]

Unfortunately, these are not exceptional cases. They are part of a growing pattern involving anti-Christian discrimination in public schools that originated with relatively modern rulings of the United States Supreme Court. Before we examine the modern era, it will be helpful to familiarize ourselves with the history of education in America and how the nation's education framework developed from a private into a public system.[13]

Development of Public Education

During the first colonial settlements, American education was decentralized and mostly private—though there was a movement for compulsory education motivated, ironically, by the colonists' belief in the importance of Christian study. But as we'll see, around the middle of the nineteenth century, starting in New England, the nation began to establish publicly run and funded schools.[14]

Today our government-controlled education system bears no

resemblance to the decentralized scheme preceding it. While many people regard public schools as marking a great progressive leap forward for America, the record is much more dismal. Albert Shanker, a former president of the American Federation of Teachers, reflected on this change for the worse: "It's time to admit that public education operates a planned economy, a bureaucratic system in which everybody's role is spelled out in advance and there are few incentives for innovation and productivity. It's no surprise that our school system doesn't improve: It more resembles the communist economy than our own market economy."[15]

In early colonial America, parents largely controlled their children's education, as there were no regulatory boards and no system for teacher certification. Colonial America had common schools that were partially financed through local taxes, but the majority of funding was private. During that time, religious organizations and philanthropists helped to establish free schools for the destitute.[16] The first common schools in America were Christian. This was a completely natural development, because many early settlers came to America as religious congregations seeking to escape religious persecution and to establish their own churches, local governments, and schools. In fact, these early schools were established for the very purpose of Christian religious instruction. There is a simple reason for this. The settlers viewed illiteracy as a great evil because it denied people access to the Bible.[17] Parents wanted to teach their children to read so they could read the Bible, which provided information essential to their daily lives and eternal salvation.[18]

Character and Textbooks of the Early Schools

In all the early American schools, including colleges, teaching was restricted mostly to religious instruction. The schools assumed little responsibility for teaching subjects like science, secular literature, or art.[19] The Bible, used for teaching both reading and religion, was the chief textbook in the lower grades, and homes or churches were the classrooms.[20] Other textbooks were hornbooks, the *New England Primer,* and the *Bay Psalm Book.*[21]

A hornbook consisted of a sheet of parchment pasted to a flat piece of wood with a handle, laminated with animal horn. Hornbooks featured the alphabet and also referenced the Trinity and the text of the Lord's Prayer.[22] In 1690, the *New England Primer*, an explicitly Christian book, became a central textbook for the Puritans, replacing the hornbook as the chief beginner's textbook. The *Primer* contained the names of all the books of the Bible, the Lord's Prayer, "An Alphabet of Lessons for Youth," the Apostles' Creed, the Ten Commandments, the Westminster Catechism, and "Spiritual Milk for American Babes, Drawn out of the Breasts of Both Testaments for their Soul's Nourishment," by the Reverend John Cotton.[23]

The *Primer*'s Christian emphasis can also be seen in its illustrated rhyming verses for each letter of the alphabet, beginning with "In Adam's fall We sinned all," and ending with "Zaccheus he Did Climb a tree His Lord to see." The *Primer* was a staple of school instruction for more than one hundred years,[24] and was second only to the Bible in popularity, with five million copies reportedly in existence for a population of around four million people.[25] It was commonly said that the primer "taught millions to read, and not one to sin." The *Bay Psalm Book* rendered the Psalms in verse and was the New England colonists' hymnal.[26] *Webster's Blue-Backed Speller*, which was based on "God's Word" and originally published in 1783, was used for about one hundred years. Reportedly, through the years more than one hundred million copies of the *Speller* were sold.[27]

Not only were textbooks explicitly Christian, but ministers commonly doubled as schoolteachers.[28] George Washington firmly believed in the indispensability of Christian training for good government. "True religion," he said, "affords government its surest support. The future of this nation depends on the Christian training of our youth. It is impossible to govern without the Bible."[29] Noah Webster, renowned American educator and founder of the famous dictionary bearing his name, was equally convinced that Christianity and education were mutually dependent. "In my view," said Webster, "the Christian religion is the most important and one of the first things in which all children under a free government ought to be instructed.... No truth is more evident to my mind than that the Christian religion must be the basis of any government intended to secure the rights and privileges of a free people."

Fifty years after the Constitution was ratified, the Christian influence remained dominant in schools, as evidenced by the presence of the Christian-oriented *McGuffey's Readers,* compiled by minister and professor William Holmes McGuffey, in schoolhouses throughout the land.[30] It is estimated that between eighty and ninety million of these books were sold over the course of their history and at one point more than half of all American schoolchildren used them.[31]

Types of Education

Though education in early colonial America was emphatically religious, it varied in type in different areas of the country. The New England colonies, under the control of the Puritans, developed a compulsory educational system in the early 1600s. People of many different sects, none being dominant, inhabited the Middle Atlantic colonies of New York, Pennsylvania, New Jersey, and Delaware. Such pluralism made common schools undesirable, and parochial schools sprang up to accommodate the various denominations. The Southern colonies, being geographically and culturally distinct, used the English charity schools—grammar schools aimed at providing a very basic education for the poor in Britain—as their educational model.

New England Colonies

As Calvinists, the New England Puritans believed that education was a principal avenue through which children would become conversant with Scripture. They also considered it essential for society to achieve social and religious stability and to develop a particularly well-read clergy.[32] In 1636, John Harvard, "a godly Gentleman and a lover of Learning,"[33] established Harvard College to "raise up a class of learned men for the Christian ministry"[34] so that "the tongues and arts" might be taught and learning and piety maintained.[35] It has been said that 123 of this nation's first 126 colleges were of Christian origin.[36] In order to prepare children for college, town governments established Latin grammar schools. The clergy sometimes participated in the educational process by teaching certain children the classics, either by tutoring them or by taking them into their families as boarding pupils.[37]

At first, education was entirely voluntary, but people soon became concerned that too many were neglecting the religious instruction necessary to undergird society and civil government. Such parental negligence as there was in educating children was more a result of difficult living conditions than religious apathy. To keep matters from getting worse, Puritan leaders approached the state governing bodies, which in their world were subordinate to the Church, to pass a law requiring parents and masters to tend to their educational and religious duties.

In response, the colonial legislature of Massachusetts passed the Massachusetts Law of 1642, directing town officials to determine whether children were being trained "in learning and labor and other employments profitable to the Commonwealth," and if they were being instructed "to read and understand the principles of religion and the capital laws of the country." Violators were subject to fines. This was the first time in the English-speaking world that a representative body of a state government had ordered mandatory reading instruction for all children.[38]

Notably, the 1642 measure had nothing to do with schools or teachers, just instruction, the responsibility for which remained with parents. But this law didn't produce the desired results, so the colonial legislature passed another law in 1647, known as the "Old Deluder Satan Act," which gets its name from its preamble. The preamble recited the colonists' belief that "one chief point of that old deluder, Satan, [was] to keep men from a knowledge of the Scriptures." Learning, it said, was in jeopardy of "being buried in the grave of our fathers in church and commonwealth." As the Puritans believed that ignorant people were more susceptible to Satan's corruptive power, the law required every town of fifty householders to appoint and compensate a reading and writing teacher. Towns of one hundred householders were to establish Latin grammar schools to train children for college. If they did not, they would be assessed a fine.

It has been said that these two laws of 1642 and 1647, along with the earlier laws of 1634 and 1638—establishing the principle of common taxation of all property for town and colony benefits—were the bedrock upon which the public school system was later founded in America. But in no way did these laws establish an educational system remotely approximating today's level of government support and control of education.[39] It is ironic, given today's hostile climate toward any presence of Christianity in public schools, that the impetus for compulsory education was the colonists' determination to instruct their children in the Christian religion. This legislative scheme provided the model for education laws throughout New England, with the exception of Rhode Island, as its founding was grounded in a broader interpretation of religious freedom.[40] Gradually, compulsory school laws were less stringently enforced and private schools began to flourish, so that by 1720, Boston, for example, had more private schools than taxpayer-supported ones. By the end of the Revolutionary War, many towns in Massachusetts had no publicly supported schools.[41]

Middle Atlantic Colonies

Society in the Middle Atlantic colonies was extremely pluralistic. Among the various sects were contingents of Dutch Reformed, Anglican, Lutheran, Quaker, Presbyterian, Roman Catholic, and Jewish. And the people came from different nationalities, including English, Dutch,

Swedish, French, Danish, Irish, Scottish, and German.[42] Education was under control of the churches here too, but since no single denomination controlled the state, the churches operated their schools independently. The clergy often served as teachers in these parochial schools.[43] This pattern of mostly private schools persisted through the Revolution and into the first third of the nineteenth century.

Southern Colonies

Various factors, such as its agricultural dependence and plantation culture, deterred a strong sense of community in the South. These factors, along with a sparse population spread over a wide geographical area, worked against the development of formal education and led to the frequent use of tutors, mostly for the children of the elite.[44] This was in marked contrast to New England, where education was largely driven by community cohesiveness and the Calvinist belief that Christian training was essential for the good of the community. Eventually, however, formal education emerged in certain areas of the South, mainly through the enactment of laws in Virginia and North Carolina requiring orphans and poor children to receive apprentice training in the trades as well as in reading and writing. Beyond these measures, the state exerted little influence over education. Private denominational (charity) schools also sprang up, largely supported by private endowments or gifts.

Though Southern efforts at formal education paled in comparison to the New England system, Southern education was nonetheless steeped in religious instruction. Indeed, early sources confirm that "the most prominent characteristic of all the early colonial schooling was the predominance of the religious purpose in instruction.... This insistence on the religious element was more prominent in Calvinistic New England than in the colonies to the south, but everywhere, during the early colonial period, the religious purpose was dominant. There was scarcely any other purpose in the maintenance of elementary schools."[45] Virtually every school owed its existence to a religious purpose. In the absence of such purpose, many believe, the cause of education would have greatly diminished.[46] And this religious motive for maintaining schools, though waning somewhat, continued to be dominant through the Revolutionary War, after which it began to decline.

Education and the Constitution

The subject of education is notably absent from the body of the Constitution and was mentioned only once in the debates of the Constitutional Convention and then only with the issue of whether a national university should be established at the seat of government. The likely reason is that education was still largely a private issue, with exceptions, and under the control of the church. Thus, under the Tenth Amendment to the Constitution, the matter of education was left to the states. Significantly for later church/state debates, there were few, if any, free schools funded by the government at the time the First Amendment was being drafted.[47]

The federal government had expressed some interest in education just prior to the ratification of the Constitution, though, with the passage of the Northwest Ordinances of 1785 and 1787. These laws established a rectangular form of land survey for the Northwest Territories, from which new states would be carved out, laying out land in six-mile-square townships, which were further subdivided into one-square-mile sections. Congress set aside a section of each township for education and also expressly affirmed a federal commitment to education. Article III of the Ordinance states: "Religion, morality, and knowledge being necessary to good government and the happiness of mankind, schools and the means of education shall forever be encouraged." This was probably an outgrowth of the gradual shift in the initial religious purpose in education to a more politically based belief that maintaining an educated citizenry was essential to the republic.[48] (This shift came to full flower in the decades preceding the Civil War.)[49] As states were added to the union, beginning with Ohio,

Congress donated a section in each township to the state for the maintenance of schools within the township, in exchange for foregoing state taxation of the public lands.[50]

Despite the land grants of the federal government, except in New England and New York, there was little national consciousness with respect to education through the first quarter of the nineteenth century,[51] and there were few public schools. The public schools that did exist were funded by parents whose children attended the schools, or sometimes by local taxes. That private schools existed in most communities was a testament to the view that education was primarily the parents' responsibility. Private schools, still motivated by the religious interests of the sects establishing them, remained dominant. In some states, the private school "lobby" was so powerful that it was able to secure public aid.[52]

The success of private schooling was phenomenal, with literacy in the North increasing into the middle to high ninety percent range and reaching as high as eighty-one percent among whites in the South between 1800 and 1840.[53] The initial pressure for government-controlled education began in Boston in 1817, as a result of lobbying by those who contended that impoverished parents were unable to afford private schooling for their children. The Boston School Committee, however, urged against public schooling after its own survey revealed that ninety-six percent of Boston children were in school even though the schools were private and there were no truancy laws. But public school advocates persisted, and by 1818 succeeded in making Boston the first city in America to establish an entirely publicly funded school system.[54]

Around 1825 a serious battle began for the development of tax-supported, publicly controlled and directed, nonsectarian common schools. Before then, such schools were merely a distant hope among "reformers."[55] It wasn't until the 1850s that public education—in the sense of being government-sponsored, -operated, and -controlled—started to gain national prominence, first in New England and then in the rest of the nation. Prior to that time, America's education system had remained decentralized.[56] While one of the main purposes of government-controlled schooling was to provide a safety net so that even the poorest of children could go to school, in practice, government schools didn't effect an increase in school enrollment. Rather, they wiped out many private schools whose sponsors could not support them while simultaneously supporting public schools through taxation.[57]

One of the prime movers in this transformation was Massachusetts legislator Horace Mann. Mann was raised Calvinist, but at the age of twelve rejected his Calvinist background and eventually became a Unitarian. Mann fought to diminish the Calvinist influence in the schools,[58] and was instrumental in a reform movement that eventually led to centralized control of education. When he was president of the state senate, he played a major roll in establishing the Massachusetts Board of Education in 1837, and served on it until 1848.[59]

Mann was such an idealist in his views of the social engineering possibilities for government-run schools that he envisioned a society where ninety percent of the crimes would be eliminated.[60] His influence extended well beyond Massachusetts; his energetic activism greatly contributed to the ignition of a crusade for public education in almost every state.[61] During this time, the character of education became increasingly nonsectarian and secular, with a steadily decreasing focus on religious instruction.[62] Many Protestant leaders attributed this trend to the workings of Mann, and people began to attack him for introducing secularism into the schools. Some claimed that the Massachusetts Board of Education intended to take the Bible out of schools and to leave students' religious instruction to the home and the Sabbath schools.[63] While Mann denied any desire to remove the Bible, many today believe he was very influential in planting the seeds of secularism in our public schools. Secularism was part of a philosophical movement known as "humanism," whose influence on public education is explored in Chapter Three.

The Genesis of the "Wall of Separation" —*Everson v. Board of Education*

In the mid-1940s, New Jersey resident Arch Everson filed a lawsuit against Ewing Township to prevent state tax revenues from being allocated to transport parochial students to their Catholic high school in Trenton. This lawsuit culminated in the landmark Supreme Court case of *Everson v. Board of Education* (1947).[64] The court, ironically, given the legacy of the case, denied Everson's claim, but it did so in language that proved to be the best weapon ever handed to those looking to strip Christianity from the public schools or public life.

In his majority opinion in *Everson*, Justice Hugo Black is the one who firmly incorporated—out of context, many would argue[65]—Thomas Jefferson's "wall of separation" language into American jurisprudence.[66] "The First Amendment," said Black, "has erected a wall between church and state. That wall must be kept high and impregnable. We could not approve the slightest breach."[67] Justice Black gave the separation language its first real teeth, delineating its initial parameters. Black wrote:

> The "establishment of religion" clause of the First Amendment means at least this: Neither a state nor the federal government can set up a church. Neither can pass laws which aid one religion, aid all religions, or prefer one religion over another. Neither can force nor influence a person to go to or to remain away from church against his will or force him to profess a belief or disbelief in any religion. No person can be punished for entertaining or professing religious beliefs or disbeliefs, for church attendance or non-attendance. No tax in any amount, large or small, can be levied to support any religious activities or institutions, whatever they may be called, or whatever form they may adopt to teach or practice religion.

> Neither a state nor the federal government can, openly or secretly, participate in the affairs of any religious organizations or groups and vice versa.[68]

Author Gerard V. Bradley noted that *Everson* "effectively opened the modern era of church/state jurisprudence."[69] Constitutional scholar Paul G. Kauper underscores the point. *Everson*, according to Kauper, "stands as a key decision in laying the foundation for judicial review of all governmental practices supportive of religion. The beginning of an impressive and influential body of case law, it nationalized the restrictions embodied in the Establishment Clause of the First Amendment and opened up a new and comprehensive surveillance of state and local laws and practices dealing with religious matters."[70] Professor Daniel L. Dreisbach goes so far as to say, "Any informed discussion of the constitutional prohibition on 'an establishment of religion' must contend with the reasoning and holding of *Everson v. Board of Education*."[71] The *Everson* court's "version of history" and "separatist construction of the First Amendment," according to Dreisbach, "laid the foundation" for later First Amendment cases involving released-time, school prayer, "the continuing controversies over religious expression and instruction in public schools," and other lines of cases.[72] Indeed, American courts have, on the whole, expanded the separationist concept over time. But the courts' unwillingness to go even further in certain areas has not prevented the education establishment from pushing the envelope of separation to new heights. That establishment, when unchallenged, has become a law unto itself, as this chapter will amply show.

The Prayer Police

For most people, the rising wall of separation wasn't apparent until the Supreme Court outlawed state-sponsored prayer in public schools in *Engel v. Vitale* (1962).[73] The problem arose when the New York

Board of Regents tried to compose an innocuous, nondenominational prayer that could be recited in New York public schools. The text of the prayer was simply, "Almighty God, we acknowledge our dependence upon Thee, and we beg Thy blessings upon us, our parents, our teachers and our Country." Ironically, some Christians who might otherwise support school-sanctioned prayer are against prayers like this one, precisely because they are so neutral and devoid of any particularly Christian characteristics.

It is important to understand that the board was adamant that no child should be compelled to join in the prayer, or even encouraged to do so.[74] Yet when the New York suburban school board of New Hyde Park adopted the prayer, the Supreme Court ruled it unconstitutional. It is inarguable that the principle established in *Engel*—that state-sponsored school prayer is constitutionally forbidden—is now firmly rooted in modern constitutional law. Lower courts are bound by the principle of *Stare Decisis* to follow that precedent. (The Supreme Court is also guided by *Stare Decisis*, but it has the power to reverse its earlier holdings.) That *Engel* is now the law of the land doesn't alter the fact that many still believe that the Supreme Court wrongly decided it in the first place, based on its misreading of the Constitution and American history. Nothing better highlights this than reference to the learned rulings of the lower New York courts in that case, all of which found the prayer constitutional. Their honest pronouncements, though rendered a legal nullity by the Supreme Court, are instructive for all who long for constitutional interpretation according to the framers' original intent.

First Amendment scholar George Goldberg aptly observed, "Of the first thirteen judges who considered the constitutionality of the Regent's Prayer, among whom were some of the most learned appellate judges in the nation, eleven found it valid, a batting average of .846; and some of them felt strongly that any other decision would be historically wrong and itself constitutionally objectionable."[75] The chief judge of the New York Court of Appeals minced no words:

> Not only is this prayer not a violation of the First Amendment . . . but holding that it is such a violation would be in defiance of all American history, and such a holding would destroy a part of the essential foundation of the American governmental structure.[76]

And as Goldberg noted, the language of one of the concurring judges was even stronger:

> It is not mere neutrality to prevent voluntary prayer to a Creator; it is an interference by the courts, contrary to the plain language of the Constitution, on the side of those who oppose religion.[77]

Some like to point out that *Engel* has been widely misunderstood. It did not, they say, "take God out of the schools." It merely prohibited state-sponsored prayer. Even the current Supreme Court has said as much.[78] But such analyses are oversimplified. It's one thing to say that only state-sponsored prayer is outlawed and another to define the parameters of state sponsorship. Suffice it to say, it doesn't take much state activity at all to trigger state sponsorship under modern precedent. The 1985 case *Wallace v. Jaffree* held that public schools may not set aside a period of silence at the commencement of the school day if there is the mere suggestion that students might use the time for prayer.[79] It strains the imagination to conceive how moments of silence constitute state endorsement of religion, especially a particular religion. But the law is nonetheless what the Supreme Court says it is.[80]

While the court can protest that it has not unduly restricted religious freedom, its "modern" decisions, beginning with *Everson* and continuing through *Engel* and *Wallace*, have greatly emboldened those hostile to Christianity to scrub away prayer and other religious expression from our public schools.

Not in Our Cafeteria

The parents of Raymond Raines, a fourth grader at Waring Elementary School in St. Louis, Missouri, taught Raymond to pray before eating, which he did faithfully each day. By all accounts Raymond was a well-behaved, respectful, and studious young man. When a teacher saw Raymond in the school cafeteria at lunchtime bowing his head to thank God for providing his food, the teacher allegedly ordered him out of his seat and sent him to the principal's office. The teacher, according to reports, apparently made no effort to downplay this scene, as Raymond was singled out in full view of the other students present.

Raymond says the principal told him that it was against the rules to pray in school and ordered him not to do it again. But since Raymond's parents had instilled in him the importance of praying at mealtime he continued to do so. On two further instances—three in all—he was allegedly taken from the cafeteria and disciplined. The school administration segregated him from his classmates, subjected him to ridicule for his religious beliefs, and eventually gave him a weeklong detention.[81] This incident gained national notoriety when U.S. Representative Newt Gingrich, then House Speaker-elect, discussed the case on NBC's *Meet the Press.*

Raymond and his mother filed suit in 1994 against the city schools and the principal for violating his constitutional right to freely exercise his religion. School district officials continually maintained that Raymond had been disciplined for reasons other than school prayer.[82] But a representative of the Rutherford Institute, a public interest law firm specializing in religious freedom cases, which was defending Raymond, testified before the Senate Judiciary Committee that Rutherford had obtained "at least four sworn statements from witnesses who were in the cafeteria when Raymond was disciplined, as well as other pieces of information to substantiate Raymond's claims."[83] The parties settled the lawsuit when the school board agreed to adopt a policy governing students' prayer rights. The policy permits students to pray at school in a nondisruptive manner when not involved in a school activity.[84]

Just Keep It to Yourself

In 1997, United States district judge Ira DeMent issued an injunction against the DeKalb County, Alabama, school board from organizing, sponsoring, or encouraging school-sanctioned religious activity. Fair enough. Most of us can agree or at least live comfortably with the notion that public schools shouldn't endorse religious activity. But the court went further, issuing an additional injunction prohibiting the school from permitting any prayer or devotional speech that was uttered aloud—even if it was voluntary. Under the order, any prayers spoken "aloud in the classroom, over the public address system, or as part of the program at school-related assemblies and sporting events, or at a graduation ceremony" were prohibited—even if the school in no way endorsed them. The court also appointed an attorney to serve as a prayer monitor to oversee the school to make sure the order was carried out.[85]

Happily, on two separate occasions, the Eleventh U.S. Circuit Court of Appeals vacated that part of the district judge's order prohibiting voluntary, vocal prayer. The court did not, however, reverse the order appointing the prayer monitor.[86] Over a period of eight months alone the court-appointed prayer policeman cost the school some $62,000.[87]

But before you get too sanguine about our courts allowing voluntary or student-initiated prayer, understand that it is not all that clear what constitutes "voluntary" in our mucked-up First Amendment jurisprudence. And it became less clear after the Supreme Court issued its ruling in *Santa Fe Independent School District v. Doe* (2000).[88] There, the court, in a 6-3 decision, struck down a Texas school district's policy that allowed a student, elected by his classmates, to deliver a public invocation before the home high school football game.

The controversy initially arose when Santa Fe's student council chaplain delivered a prayer over the public address system prior to every home varsity football game. This upset certain Mormon and Catholic students, who sued to challenge the practice. Before the hearing, the school board changed its policy and provided for two separate student elections, presumably to dissociate the school from the process. In the first, the students would decide whether an invocation or message should be given at all. If so, the second election would determine which student would deliver it. But this bifurcated procedure turned out not to be enough to insulate the prayer. Both the Fifth Circuit Court of Appeals and the United States Supreme Court invalidated the policy as violating the Establishment Clause of the First Amendment.

The Supreme Court did not buy the school district's argument that the invocation was private speech because the students, not the school administration, voted to have it. The court reasoned that because the district sanctioned the election, which permitted the majority to prevail, the religious views of the minority candidates "will never prevail" and "their views will be effectively silenced." Nor was the court persuaded that the invocation should be considered private because it was delivered at an extracurricular event where student attendance was not mandatory. "For some students, such as cheerleaders, members of the band, and the team members themselves, attendance at football games is mandated, sometimes for class credit." The court also factored in the peer pressure driving many students to the game. "The Constitution demands that schools not force on students the difficult choice between whether to attend these games or to risk facing a personally offensive religious ritual."[89]

Chief Justice Rehnquist, in his stinging dissent, joined by Justices Scalia and Thomas, said that the majority had distorted existing precedent to invalidate the policy. He said that the policy "permits many types of messages, including invocations. That a policy tolerates religion does not mean that it improperly endorses it." But Justice Rehnquist got to the real nub of the problem when he commented on the majority's overt antipathy toward religion in public life, an antipathy—as this case alone shows—that has permeated the highest reaches of our judicial system. Rehnquist wrote:

> "But even more disturbing than its holding is the tone of the Court's opinion; it bristles with hostility to all things religious in public life. Neither the holding nor the tone of the opinion is faithful to the meaning of the Establishment Clause, when it is recalled that George Washington himself, at the request of the very Congress which passed the Bill of Rights, proclaimed a day of 'public thanksgiving and prayer, to be observed by acknowledging with grateful hearts the many and signal favors of Almighty God.'"[90]

Rehnquist might have gone further. Not only did Congress proclaim a public day of prayer, *it did so just one day after it passed the First Amendment itself.* As scholar M. Stanton Evans poignantly observed, "Indeed, in one of the greatest ironies of this historical record, we see the practice [officially sponsored prayer] closely linked with the passage of the First Amendment—supplying a refutation of the Court's position as definitive as could be wished."[91]

This case dealt a significant blow to religious freedom by holding that a public school, merely by allowing students to hold an election to determine whether there would be a prayer at all, violated the Establishment Clause. But the flipside of the coin and what the court failed to acknowledge was that by invalidating the school's election process, the state—through the agency of the court—denied students their religious freedom. The court's assertion that the election would effectively silence the views of the minority was unimpressive. To allow the majority of students to enjoy a prayer of their choosing does not silence those who elect not to participate or prevent them from praying their own prayer. They are free to worship or not as they please, including silently to themselves during the majority prayer. Why should a minority deprive the majority of their religious freedoms just because they don't want to participate? While the Bill of Rights certainly aims to protect the minority against the "tyranny" of the majority, it is not intended to oppress the majority at the hands of a vocal minority. Banning this prayer denied the majority of students their free exercise rights while doing nothing to protect the killjoy minority.

The court's ruling in *Santa Fe Independent School District v. Doe*, it should be noted, sparked some student defiance around the country. In Poca High School in West Virginia, for instance, more than 200 students and parents at a football game stood up on cue and joined in when placekicker Jason Legg began the Lord's Prayer from the fifty-yard line. He said, "For me, it's the only time some fans will see somebody witness to them. They come to watch a football game, and they see the teenagers doing something good, maybe it will spark something in them—maybe that's something they will want to check into."[92]

Legg was not trying to violate the Supreme Court's decision, but to organize a method to lead students in prayer without running afoul of the *Santa Fe* case. The students even avoided using the school's intercom system to broadcast the prayer. The school's superintendent, Sam Sentelle, who approved of the student-led prayer, acknowledged that "a government institution cannot foster religion. I cannot tell you what to pray, or not to pray. As long as the principal doesn't tell them to go out, or it's not disruptive, it's okay," said Sentelle.[93]

The proscription against "public" prayer has extended beyond high school classrooms, auditoriums, and sporting events. Now we see it rearing its head in kindergarten settings, where the prayer police are on the beat to suppress any renegade attempts at vocal prayer. On January 15, 2002, kindergartner Kayla Broadus recited a familiar prayer at her school in Saratoga Springs, New York, while holding hands with two students sitting next to her at her snack table. "God is good. God is great. Thank you, God, for my food." This didn't sit well with her teacher, who silenced and scolded her, then dutifully reported the infraction to the school's lawyer, Gregg T. Johnson. Johnson concluded Kayla's behavior was a violation of the "separation of church and state." The school principal sent a letter saying, "Please be advised that Kayla will not be permitted to ask other students to join her in prayer prior to snacktime or lunchtime. Kayla is certainly free to silently say her prayer before a snack or lunch." The school board then launched into action, issuing a press release stating that Kayla was prohibited from praying aloud in school. Kayla's mother, Cheryl Broadus, filed a federal lawsuit on Kayla's behalf through the Rutherford Institute, and obtained a temporary restraining order against the school. Rutherford president John W. Whitehead observed that the school officials' understanding of the First Amendment religion clauses was upside down. "Saratoga Springs school officials claim the Constitution requires them to be alert to personal student discussions and immediately censor any student expression that appears religious," said Whitehead. "In fact, the Constitution requires the opposite."[94]

The lawsuit was settled without trial, with the school district acknowledging Kayla's right to pray out loud, so long as she did not disturb her classmates or invite them to pray with her. Whitehead was pleased with the settlement, but expressed regret that it took a federal lawsuit to vindicate Kayla's civil rights. Whitehead had it just right when he said, "Any censorship of personal religious speech in a public school—even though it is couched in terms of separation of church and state—teaches children that religious persons are second-class citizens, and this is fundamentally wrong."[95] Following the settlement, a defiant school board refused to admit any wrongdoing, claiming that it had always permitted "nondisruptive audible prayer at school."[96] But Thomas Marcelle, another attorney representing the Broadus family, disputed that claim. "The school district," said Marcelle, "said she could only say grace silently."[97] There seems to be a recurring pattern in religious discrimination cases. When its perpetrators are caught in the act they invariably offer some excuse for suppressing the students' freedoms. In Kayla's case, this wasn't about disruption and the school should be ashamed for suggesting so. It was about the district's hyperventilation over "church and state" issues, a hyperventilation caused by a combination of prejudice against the free exercise of religion and ignorance that this right is guaranteed by the Constitution.

Prayer-Free Pomp and Circumstance

Even under conservative Chief Justice Rehnquist—though not because of him—the Supreme Court has added further restrictions on school prayer.[98] In *Lee v. Weisman* (1992),[99] the court, in a 5-4 decision, held that it is unconstitutional for public schools to include prayers given by clergy at their official graduation ceremonies. In this case, the principal, Robert E. Lee, had made the decision that a prayer should be given and selected the clergy member who was to deliver the prayer. That was too much involvement by the state for the narrow majority's comfort.

Lower courts have split on whether school board members or superintendents may, as part of a graduation address, recite the Lord's Prayer or other prayers. In a case in a Nebraska high school, a board member, whose son was in the graduating class, was permitted to lead students in the Lord's Prayer in his graduation address, but the ACLU is appealing the District Court's ruling. In another Nebraska school district, however, the state Department of Education reprimanded the superintendent for leading students in prayer at a graduation event.[100]

But what about student-initiated prayer at graduation ceremonies? Well, it's a little less clear, with conflicting decisions in lower court jurisdictions and with a great deal of murkiness as to what constitutes student-initiated prayer as distinguished from school-sponsored prayer. The Eleventh Circuit Court of Appeals, for example, in *Adler v. Duval County School Board* (2001)—see below—ruled that student-led prayers at graduation ceremonies, unrestricted as to content, are constitutional.[101] The Ninth and Fifth Circuits have held that student-led prayers are only permissible if they are nonsectarian and nonproselytizing.[102] The Ninth Circuit found that the school district's "plenary control over the graduation ceremony" meant that it "would have borne the imprint of the district." The Third Circuit, meanwhile, ruled that student-led prayers at graduating ceremonies are unconstitutional, and at least implied their constitutionality wouldn't be saved even if they were nonsectarian and nonproselytizing.[103] With this hodgepodge of opinions it is no wonder, then, that throughout the various jurisdictions, uncertainty reigns.

The Eleventh Circuit case of *Adler v. Duval County School Board* (2001) arose in Florida, where some students and their families were upset when the Duval County School District permitted its seniors to elect one of their classmates to deliver a religious message at graduation festivities. A student in one of the county's high schools chose to deliver a Christian-based message. In her remarks, the student thanked Jesus for "dying for our sins" and thanked God for "raising him from the dead three days later so that through your son's death we may be at peace with you and thereby may have fellowship with you." A group of offended students and their parents filed a suit, which ultimately failed, because, according to the Eleventh Circuit Court of Appeals, the students selected the speaker and school officials did not preview the remarks for approval, thus maintaining the school's neutrality. The United States Supreme Court refused to take the case, which means that student-led prayer at graduation ceremonies is probably safe, for now, in that circuit.[104]

In another case, a Pennsylvania graduating high school senior actually had to threaten her school with a temporary restraining order before it would let her allude to her Christian faith in her graduation speech. The principal of Hollidaysburg Area Senior High School told salutatorian Shannon Wray that it might be offensive to some if she spoke about Christ and asked her to rewrite her speech to make it more "inclusive" and "diverse." But it was the school's instructions to her—that her speech should focus on her life's path to graduation—that had led her to discuss her religion in the first place. And this is a crucial point: Christ was central to her life and it would have been intellectually dishonest of her not to emphasize that in her message. Yet those who would erect an enormous wall of separation between religion and public life force people into such dishonesty. According to Wray's attorney, Joel Oster, she wanted to "talk about what her religion meant to her and how it allowed her to get to the point where she was.... She felt like if she had to give a speech with the religion struck out, it would be an incomplete speech; it would be a lie."[105]

Wray insisted that she wasn't trying to proselytize, but to share the reason for her success in school, the single greatest factor of which, she believed, was her dependence on Christ. The school finally retracted its demand that she delete the paragraphs touching on her Christianity when attorneys for Liberty Counsel said that interfering with the content of Wray's speech would lead to them to request a federal restraining order. Amazingly, even after the school backed down, the superintendent faxed Wray another message imploring her to delete those portions because to include them wouldn't be "fair" to everyone at the ceremony. There were separate rumblings that the school might end the tradition of having valedictorians or salutatorians giving graduation speeches lest future students make Christian allusions.[106] Again, the prevailing assumption in these schools seems to be that Christianity is intolerably offensive to all but Christians.

So as we can see, even when the courts permit or grudgingly tolerate a degree of religious expression in the schools, that's no guaranty that recalcitrant classmates and administrators will make it easy for students wishing to freely exercise their religion. But such obstacles aren't stopping some students. In 2001, the valedictorian at Norfolk High School in Nebraska led her fellow students in prayer—and received a standing ovation for her courage.[107]

In some cases the courts have upped the ante for "disobedient" Christians. In West Virginia, a federal district judge not only outlawed a student-led graduation prayer at St. Albans High School in Kanawha County; he ordered the offending school system to pay $23,000 in legal fees to the eighteen-year-old atheist who brought the suit.[108]

The judge's initial order banning the student-led prayer and saying that the plaintiff would likely suffer irreparable harm if he were exposed to the prayer did not sit well with many of the students, more than one hundred of whom disobeyed the order. Following the lead of one student, they stood, bowed their heads, and recited the Lord's Prayer during a moment of silence. This prompted many relatives in attendance to give the students a standing ovation. At the beginning of the ceremony, one parent shouted "God Bless America" from the bleachers, to which the crowd replied, "Amen." And during the recitation of the Pledge of Allegiance, many in attendance, students and parents, enunciated "under God" louder for emphasis.[109]

The atheist student plaintiff, who ostensibly was in jeopardy of irreparable harm, didn't even bother to attend the graduation ceremony. He said, "I have no use for that pretentious, self-congratulatory ceremony. To me, this ruling is much more significant."[110]

In so many of these cases denying the students' right to pray at school events, the courts engage in lofty rhetoric about the Establishment Clause and in the process almost completely ignore the underlying religious freedom issues. Every time a student's right to invoke God is denied, often due to overblown concerns about the indirect involvement of the state in religion, we must remember that his speech and religious freedom are being suppressed. A case at Amador Valley High School in Pleasanton, California, illustrates the point. The school administration invited the school's salutatorian, Nick Lassonde, to give a graduation speech. Nick was excited at the invitation and viewed it as an opportunity to tell his classmates how important his Christian faith was to him. The principal required Nick to submit his speech in advance for review. Predictably, though Nick was told before that he could speak on any topic he chose, the principal demanded that references to Nick's faith be deleted. According to the school's attorneys, those references were forbidden because they constituted "proselytizing" or "preaching." Nick was told he could either rewrite his speech as directed or he wouldn't be permitted to speak.[111]

Nick was disheartened because, like Shannon Wray in the Pennsylvania case, he believed he could not fully express who he was as a person without revealing the thing most important to him, his faith in Christ. He felt that he had been censored and denied his speech and religious rights. "I felt, and still feel," said Nick, "that I was denied a right I had earned, the right to express who I am and how I came to achieve the honor of being salutatorian, based solely on my Christian viewpoint.... I felt, and I still feel, that the censored portions were the most important part of the speech, for they contained the central message that I felt not only explained who I was as a person, but answered the question implicitly addressed in any graduation speech: how others could follow my example of success and happiness. I believed, and sought to state, that success and happiness in this life depend not on material wealth or personal fulfillment, but upon knowing who God is as our Creator and Heavenly Father...."[112]

Nick's father said that it would have been disobedient to accept a public honor without giving the glory to God. He added that the school's censorship of these portions of Nick's speech "made me feel that our views as a Christian family were disfavored by the district... as being too offensive to state publicly."[113]

Again, the underlying purpose of both religion clauses in the First Amendment, the Free Exercise Clause and the Establishment Clause, is to protect religious freedom. As we can see in the cases, these clauses are often in tension. That tension, generally speaking, should be resolved in favor of maximizing religious expression. In considering cases like Nick's, we have to ask ourselves whether the suppression of the religious content of his speech furthered or limited the cause of religious expression. Had the school permitted Nick's speech to be delivered in its entirety, would anyone's religious freedom likely have been violated? Just as with the non-participating students in the Santa Fe football prayer case, how can it reasonably be argued that the religious freedom of other students, even those who violently disagreed with the tenets of Christianity, would be abridged by sitting through a speech endorsing Christianity? It is an absurd stretch to conclude that by simply allowing that speech, the state, through the agency of the school, somehow affirmatively endorsed Christianity and thereby intimidated non-Christians. Yet by disallowing those parts of the speech the school clearly suppressed Nick's right to express himself. And in so doing, it didn't just violate his rights in the abstract. The omitted segments were highly relevant. The thrust of his speech was gutted when he couldn't share his foundational beliefs.

It is not just formal prayer at graduation ceremonies that alerts the prayer police. They are also opposed to individual students and high school choirs singing the Lord's Prayer at graduation ceremonies. Two students at Windsor High School in Virginia wanted to sing "The Prayer," an inspirational song, at their graduation ceremony. The song, which mentions God once and talks of faith, has been recorded by Christian and mainstream singers alike, including Celine Dion. School officials refused to let the students sing the song because it would "violate the requirements of separation of church and state." When the students asserted their First Amendment "free exercise" rights, the school simply banned all singing at the ceremony.[114]

In another such case in Woodbine, Iowa, involving a school choir, the complaining students (members of the choir), who were reportedly from an atheist family, didn't want "to be forced" to sing the Lord's Prayer. The Iowa Civil Liberties Union filed a lawsuit on their behalf. Neither the disgruntled students nor the ICLU were satisfied with the choir's offer to compromise by adding a "nonreligious" song "to balance things out."[115] The school superintendent, Terry Hazard, said that the song was selected for its musical content, not its religious value. But one of the objecting students disagreed. "The prayer which they are having us sing for graduation is basically forcing us to sing praise to a God that we don't even believe in," said Donovan Skarin.[116] "The novelty here is that the prayer is to be sung. That's still unacceptable," said Rand Wilson, ICLU legal director.

The U.S. District Court granted the injunction banning the singing of the Lord's Prayer, ending the school's thirty-year tradition.[117] School officials announced that they would not appeal the court's decision. Does this decision mean that choir members can prevent their choirs from singing, for example, "God Bless America" or "The Battle Hymn of the Republic" or the bulk of the greatest classical choral music ever written? This extreme banishment of God from the classroom means the exclusion of much of the most important art, culture, history, and civilization of the West, and, rock bottom, that's a failure of education, all based on an anti-Christian bias and a tendentious reading of the Constitution.

A "Subversion of School Policy"

In addition to forbidding school choirs from singing the Lord's Prayer or other religious songs at graduation ceremonies, some schools restrict the outside activities of their choirs as well. To commemorate the first anniversary of the September 11 massacre, the Central Baptist Church in Sanford, Florida, organized a memorial service honoring the victims of the attacks. The church invited the local school board members, other community leaders, and the general public. The church asked the Seminole High School Gospel Choir to perform at the ceremony, which was to be held at the church. The gospel choir had been established twelve years before as a result of community demand for this type of music. The school district has three other choirs, all of which are secular. All four of the choirs are highly acclaimed and have received a number of trophies in competition. The gospel choir had some eighty-five members, every one of whom participated on a purely voluntary basis.[118]

School officials, upon hearing of the invitation, barred the choir from participating. They didn't stop there, saying the voluntary participation by individual choir members was also forbidden as "subversive of school policy." The choir director said the students were heartbroken because they had been rehearsing diligently in anticipation of the service. Their names had already been printed in the program because the school was late in informing the church that the choir would be forbidden to attend.[119]

The school district, in response to the controversy, quickly adopted a new policy that officially prohibited the school choir from taking part in any event located in or sponsored by a church. Reportedly, the district was even considering banning the gospel choir altogether.

The school's hostility toward religion went further: it prohibited choir members from praying among themselves prior to their practice sessions. When the students asked, then, whether they could share a moment of silence, the answer was no. This is when Liberty Counsel intervened on behalf of the aggrieved choir members. Liberty's president, Mathew Staver, happened to be the keynote speaker for the memorial event and was appalled with the school district's treatment of the choir. "I was shocked by the situation—not only because I believe it's blatantly unconstitutional, but it's also unbelievable that it would come on the day that they were going to celebrate those who died during the September 11, 2001, terror attacks, and honor them in a patriotic celebration and a memorial service as well," said Staver.

Many citizens of Sanford were none too pleased, on the whole, with the school board's decision. They were especially upset with school superintendent Paul Hagerty's proposal to create a separate, after-school club that would be permitted to sing at religious events, provided it was clear that in so doing it did not represent the school or district. When residents appeared at a school board meeting and registered their strong support for the choir, three members requested an audience with Hagerty to discuss the issue. Following the meeting, Hagerty reversed himself, maintaining the choir's status and saying that it could perform at churches, so long as students were permitted to opt out if they didn't want to participate.[120] Of course, Mathew Staver didn't consider this qualifier to be a significant burden. The choir members, he said, were always agreeable to such a provision. But Staver views it as a moot point. "No one has ever requested to opt out," he said. "They're in the gospel choir so they can sing gospel music. So, they're not going to opt out whenever they get an opportunity to sing gospel music at a religious event."[121]

You've Got (Prayer in Your) Mail

The prayer police aren't just after students. School employees are also fair game. LaDonna DeVore, a receptionist in the administrative offices of Highland Park Independent School District in Dallas, Texas, sent a personal group e-mail message from her office computer that included, God forbid, President Bush's National Day of Prayer Proclamation. DeVore's accompanying note said, "The following proclamation by our president is an incredible statement by the leader of the free world, and I encourage you to pass this on to your friends and colleagues to set the stage for the National Day of Prayer this Thursday, May 2."[122]

According to a school administrator, the e-mail violated the district's policy of banning e-mail messages for "commercial, for-profit purposes, political purposes, religious worship, or proselytizing." School officials admonished DeVore over the "inappropriateness" of the e-mail and told her that further violations could result in discontinuance of her e-mail privileges. The school district had no problem with its employees sending non-work-related messages over its e-mail system, including jokes, secular messages of encouragement, event invitations, and chain messages.[123] But forwarding a national day of prayer proclamation from the president of the United States was strictly forbidden. After the American Center for Law and Justice (ACLJ) brought a lawsuit on DeVore's behalf in the U.S. District Court in Dallas, the school agreed to amend its communications policy to remove the provisions prohibiting "religious worship or proselytizing."[124] The district admitted that the religious content of the e-mail was constitutionally protected. DeVore's attorney put this case in perspective. "All this individual did, in effect, was distribute the text of the president's message, and the school district is saying that raises serious constitutional issues," said ACLJ attorney Stuart J. Roth. "She's just passing on the president's proclamation. He's our president; he's a government employee, just like she is."[125]

Conclusion

When you consider that the first common schools in this country were established for the purpose of Christian instruction, the current climate of hostility toward all things Christian in the public school environment is sobering. Legitimate concerns about government-sponsored religion have been blown out of proportion to the point that voluntary student activity involving the Christian religion—without the slightest nod of endorsement by the state—is prohibited. While separationist extremists operate under the freedom of religion banner, the fact is that they are on a campaign to smother religious freedom for Christian students. In the next chapter we'll see further examples of discrimination against Christians in public schools covering a broad scope of activities. The sheer number and variety of these cases prove that the separationists are determined to purge public schools of Christian thought, symbols, and expression.

chapter TWO

Christianity Out, Part 2

FOLLOWING THE 1999 MASSACRE at Columbine High School, school officials gave students and their families an opportunity to paint tiles with images and words above student lockers. But the administrators were apparently surprised that some families chose to mourn the dead with Christian symbols and verses. They removed some ninety of the 2,100 painted tiles because they contained such "objectionable" phrases as "God is Love" and "4/20/99 Jesus Wept." The parents of two slain students, Daniel Rohrbough and Kelly Fleming, were among those affected. The families sued and the federal district court held in their favor, ordering the tiles returned to the walls.[1]

But that wasn't the end of it. Just one day after a federal appeals court in San Francisco ruled the Pledge of Allegiance unconstitutional, the Tenth Circuit Court of Appeals reversed the district court, and held that school officials had been within their rights to ban the tiles. The court referred to the tiles as "school-sponsored speech"—even though the school was not involved with suggesting content and did not censor any other viewpoint. But the Court defended its viewpoint discrimination, stating, "If the [school] district were required to be viewpoint neutral in this matter, the district would be required to post tiles with inflammatory and divisive statements, such as 'God is Hate,' once it allows tiles that say 'God is Love.'"[2]

The families' attorney, John W. Whitehead of the Rutherford Institute, said that the Court of Appeals "has said, in essence, that the Constitution allows public officials to search out and censor religious speech simply because it is religious. This is hostility toward religion, not tolerance and inclusion of all." Rutherford correctly noted that the school district initiated the undertaking in the first place by inviting students and families to decorate the walls and thereby opened the memorial project to community members.[3] It is inconceivable that the school didn't anticipate an outpouring of religious expression following the tragedy. One of the plaintiffs remarked, "The school district apparently believes in freedom from religion instead of freedom of religion."[4] Regrettably, the Supreme Court declined to review the case and resolve the conflict that exists in various jurisdictions over whether schools may engage in viewpoint discrimination.[5] So a ruling that equates "God is Love" and "Jesus Wept" with "inflammatory and divisive" speech will stand. Once again, exaggerated concerns over church/state separation trumped religious freedom.

Meanwhile in Syracuse, New York, Antonio Peck's kindergarten teacher at Catherine McNamara Elementary School gave Antonio the assignment of creating a poster that would depict what could be done to save the environment. Antonio drew a picture of Jesus Christ praying and captioned the drawing, "The only way to save the world" and "Prayer Changes Things."[6] The teacher refused to display the poster, saying it promoted one religion over another. (Of course Anthony was promoting his religion over others, but it was Anthony doing the promoting, not the school.) Anthony went back to the drawing board and sketched people picking up garbage with a robed man beside them, kneeling with his hands raised to heaven. The robed man was not identified as Jesus. The teacher agreed to display the second poster, but on the condition that the part showing the robed man was folded over so that it could not be seen.[7] The Pecks have sued the school for religious discrimination and denial of free speech. Antonio's attorney, Erick Stanley, explained, "One thing we are arguing is that... the school's censorship of that was related to nothing other than a hostility to religion. Religion is a part of his everyday life, and he didn't understand why his picture was inappropriate in school."[8] And indeed, it was not inappropriate. What is inappropriate is the attitude of the public schools that every free expression of religion needs to be either suppressed or covered with a fig leaf. Who was acting more like a child here, the student who innocently incorporated religion into his poster or the school that required the religious part to be covered?

Christophobia

A Montana school district prevented a motivational speaker from speaking to students at Dillon Middle School simply because he was a Christian, even though he was to make a strictly secular presentation. School officials had originally invited Jaroy Carpenter to speak to help students cope with a number of teen suicides and accidental deaths, but rescinded the invitation when a school board member complained about church/state implications. Please! Carpenter is a former public school teacher who goes from school to school speaking to students at assemblies about things that matter: living with integrity and good behavior. He teaches students the importance of honesty and of respecting one another. He also discourages them from degenerate lifestyles and behavior, such as using drugs, and tries to instill in them that they must be responsible and accountable for their own actions, which have consequences. He is said to lace his talks with "slapstick humor and offbeat anecdotes" and almost always captures the attention of the students.[9]

After canceling Carpenter's talk, other area schools did likewise, folding like scared rabbits. They were reportedly concerned that this Christian man might inject his religion into his speech, though he "has made more than 200 secular presentations at school assemblies around the country and has never addressed religion or sought to proselytize those in attendance."[10]

This school's decision represents the kind of thinking that breeds discrimination against Christians because it says we will bar Christians from participating just by virtue of who they are and what they believe. As Carpenter's attorney, John W. Whitehead, aptly summarized: "By withdrawing its invitation to address a public school assembly simply because Jaroy Carpenter is religious or happens to be associated with a religious ministry, this school district is essentially saying that religious persons must be kept off campus even though they have valuable insights and experiences to share with schoolchildren on subjects other than religion."[11]

No Can Do

At a high school in Hampton, Virginia, Warriors for Christ, a student club, organized a canned food drive to raise funds for the local YMCA women's shelter. But authorities apparently concluded the project was tainted because the students decided to call it the "Easter Can Drive."[12] No, no, no! Such language could not be tolerated in Kecoughton High School. Administrators demanded that the drive be renamed the "Spring Can Drive" because some might find the invocation of Easter offensive. But which is more offensive, a Christian club attaching a Christian name to its philanthropic activity, or school officials declaring that words depicting sacred Christian holidays are offensive? And where is the tolerance? Do you think the school would have dared prohibit a group of Muslims from naming an activity after Ramadan? Even Americans United for Separation of Church and State reportedly believes the Christian group has the right to use "Easter" in naming the food drive.[13] Now that is remarkable! The principle established in this case is that Christian symbols are sufficiently offensive to non-Christian students to justify the suppression of the Christian students' religious freedom.

Ho Ho Ho, Christmas Must Go

If Easter is controversial, so is Christmas. The chancellor of the New York City Department of Education prohibited the display of Nativity scenes in New York City schools during Christmas, but allowed displays of the Jewish menorah and the Islamic star and crescent. The excuse, of course, was "diversity" and "multiculturalism"—"to promote understanding and respect for the diverse beliefs and customs relating to our community's observance of the winter holiday." But the most important cultural institution shaping Western civilization and the lives of these very students is verboten; indeed, the city officials even refer, in Orwellian language, to "the winter holiday," which is not what most of these students will be celebrating, rather than Christmas. One principal, in accordance with the New York chancellor's policy, sent out a memo urging teachers to bring Jewish, Islamic, and Kwanzaa symbols to school, but references to Christianity were conspicuously absent. Again, the celebrated virtues of tolerance and diversity are accorded to all but Christians.

School officials will often agree to allow Christmas trees, which have become secular as much as religious symbols (according to the Supreme Court), but emphatically refuse Nativity depictions.[14] Richard Thompson, chief counsel for the Thomas More Law Center, said, "When you disallow the Nativity scene by calling it religious and allow other symbols categorized as religious, then you are underlying the fact [that] it becomes a less favorable religion... [and it] shows a callous indifference and hostility toward Christians during one of their holiest seasons.... This policy relegates Christians to second-class citizens." New York's discrimination has outraged many Christians, including Catholics. "It is outrageous that New York City public school officials allow some religious symbols in the schools every December while banning others," said William Donohue, president of the Catholic League. "Catholics are sick and tired of being discriminated against by bureaucrats who tell us we should be satisfied with a Christmas tree in the schools."[15]

Repeatedly, in the name of inclusiveness and tolerance, Christmas is targeted for special discrimination. In Frederick County, Maryland, a school employee was barred from distributing Christmas cards with a Christian message. A fourth grader in Ephrata, Pennsylvania, was forbidden from handing out religious Christmas cards to his classmates.[16] And two parents whose families don't celebrate Christmas complained when a Canandaigua Primary School teacher near Rochester, New York, asked students to bring items from home for a class Christmas party. In response, the eagerly compliant principal issued a memo advising that it is more appropriate to use secular words such as "holiday" than "Christmas." That memo in turn caused rebellion from Christian parents in the community, which prompted the district superintendent, in a refreshing display of courage, to issue a superseding memo clarifying that the term "Christmas" would not be banned.[17]

In Portland, Oregon, one student's mother complained that the local public school had actually made her son feel guilty about celebrating Christmas. A school district in California has forbidden teachers to utter the word "Christmas" in class and instructed them not to wear Christmas jewelry. One of the teachers, who had conducted a classroom program called "Christmas Around the World" for more than two decades, was reportedly so discouraged she considered retiring.[18]

Elsewhere around the country, school districts have discontinued references to "Christmas break" in favor of the politically correct and "inoffensive" "winter break" or "holiday break." So radioactive is Christmas that a New Jersey third grade teacher, under pressure from the ACLU, canceled a class field trip to see the play "A Christmas Carol" on Broadway.[19] The ACLU contended that the play excluded certain aspects of the community (non-Christians). Instead, the teacher took the class to "The Great Train Race."[20]

Even in the Bible Belt, such anti-Christian discrimination abounds. In a Tupelo, Mississippi, elementary school, children had to sit through an assembly where Kwanzaa was celebrated, Chanukah was taught, and students were led to chant "Celebrate Kwanzaa." In contrast, in the Christmas hymns that were permitted, officials removed any references to Jesus Christ or specifically Christian content and renamed the Christmas tree a "giving tree."[21] A more draconian restriction on Christmas songs occurred at Pattison Elementary School in Katy, Texas. Pattison not only banned the singing of Christmas songs, but threatened grade reductions for students who refused to participate in singing songs of other faiths.[22]

One story illustrates the impact this anti-Christmas attitude is having on children. During the 2002 Christmas season in Scottsdale, Arizona, a man was singing "We Wish You a Merry Christmas" with his five-year-old daughter, who interrupted to insist that they sing "We wish you a happy holiday," because, she explained, one of her teachers doesn't celebrate Christmas. A few days later, when attending the school concert, the father discovered that indeed there were no references to Christmas or Christ—or any other hints of Christian meaning in any of the songs. This obsession not to offend is remarkable, considering that it's hard to comprehend how the celebration in song of a holiday for one religious group (a very large one at that) would threaten those of other religions. The spirit of the season is, to borrow a term, inclusive, not exclusive. But even more noteworthy is that according to a 2000 Gallup Poll some ninety-six percent of Americans celebrate Christmas.[23]

Britney & *Nsync In, Christ Out

It's one thing for Christophobes to be nervous about Easter and Christmas, given their obvious association with Jesus Christ, but surely holidays like Valentine's Day should escape their scrutiny. Well, not quite. A public school in Milwaukee, Wisconsin, permitted its students to exchange valentines of all varieties, including those showcasing pop stars Britney Spears and *Nsync. All varieties, that is, except one honoring Jesus Christ. Eight-year-old Morgan Nyman was told she could not pass out her homemade cards saying "Jesus loves you" or "Freely rely on God."

Mark Vetter, the school district's attorney, said, "We think that violates the separation of church and state and would be unconstitutional and impermissible for us to do."[24] He said the school would have had no problem with Morgan passing out her valentines during lunchtime or before or after school. Yet there was no such prohibition for the distribution of secular cards, and if the school was not "endorsing" Britney Spears, it certainly was not "endorsing" Morgan's religious cards either.[25]

Morgan's lead attorney, Mathew Staver, agreed that, "If the literature disrupted the ordinary operation of the school, the school has certain authority to be able to restrict that literature."[26] But, Staver added, there was never any suggestion that Morgan's literature was disruptive. "What was disruptive was the principal ordering that the literature be taken back up or confiscated."[27]

When Morgan and her parents sued the school for violation of her constitutional rights, the school district agreed to apologize publicly to Morgan and to revise its policy clarifying students' rights to express their religious beliefs during school and the types of religious materials they are permitted to distribute. But even after issuing the apology, defiant school officials insisted they hadn't done anything wrong.[28]

That Evil Bible

Many local school districts become rather nervous when students try to give Bibles away on school grounds. There have been several cases of school districts prohibiting students from distributing Bibles to fellow students, even if they did so when classes were not in session. The "Truth for Youth Bible," a New Testament translation geared toward teens, was the focus of one such case in Davenport, Iowa, and other cases in Missouri. In the "Show Me" state, one principal chastised students for attempting to distribute Bibles. And another principal confiscated some one thousand of the Bibles, which the students had purchased with money they had raised. At yet another school, the principal, school administrators, and police confronted students gathered around the flagpole before the school day had begun and threatened to arrest them if they didn't quit handing out Bibles.[29]

Such actions bring to mind Communist China rather than the states of "fly-over" America. These repressive measures are even more absurd when one remembers that Congress once funded a project to provide Indians with a Christian education and in 1780 made an effort to print an American Bible.

The Bible Is "Garbage" and the Ten Commandments Are "Hate Speech"

A teacher at Lynn Lucas Middle School in the Houston, Texas, area reportedly shouted, "This is garbage," as she threw two students' Truth for Youth Bibles in a trash can. According to Liberty Counsel's report, the two sisters were carrying the Bibles when they walked into their classroom one morning, where their teacher met them at the classroom door. She noticed the Bibles and promptly escorted the students to the principal's office. She then paged the girls' mother and threatened to call child protective services because the Bibles were not allowed on school property. One of the girls became hysterical at the teacher's bizarre behavior. When the mother arrived, the teacher waved the Bibles at her and exclaimed, "This is garbage," then threw them into the trash can. She said the girls could not bring Bibles to school. In a separate but similar incident at the same school, officials confronted three students whose books had the Ten Commandments displayed on the covers. They threw the covers in the garbage, claiming the Ten Commandments were hate speech that might offend other students. Liberty Counsel filed a federal lawsuit seeking an injunction and damages against the school board officials. School officials denied the claims.[30]

Distribution is just one of the many ways the Bible can get you into trouble in public schools today. Some schools also prohibit students from discussing stories from the Bible in class. Elizabeth Johnson, an eleven-year-old sixth grade student in the Boulder Valley School District in Colorado, chose to do a report on the Book of Exodus for her assigned oral book report. "I like the Bible, so I chose that," she said. The teachers stopped her, saying that some students might find the Bible "offensive." She was even told that she couldn't bring her Bible to school. The incident deeply upset the little girl, who said, "After that I felt like I never wanted to choose the Bible.... I should never choose the Bible and it didn't make me feel so good." After attorneys with the Alliance Defense Fund got involved and word reached the media, the school district reversed itself and allowed Elizabeth to do her book report.[31] A jubilant Elizabeth explained later, "I just wanted to do how he [Moses] rescued the slaves, and how he was born."

A similar event occurred in Medford, New Jersey, where first grader Zachary Hood was denied permission to read his favorite Bible story to classmates at the Maurice & Everett Haines School. Zachary's teacher said he would only be allowed to read the story to her in private. Zachary's mother, Carol Hood, filed a lawsuit on his behalf through the Becket Fund for Religious Liberty that was ultimately settled for $35,000. Even after the case was settled in the Hoods' favor, school officials were defiant, even cocky. Superintendent Susan Mintz said the decision to settle was made by the district insurance provider and that she was confident the district would have prevailed had the case gone to trial. "We would have won without question," said Mintz.[32]

It's not just the Bible, but Christian books in general that distress some public educators. Laura Greska, a seven-year-old second grader at Northwest Elementary School in Massachusetts, brought the book *The First Christmas* to class to fulfill an assignment about her family's Christmas traditions. Sounds straightforward enough, right? Think again. The book centered on the birth of Jesus Christ and was thus "religious," so Laura was forbidden to share it with the class.

Laura's parents were appalled at the school's attitude toward Christianity. "They teach tolerance, which is great," said Laura's mother, Jessie Greska, "but not on a Christian's behalf?" After unsuccessful efforts to resolve the matter with school administrators, the Greskas asked attorneys with the American Center for Law and Justice for assistance. Vincent McCarthy, the ACLJ attorney handling the case, made a telling observation. "The actions of the school district are not only unconstitutional," he said, "but send a disturbing message to all elementary school students—that religious beliefs must be treated the same way the school handles profanity or offensive behavior not permitted at school."[33]

Another case extended the Bible-as-dangerous mentality a step further. Fourth grader Joshua Burton got himself into trouble for reading his Bible silently in class during free time. The teacher disputed this, saying Joshua was reading the Bible when he was supposed to be working on assignments, but once Joshua filed suit the school eventually agreed to pay the boy's $10,000 in legal fees.[34]

New Guidelines

On February 7, 2003, Education Secretary Rod Paige issued new student free speech guidelines as part of President Bush's No Child Left Behind Act. The guidelines provide that schools—under the threat of losing their federal aid—must allow students their right to free expression, including religious expression such as voluntary prayer and Bible reading in school. In his letter introducing the guidelines, Mr. Paige wrote, "Public schools should not be hostile to the religious rights of their students and their families . . . . Among other things, students may read their Bibles or other scriptures, say grace before meals, and pray or study religious materials with fellow students during recess, the lunch hour, or other noninstructional time to the same extent that they may engage in nonreligious activities."[35]

"Candy Canes, Sweatshirts, and Jewelry, Oh My!"

Yes, to many the Bible is now offensive and so are candy canes with a Christian message. For four years, a Bible club at a Reno, Nevada, high school had distributed candy canes containing the words "Jesus Loves You" without incident. But in 2002 the school administration denied the club permission to dispense the candy because the message was "potentially offensive." To its credit, the school reversed its position when the Pacific Justice Institute intervened.[36] One wonders, though, whether the school was even aware that the candy cane itself was invented as a Christian symbol, representing the shepherd's crook of a bishop.

Indeed, candy canes are a big issue—for school districts anyway—across the country. School administrators at Westfield High School in the Boston area suspended six students for passing out candy canes with Bible verses on the attached card before class.[37] The cards also included information about Bible club meetings and the story of the candymaker who popularized the candy in America as a Christian witness. (The cane now represented not only a shepherd's crook, as it had in Europe for centuries, but J for Jesus, white for purity, and red for Christ's redemptive blood.)

The students had requested permission to hand out the candy, but said the principal denied it because it might be "offensive" to other students.[38] The school claimed that its refusal was based on a policy barring students from passing out non-school-related literature on campus.[39] Administrators warned the students that they might face punishment for insubordination. The students, believing that God had called them to share the Gospel, went ahead and risked punishment. One reason they did so was that the previous year they had been told that the only message the candy could contain was the generic "Happy Holidays." They thought it would be wrong to dilute their message again.[40] And they are right. The Constitution protects the free exercise of religion; it was never intended to require that religious holidays be treated as secular ones. When the students filed a federal lawsuit against the school district, district judge Frank Freedman issued an injunction prohibiting the school from disciplining the students.[41]

Even five-year-old pre-kindergartners can get into trouble over candy canes. A case now pending in the Third U.S. Circuit Court of Appeals involves the right of five-year-old Daniel Walz of Egg Harbor Township, New Jersey, to give his classmates pencils and candy canes containing Christian messages. Daniel's teacher confiscated the pencils for fear that their messages could offend students who do not belong to an organized religion.[42] Of course, one has to wonder which is more offensive to the Constitution of the United States: a five-year-old passing out candy canes to his classmates or a teacher confiscating the candy canes because they are Christian.

Matters of apparel are also at issue. Students at a high school in McArthur, Ohio, were told to remove bracelets with the letters "WWJD," which stand for "What Would Jesus Do," because they might offend some students. The school reversed itself, however, and permitted the wearing of the bracelets following a letter by the National Legal Foundation to the assistant principal.[43]

School administrators of Walker County School District in Birmingham, Alabama, told eleven-year-old Kandice Smith that she couldn't openly wear a cross necklace to Curry Middle School under the school's dress code. The school claimed that it wasn't intending to infringe on Kandice's free speech or religious expression rights, but to discourage gang activity. It is difficult to understand how a cross necklace could encourage gang activity, but Kandice was nonetheless risking detention or suspension if she didn't remove or conceal the necklace. The school settled after a lawsuit was filed, agreeing to revise its dress code "to mandate religious accommodations in accordance with the Alabama Religious Freedom Amendment."[44]

Gelsey Bostick, a third grader at Asa Adams School in Orono, Maine, caused a stir at her school when she wore a T-shirt and sweatshirt both bearing the name "Jesus Christ." Gelsey's teacher asked her to turn the shirts inside out because they were causing a commotion. The teacher attributed part of the disruption to the fact that one of the students in the class was named Jesus, which caused the other students to "chatter." But, the teacher also said the words on Gelsey's shirt offended one of the students. Gelsey's mother, Cynthia Bostick, a professor of psychiatric nursing at the University of Maine, was upset that she wasn't contacted about her daughter having to wear her shirts inside out. The school changed its position when the Thomas More Center intervened. The school insists, however, that it was not engaging in religious discrimination, but that the shirts were disrupting the class because some students interpreted the words as "swear words." Perhaps the students could have been told otherwise, but evidently that was asking too much. "There were no religious overtones," said Principal Susan O'Roak. "If kids are focused on the shirt, they're not focused on the lesson."[45]

Bible Clubs

What about student Bible clubs? Should they be allowed to meet on school property? Or does their obviously religious purpose make them intolerable? Northville High School in Michigan told Connect for Christ, a student Bible club, that it could no longer meet during seminar period at school, but continued to permit other noncurricular clubs to meet. The principal said that because the Bible club was "religion-based" it could meet before or after school, but not during.[46] Two of the club's students, Nicollete Pearce, a senior, and her brother Matthew, a ninth grader, brought a federal lawsuit for religious discrimination, which resulted in a consent decree authorizing the club to resume meetings. The school, according to the order, must give the club the same access to school facilities as other noncurricular clubs at the school. The decree also required the school to train teachers and administrators on the Federal Equal Access Act (see below) and not to single out members of the Bible club for selective enforcement of school policies. While such discriminatory school policies are probably casually dismissed by some as inconsequential, one need only look at what happened to attendance when the ban was in effect to understand the real impact such discrimination can have on the lives of Christian students. In the initial aftermath of the ban, the club's membership decreased roughly ninety percent, but following the court order, attendance doubled.[47]

There are scores of such Bible club stories, but it's hard to top one out of Panama City, Florida. There, a school principal, on her own initiative, unilaterally changed the name of a student Bible club from "Fellowship of Christian Students" to "Fellowship of Concerned Students," in deference to the gods of political correctness. She also prohibited the club from advertising. In effect, she was saying the school would hold its nose and permit the club to exist on the condition that it dilute its name to disguise its Christian nature.[48]

Yet some values aren't discouraged in public schools. In fact, schools often go out of their way to concoct justifications for their discriminatory treatment in favor of some value-based organizations and against Christian groups. One such arbitrary and phony excuse is that the subjects and activities of the non-Christian clubs correspond to the school's curriculum. School officials at Monarch High School in Louisville, Colorado, for instance, prohibited a group of students from forming a Bible club at the school because it was limiting recognition of student organizations to those that "directly relate to the regular curriculum and the educational goals of the school district." But it allowed other groups to form, including the Gay/Straight Alliance Club, the Multicultural Club, Peace Jam, and Amnesty International. In pressing for recognition, the Christian group maintained that its club would directly relate to the school's curriculum as an extension of courses relating to the Bible in history, literature, and philosophy. School administrators rejected the students' perfectly reasonable argument, betraying the school's apparent opinion that partisan political groups and homosexual organizations have more to do with real education than does the sourcebook of the Judeo-Christian tradition, which proves the school is intellectually bankrupt as well as discriminatory against Christians.[49]

Unequal Access

In 1984 Congress passed a law requiring federally funded high schools to provide equal access to all noncurricular student-led groups wishing to meet on school grounds. The law is based on *Wid-*

mar v. Vincent (1981), a Supreme Court case that prohibited publicly funded universities from discriminating against religious groups in the use of campus facilities.[50] It is a matter of equal treatment: if the university opened its facilities to some groups, it had to for religious ones. The court didn't even consider the rights of the various parties under the religion clauses of the First Amendment, the Free Exercise Clause, and the Establishment Clause. With the Federal Equal Access Act Congress sought to extend this principle, by statute, to federally funded high schools.[51]

A few years later, some recalcitrant school administrators challenged the constitutionality of the Equal Access Act. Westside High School in Omaha, Nebraska, argued that the Equal Access Act violates the First Amendment Establishment Clause. The case went to the United States Supreme Court in *Board of Education of the Westside Community Schools v. Mergens* (1990), where the Court, in an 8-1 decision, ruled against the school.[52] The act is now firmly rooted in our law.[53] It is referred to in the Department of Education Guidelines for Religious Expression, which provides that:

> Student religious groups at public secondary schools have the same right of access to school facilities as is enjoyed by other comparable student groups. Under the Equal Access Act, a school receiving Federal funds that allows one or more student noncurriculum-related clubs to meet on its premises during noninstructional time may not refuse access to student religious groups.

In a more recent case, the Supreme Court held that public elementary schools may not deny access to Christian organizations and Bible clubs for after-hours meetings at the school.[54]

But despite the Equal Access Act, the court's validation of it, other cases permitting Bible clubs to meet, and the unambiguous Department of Education Guidelines, many public school administrators continue to act as though they are required to discriminate against Christian students. Los Angeles Unified School District (LAUSD), for example, denied requests from the San Fernando Valley of Child Evangelism Fellowship to form a Bible club called the "Good News Club." Liberty Counsel's Mathew Staver, representing the group, said, "The LAUSD seems to think it's above the law. A policy excluding persons or groups because of their religious viewpoint is unconstitutional. This underscores that educators need education." LAUSD policy, said Staver, permits groups or individuals to "meet and discuss any subjects and questions which appertain to the educational, political, economic, cultural, artistic, and moral interests of the community in which they reside." Yet the school concluded that a Bible club doesn't qualify.[55] An analogous situation occurred in Marion, Massachusetts, where the school allowed every conceivable group to use its school auditorium except for the South Coast Community Church.[56]

School officials in Crosby, Minnesota, prohibited a Christian group called the "Lunch Bunch" from passing out flyers or posters to advertise its meetings at Crosby-Ironton High School. Club members Katie Hodges and Jonathan Friesner were trying to publicize the club's annual "See You at the Pole—National Day of Student Prayer" (SYATP), which is a national celebration. In fact, a week after the September 11, 2001, terrorist attacks on America, more than three million students participated in the event in all fifty states.[57] Yet the school principal denied Katie and Jonathan permission to distribute the leaflets unless they substituted "praise" for "prayer." On a separate occasion he also prohibited the club from promoting a Bible study.[58]

Banning Christian groups from distributing flyers and teachers from handing out permission slips about their meetings is a common occurrence around the country. In one case in New Jersey, it took a federal court order to compel the school district to require teachers to distribute flyers and permission slips to students concerning Bible club meetings.[59]

Released-Time Programs

Hundreds of public schools across the nation allow students, with permission from their parents, to take Christ-centered Bible instruction off campus during the school day. Such arrangements, known as released-time programs, have been around since 1914, when Gary, Indiana, school superintendent William Wirt originated the concept. It has been estimated that as many as 600,000 students in thirty-two states participate in these programs.[60] The United States Supreme Court held, in *Zorach v. Clauson*(1952),[61] that they are permissible under the Constitution so long as the teachers are not state-approved, public money is not involved, and there is no state coercion. This was the case, by the way, in which that darling of all liberal Supreme Court justices, William O. Douglas, made his famous statement that, ironically, would be used by proponents of religious liberty for years to come:

> We are a religious people whose institutions presuppose a Supreme Being.... When the State encourages religious instruction or cooperates with religious authorities by adjusting the schedule of public events to sectarian needs, it then follows the best of our traditions. For it then respects the religious nature of our people and accommodates the public services to their spiritual needs. To hold that it may not would be to find in the Constitution a requirement that the government show a callous indifference to religious groups. That would be preferring those who believe in no religion over those who do believe.... But we find no constitutional requirement which makes it necessary for government to be hostile to religion and to throw its weight against efforts to widen the effective scope of religious influence.... But it can close its doors or suspend its operations as those who want to repair to their religious sanctuary for worship or instruction. No more than that is undertaken here.[62]

California statutes authorize released-time programs. Under the program in the Pomona Unified School District in Pomona, California, students are released from school one hour per week to attend classes on religious instruction off campus. Recently, anti-Christian sentiment has reared its head, apparently making some in the school district feel the need to subtly discourage the program. For ten years the Pomona district allowed teachers to distribute permission slips for the program to students. But in 2002, the district reversed itself, specifically forbidding teachers from making permission slips available and forbidding students from passing them out to other students.[63]

"It is outrageous," observed attorney Brad Dacus, "for a school district to trounce upon the ability of elementary school children to invite their peers to attend something that is very dear to them. Such policies only further the anti-religious stigma often created by public schools."[64] There is no constitutional excuse for the district's behavior. As Dacus notes, "The mere providing of permission slips for possible activities of outside organizations in no way connotes an endorsement of those organizations, but merely is an administrative necessity for allowing outside activities and outside organizations to make contact with parents."[65]

God (Better Not) Bless America

Not just purely religious expressions are forbidden on school grounds, but anything—words, symbols, or messages—that can be associated with Christianity. When Breen Elementary School in Rocklin, California, placed the message "God Bless America" on the school marquee after the terrorist attacks of September 11, 2001, the ACLU accused the school of committing a "clear violation of the California and United States constitutions, as well as the California Education Code." "It must be replaced immediately," said the ACLU staff attorney.

According to the ACLU, the message divided students along religious lines, harming and isolating students of minority faiths. This is a time, said the attorney, that schools "should be supporting" minority faiths "and the values of pluralism and tolerance." The school district's attorney, Phillip Trujillo, disputed this characterization, saying, "It's simply not a religious expression. It's instead a patriotic expression." Mike Forbes, president of the district's board of trustees, said he was "disgusted" by the ACLU demand. The ACLU's action outraged students, parents, and some administrators, who came together at a rally 250 people strong, dressed in red, white, and blue in support of the sign's message.[66] The school defiantly (and courageously) decided to continue displaying the sign.[67] "They picked the wrong issue, they picked the wrong time, and they picked the wrong community," said Forbes.

It is quite a stretch to say that an innocuous sign whose primary thrust is patriotic, not religious, violated the Establishment Clause because it contained a polite, nonsectarian exhortation to the Almighty to bless our nation, which was under attack. American presidents have routinely invoked the blessing for two hundred years. The sign didn't say, "The Triune Godhead blesses America," or "Jesus Christ Blesses America." It was a neutral reference to God folded into a patriotic message. Even the California Supreme Court has said that the phrase "God Bless America" is a traditional, nonreligious patriotic phrase.[68] The only people likely offended by such a message are those looking to be offended—and that noisy minority has no constitutional right to abolish the Free Exercise Clause of the First Amendment.

Hanging Ten

People often say that the United States Supreme Court has banned displays of the Ten Commandments in public school classrooms. But that's not quite accurate. In *Stone v. Graham* (1980), the court held that states may not *require* that the Ten Commandments be displayed in public classrooms, as that would violate the Establishment Clause of the First Amendment. It did not go so far as to say that public school classrooms would not be *permitted* to hang such displays on their own, though lower courts have so held.[69] In *Stone v. Graham*, the court ruled that the Kentucky statute in question had no secular legislative purpose and "the pre-eminent purpose for posting the Ten Commandments on schoolroom walls is plainly religious in nature. The Ten Commandments are undeniably a sacred text in the Jewish and Christian faiths and no legislative recitation of a supposed secular purpose can blind us to that fact."[70]

Justice Rehnquist wrote a strongly worded dissent, criticizing the majority for concluding without considering any evidence that the statute had no secular legislative purpose and that the preeminent purpose for posting the commandments was plainly religious. While Rehnquist conceded the majority's conclusion that the Decalogue is "undeniably a sacred text," he asserted that it is "equally undeniable... as representatives of Kentucky determined, that the Ten Commandments have had a significant impact on the development of secular legal codes of the Western World." Rehnquist argued that the Establishment Clause didn't require the public sector to be "insulated from all things which may have religious significance or origin."[71]

In another case in 2001, U.S. District Judge Jennifer Coffman ordered the Ten Commandments removed from public buildings in three Kentucky counties, saying that the Ten Commandments' history "bolstered the reasonable observer's perception of the state endorsement of religion."[72]

The counties initially complied with the order and then re-posted the Ten Commandments along with the Declaration of Independence and the Bill of Rights. Judge Coffman didn't accept the revision and again ordered the removal of the display. Mathew Staver of Liberty Counsel announced that the case would be appealed. In the meantime the ACLU is filing similar lawsuits, county by county, across the nation.[73]

Some local governments and state legislatures are fighting back. On July 17, 2001, the North Carolina senate, by a vote of 44-6, passed a law allowing public schools to post the Ten Commandments in the classroom as part of a larger display.[74] Not long after, the North Carolina house passed the measure 94-18 and Governor Mike Easley announced he would sign the bill into law.[75] There appears to be a nationwide movement among state legislatures to consider similar legislation.[76] And in 2002, in West Union, Ohio, a school board voted to appeal a federal court order to remove from public schools stone tablets of the Ten Commandments that had been on display since 1997.[77]

On the federal level, Congressman Robert Aderholt has introduced a bill entitled The Ten Commandments Defense Act. Aderholt's purpose behind the act is to "return to the individual states the power to make the decision of whether the Ten Commandments may be displayed on or within publicly owned buildings." The bill, says Aderholt, doesn't force the states to do anything, but merely provides them the option. The congressman earlier introduced similar legislation that passed by a handy margin (248-180). The bill never became law, however, because it was attached as an amendment to another bill that was stalled due to different versions in the House and Senate that couldn't be reconciled.[78]

"Under God"

In September 2001, the Wisconsin state legislature enacted legislation requiring Wisconsin school districts to have students either recite the Pledge of Allegiance or sing (or have played) the national anthem daily. The following month, on October 8, 2001, the Madison, Wisconsin, school board, by a vote of 3-2, banned student recitation of the Pledge of Allegiance in public schools and prohibited students from singing the national anthem and substituted an instrumental version. Board member Bill Keys said the words "under God" in the pledge were offensive to some and that many were opposed to the militaristic themes in the "Star-Spangled Banner." "What I wanted to do was eliminate that which would be repugnant to those who believe very strongly and would have their personal and political beliefs violated by group coercion," said Keys.[79] And, of course, he found a way to inject the familiar buzzword "inclusive" into the mix. He said, "We have a large number of people who refuse to take religious oaths to something other than what they believe in. We were trying to satisfy the state law and be as inclusive as possible."[80] One board member, however, rejected the charge that the pledge was predominantly religious. Member Ray Allen said, "For a few minutes every morning, everyone joins together in an exercise that I believe binds us together. I don't think the pledge is about religion. I think it is a commitment to our democracy."[81]

One Madison resident in favor of the ban said that it was unfair to divide students with different beliefs over the pledge issue. "It's bad enough Osama bin Laden has declared a holy war on us," said Laura Brown. "It's a heck of a lot worse if we declare war on each other in the name of God."[82] It's difficult to understand how one can come to the conclusion that those favoring recitation of the pledge are divisive, much less engaging in a holy war. Such excessiveness and disproportion often drive the anti-religion crowd. Subsequent events in Madison, though, convincingly proved that Laura Brown's radical view was in the minority—a very small minority—at least in Madison.

The school board received more than 20,000 e-mails and phone calls, almost all of which expressed opposition to the board's banning of the pledge and anthem.[83] Governor Scott McCallum denounced the school board as "oddballs," and one state legislator threatened to propose cutting state funding.[84] Just a week after its decision, under intense community pressure, the board reversed itself. Following a late-night meeting that overflowed the Madison High School 800-seat auditorium with irate citizens, the board, by a vote of 6-1, determined that the district's students would begin each day by reciting the Pledge of Allegiance, effective immediately. At the meeting, 165 separate people spoke before the board. Before the meeting began, the citizen audience spontaneously erupted into a recitation of the pledge, over some scattered booing. Upon its completion, the crowd applauded and waved American flags. One person in attendance, Dan Neviaser, who had volunteered to serve in World War II, was blunt. "In this time of stress and fear," said Neviaser, "we need our 'Star-Spangled Banner,' we need our Pledge of Allegiance. You know what we don't need? Our school board."

The controversy over the Pledge of Allegiance and saluting the flag is actually an old one. In 1940, the Supreme Court chose to hear a case involving the suspension of two Jehovah's Witness schoolchildren, aged ten and twelve, for disobeying the school district's requirement that they salute the flag. So the students' father brought an action to enjoin the authorities from violating his children's religious freedom by requiring them to participate in the flag-salute ceremony as a condition to attending the school. As Jehovah's Witnesses, they held that the flag was a graven image to which they shouldn't bow. In *Minersville School District v. Gobitis* (1940),[85] the court upheld the school district's position. It ruled that the school district's interest in promoting national unity outweighed the religious freedom of the Witnesses. "National unity," said the Court, "is the basis of national security." But just three years later, the court properly corrected itself in *West Virginia State Board of Education v. Barnette* (1943),[86] holding that the states (and local school districts) cannot compel students to salute the flag and recite the Pledge of Allegiance.

In 2002, the pledge issue came up again in a nationally celebrated case in California, *Newdow v. United States Congress* (2002).[87] Michael Newdow sued his daughter's school district for unconstitutionally endorsing religion because her teacher led the class in reciting the Pledge of Allegiance. He also challenged the constitutionality of a 1954 act of Congress that added the words "under God" to the pledge. Newdow, an avowed atheist, argued that his daughter, over whom he did not have custody and who lived with her Christian mother, was injured just by having to watch and listen to other students reciting the pledge—even though she was not required to participate. The liberal three-judge panel of the Ninth Circuit Court of Appeals agreed. "In the context of the pledge," said the court, "the statement that the United States is a nation 'under God' is an endorsement of religion . . .

Furthermore, the school district's practice of teacher-led recitation of the pledge aims to inculcate in students a respect for the ideals set forth in the pledge, and thus amounts to state endorsement of these ideals. Although students cannot be forced to participate in recitation of the pledge, the school district is nonetheless conveying a message of state endorsement of a religious belief when it requires public school teachers to recite, and lead the recitation of, the current form of the pledge."[88]

It's probably not an exaggeration to say that no case since *Engel v. Vitale* (1962)—the school prayer case—has caused such a public uproar, with the possible exception of *Roe. v. Wade* (1973), one of two companion abortion cases.[89] President George W. Bush, according to then White House press secretary Ari Fleischer, thought the ruling was "ridiculous." The president said that the decision was "out of step" with the country's history. "The Supreme Court itself begins each of its sessions with the phrase 'God save the United States and this honorable court,'" said Fleischer. "The Declaration of Independence refers to God or to the creator four different times. Congress begins each session of the Congress each day with a prayer, and of course our currency says, 'In God We Trust.' The view of the White House is that this was a wrong decision and the Department of Justice is now evaluating how to seek redress."[90] "America," said President Bush, "is a nation that values our relationship with the Almighty. We need common-sense judges who understand that our rights were derived from God."

Even the ordinarily left-leaning *New York Times*, *Los Angeles Times*, and *Washington Post* editorial pages mildly criticized the ruling. The *New York Times* wrote, "This is a well-meaning ruling, but it lacks common sense."[91] The *Los Angeles Times* said, "The Cold War insertion of the phrase in 1954 clearly was driven as much by ideology as religion. That said, for all the overheated and dire predictions voiced then, the 'under God' phrase has in no way led to establishment of an official state religion."[92] And the *Washington Post*: "We believe in strict separation between church and state, but the pledge is hardly a particular danger spot crying out for judicial policing."[93]

Congress also made a point of expressing its disgust with the decision. Shortly after the ruling, 150 House members assembled on the front steps of the Capitol and recited the pledge. The Senate unanimously enacted an immediate non-binding resolution condemning the decision (99-0). Senator Kit Bond of Missouri crisply remarked, "Our Founding Fathers must be spinning in their graves. This is the worst kind of political correctness run amok. What's next? Will the courts now strip 'so help me God' from the pledge taken by new presidents?"[94] Dennis Hastert, Speaker of the House, said the ruling underscored the need for the Senate to "confirm some common sense jurists."[95]

The Senate didn't stop with its non-binding resolution. The next day it passed Senate Bill 2690 (this one was binding), again by a vote of 99-0. The bill affirmed that:

> On June 15, 1954, Congress passed, and President Eisenhower signed into law a statute, that was clearly consistent with the text and intent of the Constitution of the United States, that amended the Pledge of Allegiance to read, "I pledge allegiance to the Flag of the United States of America and to the Republic for which it stands, one Nation under God, indivisible, with liberty and justice for all."

As *National Review*'s Byron York aptly observed, "The interesting thing about the wording is that it declares Congress's action in 1954 as being *clearly consistent with the text and intent of the Constitution*." The bill goes on to codify the pledge with "under God," reaffirms the national motto, "In God we trust," and pointedly condemns the Ninth Circuit decision for its "erroneous rationale" and "absurd result."[96] The House of Representatives passed the bill as well, with only five members voting against and four members abstaining, all nine being Democrats. On November 13, 2002, President Bush signed the bill into law.

The first two chapters have shown that Christianity is increasingly banned from our public schools—even when there is little evidence of school sponsorship of the religion. Nevertheless, many Christians might be able to countenance the ridiculously expansive interpretations of the Establishment Clause that preclude Christian religious freedom in the name of safeguarding it, were it not for the other half of the story. Chapters Three and Four tell this other half: that the education establishment often doesn't apply the same scrutiny of values-teaching in public schools when the values are secularly based or based on other major religions. If the separationists insist that there be a "wall of separation" between church and state, why don't they demand that it be applied across the board—against secular humanism, which even the Supreme Court has identified as a religion, and against other major religions? The answer, I'm afraid, is that what really motivates them is not an affinity for the separation principle, but a worldview that simply will not tolerate Christianity.

chapter Three

Secularism In, Part 1

Humanism

TO UNDERSTAND THE SECULAR VALUES the education establishment is actively promoting in our public schools, we need to review the humanistic movement in America that began in the nineteenth century. In 1876, former rabbi Dr. Felix Adler helped to establish the Society for Ethical Culture in New York City. This led to many other such societies that were later unified in the American Ethical Union, also founded by Adler, in 1889. The American Ethical Union was a seedbed for what would become "secular humanism," a philosophy that teaches that God does not exist, and that man is perfectible, self-sufficient and the measure of all things. By the early twentieth century, humanism had already begun to manifest itself in America's cultural institutions and public schools. In 1929, a former Baptist, then Unitarian preacher, Charles F. Potter, founded the First Humanist Society of New York. The next year, he wrote *Humanism: A New Religion*, which stated flatly, "Education is thus a most powerful ally of Humanism, and every American public school is a school of Humanism. What can the theistic Sunday-schools, meeting for an hour once a week, and teaching only a fraction of the children, do to stem the tide of a five-day program of humanistic teaching?"[1]

If humanism crept in as a natural byproduct of the secularism successfully promoted by Horace Mann in the public schools in the late nineteenth century, by the time America was in the Great Depression, it had achieved a level of mainstream acceptance in American culture. In 1933 the *Humanist Manifesto* was published and signed by thirty-four national figures, bringing humanism to a level of prominence in American culture. Educator John Dewey was among the signatories of this document that rejected traditional Christian beliefs and endorsed, as an alternative, those of naturalism, materialism, rationalism, and socialism.[2] The *Humanist Manifesto* expressed the humanists' goal: "to evaluate, transform, control, and direct all institutions and organizations by its own value system." As one writer has noted, the humanists' stated purpose was to effect a cultural revolution by substituting humanism for Christianity as the cultural foundation of America.[3]

Through the years the humanists succeeded in a big way. They have made significant inroads into many of our cultural institutions, not least the education system. In education, humanism became a great motivator, the great cause to which educators could devote their lives by influencing students, and also provided a coherent organizing principle, giving education a larger purpose. John Dewey's books were practically mandatory reading in teacher training colleges, making humanism the mainstream philosophy of public education. Humanism, not posing as a traditional religion, could enforce its own values under the guise of neutrality and without much scrutiny. Its precepts have come to inform the entire public school curriculum, as meticulously documented by Samuel L. Blumenfeld's *NEA: Trojan Horse in American Education*.[4] Yet, the strict separationists don't call education's endorsement of this values-driven worldview an encroachment on the Establishment Clause. That they don't reveals that their true interest lies in promoting secular values, rather than enforcing a strict separation of church and state.

Indeed, secular humanism is values-based. John Dewey described it as our "common faith." Canada's Christian Heritage Party leader Ron Gray observed, "We must not make the mistake of thinking that 'secular' means 'neutral.' Secularism is a religious worldview, the most bigoted faith on earth: its goal is to extirpate every other faith."[5] The first *Humanist Manifesto* referred to humanism as a religion. Even the United States Supreme Court, in *Torcaso v. Watkins* (1961),[6] recognized secular humanism as a religion: "Among religions in this country which do not teach what would generally be considered a belief in the existence of God, are Buddhism, Taoism, Ethical Culture, Secular Humanism and others."[7]

Humanist principles cannot be fairly be reconciled with Christian ones—they are "radically at war with biblical religion."[8] Humanists themselves make this quite clear. In *Humanist Manifesto III*, released in 2003, they affirm their beliefs in the self-existence of nature, a denial of the supernatural, and the "finality of death."[9] In fact, humanism subscribes to the notion that man's idea of religion itself was sparked by his interaction with the natural environment, as opposed to the distinctly Judeo-Christian view that God revealed Himself to man. Biologist and humanist Julian Huxley called it "Religion without Revelation." Moreover, humanism "affirm[s] that moral values derive their source from human experience and [not from God].[10]

History Revisionism: Excising Christianity

It's one thing to prohibit public schools from endorsing a particular religion, but does that mean that all references to Christian influences in our history should be expunged from our textbooks? Federal law is clear that schools may teach *about* religion, and schools are certainly not required to falsify history and delete Christianity from our heritage. Nevertheless, there has been a conscious decision to sanitize our history textbooks of information concerning the dominant presence of Christianity in colonial culture.

When Noah Webster wrote his *History of the United States*, published in 1832, he could state, "Almost all the civil liberty now enjoyed in the world owes its origin to the principles of the Christian religion... The religion which has introduced civil liberty is the religion of Christ and His Apostles, which enjoins humility, piety, and benevolence; which acknowledges in every person a brother or sister and a citizen with equal rights. This is genuine Christianity, and to this we owe our free constitutions of government."[11] As a leading American educator of his time, he could rest assured that this view was also routinely taught in the schools. It is not taught today.

The New Jersey Department of Education removed references to the Pilgrims and the *Mayflower* from its history standards for school textbooks.[12] The problem is that "Pilgrim" suggests religion, according to Brian Jones, vice president for Communications and Policy at the Education Leaders Council in Washington. Other historical events involving Christian worship or expression are also often taboo. "It's getting more difficult," said Jones, "to talk about the Bible and the Puritans"—or at least to talk about them accurately.[13]

A study by New York University psychology professor Paul Vitz documented the purging of religion from public school textbooks.[14] In examining sixty widely used social studies textbooks (used by eighty-seven percent of public school students), Vitz didn't find one that imparted the spirituality of the Pilgrims.[15] Vitz wrote, "Are public school textbooks biased? Are they censored? The answer to both is yes, and the nature of the bias is clear: Religion, traditional family values and many conservative positions have been reliably excluded from children's textbooks[16].... There is not one story or article in all these books in which the central motivation or major content is connected to Judeo-Christian religion[17].... In grades one through four these books introduce the child to U.S. society—to family life, community activities, ordinary economic transactions, and some history. None of the books covering grades one through four contains one word referring to any religious activity in contemporary American life."[18] Vitz concluded, "Religion, especially Christianity, has played and continues to play a central role in our culture and history. To neglect to report this is simply to fail to carry out the major duty of any textbook writer to tell the truth."[19]

One book had thirty pages on the Pilgrims, including the first Thanksgiving. But there was not a single reference to religion, even as part of the Pilgrims' lives. Another textbook described the Pilgrims simply as "people who make long trips." Another said that after their first year, the Pilgrims "wanted to give thanks for all they had," omitting that they were thanking God.[20] Dr. Vitz said, "It is common in these books to treat Thanksgiving without explaining to whom the Pilgrims gave thanks.... The Pueblo [Indians] can pray to Mother Earth, but Pilgrims can't be described as praying to God—and never are Christians described as praying to Jesus..."[21]

Indeed, many public schools now portray Thanksgiving as a multicultural harvest feast in which American colonists gave thanks to Indians. But this is "feel-good" myth. In fact, the Pilgrims' earliest thanksgiving celebrations, beginning in 1621, were expressing gratitude to the God of the Bible. When they landed at Plymouth in December 1620, the severity of the winter killed almost half of their people. But the next autumn's harvest was plentiful and in gratitude they held a three-day celebratory feast of thanksgiving to God. In 1623, Massachusetts Governor William Bradford set apart a day for prayer and fasting to praise God for the rain that had saved the colony's crops from a threatening drought.[22]

President George Washington's first proclamation was the declaration of a national Thanksgiving Day, explicitly devoted to giving thanks to God. But Thanksgiving wasn't celebrated as an annual holiday until President Lincoln established it as such. In his Thanksgiving Proclamation setting aside the last Thursday of November as a national holiday he wrote, "I do therefore invite my fellow citizens in every part of the United States, and also those who are at sea and those who are sojourning in foreign lands, to set apart and observe the last Thursday of November next, as a day of Thanksgiving and Praise to our beneficent Father who dwelleth in the Heavens."[23]

Despite the undeniable Christian origins and purpose of Thanksgiving Day, in 1995 the National Education Association passed a resolution affirming its belief "that Thanksgiving is the recognition of unity and the rich American diversity that was embodied in the settlement of America. This Association further believes that this national holiday must celebrate the coming together of peoples and the inclusion of all immigrants as a part of this great diverse country."[24] Whatever the merits of celebrating "diversity," as the education establishment uses that term, there is no excuse for misleading students about the stated historical purpose of the Thanksgiving holiday. And such rewriting of history is dangerous. If Noah Webster is right that the source of our freedom is the Christianity that shaped colonial America, then to deny students that perspective is to make students less well prepared to defend our liberty, or even recognize when it is being infringed.

"More Important Subjects"

It's not just Christianity per se that is given short shrift. Our founding fathers are also in disfavor with the popular culture and so are sometimes written out of history or downplayed to the point of ignoring their contributions. As Dr. Paul Vitz demonstrated, history and social studies, along with other subjects, are manipulated in public schools to conform to the ideological bent of the education establishment. The New Jersey Department of Education recently omitted America's founding fathers, including George Washington, Thomas Jefferson, and Benjamin Franklin, from the revised version of the state's history standards until an outpouring of public objections caused it to reverse its decision.[25]

Such actions are hardly unique to New Jersey. James Rees, executive director of Mount Vernon, George Washington's estate, says that history textbooks in Virginia schools in the 1960s contained ten times more coverage of Washington than modern texts. "It's shameful," said Rees, "how little we teach our children about Washington and other founding fathers."[26] Some argue that this practice of removing these references is ideologically driven. John Fonte of the Hudson Institute says that New Jersey is not concerned with teaching the basics of

American history. "Obviously," said Fonte, "there are anti-patriotic forces at work at the New Jersey legislature."[27]

The anti-traditional establishment is often more concerned with indoctrinating students in its worldview than with teaching the essentials of core subjects. A brief perusal of the NEA's 1995–1996 handbook well illustrates the point. The union shamelessly speaks out on policy issues having nothing to do with education, from endorsing the pro-choice position on abortion to stricter gun control legislation.

The National Council of Social Studies (NCSS), with 26,000 members nationwide, is another arm of the education establishment. It consists of teachers from various disciplines, including history, geography, political science, and economics. The NCSS holds itself out as the organization that helps prepare students for citizenship. Its self-described mission is to "provide leadership, service, and support for all social studies educators." And training social studies teachers, boasts the NCSS, has profound consequences for America: "Social studies educators teach students in the content knowledge, intellectual skills, and civic values necessary for fulfilling the duties of citizenship in a participatory democracy."

A credible case can be made, however, that instilling student pride in American history is not the goal of the group. Education expert and author Kay S. Hymowitz, of the Manhattan Institute, attended the NCSS's annual conference in November 2001. Keynote speaker James Loewen, wrote Hymowitz, "warned against patriotic displays like the singing of 'God Bless America.' The Swedes," he noted, "and the Kenyans don't think God blesses America over all other countries."

Hymowitz also shared an exchange that took place at a meeting of the New York chapter of NCSS between a teacher and Alan Schulman, a member of a panel on "The Impact of September 11 on Social Studies Professionals." When the teacher explained that her students had been anxious to learn more American history after the terrorist attacks, Schulman responded, "We need to de-exceptionalize the United States. We're just another country and another group of people."[28]

Sadly, this educator's attitude is not unusual among those in his profession. In 2002, the California assembly debated a bill that would require testing high school students on the essentials of American history, including the Declaration of Independence, the Constitution, and the Gettysburg Address. Members from the Claremont Institute—an organization that established the Teaching Teachers Project to restore the teaching of America's founding principles to public schools—testified in favor of the legislation. They stressed how important it was to our society that students be educated in civics. They also reported that during their testimony, "several liberal members of the legislature were so uninterested they simply walked away." Worse, they related the testimony of a state teachers' union spokesman in opposition to the legislation. This man opined that the Declaration and Constitution are "non-essential materials," and that schools have "more important subjects they need to be teaching."[29]

There are countless additional examples of what Claremont's Brian Kennedy describes as "a vast nationwide movement to declare irrelevant America's past and the principles on which it was founded."[30] One high school American history textbook, said Kennedy, devotes a mere six lines to George Washington, but six and a half pages to Marilyn Monroe.[31] Elsewhere, the California Teachers Association at one point eliminated from its calendar a reference to the Fourth of July, but included an entry for "Internment of Japanese Day." It featured a Buddhist Nirvana Day, but omitted Christmas and Thanksgiving.[32] And some want to tell us that multiculturalism doesn't reek of an anti-American and anti-Christian bias?

National Curriculum Standards

Sadly, this bias is reflected in the NCSS's National Standards for Social Studies Teachers.[33] These social studies curriculum standards, ironically, are called "Expectations of Excellence" and are used by state education authorities throughout the country in formulating their own state standards.[34] They are based on ten "themes," such as "Time,

Continuity, and Change" and "Global Connections." Disturbingly, as Kay Hymowitz points out, this "yawning list of 'performance expectations'... includes no American history, no major documents, and only a smattering of references to government."[35] Hymowitz is right. A read-through of the "standards" shows they are so general as to be meaningless. Such non-specific criteria can hardly be considered standards, which may help to explain why our students are so ignorant of history.

Even after the standards were implemented, national test scores remained abysmally low, as revealed when the Education Department released scores from the National Assessment of Education Progress (NAEP) tests, referred to by many as "the nation's report card." The results of the 2001 NAEP tests showed that a startlingly low percentage of fourth graders are proficient in history (eighteen percent)—let alone the other major disciplines: reading (thirty-two percent), math (twenty-six percent), and science (twenty-nine percent). Only seventeen percent of eighth graders scored "proficient" in history and a dismal eleven percent of twelfth-grade history students ranked "proficient." And in case you're wondering about the other nine grades, don't. Only fourth, eighth, and twelfth graders were tested as sample groups.[36] Focusing on history, the *Washington Post* reported that these deplorable history test results occurred though the number of states who adopted the standards "doubled in the 1990s from twenty to forty-six."[37]

So much for the NCSS's teaching students those things "necessary for fulfilling the duties of citizenship in a participatory democracy." Historian Diane Ravitch, a member of the National Assessment Government Board overseeing the NAEP, understood the implications of these test results. "Since the seniors are very close to voting age..." said Ravitch, "one can only feel alarm that they know so little about... history and express so little capacity to reflect on its meaning."[38] This is hardly surprising, considering that our students are denied instruction on essential facts about America's founding and that their textbooks, as documented by Dr. Paul Vitz,[39] notably lack patriotic stories. Indeed, how can we expect anything different from students who are spoon-fed the type of anti-American bilge on display at the NCSS annual conference and which was so clearly reflected in their national standards? This group not only doesn't inspire the study of American history by instilling national pride. It actively discourages it, by often placing America in a bad light.

Rejecting the Unique American Culture

C. Bradley Thompson, chairman of the Department of History and Political Science at Ashland University in Ohio, attended the annual meeting of the American Historical Association, the largest organization of academic historians in America. Thompson said that what he saw and heard shocked him. The ideas expressed at this conference, he noted, were "utterly subversive of American culture and values" and "will eventually make [their] way into your child's classroom." He said there were over 200 panels, but not one of them covered such subjects as the American Revolution, the Civil War, or the two World Wars. What was covered to the saturation point were topics "ranging from the banal to the bizarre and perverse." Thompson provided these examples: "Meditations on a Coffee Pot: Visual Culture and Spanish America, 1520–1820," "The Joys of Cooking: Ideologies of Housework in Early Modern England," and "Body, Body, Burning Bright: Cremation in Victorian America."[40]

As if all that weren't disturbing enough, Thompson related that sex was the dominant theme throughout. "Historians at America's best universities," he lamented, "are obsessed with it." The titles of certain papers and discussion topics make the point. Consider these: "Strong Hard Filth and The Aroma of Washington Square: Art, Homosexual Life, and Postal Service Censorship in the Ulysses Obscenity Trial of 1921;" "Solitary Self/Solitary Sex;" "Constructing Masculinity: Homosexual Sodomy, Ethnicity, and the Politics of Penetrative Manhood in Early Modern Spain."[41]

But the historians' sexual obsession, according to Thompson, is "the least of their vices." Academic history, said Thompson, is "driven by a hatred of America and its ideals." Routinely, he said, teachers tell their students that the colonists engaged in genocide when settling America and that the founding fathers, far from being admirable and learned gentlemen, were "racist, sexist, classist, homophobic, Eurocentric bigots." Further, America's expansion westward was capitalist pillage.[42]

Regrettably, Thompson's words ring true. But even when America and its culture and values are not disparaged, its distinguishing qualities are certainly not championed. Kay Hymowitz describes it this way: "That a professional association of teachers [the NCSS] would do nothing to encourage kids to think of themselves as Americans with a common history and common ideals will surprise no seasoned observer of the nation's schools. Like many in the education establishment, the NCSS regards promoting an American civic identity, particularly in minority children, as 'ethnocentric,' an example of an 'assimilationist ideology.'"

Unfortunately, Hymowitz is correct. The NCSS's "Curriculum Guidelines for Multicultural Education"—for the consumption and guidance of social studies teachers throughout America—are rife with admonitions to promote multiculturalism and de-emphasize our distinctly American culture, which, the guidelines emphasize, has no more value than any other culture. Guideline 19 shows how the NCSS pushes these other cultures. "Schools should provide opportunities to participate in the aesthetic experiences of various ethnic and cultural groups... The immersion of students in multiethnic experiences is an effective means for developing understanding of both self and others."

The multicultural flavor of these guidelines is taking hold in many of our public schools around the nation. The *Washington Times Weekly* reported that an examination of seven widely used world history textbooks revealed that public school classrooms "sanitize the problems of Islam" in comparison to their treatment of Western civilization. The study was conducted by the American Textbook Council, which speculated that the special treatment of Islam might be the result of lobbying by the Council on Islamic Education. The report said the books make no effort to hide the warts and blemishes in Western history, such as slavery, the delay of women's suffrage, and others. But, it said, "subjects such as jihad and the advocacy of violence among militant Islamists to attain worldly ends, the imposition of [Shariah] law, the record of Muslim enslavement, and the brutal subjection of women are glossed over."[43]

One such textbook, *Across the Centuries*, was accompanied by "Islam simulation materials" in California schools, where the state legislature mandated three weeks of Islam studies for seventh grade students as part of a statewide curriculum. This textbook, like so many others, presents a biased view in favor of Islam and against Christianity. Conspicuously omitted from the book is any mention of the history of Islamic conquest—the Moors' invasion, the Battle of Tours, and the execution of Jews in Quarayza.[44]

With the book's simulation materials, students weren't just required to learn *about* the religion; they were forced to pretend they were Muslims, praying in the name of Allah, the Compassionate, the Merciful, and to chant "praise to Allah, Lord of Creation." They were required to take Muslim names, simulate their own jihad (a holy war against Islam's enemies) through a dice game, and plan a pilgrimage to Mecca. At Byron/Excelsior Public School, a middle school in the Oakland area—where students, incidentally, rank very poorly in English comprehension—students were taught to write Islamic sayings in the Arabic language.[45] Teachers further encouraged students to dress in Muslim garb and to use Muslim phrases such as "Allah Akbar," meaning "God is great." They even had to memorize Islamic prayers, fulfill the Five Pillars of the faith, and engage in lunchtime fasts during Ramadan, the Islamic holy month, all of which counted toward their grade in the class. Teachers told students that during this course in Islam "you and your classmates will become Muslims."[46]

On behalf of parents and four students, the Thomas More Law

Center filed suit against the Byron/Excelsior school. Chief Counsel Richard Thompson explained, "Although it is constitutional for public schools to have an instructional program about comparative religion or teach about religion and utilize religious books such as the Bible in courses about our history and culture, the Byron Union School District crossed way over the line when it coerced impressionable twelve year olds to engage in particular religious rituals and worship, simulated or not."[47] On a particular note of irony, the Thomas More Center filed this suit the very week the Ninth Circuit Court of Appeals outlawed the Pledge of Allegiance in the same state.

Jay Sekulow and Gene Kapp of the American Center for Law and Justice interviewed Elizabeth Lemings, the mother of one of the students, on their radio program. Lemings teaches in the Byron school district herself. Her comments make it clear that students were required to engage in the *practice* of the Islamic faith—an actual worship experience—in a way that had it involved the Christian faith, the ACLU would have combusted with outrage. Lemings explained that her son had to wear his Muslim name, "Ishmael," on a nametag around his neck. "They were graded on fulfilling the Five Pillars of faith: There was a 'caravan log' that they had to keep as they did their 'pilgrimage.' They also had a 'faith grade,' a 'prayer grade,' an 'alms-giving grade,' and a 'fasting grade' along with the 'pilgrimage grade.'"[48]

Wards of the State

One of the problems of public education is that it inevitably teaches values; and all too often those values are not those of the parents but of education bureaucrats whose values and ideas can be very different from what parents want for their children. The great British historian Christopher Dawson noted this as a growing trend of the twentieth century and expressed it eloquently and sadly in these words: "[M]odern education and propaganda give the community such control over the thought and emotion of the individual that religious emotion and belief no longer have free play. The inner world of spiritual experience has been opened up by the child psychologist and the schoolmaster and has become public property, so that the child can literally no longer call its soul its own." When the schools work against parents, they tacitly assert, in the words of author Dr. Samuel Blumenfeld, "that children [are] owned by the state."[49] And the morality of the state can be at stark contrast with traditional Christian morality and with the values Christian parents try to impart to their children. In the state of Massachusetts alone:

- A public school freshman health textbook in Silver Lake said, "Testing your ability to function sexually and give pleasure to another person may be less threatening in the early teens with people of your own sex... You may come to the conclusion that growing up means rejecting the values of your parents." (Reportedly, students were not allowed to take this book home.)

- After sitting through a week's worth of compulsory school assemblies during "Homophobia Week" in Beverly, a fourteen-year-old told her dad he was homophobic. Another student reportedly expressed his revulsion with the school events in a local newspaper, saying, "I felt disturbed and nauseated. I witnessed biased testimonies by gays and the public mocking of a priest in our auditorium." Needless to say, parents were not alerted to the school's festivities glorifying homosexuality.

- Also in Beverly, after a parent had removed a child because sexual harassment instruction was substituted for algebra class for four days, the teacher cajoled the student to return anyway, saying, "Your parents don't have to know."

- In Manomet, an eighth grade student informed his health instructor that materials he had distributed to the class conflicted with his parents' beliefs, but the teacher dismissed the student's concern. "If you have any trouble with your parents," he said, "tell me and I'll handle them."

- A principal in Newton would not abide by parents' directions to remove their children from a condom-distribution program, telling them, "It's too important."

Another example of schools keeping parents out of the loop occurred in St. Louis, Missouri, where a mother, Debra Loveless, was barred from attending a school-sponsored assembly at Metro High School organized by the Gay, Lesbian, and Straight Education Network (GLSEN). GLSEN holds itself out as the country's largest consortium of educators, parents, and students dedicated to preventing "discrimination based on sexual orientation and gender/identity expression in K-12 schools."[50] Loveless had tried to attend the event herself after deciding not to let her daughter attend but was prohibited from doing so. Loveless filed suit against the school district. Before trial, her attorneys, with the American Center for Law and Justice, worked out a settlement agreement with the school whereby it agreed to revise its policy so as not to bar parents from attending events based on their beliefs about the event. School officials, under the revised policy, reserve the right to remove disruptive parents.[51]

Considering the vulnerability of young children, the potential ramifications of the deliberate exclusion of parents from input and control are sobering.

New Age

While we now expect public schools to impose a strict prohibition on Christian symbols, practices, and expressions, other values-laden instruction is routinely given. In a federally funded health program for public secondary schools, the "Teenage Health Teaching Model," teachers are instructed to emphasize the students' choice on whether to engage in the "legitimate options" of smoking, drinking, and drugs, based on what they believe is "right for them." Many parents, who are legally responsible for their teenage children, might not approve of the public schools telling their sons and daughters that underage drinking and the use of illegal drugs is something for them to consider if it is "right for them." But that's not all this program teaches. It tells students there are many positive ways to express anger, such as sex, screaming, locking oneself in a room, meditating, slamming doors, and throwing things.[52]

The idea that "meditation" and relaxation techniques are something schools should encourage is increasingly widespread, but also carries some disturbing baggage with it. One mother was reportedly driving her kids to school when she realized her second grade daughter was uncharacteristically quiet, even though her brother was bothering her. The daughter's eyes remained closed and she was unresponsive when the mother called her name. When the mother "shook" her little girl out of her trance she calmly explained, "Don't worry, Mommy, I was relaxing, painting my mind picture, and was with my friend Pumsy." She said that she had learned to do this at school.[53]

"Pumsy" advocates claim that "Pumsy" is in some forty percent of the nation's public schools. Pumsy teaches students to relax by going on fantasy trips to receive "counseling" from their imaginary friends, which include Pumsy, a dragon. There is also a similar program using "DUSO," a dolphin. Parents have challenged these activities around the nation, mostly successfully. Because of the controversial DUSO program, the New Mexico senate passed a law calling for the elimination of psychological or mind-altering techniques in public schools.[54]

Some Christians have objected to these programs because of what they believe are their humanist and New Age themes. While Pumsy may include *some* good, it also sends a subtle message that children can find an ultimate source of wisdom (and goodness) within themselves. Just by tapping on that inner reservoir, they'll automatically begin to behave better and achieve greater fulfillment.[55] A passage from the Pumsy student storybook reads: "Your clear mind is the best friend you'll ever have. It will always be there when you need it. It is always close to you and it will never leave you. You may think you have lost your clear mind, but it will never lose you."[56] Students are encouraged to believe that they can eliminate negative feelings and urges not by dealing with them or confronting the source of whatever might be troubling them, but by ignoring them and looking within for their "clear mind." Many Christians have also objected to these lessons because they seem to convey the message that guilt is an artificial human construct, not a natural (and sometimes even healthy) response to immoral or inappropriate behavior.

Hinduism, Mother Earth

Pumsy and DUSO aren't the only vehicles for injecting nontraditional values into our public schools. In White Plains, New York, in 1999, a group of Roman Catholic parents sued the Bedford School District for introducing New Age themes in the schools. One complaint was that a third grade teacher asked students to make "worry dolls" during a lesson on India. Some believe that worry dolls can ward off evil spirits. Another objection was that the teacher asked the children to make paper representations of Ganesha, a Hindu god. Perhaps the worst example involved an Earth Day assembly where the students were told: "The mother of us all is the earth. The father is the sun."

While the judge did strike down these three practices, he let twelve others stand, such as yoga exercises, meditation, and lectures on crystals.[57] The yoga exercises were taught by a "yogi," Sikh minister Agia Akai Singh Kalsa. The minister denied, as they always do, that his lesson had anything to do with religion.[58] Most noteworthy here is how effortlessly a Sikh minister, Hindu practices, New Age beliefs, and yoga were introduced in the school. Would the school—or the judge in his compromise ruling—have been so lenient if the Roman Catholic parents had tried to insert a curriculum with a Catholic priest teaching how to pray the Rosary, venerate the Virgin Mary, and pray the Stations of the Cross? Somehow, I don't think so. It has become a natural knee-jerk reaction of the public schools to have one exclusionist standard for Christians and one inclusive, "tolerant" standard for every other system of belief.

Native American Spiritism and Rituals

At the American Indian Magnet School, a public school in St. Paul, Minnesota, magic "dreamcatchers" (to protect students from evil spirits) are displayed in many classrooms. So are mystical "spiritualized" drawings of the earth. Stones on the playground are arranged in a ring for the performance of Medicine Wheel ceremonies.

At least one student's mother was appalled at this apparent establishment of Native American spirituality at the school, along with the derogation of Western civilization and the wonders of pagan practices.[59] She sat in on one of the classes and witnessed, among other things, a ritual drumming and dance in which students were taught that women are forbidden to make contact with the drum for fear of offending the female spirit within it. Her student guide for the day affirmed her own belief in the Ojibwe creation story she had learned at the school. And a fourth grade teacher explained that an amber crystal in the center of the dreamcatcher was a "sacred circle" with a magical spider web inside. The crystal, she said, symbolized the importance of people being aligned with the spiritual energy of the earth. This same teacher, in discussing the school, gushed, "Here you not only are involved in education, but receive a deep spiritual experience that's not available at other public schools."[60]

It is true that this Native American school is designed to improve the "alarmingly high" dropout rate among Native American students in Minnesota. But again it is hard to imagine that if there were an alarmingly high dropout rate of black Baptists in Minnesota, a school focused around black Baptist spirituality would be approved by the school district or by the courts. This would no doubt be contested as violating the Establishment Clause of the First Amendment. But if that is how the law would be applied to Christianity, why is it not equally applied to Native American spirituality? It is cases like this that highlight how our school districts and courts speak the language of George Orwell's *Animal Farm*: some religions "are more equal than others."

Welcome to Human Sacrifice Day!

That's essentially what an elementary school in Pleasantville, Pennsylvania, said, when it organized a school performance entitled "Bizarre Bazaar" in which third, fourth, and fifth graders were to participate in dramatic re-creations of Aztec human sacrifice. Parents were appalled that human sacrifice would be portrayed in school theater for young, impressionable students. Keith Klinger, one of the objecting parents, said he was "very disappointed that those in charge . . . didn't see anything wrong with this type of production, especially around Christmas."[61] But, of course, to many public school administrators, Christmas is generally considered more controversial than human sacrifice.

McNear Elementary School in Petaluma, California, arguably went further by sponsoring an el Dia de los Muertos (Day of the Dead) celebration. Parents and others strongly disapproved of the program, not because it taught about the cultural significance of this traditional Mexican holiday, but because students were encouraged to take part in rituals related to it, such as creating altars and bringing photos of deceased family members to school. Children were led to place the pictures of their dead relatives and pets on the altar in remembrance of them. Objecting parents considered this a form of religious activity. One outraged parent remarked, "They can teach about it, but they're not supposed to be celebrating. . . . I have the right to send my daughter to school to learn math, reading, and writing without having a religious ritual shoved down her throat."[62]

What about the parents' concern over the religious implications of the holiday? As it turns out, "Day of the Dead" is an ancient Meso-

American holiday, celebrated on November 1 and 2, "that honors death by emphasizing it as an important part of the cycle of life."[63] Some go so far as to worship the dead. Many believe that during this period the spirits of the departed return to their homes to visit family and friends. Some practitioners provide a wash basin and clean hand towel to allow the visiting souls to freshen up before a feast they provide for them. The smell of burning incense and the light from many candles are arranged to assist the spirits find their way.[64]

The United States Justice Foundation (USJF) officially objected to the event as an endorsement of particular religious views. USJF's chief litigation attorney, Richard Ackerman, noted the hypocrisy of those who are so adamant about restricting Christian expression while having no problem with the promotion of other religions in public schools. "This is irresponsible," said Ackerman. "As a Christian parent, I would be beside myself if my child came home and said, 'Hey, we put offerings on the altar of the dead in class today.'... I just can't even imagine if they had a Palm Sunday event. People would be freaking out."[65]

Death Education

"Death education" is another avenue through which certain favored spiritual influences have been infiltrating public schools. Tara Becker is a former student of Columbine High in Littleton, Colorado, the school where the horrible student-on-student mass murder occurred. At a pro-family conference in 1985, Becker told of her exposure to death education at Columbine. According to Jayne Schindler, a conference attendee, "Tara explained that the subject of death was integrated into many of the courses at her high school. She said that death was made to look glamorous, that living was hard and that reincarnation would solve their problems. Students were told that they would always return to a much better life form. They would return to the 'Oversoul' and become like God."[66]

The next part is shockingly worse. Schindler related Tara's description of a "suicide talking day" that the school arranged following the suicide of one of the students. That day teachers and students talked about death in every class. Teachers assigned students the task of writing their own obituaries and suicide notes. "They were told to trust their own judgment in choosing whether to live or die." Largely as a result of this orientation, Tara said that she began to contemplate suicide as an option, to end her problems. Suicide, she thought, would liberate her spirit from being enslaved to her body. It would also help to relieve the world's population problem.[67] That qualifies perhaps as the ultimate in politically correct education: suicide to relieve global overpopulation.

Phyllis Schlafly's Eagle Forum produced a two-hour video on Tara's experiences, which led to an ABC-TV 20/20 program on the subject. On that program Tara explained that she never would have considered suicide prior to the class instruction on death education because she wasn't brave enough. But the things students learned in class, she said, "taught us how to be brave enough to face death." "We talked about what we wanted to look like in our caskets." 20/20 reported that ten percent of public schools offer death education, but since there is no approved curriculum, teachers often receive their entire training in a one-day workshop.[68] Robert Stevenson, an expert in counseling and education, confirmed this, noting that "anyone with a teacher's license can walk in off the street and start teaching death ed. Some people teach these courses as their own form of self-therapy."[69]

As far back as 1988, the *Atlantic Monthly* reported that thousands of schools across the country offer courses treating death and dying explicitly. Many schools, however, "blended some of the philosophies and techniques of death education into health, social studies, literature, and home-economics courses." The formal death education classes, according to the article, were widely varied in form and content. Some lasted just a few days. Others, however, were full-semester classes "that systematically explore the physical process of death, students' feelings about death and bereavement, the social rituals that surround death, the causes of suicide and its prevention, euthanasia, the right to die, the economics of funerals, and methods of interment and cremation."

One writer related a disturbing story of death instruction in a Massachusetts school that provides a glimpse of the attitudes that teachers in this field are imparting to students. An inordinate number of students at this particular school had committed suicide, which led to an investigation by an educational consultant. He met with the teacher of the school's death education course and was shocked when the teacher told him that fewer suicides at the school would not necessarily be an improvement. The death teacher "reasoned" that if students made the decision to commit suicide on their own, it would be a tribute to their courage in making "an independent decision."[70]

The *Atlantic Monthly* unearthed the roots of death education in a National Education Association report entitled "Education for the '70s." The report stated: "Schools will become ethics clinics whose purpose is to provide individualized psycho-social treatment for the student, and teachers must become psycho-social therapists."[71] It also quoted from a 1977 piece in *The School Counselor* magazine, which argued that schools should offer death education because "Americans handle death and dying poorly and we ought to be doing better at it. . . . Change is evident, and death education will play as important a part in changing attitudes toward death as sex education played in changing attitudes toward sex information and wider acceptance of various sexual practices." But why is "changing attitudes toward death" and "changing attitudes" to a "wider acceptance of various sexual practices" a legitimate function of a public school? That is, why should thoughts about death, suicide, and sexual activity that are at odds with Christianity have a privileged place of instruction in the public schools? Why is it that explicitly Christian teaching about death and suicide and sexual activity would be prohibited by most schools for fear of the Establishment Clause of the First Amendment, yet what is at essence anti-Christian teaching is not only allowed but promoted as necessary to "change attitudes?" The First Amendment was never intended to mandate anti-Christian teaching and shouldn't be used as a defense for it.

This chapter has documented many of the anti-Christian and non-Christian values American public schools readily endorse. Chapter Four details more of them, with a particular emphasis on those being promoted by homosexual activists. While they usually profess the innocuous goal of mere equal rights, respect, and dignity, their methods involve an unmistakable push to ostracize Christian thought and traditional Judeo-Christian values. The mere expression of Christian belief, in some cases, is deemed to be harassment and hate speech. It is especially in this context that the secularists' notion of tolerance is exposed as the fraud that it often is.

chapter Four

Secularism In, Part 2

Sex Education

WITH ALL THE PROBLEMS ACCOMPANYING teenage sexual activity, one would think our education establishment would err on the side of discouraging promiscuous sex. In addition to student pregnancy and the escalation in sexually transmitted diseases (STDs), a recent Heritage Foundation study reveals that sexually active teenagers are far more prone to depression and likely to commit suicide than those who refrain from sex.[1] Yet sex education is captive to another agenda. It is another tool being used by the social engineers to remold American society through the education system. Today's sex education is radically different from the type offered in public schools a generation ago. Now, students are often exposed to presentations on homosexuality and other so-called alternative lifestyles under the assumption that to exclude such topics would be an imposition of religious or sectarian values—as if including them isn't.

While the ostensible purpose of these courses is to help prevent student pregnancy and STDs, student exposure to "alternative lifestyles" along with the promotion of "safe sex" through condom usage can promote rather than discourage such negative consequences. Indeed, while sex education has been touted as the answer to curb widespread promiscuity among teenagers, many believe it has done the opposite. Teens are more exposed to and more educated about sex than ever before and yet their sexual experimentation has increased rather than subsided. The consequences have been devastating. Studies show that comprehensive sex education not only leads to sexual experimentation,[2] but often conceals the risks of "protected sex" for both STDs and unwanted pregnancies.

Certain groups such as Planned Parenthood and SIECUS (the Sexuality Information and Education Council of the United States) have feverishly lobbied Congress to accept the dogma that "safe sex" training and condom-based sex education are not only best for children, but are supported by the majority of parents. Recent polling data, however, show the opposite: parents don't buy the canard that abstinence education is unrealistic nor that "comprehensive sex education" is the better choice. Dr. Janice Crouse, in describing the new data, says that previous polling data from these lobbying groups were based on "deception and dishonest interpretation."

Most parents become outraged when given concrete examples of materials actually used in these vaunted sex education courses, such as those from the sex education guidelines developed by SIECUS and others. Those guidelines provide that 1) children ages 5-8 be taught that it feels good to touch and rub body parts; 2) those 9-12 be taught that homosexuality is as satisfying as heterosexuality; 3) 15-18-year-old students be taught that using erotic photographs, movies, or literature will enhance sexual fantasies.[3] Dr. Crouse also provided the results of a recent Zogby poll confirming that parents approve or strongly approve of abstinence education (by a 4.6 to 1 margin) and disapprove or strongly disapprove of comprehensive sex education (by a 2.4 to 1 margin).[4] Yet the homosexual lobby continues to pursue its campaign to oppose abstinence education.

Demoting Abstinence

In 1997, Louisiana Governor Mike Foster began the Governor's Program on Abstinence, in which he authorized the expenditure of $1.6

million of federally allocated money per year for five years to abstinence-only sex education programs aiming to lower the state's teenage pregnancy rate. The money was made available from the federal government through the 1996 Welfare Reform Act. The Louisiana ACLU went ballistic, charging that the abstinence programs were Christian-oriented and that spending federal money on them was illegal. Joe Cook, the executive director, said, "We want them to take the appropriate steps to make sure that tax dollars are not being used to preach religion."[5] Following a lawsuit by the ACLU a settlement was reached whereby the Governor's Program on Abstinence agreed to ensure that federal funds would not be used to promote religion.[6]

A reasonable case can be made that federal monies ought not to be used to promote religion. But, just because Christians support the abstinence message doesn't mean that message is religious. Moreover, it appears that other states have an aversion to the abstinence message regardless of whether federal grants are involved. The secularist viewpoint does not readily tolerate the abstinence theme, as a recent incident involving the New Jersey Education Association (NJEA) demonstrated.

New Jersey has experienced its share of problems related to teenage sexual behavior. The problems were so severe that the New Jersey legislature passed a law that mandates the stressing of abstinence when sex education is taught in public schools. The NJEA invited three experts on teenage sexual activity to speak at its annual convention but withdrew the invitation when it discovered they promote the abstinence message. The New Jersey Coalition for Abstinence Education (NJCAE), which is part of the New Jersey Family Policy Counsel, was scheduled to present a workshop for teachers at the convention, as were New Jersey doctors Joanna Mohn, M.D., and James Thompson, M.D.[7]

NJCAE's director, Bernadette Vissani, expressed concern that NJEA was censoring the abstinence perspective. NJEA's spokeswoman, Karen Joseph, said the union prefers comprehensive sex education, whereas the NJCAE employs an abstinence-only approach.

"The abstinence-only approach is unrealistic," said Joseph. "It's the same as saying, 'If we prohibit driving, we will eliminate all traffic accidents.' While that's true, it's unrealistic. We should be teaching safe driving and providing people with tools that will bring about safe driving. The same thing applies here."

One has to wonder about educators who teach that sex is like driving—that is, entirely about mechanics—as opposed to doctors who would acknowledge that there is more to it than that. Isn't it rather superficial for purported educators to ignore that powerful human emotions are involved, let alone profound moral teachings that almost every major religion has promoted?

Joseph's driving analogy also fails because these "comprehensive" sex education programs do not adequately, if at all, alert children to many of the potential consequences of teenage sex—dangers that exist even when contraception is used, as pediatrician Dr. Meg Meeker recently pointed out in her stunning book *Epidemic*. Dr. Meeker shows that the assumed safety of contraceptive devices has led to an epidemic of sexually transmitted diseases among teenagers who have never been told that contraception will not protect them from many of the extremely serious health perils that can become a lifetime legacy of teenage sexual activity.

Driver's education, we know, focuses heavily on safety issues. But it's highly doubtful that comprehensive sex education sufficiently emphasizes that certain reliable research has shown that condoms have a fifteen percent failure rate for pregnancy.[8] In fact, increased condom use by teens has been associated with increased out-of-wedlock birth rates.[9] Condoms are also believed to have a fifteen percent failure rate for HIV transmission.[10] In addition, comprehensive sex education does not likely reveal that HPV (Human Papillomavirus), which is frequently contracted as a result of teenage sexual activity, is the major cause of cervical cancer, which kills approximately five thousand American women each year—and that there is no scientific proof that condoms protect against it.

It is also misleading to suggest that the NJCAE teaches "abstinence only." According to Vissani, its approach is abstinence-centered but does not omit information about contraceptives. It shares scientific information on the actual health risks associated with teenage sex and attempts to correct the dangerous myths that exist about "protected" sex. It stresses that teenage sexual activity itself is high-risk behavior, and it aims to reduce that behavior.

The scandal of the comprehensive approach is that it puts kids at greater risk of pregnancy and disease by downplaying abstinence and promoting the use of condoms without informing kids about the real health risks involved. How can it be argued that such programs don't encourage reckless behavior when they preach the euphemism of "protected" sex, which gives kids a false sense of security?

According to a four-year study reported in the April 2003 issue of the *Journal of Adolescent and Family Health*, the principal reason for the decline in birth and pregnancy rates of teenage girls is abstinence, not condom use. The report concluded that abstinence accounted for one hundred percent of the teen birthrate decline and sixty-seven percent in the decline in the pregnancy rate for single teens. The study refuted findings of the Alan Guttmacher Institute, frequently cited in the last few years, that seventy-five percent of the decline in pregnancy rate is attributable to contraceptive use and twenty-five percent to abstinence.[11] Research—ten separate scientific evaluations[12]—has suggested that abstinence-centered education has been highly effective (much more effective than "safe sex" and condom distribution programs) in reducing sexual activity rates, sexually transmitted diseases, teenage abortion rates, and the number of children born into single-parent families.[13] Yet most conventional "safe sex" programs place little or no emphasis on encouraging people to abstain from early sexual activity.[14] It would appear that the education establishment's fear of religious values outweighs statistical and medical truth to the point of actively putting teenagers' health at risk. Christianity and other major religions do teach the virtue of chastity, but that shouldn't be grounds to deny students potentially life-saving information. Or can we no longer teach children not to steal or murder because those admonitions are contained in the Ten Commandments?

Even if the New Jersey teacher's union disagrees with the claims of abstinence-centered sex education, shouldn't it at least be willing to expose its teachers to legitimate opinions from both sides of the issue in the name of, if nothing else, diversity? Or does its ideology compel it to silence the other side—the one that is supported by empirical evidence? Sadly, it's just another example of the same people who promote "diversity" and "tolerance" being the most intolerant and close-minded against anything remotely linked to religion. In this case, their dogmatism has deadly consequences. But their propaganda continues unabated.

Advocates for Youth (AFY), an organization promoting "gay, lesbian, bisexual, and transgender" practices for teens and children met at a conference in December to launch a campaign opposing federal abstinence funding. One speaker at the conference, Pat Schiller, a longtime advocate of sex education, said, "Sexuality is a pleasurable experience whether you're two, six, or sixteen." Wayne Palowski, director of training for Planned Parenthood of America, added, "Boys should be encouraged to use condoms and masturbate at home so they will develop skills for future sex acts." Palowski also reportedly advocated that schools teach masturbation skills as part of sex education classes.[15]

Promoting the Gay Agenda

It is no secret that gay activists are promoting the homosexual agenda in schools, with the idea that a transformation of students' attitudes about the behavior will lead not only to its acceptance in our society, but perhaps even an increase in the number of practicing homosexuals. Activists have developed "marketing" strategies to accomplish their aims, such as "conversion." Paul Rondeau, a doctoral student at

Regent University, explained that one method to "convert" children into accepting the gay lifestyle is to wear society down from constant barrages "to the point where just accepting homosexuality is much less of a burden than continuing to fight it.... Whoever captures the kids owns the future."[16]

This emerging presence of homosexual propaganda in schools may owe its origin to the efforts of Marshall Kirk and Erastes Pill, two gay activists who concocted an elaborate homosexual spin campaign in 1987 with the publication of their piece, "The Overhauling of Straight America." The article first appeared in the November 1987 issue of *The Guide*, a magazine of "Gay Travel, Entertainment, Politics, and Sex." It makes clear the authors' purposes: to systematically normalize the homosexual culture and demonize any who obstruct such efforts. The first step, they said, is to desensitize the public—to get the public to "view homosexuality with indifference instead of with keen emotion."

The authors told the gay community that if it could simply condition society to "shrug [its] shoulders" with indifference about homosexuality, "your battle for legal and social rights is virtually won." To accomplish this, the authors proposed a "large-scale media campaign" to "change the image of gays in America," consisting of six elements.

1) "Talk about gays and gayness as loudly and as often as possible." The theory is that sufficient exposure will make the behavior look normal. And the authors suggested methods for overcoming objections of conservative churches. There are only two ways, they said "to confound the homophobia of true believers." The first is to "use talk to muddy the moral waters. This means publicizing support for gays by more moderate churches, raising theological objections of our own about conservative interpretations of biblical teachings, and exposing hatred and inconsistency." Sound familiar? The second way is to "undermine the moral authority of homophobic churches by portraying them as antiquated backwaters."

2) "Portray gays as victims, not as aggressive challengers." The authors say, "In any campaign to win over the public, gays must be cast as victims in need of protection so that straights will be included by reflex to assume the role of protector." Does the advent of "safe zones" and "safe schools" ring a bell? One school in Minnesota has fifty classrooms that have been designated as "safe zones" (physically marked with pink triangles), meaning that students who have questions about their sexuality can talk to the teachers in those rooms "safely"—without risk that the teachers will criticize homosexuality. The teacher can then refer the students for outside counseling with a pro-homosexual consultant or to a gay activist group. Mostly this is done without parental involvement, much less consent.[17]

3) "Give protectors a just cause." The authors acknowledge that homosexuals won't make much headway by demanding "direct support for homosexual practices." Instead, they should "take anti-discrimination" as their theme. The idea is to turn the tables on heterosexual society—making those who oppose them look like hardened bigots.

4) "Make gays look good. To offset the increasingly bad press that these times have brought to homosexual men and women, the campaign should paint gays as superior pillars of society.... The honor roll of prominent gay or bisexual men and women is truly eye-popping. From Socrates to Shakespeare, from Alexander the Great to Alexander Hamilton...." Now you know another reason that many of our public school teachings on these men have been re-oriented, so to speak.

5) "Make the victimizers look bad." Listen to this: "At a later stage of the media campaign for gay rights—long after other gay ads have become commonplace—it will be time to get tough with remaining opponents. To be blunt, they must be vilified.... Our goal here is twofold. First, we seek to replace the mainstream's self-righteous pride

about its homophobia with shame and guilt. Second, we intend to make the anti-gays look so nasty that average Americans will want to dissociate themselves from such types." Now, get this further advice as to how to implement this strategy. "The public should be shown images of ranting homophobes whose secondary traits and beliefs disgust middle America. These images might include: the Ku Klux Klan demanding that gays be burned alive or castrated; bigoted southern ministers drooling with hysterical hatred to a degree that looks both comical and deranged; menacing punks, thugs, and convicts speaking coolly about the 'fags' they have killed or would like to kill; a tour of Nazi concentration camps where homosexuals were tortured and gassed."

6) "Solicit Funds: The Buck Stops Here," which provides fundraising suggestions.

If the authors are to be evaluated on the success of their campaign, they deserve exceedingly high marks. The California legislature recently enacted the California Student Safety and Violence Prevention Act, which requires the state education curriculum to be modified to enable students to acknowledge homosexual, lesbian, "transgender," and bisexual historical figures and events. Here again, the pretense is to prevent violence, but the actual purpose is, inevitably, indoctrination.[18] Other states, such as Florida and New York, are considering similar bills, both called the "Dignity for All Students Act."[19]

Indeed, homosexual activists have made great strides in public schools. One of the ways they are forcing their agenda into schools is through so-called anti-harassment or anti-bullying policies, explored below. Through this vehicle and others, their goal is not simply to end the mistreatment of gays or to prevent bullying, but to force heterosexual society to accept their behavior as normal—as just another equally valid lifestyle.

Some states are officially supporting this agenda. In West Virginia, the attorney general's office organized the Civil Rights Team Project to squash school bullies, but some believe that it is nothing more than a veiled program to advance the homosexual cause. Kevin McCoy, president of the West Virginia Family Foundation, points to the Civil Rights Team Project's training manual as proof. According to McCoy, the manual recommends that teachers "wear a 'LesBiGay positive' button or a T-shirt with a 'Straight, but not Narrow' slogan or a pink triangle; tell students not to assume all their classmates are heterosexual, but acknowledge that some students are homosexual and bisexual; avoid using traditional terms such as boyfriend, girlfriend, wife, or husband, and broaden their language to include 'partner, lover, significant other.' Teachers are also advised to use the phrase 'permanent relationship' instead of 'marriage;' identify the contributions of homosexuals in history, literature, art, science, and religion and expand libraries to include books related to sexual diversity."[20] Advocates of the program nevertheless deny that it seeks to promote the gay agenda—apparently hoping that the covering language of "civil rights" will give them a free pass from closer scrutiny, pigeonholing opponents as "anti-civil rights."

Effective January 1, 2001, California enacted two bills, AB1785 and AB1931, that opponents say will expose students to "information and activities designed to influence [their] views about human sexuality and gender identity, including areas of homosexuality, bisexuality, transvestitism, transsexuality, and other alternative lifestyles." AB1785 encourages the adoption of curricula to promote "tolerance" education in public schools at every grade level, beginning with kindergarten. Gary Kreep of the United States Justice Foundation described the measure as "a dagger aimed at the innocence of our children," that would "isolate and target those who do not agree with the homosexual lifestyle." AB1931 provides for taxpayer-funded grants to take children on field trips where they can learn about "diversity" and "tolerance." Included in "diversity" is the category of "sexual orientation." Ultimately, the aim of the bills is clearly values-based: to inculcate in children the notion that homosexual behavior is normal and morally acceptable. In response, pro-family groups developed "opt-out" forms that would allow parents to remove their children from objectionable courses. California law already permits the use of such forms for sex education classes, but the new opt-out form is broader and covers all other courses the parents might find objectionable.[21]

Nevertheless, under these laws and subsequent California legislation and administrative guidelines, California public school students are often introduced to the gay lifestyle while their teachers are encouraged to take "tolerance" training. Karen Holgate of the Capitol Resource Institute describes one school district that is using a course called Preventing Prejudice, which features lessons on "coming out" and "what is a boy/girl?" Holgate said, "This whole movement is not about tolerance. It's about redirecting the hate towards anyone who does not agree that homosexuality is a normal, positive and healthy lifestyle."[22]

Speaking of normal lifestyles, in 2000 the gay activist group GLSEN (Gay, Lesbian, and Straight Education Network) and the Massachusetts Education Department co-hosted a TeachOUT at Tufts University in Boston. At the conference the organizers taught public school teachers how to incorporate positive messages about homosexuality into the curriculum. But more controversial were the instructions to children as young as fourteen on various homosexual practices, including "fisting." This outrage led to two Department of Education instructors being fired, but that didn't deter GLSEN from planning another TeachOUT shortly thereafter.[23]

Another indoctrination technique is the use of pro-homosexual videos in elementary and middle schools. Debra Chasnoff and Helen S. Cohen produced a three-part series entitled "Respect for All." The first video, "That's a Family," reportedly exposes student viewers to multiple types of families, including "divorced, single parent, adoptive, multiracial, multigenerational, and stepfamilies, and intertwining gay and lesbian families." Chasnoff and Cohen are optimistic that the "impact of this project will be tremendous." They say, in a 1999 fundraising letter, "Giving elementary school students the opportunity to hear the word 'gay' and 'lesbian' described in a matter-of-fact way by their peers, and experience gay and lesbian families in the context of... [a] diverse group of other families, could have a profound effect on their values and behavior for the rest of their lives."[24] Another word for this is propaganda, and one wonders why the public schools should be peddling it.

Educators are certainly lining up to implement the gay-indoctrination agenda. A middle school in Elk Grove, California, sponsored a pro-homosexuality event involving several single-person skits. The subjects included the rape of a girl and a gay football player who emphasized that he was "born" that way. Parents were not notified of the event and one related that his son had been told at school, "It's okay if you don't like girls, because that means you're gay."[25]

At Pleasant Valley Elementary School and San Ramon Elementary School in Novato, California, similar activities took place. Parents were outraged that their second through sixth grade students were being subjected to plays with pro-homosexual themes without their knowledge. The plays were called "Cootie Shots: Theatrical Inoculations Against Bigotry." In one of the skits a boy was wearing a dress and discussing cross-dressing. In another, dealing with homosexuality, a female character became involved with a princess instead of a prince.[26]

Sometimes, gay activists, among themselves at least, don't conceal their agenda to indoctrinate students with the goal of transforming society. Nor do they hide their hostility toward opposing viewpoints. At a GLSEN convention in October 1999 in Atlanta, speakers underscored their plan. Deanna Duby of the National Education Association, speaking at the convention, said, "The fear of the religious right is that the schools of today are the governments of tomorrow. And you know what? They're right." Speaker James Anderson, GLSEN's communications director, added, "We're going to raise a generation of kids who don't believe [the claims of] the religious right."[27]

GLSEN should be proud of its progress. Many schools have adopted the "safe school" concept GLSEN fosters, meaning that schools are only safe if students who disapprove of homosexuality are denied their free speech on that issue. Anyone voicing an opinion against homosexuality, no matter how compassionately framed, is perpetrating "hate." One junior named Jonathan at a Vermont high school challenged his teacher's assertion that homosexuality was genetic. The teacher's response was, "What's wrong, Jon, are you homophobic? Did you know that a lot of people who are afraid of gay people are actually gay themselves?"[28]

GLSEN has come a long way in just the last few years. With a $3.5 million budget, it has become a formidable force in public schools, striving to actualize its agenda as laid out in its publication, *Institutionalized Heterosexism in Our Schools: A Guide to Understanding and Undoing It*. This document reveals that the homosexual lobby is becoming bolder. Heterosexism is defined as "the belief that heterosexuality is 'normal,' and that homosexuality is 'sick' or 'immoral.'" The term, it says, is not meant to replace "homophobia." "Heterosexism" is a more expansive word that doesn't connote an equal level of hatred, and can even encompass "seemingly innocent thoughts and behavior based on the belief that heterosexuality is the norm." These seeds have taken root, as shown by an incident at a high school in Arcata, California, where children were made to sit in a circle and respond to the question: "Do you believe homosexuality is a sin and therefore wrong?"[29] Think about that for a minute: the public schools that so assiduously try to erect a separation between school and religion are nevertheless willing to invoke religion, in essence—the idea of "sin"—in order to debunk religious beliefs as ignorant or intolerant or wrongly understood by traditional believers. Certainly no values instruction there!

Another example of gay tolerance on display occurred at Pioneer High School in Ann Arbor, Michigan. In 2002 the school celebrated "2002 Diversity Week," which included a number of activities, such as an all-school assembly with student speeches and panel discussions on such topics as "Homosexuality and Religion." The school required students to submit the text of their speeches to the administration for approval. When student Betsy Hansen submitted her speech, school officials removed all remarks critical of homosexuality. Betsy was also forbidden to articulate her Roman Catholic view on homosexuality during the panel discussion—even though the panel was supposed to talk about homosexuality and religion. Officials informed her that her "negative" message would conflict with and "water down" the "positive" religious message they were trying to convey—that religion and homosexual behavior are compatible and that homosexual behavior is neither sinful nor immoral.[30] Thus we have a public school instructing a Christian student about what her religion really means—as opposed to what she might think it means or what her parents or her pastor or priest might tell her. This is more than indoctrination; it is the use of a public school to perpetuate falsehood.

Yet another revolting example of such propaganda and "tolerance"—some readers might want to skip the paragraph that follows—occurred in Newton South High School in Newton, Massachusetts in 2001. A teacher there told the *Boston Globe* that he had subtly introduced "bisexual, gay, lesbian, and transgendered" subjects in class. He distributed the novel *The Perks of Being a Wallflower* by Stephen Chbosky and instructed the class to write an essay on it. The book features such subjects as bestiality (between boy and dog), man-boy sex, anal sex between boys, male masturbation, and female masturbation using a hot dog. When a parent objected, school officials treated her as an ignorant pest.[31]

Suppressing Christian Speech at School–The Anti-Harassment Subterfuge

As we've seen, the gay and lesbian lobby has been quite successful in securing tolerance for itself and intolerance against Christians, particularly in public schools. The lobby pushes "anti-harassment" policies, which are deceptively titled because they do more to chill politically incorrect speech disapproving of homosexual behavior than to prevent harassment. Under these policies, students who express their opposition to homosexual behavior are subject to punishment.

Pennsylvania State University professor David Warren Saxe decided to challenge such an "anti-harassment" policy at a Pennsylvania high school on behalf of two Christian students over whom he had legal guardianship. In striking down the school's policy, the Third Circuit Court of Appeals ruled that there is no "harassment exception" to the First Amendment free speech clause. The Constitution, the court ruled, does not protect people from being offended by others and their opinions. The court stated, "No court or legislature has ever suggested that unwelcome speech directed at another's values may be prohibited under the rubric of anti-discrimination. . . . By prohibiting disparaging speech directed at a person's values, the policy strikes at the heart of moral and political discourse—the lifeblood of constitutional self-government (and democratic education) and the core concern of the First Amendment. That speech about 'values' may offend is not cause for its prohibition. . . ."[32] But not all courts are in harmony on this issue.

On January 16, 2001, a sophomore at Woodbury High School in St. Paul, Minnesota, tested his school's commitment to tolerance by wearing a sweatshirt with a "Straight Pride" logo. The student, sixteen-year-old Elliot Corbett, a devout Christian, insisted the shirt was not intended to disparage other lifestyles, but to make a positive statement about heterosexuality, since the school caters to homosexual students in various ways, such as creating gay "safe zones" on campus. The school principal told Elliot to take off the shirt because it violated the provisions of the school's dress code that prohibit written or graphic depictions that offend others. The principal said that his logo was both offensive and a safety risk. The Corbetts sued in federal court and obtained an order requiring the school to allow Elliot to wear the shirt.[33]

In another case briefly alluded to above, the Gay-Straight Alliance club at Pioneer High School in Ann Arbor, Michigan, demanded the school board take action against the Pioneers for Christ club for refusing to adopt the school's "non-discrimination" policy in its mission statement. The Thomas More Law Center defended the Christian club, saying the policy would have prevented members from expressing their views against homosexuality. In the face of this challenge, the school board wisely decided to amend its policy.[34]

But a few isolated victories for religious expression haven't eradicated the nationwide pattern of intimidation being employed by the homosexual lobby. In California, the ACLU and the Gay-Straight Alliance Network pressured the Visalia Unified School District to adopt a pro-homosexual policy that calls for punishment of any student or teacher who speaks out against homosexuality. The district has gone so far as to assign its teachers special training to accept homosexuality, such training to be administered by the Intergroup Clearinghouse, an outfit that professes to teach "tolerance." The Gay-Straight Alliance, on the other hand, will teach the students.[35] This all arose when student George Loomis alleged he had been abused and harassed by a Spanish teacher, who, Loomis alleged, made an issue of him wearing an earring in class and made disparaging remarks about his sexual preference. This, said Loomis, led to other students calling him names and demeaning him. The school disciplined the teacher, but that apparently wasn't enough to satisfy Loomis, who filed a lawsuit. As a result of the settlement the school district agreed to pay him $130,000 and adopt "professional development training."[36]

Conservatives are concerned that this gay sensitivity training will consist of more than lectures about tolerance and treating people civilly. They fear it will venture into the area of indoctrination, crossing the line from tolerance to forced acceptance of the morality of homosexuality, which means dictating the personal beliefs of students.[37] The Pacific Justice Institute (PJI) has pledged to represent all parents that choose not to subject their children to the mandatory "pro-gay" training. It has also agreed to represent administrators and teachers who disapprove of the training on the basis of their religious beliefs. "It is especially important," said PJI's Brad Dacus, "that the district accommodate and respect the objections of employees of religious faith, as well as those parents who wish to opt their children out of a course of instruction that is inconsistent with the children's moral or religious upbringing."[38]

A visit to the Gay-Straight Alliance Network's website shows why parents worry about the group indoctrinating students. The site has a section entitled "Creating Peer Education Workshops." In it, as well as in numerous others on the site, the acronym LGBTQ appears, as in "One of the most unique aspects of the Gay-Straight Alliance model is that it brings together LGBTQ individuals and straight allies to combat homophobia." The acronym stands for "Lesbian Gay Bisexual Transgendered Queer."

In many cases, the terminology on these web pages is hardly neutral. The term "anti-homophobia" is used liberally. One link is titled, "What Every Super-Rad Straight Ally Should Know." It takes you to a list of "Ten Ways Homophobia Affects Straight People."

Number One, for example, reads: "Homophobia forces us to act 'macho' if we are a man or 'feminine' if we are a woman. This limits our individuality and self-expression." Number Five states: "Homophobia causes youth to become sexually active before they are ready in order to prove they are 'normal.' This can lead to an increase in unwanted pregnancies and STDs (Sexually Transmitted Diseases)." Suffice it to say that many public schools today are more likely to teach that "homophobia" leads to STDs than that abiding by Judeo-Christian morality helps prevent STDs—illustrating how our schools are shifting from education to propaganda.

The Politics of the NEA

The gay agenda has received quite a boost from the National Education Association (NEA) in recent years. Indeed, the NEA has been instrumental in promoting most of the "progressive" ideas of the education establishment. The NEA describes itself as "America's largest organization committed to advancing the cause of public education." Was it advancing that cause when it adopted a plan on February 8,

2002, to make schools safe and hospitable for gay, lesbian, bisexual, and transgendered students and education employees?[39]

The NEA's press release promoting the plan said the union would endeavor "to provide students, education employees and the general public with accurate, objective and up-to-date information regarding the needs of, and problems confronting, gay, lesbian, bisexual, and transgendered students." Any such information, according to the statement, would be "nonjudgmental in terms of sexual orientation/gender identification." "Nonjudgmental," of course, in instances like this means substituting one judgment for another: that is, approving the "judgment" that homosexuality is morally neutral behavior and disapproving the "judgment" that it is not.

In fact, the NEA is colluding with gay activist groups to promote gay issues in every state in the Union. It encourages public schools to arm their principals with "Just the Facts," a so-called primer on sexual orientation and youth that it has formally endorsed. Here are a few passages from the primer: "Sexual orientation is one component of a person's identity, which is made up of many other components, such as culture, ethnicity, gender, and personality traits.... Gay, lesbian, and bisexual youth must also cope with prejudiced, discriminatory, and violent behavior and messages in their families, schools, and communities. Such behavior and messages negatively affect the health, mental health, and education of lesbian, gay, and bisexual young people. These students are more likely than heterosexual students to report missing school due to fear, being threatened by other students, and having their property damaged at school."

The brochure goes on to say that such treatment leads to isolation and lack of support, which in turn accounts for "higher rates of emotional distress, suicide attempts, and risky sexual behavior and substance abuse" among gays. Since gays are afraid of being harassed or hurt, the primer urges schools to create an environment that is "as open and accepting [of gays, lesbians, and bisexuals] as possible, so these young people will feel comfortable sharing their thoughts and concerns."[40]

No one approves of actual bullying or harassment of any groups or individuals for any reason, including sexual orientation. The problem some have with the message of "Just the Facts" and related propaganda is that it assumes that the "higher rates of emotional distress, suicide attempts, and risky sexual behavior and substance abuse" are the result of "bullying" rather than something that might be linked to the lifestyle behaviors themselves. Beyond that, though, the real civil rights issue here is the discrimination against students who uphold traditional religious beliefs about homosexuality. There is no legitimate reason for the public schools to assume a charter to reshape the religious beliefs of students or to deny them the right to freely dissent from this propaganda. "Bullying" is legitimately punishable—and always has been. But the idea that traditional religious beliefs should be subverted by the public schools as a matter of course and duty is ominous.

Many believe the NEA and its rival union, the AFT (American Federation of Teachers), are the strongest forces standing in the way of true education reform. Together, these unions represent some three-fourths of all public school teachers (K-12) in this country. One expert estimated in 1996 that their combined annual revenues were in the neighborhood of $1.3 billion, exclusive of their political action committees (PACs), various foundations, and special purpose organizations. With that amount of cash and thousands of highly paid staff employees, they wield enormous political power—primarily over educational issues—though their influence is not limited to that.

Since the NEA established its PACs in 1972 it has supported and endorsed every Democratic presidential candidate. While it claims to be bipartisan, it overwhelmingly endorses Democratic candidates at the congressional level as well. In 1996 the NEA employed more political operatives than both major political parties combined.[41] The union has even developed a handbook on dealing with the "radical right's crusade against the public schools."[42] The text opens, "They won't go away. No matter how bizarre we believe their beliefs to be, no matter how illogical and inconsistent their goals appear, and no matter how often we reassure ourselves that 'this too, shall pass,' the political, social, and religious forces that make up the radical right in contemporary American society will not go away."

Later in the body of the document the tirade continues: "The overriding goal of the radical right is to impose a new political, social, and religious order on the nation. The ideal New America, for the radical right, would be one in which citizens conformed to the right-wing views on everything from foreign policy and constitutional interpretation to the selection of textbooks in our classrooms."

The position paper goes on to trash the so-called radical right's supposedly inconsistent opposition to abortion and support for gun rights and capital punishment.[43] A more interesting inconsistency is what these issues have to do with education and the interests of teachers. In its own published statements, such as this one, the NEA reveals itself to be a crass political arm of the left wing, distracted by various and sundry political views having nothing to do with its mandate. And when it does discuss education in literature such as this, it is in terms of partisan name-calling, suggesting that when "stars of the radical right" like Phyllis Schlafly come to town, "that's a pretty sure sign that plans are underway for some kind of assault on the schools or the Association or both."

The NEA, as has been noted, spends an inordinate amount of time *off* the education message. It actively supports "reproductive freedom," the current euphemism for "abortion rights." Dictating these views to teachers sometimes forces the union to confront dissent. Dennis Robey, a teacher, put union officials on notice starting in 1995 that he objected to supporting the NEA because of its positions on abortion, homosexual rights, and its efforts to interfere with parental rights. He thus asked for an exemption from dues on the basis of his religious beliefs. The union, in the 1999–2000 school year, not only rejected his claim, but also submitted him to "probing questions about his personal relationship with God [and] his religious affiliation."

Robey fought back and in October 2000 the Equal Employment

Opportunity Commission ordered the NEA to curtail its annual questioning of teachers who request their dues to be paid elsewhere for religious reasons. Stefan Gleason, vice president of the National Right to Work Legal Defense Foundation, said of the decision, "For years the NEA union has used this particular illegal scheme to intimidate and harass teachers of faith who dare to challenge their radical agenda. The EEOC's finding of a violation further underscores that the nation's largest teacher union has systematically persecuted people of faith."[44]

Another case involved school psychologist Kathleen Klamut of Ohio. She also tried to have a portion of her union dues diverted to charity because she opposes abortion, which she saw the NEA as supporting. She too met with resistance. After an eighteen-month-long fight, the OEA, the Ohio counterpart of the NEA, relented and granted Klamut's request.[45] But again, the fundamental question is: why is a pro-abortion agenda a legitimate interest of a teacher's union? Regardless, should the NEA seek to force its political views into public schools?

The NEA is also fully supportive of what are called the "multicultural" and "diversity" agendas. In two resolutions issuing from its 1999 convention it affirmed its commitment not only to "diversity"-based curricula, but to their introduction in early childhood (from birth through age eight) education programs. In its resolution it stated "that a diverse society enriches all individuals." Part of this enriching diversity, it went on to say, is people with differences in "sexual orientation."

In a separate resolution on "Sex Education" it stated "it is the right of *every individual* to live in an environment of *freely available information* and knowledge about sexuality." It further encouraged the establishment of sex education programs to include information on many things, including "diversity of sexual orientation" and "incest."[46]

Given the poor educational performance of America's public schools—a performance that was famously encapsulated in the phrase "a nation at risk"—it might be better if the nation's leading teachers' union were more concerned with reading, writing, and arithmetic—and leaving the moral beliefs of Christians alone.

Conclusion

The War against Christianity in education isn't limited to the K-12 public schools. Battles are also raging on university campuses throughout America. Academia is dominated by administrators and professors who are often hostile to Christianity and the Christian worldview. Our finest education institutions are sometimes so preoccupied with indoctrinating students that true academic freedom and inquiry are lost in the process. Just like our public grade schools and high schools, our colleges have become radically secularized. Christianity is impugned and its ideas ridiculed, distorted, and suppressed. By contrast, competing secular values are trumpeted. If so-called progressives were true to their professed commitment to enlightenment and academic freedom, they would recoil in horror at the thought-tyranny dominating our politically and philosophically monolithic educational institutions today.

chapter Five

The Battle for the Academy

WHILE ALMOST ALL OF AMERICA'S FIRST COLLEGES and universities, including Harvard and the other Ivy League schools, were founded as Christian institutions,[1] today secular liberals who are openly hostile to Western civilization, traditional values, and Christianity dominate their campuses. Just as with the teachers in our public schools, university professors inject their biases into their classrooms. There is hardly any pretense of values-neutrality, as secularists present their indoctrinating materials to students throughout the land, sometimes subtly, and other times overtly. The Williamsburg Charter Survey of Religion and Public Life reported in 1988 that "nearly one out of three academics said that Evangelicals are a 'threat to democracy.'"[2] It seems that in the fifteen years since that survey, this anti-Christian sentiment has only intensified.

This is sobering, considering the enormous influence professors have on society. And it's outrageous, in view of the contrasting ideological and theological makeup of the parents whose students attend these universities and whose funds support them. Because of difficulties in polling and the fluid nature of public opinion, it is difficult to ascertain with certainty the percentages of the American public that are politically conservative, liberal, moderate, or simply apathetic. The same is true in determining the theological inclinations of the populace, since nominal religious and denominational identification doesn't necessarily correspond with peoples' actual beliefs.

But one thing is certain. The American public is anything but monolithic with respect to religion. And, by any measure, a strong majority consider themselves Christians.[3] Yet their views are grossly underrepresented in our venues of higher learning. While these institutions present themselves as open to all viewpoints, they are largely dogmatic propaganda centers with an antipathy for the values that a substantial portion of the American people holds sacred. And it's disgraceful. In writing about this glaring imbalance, author and Berkeley professor emeritus of law Phillip E. Johnson said, "Although most Americans are at least nominally theists and a substantial portion build their lives on theistic principles, naturalistic philosophy rules the academic roost absolutely. The idea that God might really exist is rarely seriously considered," but "classroom advocacy of atheism is common and everywhere assumed to be protected by academic freedom. Many philosophy professors make a career of fashioning arguments that support or assume atheism and students frequently tell me about courses that incorporate heavy-handed ridicule of theistic religion."[4] James Tunstead Burtchaell, in a *First Things* article entitled "The Decline and Fall of the Christian University (II)," called it the "learned disdain for faith,"[5] and historian Paul Johnson wrote of the "extreme secularization" of the academy.[6]

Some campus insiders contend that Christian professors in general are denied the freedom to express their beliefs. George Marsden, a Notre Dame history professor, said, "In the most prestigious parts of American academia, religious scholars are given less of a voice than are, for instance, Marxist scholars. That is astonishing given the relative sizes of their respective constituencies in the American population."[7] Christian evangelist Chuck Colson laments the absence of true academic freedom and inquiry. "We are left with a disturbing paradox," he said. "While higher education is better funded and more accessible than ever before, it has nothing left worth teaching. Our educational establishment seeks to instill a passion for intellectual curiosity and openness, but allows for the existence of no truth worth pursuing."[8]

In addition to the pronounced secular bias, Christians in American colleges are subjected to rampant discrimination in a variety of forms, as this chapter documents. Ironically, the discrimination often occurs in the name of "tolerance" and "diversity." Or as David French of the Philadelphia-based Foundation for Individual Rights in Education (FIRE) put it: "Experience teaches that religious individuals and organizations are most often victimized by university policies that, in theory, were enacted to *promote* tolerance, diversity, and fairness."[9]

Professors on the Attack

One would think that, of all people, university professors would be guardians of academic freedom and tolerance for the diversity of ideas in the classroom. But the reality on campus is quite different. Usually the educational experience is centered in the classroom, and classrooms, of course, are under the near-dictatorial control of professors, many of whom use their classrooms as controlled settings in which to impose their anti-Christian bigotry on sometimes unsuspecting young students.

Mike Adams, an associate professor of Criminal Justice at UNC-Wilmington and a self-described former liberal and agnostic, attests to this. In an article entitled "Campus Crusade Against Christ," Adams wrote that he was "taken aback by the prevalence of anti-Christian sentiment as well as the degree of comfort professors felt in expressing it both inside and outside the classroom." Adams provided a number of examples of anti-Christian hostility he observed firsthand, among them professors who place on their office doors emblems depicting a "Darwin fish" swallowing a "Jesus fish," which signifies the validity of evolution theory and the supposed invalidity of Christianity. Other professors display bumper stickers saying, "Homophobia is a social disease." Adams also noted attitudes that professors display out of the public's hearing and view, such as their anti-Christian bias in job recruitment. Some objected to candidates, for example, because they "seemed too religious" or "too much of a family man."[10]

Consider also the career-oriented hostility of Professor Michael Dini at Texas Tech. Dini, an associate professor in biology, refused to write medical school letters of recommendation for students who wouldn't acknowledge their acceptance of the theory of evolution. Dini even published his policy on a web page, which warned students seeking a recommendation to be prepared to answer the question, "How do you think the human species originated?" Dini added, "If you cannot truthfully and forthrightly affirm a scientific answer to this question, "then you should not seek my recommendation for admittance to further education in the biomedical sciences."[11] Dr. James Brink, the university's assistant provost, supported Dini. "I think a student with a strong faith and belief in creationism should not attend a public university," said Brink, "but rather should attend a Biblically grounded university where their ideas are reinforced instead of scientifically challenged."

The Liberty Legal Institute (LLI) filed a complaint with the U.S. Department of Justice and brought a suit against the university and Dini for religious discrimination, calling the professor's policy "open religious bigotry." "Students are being denied recommendations not because of their competence in understanding evolution, but solely because of their personal religious beliefs," said Kelly Shackelford, LLI chief counsel. After the Justice Department opened an investigation into the professor's practices, Dini changed his policy, now merely requiring that students be able to explain the theory of evolution, without requiring them to affirm their personal belief in its validity. The Justice Department promptly closed its investigation, and assistant attorney general for civil rights Ralph F. Boyd Jr. said in a press release, "If the separation of church and state is to mean anything, it must surely mean that such matters of conscience are beyond the reach of government inquiry."[12]

Harvard Students' "Fear" of God

With all the anti-Christian, anti-conservative propaganda disseminated by professors in the classroom and through other aspects of campus life, not to mention the media and the dominant culture, many college students develop a pronounced aversion to Christianity and traditional values. Thus molded, they follow the example of their teachers and become fully capable of waging war on their own against any of their peers who have the audacity not to submit to the status quo.

Consider some students at Harvard University, which, as we've seen, was the first college established in America and was Christian in origin. In October 1998, Harvard student Christopher King decided to run for president of the Harvard student government to counter the cynicism pervading the campus atmosphere. King and his running mate Fentrice Driskell campaigned on a theme of building a "healthier Harvard community." The duo consciously tried to recruit individuals from diverse backgrounds to join their effort. King said, "We looked like the United Nations."

When the campaign was barely underway, a woman serving on the Undergraduate Council Election Commission asked her friends in an e-mail to pray for the candidates, and in particular for King and Driskell. Though King had not sought the endorsement, word nevertheless circulated that King was Christian, which brought out the anti-Christians in full force. They circulated posters seeking to paint King's candidacy as a glorified evangelical crusade. Earlier, King had sought advice from various "community-building" groups off campus, including Global Youth Connect, a secular organization.[13]

On the posters, King's opponents falsely attributed a proselytizing quote to Global Youth Connect that had actually originated from a website for "Connect," a Bible study group in Ohio with which King had no contact. At the bottom of every anti-King poster appeared the following bogus quote: "Our youth ministry exists to bring non-believers to Christ." Then, as if auditioning for positions on the *New York Times* editorial page, the *Harvard Crimson*'s editors followed up with a hand-wringing opinion piece endorsing one of King's opponents, in which they reinforced the credibility of the poster's quotation. Referring to the King-Driskell ticket, the editors wrote, "Their promise of 'values-driven leadership' is vague and worrisome; though King and Driskell say they want to unify the campus, their ties to religious groups have raised concerns among many students."[14]

King and Driskell lost by one hundred votes, and the anti-Christian smear may well have cost them the election. "Christianity is... an important part of who I am," King said. "But they were the ones who made it an issue.... I have struggled with the fact that in 1999 at Harvard you could be so persecuted for being a Christian."

Naomi Schaefer reported in the *Wall Street Journal* that King's experience was symptomatic of a greater problem. Schaefer quoted former student and Undergraduate Council president Beth Stewart as saying, "There is a large community of Harvard students who are extremely suspicious of and feel threatened by organized religion. Certainly, there is a prejudice against Christianity here more than against any other religion."[15] According to Schaefer's report, school newspaper president Matt Granade flatly denied that the *Crimson* had engaged in religious discrimination. "That's an unequivocal no," he said. What troubled the editors was "the religious language used in the e-mails and the woman's connections to the election commission."

As Schaefer noted in her story, "The theory seems to be: How can you embrace a community of diverse individuals if you are narrow-minded enough to believe in God?"[16] But the discrimination is even worse than Schaefer described, for the e-mail was neither written nor solicited by King. Rather, Christianity and prayer requests are viewed as so obnoxious to students attending this school, founded primarily to promote the Gospel of Christ, that Christians dare not even profess their beliefs in these enlightened times. Moreover, so imbued with secularism are these elite students that the perpetrators of this bigotry seem completely oblivious to their infractions. When Christians are the targeted group, "diversity" is out the door and different rules apply. Today's "tolerance" unabashedly excludes them from equal dignity, respect, and treatment.

University Administrators–Challenging the Dogma

Speaking of academic freedom and tolerance, campus administrations around the country espouse it fervently but somehow cannot extend the principle to professors and others who courageously think outside the secular box. San Francisco State University took the position that a particular biology professor was no longer appropriate as a teacher of introductory biology. Professor Dean Kenyon, a leading national authority in chemical evolutionary theory, committed the unpardonable sin of exposing his students to certain points of dispute among scientists on macro-evolutionary theory. But worse, Kenyon reported the sacrilegious fact that a number of biologists admit to the existence of evidence for intelligent design in the universe.[17]

Similarly, Mississippi University for Women asked professor Nancy Bryson—the head of the school's Division of Science and Mathematics—to resign her position for exposing a group of honor students to scientific flaws in Darwinian thought in a presentation called "Critical Thinking on Evolution." The presentation covered alternative theories, including "intelligent design," and after the lecture a biology professor—who had not attended the talk—told Bryson that her talk was "religion masquerading as science." Bryson was incensed, saying, "The academy is all about free thought and academic freedom. He hadn't even heard my talk. Without knowing anything about my talk, he makes that decision. I think it's really an outrage." Encouraged by the outpouring of support from her students,[18] Bryson refused to resign, whereupon school officials sent her a letter informing her they would not renew her contract in the fall as head of the division. After coming under heavy criticism, the university reversed itself, but Bryson hardly feels secure in her position. "I'm going to be watching my back," she said.[19]

The Tolerance and Academic Freedom Charade

There was a near perfect illustration of the need for a professor to watch her back at DePauw University in Greencastle, Indiana. There, Professor Janis Price, an education instructor for fifteen years, committed the grievous sin of subjecting her students to a "hostile environment." What did that hostile environment consist of? She placed issues of Dr. James Dobson's magazine *Teachers in Focus* on a table in the back of her classroom. She advised students that the publication contained articles written from a Christian viewpoint, which they could peruse if they chose to, but they would not be required to, nor would any assignments be made concerning them.

An article in one of the magazines addressing how teachers should approach the issue of homosexuality in public schools offended a student, who complained to the administration. Vice president of Academic Affairs Neal Abraham sent Professor Price a letter of reprimand, accusing her of providing students with "intolerant" material, which "served to create a hostile environment" in violation of school policy. Abraham went so far as to characterize Price's actions as "reprehensible." He then backed up his words with action, cutting her salary by twenty-five percent and suspending her from teaching responsibilities. Abraham's explanation? The university "cannot tolerate the intolerable."[20]

One of Price's friends and fellow professors, Dr. Mary English, summed up the university's tyrannical conduct when she said that tolerance there is not a two-way street. "We have to be tolerant and politically correct in all other areas except Christianity. So it's okay to be intolerant of Christians as long as Christians are tolerant of everybody else." What's more, said English, is that DePauw is a Methodist school. That should surprise no one. Political correctness has invaded America's religious institutions as surely as it has all others.

Secular universities are similarly notorious for displaying tolerance to all ideas except those based in Christianity or Western civilization, as shown by the experience of Professor Dilawar Edwards at the California University of Pennsylvania. For his class "Introduction to Educational Media," Edwards chose instructional materials that at least one student found offensive. Among the objectionable items were books arguing that America's education establishment subjects conservatives and Christians to censorship and intimidation. Included among the books were Cal Thomas's *Book Burning*, John W. Whitehead's *The Freedom of Religious Expression in Public Universities and High Schools*, articles from the *Houston Chronicle* and the *Wall Street Journal*, and various articles by Phyllis Schlafly.[21]

As if to prove the very thesis of these materials, the administration forced the professor to discontinue using these books and other publications. In his objection to the materials, the disgruntled student charged that Edwards was using his course to advance religious ideas. Note the sophistry here: The books and materials did not seek to advance Christian ideas, or those of any other religion, but rather the principles of academic and intellectual freedom. The theme was freedom from censorship, not proselytizing the Gospel, as anyone with a high school education—or, one would think, in an administrative position on campus—could have seen.

University Groups on the Move

School officials and professors, to be sure, offer the main line of attack on Christians and Christian values, but they are closely supported by various other institutional arms of the university. The aforementioned professor Mike Adams told of the work of the Women's Resource Center at UNC-Wilmington in steering pregnant students to the rabidly pro-abortion Planned Parenthood, while trying to impede efforts of pro-life groups to provide counseling services. Notably, research has emerged showing that the majority of women who have abortions experience some kind of emotional or psychological problem. Yet groups like the Women's Resource Center and Planned Parenthood, which bill themselves as pro-choice, curiously don't seem to want pregnant women exposed to all the relevant information to enable them to make an informed and reasoned decision. Such behavior, rife on university campuses as well as in society at large, clearly bespeaks of an extreme pro-abortion mentality. This extremism is especially evident in an e-mail disseminated by a similar group, the Women's Center at UNC-Chapel Hill. The group tried to deflect criticism of "partial-birth abortion" by calling it an "inflammatory term invented by the right wing."[22]

A particularly egregious case of discrimination occurred at Washington University in St. Louis, where the Student Bar Association (SBA) denied official status and funding to a group of anti-abortion law students based on the content of the group's beliefs. According to the SBA, the group's focus was "too narrow." And just how was the Law Students Pro-Life (LSPL) organization too narrowly focused? Well, according to the SBA, the group was not authentically pro-life because it did not include in its constitution a denunciation of the death penalty. "If your group truly has the purpose they claim, they need to consider revamping the organization to encourage and facilitate discussion of the issues as a whole, and not simply the pro-life side of certain issues," said SBA president Elliot Friedman.

The Foundation for Individual Rights in Education (FIRE) wrote a letter to the administration, pointing out the "dreary intolerance and breathtaking double standard" the university was waging against the group. FIRE noted that the SBA had approved other "narrowly focused" groups, such as the Jewish Law Society, which was committed to "fulfilling the needs of Jewish students," and the Black Law Students Association, organized "to orient, assist, and otherwise support African-American students."[23] FIRE also organized a nationwide publicity campaign to bring attention to the Washington University anti-life discrimination. After twice denying the group official recognition, the SBA finally reversed itself on October 15, 2002, and granted official recognition to the LSPL organization.[24]

Targeting Individuals–Temple University's Gulag

Attacks by university professors, students, administrations, and related groups have turned the university campus into a zone of hostility toward all things Christian; individuals, organizations, and Christianity itself are subjected to inexcusable treatment.

Michael Marcavage, a student at Temple University, knows this all too well. He was unhappy when he learned in the fall of 1999 that the play *Corpus Christi*—where Jesus is portrayed as a homosexual who makes love to his disciples—would be staged on campus. Considering the play blasphemous, Marcavage set out to protest it. He posted close to one thousand flyers throughout the campus and said that he intended to hold a demonstration. On reflection, he decided to organize a counter-event rather than a protest, to show his peers "who the real Jesus is." This event was to include a performance by gospel singers, speakers, and a biblically oriented play on Christ's life called *Final Destiny*, which was to be performed by Temple's Campus Crusade for Christ chapter. *Corpus Christi* proceeded without protest, but the university allegedly reneged on its promise to permit *Final Destiny* to be performed on a campus stage. Even when Marcavage offered to pay for the event, the school refused to grant permission.

On November 2, 1999, Temple vice president William Bergman summoned Marcavage to his office to tell him that *Final Destiny* would not be performed on campus, after which the student left Bergman's office in disgust and went to the bathroom and splashed water on his face. Marcavage alleges that Bergman followed him to the bathroom, pounded on the door, and when Marcavage opened it, Bergman physically forced him to return to his office. Once back in the office, according to Marcavage, Bergman pushed him down into a chair, at which point Marcavage, now afraid of Bergman, said he wanted to leave. Bergman refused to let him leave or use the phone. Knowing that Bergman could not forcibly detain him, Marcavage said he again attempted to leave, but was tripped to the floor by Bergman. Marcavage said Bergman next forced him onto a couch and held him there against his will. University police then arrived, handcuffed Marcavage, and transported him in a police car to the Emergency Crisis Center at Temple University Hospital. After a three-hour examination, psychiatrists concluded nothing was wrong with the Christian student.

When Marcavage filed a lawsuit against Bergman and the University in December 2000, Bergman "vehemently" denied the allegations, saying everyone at Temple was treated fairly. A Temple spokeswoman said that Bergman was concerned after Marcavage had been in the bathroom for fifteen minutes and wouldn't come out, fearing he might harm himself. She also said that officials sent him to the hospital based on a campus psychologist's recommendation. Temple University Hospital documents, however, reportedly show that the campus psychiatrist "claims that she did not see any overt sign that the patient will hurt himself" and while Marcavage was upset after the incident, "there are no apparent grounds for 302 [a form for involuntary commitment]." The spokeswoman also said that the incident arose because Marcavage requested a seventy-foot stage at the last minute and was unreasonable about it. Marcavage said the university fabricated this story to discredit him.

According to Marcavage's attorney, Michael Fahling, "What had gotten Michael a ticket to the psychiatric ward were his religious beliefs and opposition to a play. How utterly chilling it is that something like this could happen at a major university by top-level officials."[25] Timothy Duggan, president of the school's Campus Crusade for Christ chapter, said that the incident against his friend Marcavage was part of a larger pattern of anti-Christian bias on campus. "The reason this had become an issue," said Duggan, "is because of the rebellion of the university to the Christian point of view."[26]

Christian Beliefs Disqualify Coach

In April 2002, the *Daily Nebraskan* reported that Stanford University denied the head coaching job to University of Nebraska assistant football coach Ron Brown because of his religious beliefs. Not surprisingly, one of the major objections to Brown was his belief that homosexual behavior is sinful. Alan Glenn, Stanford's assistant athletic director of human resources, said Brown's religion was not the determining factor, but admitted to the student newspaper that it "was definitely something that had to be considered. We're a very diverse community with a diverse alumni." Apparently not diverse enough, however, to permit the hiring of an outspoken Christian coach. Brown himself seemed to believe religion was a very important factor in the school's decision. In a column he wrote for *Sharing the Victory*, a Fellowship of Christian Athletes publication, Brown said, "After the first interview, the athletic director vacillated whether to bring me on campus for a final interview. After deliberation he decided not to, with the explanation that he did not believe that my Christian convictions would mesh well with that university.... They seemed to have no problem with the notion of squelching or eliminating one because of his representation of Jesus Christ."

Courtney Wooten, a Stanford sophomore and social director of Stanford's Queer-Straight Social and Political Alliance, said, "Wow, it would be really hard for him here. He would be poorly received by the student body in general."[27] But a Nebraska student didn't see it that way. Ryan Wilkins, president of the Association of Students, said, "The Stanford decision sends a dangerous message. He's a football coach. Judge him on whether his players play well on the field, whether his players respect him, or whether his players graduate. Don't hire or disrespect a man because he carries a Bible in his suitcase."

Coach Brown was shocked at the decision and the school's unapologetic openness about it. "If I'd been discriminated against for being black," said Brown, "they would have never told me that. They had no problem telling me it was because of my Christian beliefs." Brown noted that it was ironic that a prestigious school founded on religious principles no longer welcomes Christians. Brown was clear that he would not betray his beliefs or silence himself in the future over the school's rejection of him. "I don't believe you compromise any truth for whatever job," said Brown.[28] Brown also said, commendably, that he would not attempt artificially to separate his faith from his job. "I'm a Christian Ron Brown, period.... One thing I've tried not to do is separate my coaching from who I am. Some people have a problem with that. They want to separate my coaching from my faith in Christ. I can't do that. That would be a huge hypocrisy. You have to be who you are,"[29] he said. "This thing about following Jesus Christ isn't flag football. It's for real.... You can't straddle the line." Brown also said he believed anti-Christian discrimination is happening nationwide. Alex Van Riesen, of the Stanford chapter of InterVarsity Christian Fellowship, said the incident against Brown is not the first of its kind.[30]

Religion Disqualifies Scholarship

The same Christian beliefs that disqualify football coaches can also make students ineligible for scholarships. Michael Nash, a junior at Cumberland College in Williamsburg, Kentucky, received a Kentucky Educational Excellence scholarship based on academic achievement and college board scores. That is, he thought he received one until the school notified him otherwise in October 2002, having discovered that he would be majoring in philosophy and religion. Regulations prevented the state from making scholarship grants to theology, divinity, or religious students. But the argument that such scholarships would violate the Establishment Clause is suspect for two reasons. The student, not the school, has complete control over the decision as to what major he will pursue. Veterans, moreover, are not precluded from using their GI funds for religious studies.[31] When the American Center for Law and Justice filed suit, Cumberland College changed its position and reinstated Nash's eligibility for the funds.[32]

Christian Clubs

Academic intolerance is particularly acute in universities' discrimination against Christian groups on campus. In December 2002, Rutgers University booted from campus the Rutgers InterVarsity Multiethnic Christian Fellowship because the group required—of all outrageous things—that its leaders be Christians. The group became ineligible to receive university funds and was denied permission to meet or operate on school grounds. The university's rationale was that denying non-Christians access to leadership is unfairly discriminatory to nonbelievers and thus in violation of the university's guidelines on nondiscrimination. This non-thinking policy required student groups to be open to all students and to permit any active member to run for office. InterVarsity's charter limits leadership positions to those "committed to the basis of faith and the purpose of this organization."[33]

The university's rationale of seeking to prevent discrimination was absurd on its face. What possible reason would a nonbeliever have for joining a Christian organization, much less becoming a leader in the group? This university's action was a transparent swipe at Christians, the lone disfavored, unprotected group in the academic universe. What the university was essentially saying was that Christian groups must abandon their theological character if they want to be officially recognized and avail themselves of the benefits of such recognition, including state funds and the use of university facilities. But permitting nonbelievers to occupy leadership positions would so dilute the club's purpose and character as to render it meaningless, a fact that couldn't have been lost on university officials. But their aversion to Christianity is presumably so intense that they weren't concerned that their actions constituted flagrant violations of the club's constitutional freedoms of association, religion, and speech. Rutgers lifted its ban against InterVarsity in April 2003, shortly after the Foundation for Individual Rights in Education (FIRE) filed suit against it.

At Tufts, a similar assault on a Christian group took place, but this time at the hands of a student body. The Student Judiciary defrocked the Tufts Christian Fellowship (TCF) because it wouldn't permit a bisexual member to have a leadership position in the group. When FIRE intervened, once again the university backed down.[34]

The list of offending universities goes on, but the University of North Carolina at Chapel Hill has been particularly discriminatory against Christian student groups. Like Rutgers, the university set its sights on the InterVarsity Christian Fellowship chapter, threatening to revoke its funding and strip it of recognition because it required its officers to affirm Christian doctrine. A school administrator informed InterVarsity that its charter was inconsistent with the university's policy for such clubs to grant "openness to full membership and participation without regard to race, color, religion, national origin, disability, age, veteran status, sexual orientation, or gender."[35] Again, FIRE came to the rescue and the administration backed down. FIRE's president Alan Charles Kors said, "UNC couldn't defend in public what it was willing to do in private.... Everybody on campus would immediately see the absurdity... if an evangelical Christian who believed homosexuality to be a sin tried to become president of a university's Bisexual, Gay, and Lesbian Alliance. The administration would have led candlelight vigils on behalf of diversity and free association."[36]

As it turned out, UNC-Chapel Hill had engaged in systematic discrimination against Christian groups across the board. Through a public records request, UNC-Wilmington's professor Mike Adams learned that the university had sent seventeen letters to various Christian groups threatening to cut off their financial support. Adams said, "Very clearly you can see that, in fact, they have not been focusing on secular fraternities.... It appears that these letters are targeted toward Christian groups, and essentially telling them the same thing—namely, that they can continue to be a group as long as they are willing to cease to be Christian."[37]

Bashing Christianity

The double standard against Christians comes into yet clearer focus when we realize that bashing Christianity per se is also permissible.

Well-known Princeton bioethicist and animal rights advocate Peter Singer makes no secret of his disdain for Christianity. He regards with the contempt the biblical message that human beings are superior to other animals and life forms, which he calls "speciesism." "One of the things that causes a problem for the animal movement," said Singer, "is the strong strain of fundamentalist Christianity that makes a huge gulf between humans and animals, saying humans have souls but animals do not." But the scope of Singer's radicalism can best be seen in his belief that not all human life is sacred—that it is not immoral to murder severely disabled infants.[38] Princeton apparently has no problem with the dissemination of Singer's odious views.

Universities don't just permit the overt denigration of Christians—they also often suppress the Christian message and its values. When Dartmouth's chapter of Campus Crusade for Christ placed copies of C.S. Lewis's theological works in students' mailboxes, one university dean decried the action, saying it was an offensive imposition of religion on non-Christian students. This was no small matter to the group, which believes its reason for existence is to bring nonbelievers to Christ.[39] One wonders whether the same level of indignity would have been shown had another group representing a non-Christian religion been involved.

Censorship of messages not explicitly Christian but clearly grounded in the Christian worldview is also a common practice at universities. Officials at the University of Texas repeatedly denied permission to a pro-life student group, Justice For All, to display a huge exhibit promoting life on open areas of the campus—places that have been customarily used for student expression.[40] When a Harvard law student posted notes on school bulletin boards stating, "Smile! Your mother chose life," an employee said he was expressing "hate."[41] University of Houston officials quashed an anti-abortion rally but embraced a pro-gay rights event, saying that the gay celebration was permissible because it was akin to cheerleading or band practice and thus could be held outside the designated free speech zones.[42]

VMI Dinner Prayer

The taboos against state-sponsored prayer have also made their way onto college campuses. The Virginia Military Institute (VMI) in Lexington, Virginia, has conducted dinner prayer ceremonies since the 1950s. During the ritual, the cadets march to dinner in formation, then hear a prayer from a school chaplain, which changes daily. In May 2001, the ACLU filed suit against VMI on behalf of Neil Mellen and Paul Knick, two cadets who objected to the prayer ceremony. The school defended the tradition, saying that it was not endorsing religion because the prayer was non-denominational and voluntary for the students, who are adults. In January 2002, U.S. district judge Norman K. Moon sided with the plaintiffs in ruling the practice unconstitutional. The United States Court of Appeals for the Fourth Circuit affirmed the decision on April 28, 2003, stating, "While the First Amendment does not in any way prohibit VMI's cadets from praying before, during, or after supper, the Establishment Clause prohibits VMI from sponsoring such a religious activity." The court rejected the contention that the prayer was voluntary because the extraordinary obedience required of the cadets supposedly negated the voluntary nature of the exercise.[43] Because two students didn't feel comfortable while the rest of the students were enjoying a prayer, the entire tradition had to be scrapped, with virtually no thought given to the encroachment on the religious freedom of the participants.

Promoting Islam, Homosexuality, Pornography

Pro-Islam

The attack on Christianity is seen not just in what is prohibited on campus, but also in what is promoted. When the topic under consideration is, say, Islam, homosexuality, or even pornography, students are urged to be open, diverse, accepting. Every conceivable idea is embraced, it seems, except Christianity.

Again, UNC-Chapel Hill has shown us the way. That august university required that all freshmen and transfer students read

Approaching the Quran: The Early Revelations, a book of excerpts from the Islamic holy book. The university website described the volume as a book of "enduring interest" that introduces the literature and culture of a "profound moral and spiritual tradition." Later the website's blurb was revised, saying that reading the book would no longer be required, but that students who declined to read it because they found it "offensive to their own faith" had to write a one-page paper explaining why they chose not to read it. The inconsistency between the university's approach to the Koran and its attitude toward the Bible and other Christian materials is staggering. Can you imagine the apoplexy that would have ensued from the liberal community had this been a book about the Bible?

Some of our major universities don't have the same reluctance toward Muslim speakers as they do toward Christian ones. In fact, a willingness among universities to give even pro-terrorist Islamist speakers a campus platform, in stark contrast to the animus displayed toward Christians, could be seen in an incident at the University of Wisconsin. Dr. Michael Curtiss, a Christian second-year resident in the Wausau Family Practice program at the University of Wisconsin School of Medicine, claimed he was persecuted because he asked a couple of "innocuous questions" during a required 2002 lecture on Islam. This particular one, by two first-year Muslim residents, was on the subject of Islam and Muslim culture, and "no medical topics were discussed at all," said Curtiss. "There was no point to the lecture other than to give them a forum to expound their religious views. They wouldn't have given me two and a half hours to teach about Christianity, not that I would expect them to." During the presentation, in what Curtiss said was an acknowledged effort to evangelize, one of the men sang prayers to Allah, preached the benefits of Islam for women, and explained the Five Pillars of Islam. Some residents became uncomfortable when the Muslim speaker refused to condemn suicide bombers and admitted donating funds to their families.

Curtiss said he questioned the lecturer about six times, citing Scripture, insisting that he did so in an "informative, and non-insulting manner." Following the lecture, Curtiss alleges, one of the Islamic residents, Altaf Kaiserruddin, called him into a room and told him his contract would not be renewed. Two days later, according to Curtiss, he received a letter confirming that he was being terminated. He said that when he asked why, university officials would give no reason for their decision. Curtiss filed a complaint against the university with the Equal Employment Opportunity Commission for religious discrimination. The university denied the allegations. "The established curriculum of the Department of Family Medicine Residency Program includes occasional informational presentations about different cultures," said University public affairs spokesman Michael Felber. "The purpose of these presentations is to adequately prepare residents to deliver high quality medical care to people of different backgrounds." But, Curtiss contends, no other cultural presentations had taken place. "We don't really have Muslims here, and there's no foreseeable influx of Muslims to Northern Wisconsin."[44]

Homosexual Seminars and Gay Studies

More and more these days, it has become fashionable, if not almost mandatory, for universities to promote the idea that homosexuality is completely normal and that homosexual behavior is exempt from moral evaluation. It's simply an alternative lifestyle as routine and acceptable as heterosexuality. And woe to those who interfere with this message! Professor Mike Adams shared his experience of attending a seminar at UNC-Wilmington instructing students on how to better display sensitivity toward homosexual, bisexuals, and transgendered persons. At the seminar, two cross-dressers gave the audience instructions on how not to offend those who switch their gender identity back and forth. One of the two said that not all cross-dressers are gay and that the heterosexual ones feel superior to the gay ones, "because they're like the Catholics who think they're the only ones going to heaven." This is the rubbish passing for higher education on many of our campuses today.[45]

Examples of such madness are endless. UNC Provost Robert Shelton commissioned a report on the state of UNC-Chapel Hill's homosexual community. The report recommended promoting the development of the "lesbian, gay, bisexual, transgender, and queer (LGBTQ) community on campus," with an emphasis on encouraging "tolerance" of gays and their agenda. It reported with horror and apparent incredulity that "half the general population continues to believe that homosexual behavior is morally wrong." The implication, obviously, is that an open and tolerant university climate can't permit such archaic thought patterns. The report concludes that UNC-Chapel Hill's climate for members of the LGBTQ community in academics, support services, employee and faculty benefits, and institutional policy lags behind other "benchmark" universities in America.[46]

Of special concern was the finding that UNC did not offer majors, minors, and certainly not certificates in "sexuality studies." After all, according to the report, "Over the last three decades, the study of sexuality has become established in the U.S. and elsewhere as a rich, vibrant area of research." That says it all, does it not? The study recommended that to correct this disparity UNC must "actively encourage department chairs and faculty to revise existing courses to include material relevant to sexuality studies and to develop new courses" and to "explicitly communicate to . . . the departments that sexuality studies is a valued and legitimate area of research, teaching and scholarship." It urged the acquisition of a full-time director of sexual studies.

Note that, beyond being objectionable on their face, these recommendations carry an educational opportunity cost. One UNC alumnus put it in perspective, saying, "You find students now who have difficulty getting into core classes . . . because they are full, because they don't have money to fund more professors. It makes it very difficult for a student to successfully arrange their schedule in the course of four years . . . yet the university is using its resources to provide classes . . . that don't contribute to the intellectual climate."[47]

The dean of the College of Education at Texas A&M University proposed a "tolerance" statement for homosexuals, requiring faculty members to "celebrate and promote all forms of human diversity," including sexual orientation. It didn't simply say that homosexuals should be treated fairly, but that their lifestyle must be "celebrated and promoted." Eight professors submitted a letter of objection, saying that Christian faculty members should not be forced to "celebrate and promote" a lifestyle they believe is immoral. One faculty member countered by accusing the objecting professors of bigotry and urging that one of them be fired from his administrative position.

"Rather pompous and arrogant" is how Dean Jane Conoley characterized the letter. "Sacred texts should be used to guide our personal lives and not used in judgment of others," she explained as she stood in judgment over the professors. "I generally consider distinctions that call us to love the sinner while hating the sin to be empty, rhetorical gestures at best and covers for persecution at worst." But the objecting professors were not suggesting that they engage in judgmental behavior—merely that they not be compelled to sign on to a policy statement repugnant to their personal moral beliefs.[48]

Academic Freedom and Tolerance–Porn

Pretty much anything is a legitimate subject of academic inquiry on college campuses, besides Christianity. James Madison University, for example, held a "SexFest," which featured such enlightening endeavors as a demonstration of how to put on a condom when drunk.[49] At many universities, pornography has been elevated to a noble discipline inside the classroom. Even so-called Christian-based universities, like Wesleyan in Middletown, Connecticut, have degenerated into this practice. Wesleyan offered a course called "Pornography: Writing of Prostitutes." For the final assignment of the class a few years ago, Professor Hope Weissman told her students to produce a piece of pornography. "I don't put any constraints on it," explained Weissman. "It's supposed to be: 'Just create your own work of pornography.'"[50]

One student produced a video, training the camera's lens on a man's eyes while he was masturbating. Another turned in pictures of herself engaged in oral sex with her boyfriend. When someone finally objected, school officials initiated a review of the class to evaluate "how the course fits the College of Letters' program objectives and those of Women's Studies." The review incurred the indignation of faculty and students, who were outraged by this affront to so-called academic freedom. The administration's action "constitutes the largest attack on academic freedom at Wesleyan in at least forty years," a student editorialist charged. But pornography in the classroom is not limited to Wesleyan. Dozens of secular universities around the nation offer such courses. Constance Penley, chairman of the film studies department at the University of California-Santa Barbara, who introduced a pornography curriculum there in 1993, heralded Professor Weissman as "a very brave woman. . . . Now pornographic film can be seen as a completely normal and necessary part of a film studies curriculum."[51]

Academic Freedom and Tolerance–Speech Codes

Most people have heard of the speech codes existing on campuses across America that censor politically incorrect speech. It has been estimated that ninety percent of American universities have speech codes. Ostensibly, they are most often adopted to promote a peaceful educational environment.[52] These codes gained prominence in the 1980s, and many professors and students have felt their sting. In one disturbing case, a seventy-four-year-old professor was yanked from his classroom during class and interrogated while armed guards looked on. But that's just one example of the hundreds of cases where university authorities punished professors or students, essentially for expressing politically incorrect views. In some cases, the violation was not even one of commission, but of omission, as when a residential adviser at Carnegie Mellon was canned for refusing to put on a pink triangle (symbol of gay behavior) during mandatory "gay and lesbian sensitivity training."[53]

There is simply no room for dissent in the politically correct atmosphere of the college campuses today. The sponsors of these speech codes pretend they are vindicating minority rights and preventing harassment of protected groups, but no matter how nicely they dress it up, in the end it amounts to no less than mind control and speech regulation for political purposes.

Behind the Agenda: Left-Wing Bias

Some universities have a distorted idea of academic freedom. At the University of South Carolina (USC), so-called Guidelines for Classroom Discussion have been established in one required course (for a degree in Women's Studies). The guidelines, which set the ground rules for classroom discussion in "Women's Studies 797: Seminar in Women's Studies," require students, as a condition of participating, to "acknowledge that racism, classism, sexism, heterosexism, and other institutionalized forms of oppression exist." Students must also agree "that people—both the people we study and the members of the class—always do the best they can."

Further, the guidelines provide that, "we are all systematically taught misinformation about our own group and about members of other groups," and "this is true for members of privileged and oppressed groups." Students have to "agree to combat actively the myths and stereotypes about our own groups and other groups."[54] In this strange course, class participation counted for twenty percent of the student's grade, clearly requiring students to conform to the guideline's dictates, lest their grade suffer. Such draconian guidelines may soon be coming to a campus near you, for they have gained a measure of academic acceptance, having been published in the *Women's Studies Quarterly* and in *Teaching Sociological Concepts and the Sociology of Gender*,[55] a publication of the American Sociological Association.

While thought control is doubtlessly not as severe in all college classes, there is little doubt that most universities are bastions of politically liberal thought. Author and activist David Horowitz's

Center for the Study of Popular Culture, together with the American Enterprise Institute, conducted a survey of the political leanings of American university faculties. The findings were not surprising, but are nonetheless alarming. Over ninety percent of instructors in the arts and science departments at major universities such as Harvard, Cornell, Stanford, Penn State, Maryland, and Brown were either registered Democrats or in other left-leaning parties, including the Greens. Very few were Republicans or Libertarians. As Horowitz observed, "You can't get a good education if you only get half the story."[56]

The survey also revealed that eighty percent of Ivy League professors voted for Democratic presidential candidate Al Gore in 2000, while only nine percent cast their ballots for Republican George W. Bush. The findings were even more dramatic on certain social issues. Seventy-nine percent of the professors said they considered President Bush's political views "too conservative." Despite these findings, Harvard spokesman Joe Wrinn had the audacity to assert that "Harvard University represents a full spectrum of thought, which is the basic purpose and goal of a university."[57]

This ideological imbalance extends beyond the classroom and into the entire educational experience. Even speakers invited to give commencement addresses at major universities are overwhelmingly liberal. Young America's Foundation (YAF) released a study showing that the great majority of commencement speakers in 2002 for the nations' top fifty universities (using the *U.S. News & World Report* list) were liberals. According to the survey, conservative commencement speakers are also greatly underrepresented at schools that are not part of the top fifty.[58]

Conservatives are not merely crowded out of graduation ceremonies. Faculty often bar them from other speaking events on campus. That's exactly what happened to author Dan Flynn at Michigan State University (MSU). The university's College Republicans had invited Flynn to speak about his book, *Why the Left Hates America*. The MSU College Republicans were given approval for Flynn to speak on "patriotism" and "why America is great." But when a school bureaucrat noticed the title of the book in a flyer advertising the event, she determined it was "too hostile" and that the Republican group had misrepresented the topic of the speech. In a chilling attack on freedom of expression, she pulled the plug on the speech and threatened to call the police if Flynn went ahead with his talk. Nonetheless, Flynn did speak, and no law enforcement officers showed up to drag him away to the MSU re-education camps.[59] One official unwittingly admitted the university's censorship when he said, "First Amendment rights are not the same thing as being polite or not being impolite. There is no absolute right in the First Amendment to say anything you want anywhere you want." But who said anything about absolute rights here? How about just giving the conservative viewpoint an airing, let alone equal time?

When conservatives are permitted to speak on campus, they are often treated with scorn and contempt. When racial equality activist Ward Connerly spoke at a conference at Columbia University, along with columnist John Leo and author Dinesh D'Souza, officials resisted, by demanding thousands of dollars in extra security money for the event. Because these three speakers are known conservatives, newspapers billed the upcoming conference as racist, sexist, and a threat to civil rights, which contributed to the hateful mobs greeting the participants, who were insulted, physically threatened, and spat upon. Adding insult to injury, Columbia refused to discipline the protestors, but instead issued a memo criticizing Connerly,[60] expressing its commitment to affirmative action—though that subject had nothing to do with the conference—and banning the conference from campus. A strikingly similar incident occurred at Penn State, where militarily clad protestors interrupted conservative Star Parker's address by marching to the front of the room, blowing whistles, and conducting a ten-minute skit. University police sat by as Parker was subjected to these indignities. As if that weren't enough, a director of a cultural center on campus called Parker an "ideological whore" in the pages of the campus newspaper.[61]

Other Campus Censorship

Not surprisingly, conservative journalists are often the targets of liberal bias and intolerance on university campuses. A group of thieves stole twenty-two stacks of *Liberty's Flame*, the University of California-Davis's conservative newspaper, and dumped them in a recycling bin. Prior to the incident, the publication's writers had received insulting e-mails accusing them of bigotry and promoting segregation. Among the paper's editorial positions that inflamed campus liberals was its exposure of the allegedly anti-American goals of a Mexican group called MEChA.

Large-scale thefts of conservative newspapers have been reported in universities across the nation, including Brown, UC-Berkeley, Georgetown, and Villanova. Perhaps it would be marginally less troublesome if these acts of vandalism and censorship were condoned by only small numbers of radical students. But in case after case, faculties defend these actions. One Cornell spokesman said that burning an issue of *The Cornell Review* in 1998 was justified on First Amendment grounds—as if that were the issue. The president of Georgetown denounced its conservative paper instead of condemning those who confiscated every issue of it. At Villanova, the school's dean of students was the mastermind of the theft of the entire issue of a conservative publication.[62] And student activists at Yale stole the freshman orientation issue of the campus paper *Light and Truth* because it criticized a freshman "safe sex" program promoting risky sexual behavior in the guise of "sexual liberation." The article's sin was to condemn the program's encouragement of one-night stands and the like.[63]

Intellectual Vapidity

The left-wing bias at some universities is so pronounced that it borders on the bizarre, as witnessed by the silly and biased ideas being dished out as education all over the country. A quick spin through university curricula circa 2000, as reported in the *Washington Times*, showcased courses on:

- "Marxism: What Is to Be Learned from It?"—The work of the venerable godfather of Communism, according to the University of Virginia course description, is the "standard against which all subsequent social thought must be judged... It's worth devoting an entire semester to it."

- "Bodies Politic: Queer Theory and Literature of the Body." This Cornell University course looks into the way in which "concepts of perversion and degeneration haunt the idea of the social body," and "how... individual bodies are stigmatized, encoded, and read within the social sphere."

- "Death, Suicide and Trauma." UCLA students of this class will learn about the "definition and taxonomy of death, new permissiveness and taboos related to death; romanticization of death; role of individual in his own demise; modes of death; development of ideas of death through life... partial death, megadeath; lethally psychological autopsy; death of institutions and cultures."

- "Sex and Death," at Carnegie Mellon University. Here the students will examine "whether we need to liberate death now that (maybe) we have figured sex out."

- "Women's Studies," where Maine's Bowden College students will explore such heady questions as "Is Beethoven's Ninth Symphony a marvel of abstract architecture culminating in a gender-free paean to human solidarity, or does it model the process of rape?"[64]

An Academic Lampoons Academia

Alan Sokal, a physics professor at New York University concerned about the declining quality of our colleges, decided to conduct his own little "controlled" experiment to see how far academic standards had deteriorated. His purpose was to see whether a "leading North

American journal of cultural studies . . . would publish an article liberally salted with nonsense if (a) it sounded good and (b) it flattered the editors' ideological preconceptions." "The answer," reported Sokal in an article for *Lingua Franca*, "unfortunately, is yes." He was incredulous that the editors of *Social Text*, who published his piece, didn't realize it was a parody. In the second paragraph of the article he asserted, "without the slightest evidence or argument," that "physical reality . . . is at bottom a social and linguistic construct." Sokal later emphasized the absurdity of his claim by pointing out that he wasn't saying that our *theories* of physical reality were a social and linguistic construct, but that reality itself was. "Anyone who believes that the laws of physics are mere social conventions," quipped Sokal, "is invited to try transgressing those conventions from the windows of my apartment. (I live on the twenty-first floor.)"[65] Sokal says that as ridiculous as many of his article's statements were, its "fundamental silliness" was the "dubiousness" of its central thesis. His thesis was that quantum gravity—the still-speculative theory of space and time on scales of a millionth of a billionth of a billionth of a billionth of a centimeter—has profound political implications.

Sokal's explanation for his experiment is fascinating and bears on the postmodern relativism run amok on our campuses, which holds that there is no such thing as objective truth. He said that what concerned him was the "proliferation . . . of a particular kind of nonsense and sloppy thinking . . . that denies the existence of objective realities, or (when challenged) admits their existence but downplays their relevance." He confessed that he is angered because "most (though not all) of this silliness is emanating from the self-proclaimed Left." In a scathing denunciation of relativism, he concluded with this sobering observation: "Theorizing about the 'social construction of reality' won't help us find an effective treatment for AIDS or devise strategies for preventing global warming. Nor can we combat false ideas in history, sociology, economics, and politics if we reject the notions of truth and falsity."[66]

Fueling the Agenda: Postmodern Hogwash

Sokal's experiment and findings are a fitting lament for the deplorable moral and academic condition of many of our college campuses, which is the byproduct of the American cultural elite's rejection of absolute truths and traditional values in favor of postmodern relativism. Sokal is not exaggerating about this growing tendency on many campuses to reject the very concepts of truth and falsity.

Bridgewater State College in Massachusetts offers a history course in which a number of books are required reading. On the back cover of one of the books, the following statement appears. "It is commonplace today to suggest that gender is socially constructed, that the roles women and men fulfill in their daily lives have been created and defined for them by society and social institutions."[67] Along the lines of Sokal's parody thesis, this book argued that different roles of men and women are *all* social constructs—artificially created by society. The authors, to borrow Sokal's phrase, are denying the existence of objective realities. Reality, whether about the sexes or anything else, is reduced to a subjective phenomenon—it's whatever we choose to make it. There are no absolutes. Postmodernists devalue human life, and some of them go so far as to see human nature itself as a "social construct." As postmodern psychologist Kenneth Gergen explains in *The Saturated Self*, "With the spread of postmodern consciousness, we see the demise of personal definition, reason, authority.... All intrinsic properties of the human being, along with moral worth and personal commitment, are lost from view."[68]

Thus it is no mystery that Christianity is unacceptable to the postmodern paragons of tolerance. For the Christian worldview holds that the one and only God objectively intervened (and intervenes) in history and that its truth claims are absolutely valid and open to rational, empirical investigation. Truth, to Christians, is not a function of whatever a person says it is. Nor is a religion valid simply because someone affirms it. Postmodernists—those who peddle the euphemisms of tolerance, diversity, openness, multiculturalism, and the rest—view Christianity as inherently in conflict with their subjective assumptions about the world, including their notion that truth itself is just a tool to justify power. "We cannot," says postmodernist Michel Foucault, "exercise power except through the production of truth." So it is that postmodernists fear and oppose those who subscribe to absolute truth.

Postmodernism gives rise to such ideas as that tolerance requires us not just to permit the free expression of all ideas, but also to accept all beliefs as equally valid. This mindset discourages reason, because reason itself is tainted by our socially constructed realities. This mentality also largely rejects the evaluation of ideas on moral grounds, since no one can possibly be in a position to make such judgments. But since Christianity, by its very nature, cannot submit to such intellectual anarchy, it is a glaring exception to the rule that all ideas must be accepted as equally valid. The postmodern rule, more accurately formulated, is that all ideas must be tolerated except those that refuse to accept the doctrine that all ideas are equally valid. For all these reasons, postmodernism is innately anti-Christian.[69]

In short, "the reason postmodernists find Christians so irritating is that we keep violating the rules by speaking of our beliefs in terms of real, objective truth. This is regarded as a category mistake," says scholar and writer Nancy Pearcey.

How, you might ask, does this philosophy affect teaching in the core disciplines? Well, it's rather obvious that when you reduce truth to subjective preferences, the subject matter of any educational curriculum is devalued. If truth is merely an expression of subjective, socially constructed content formulated by those who hold power, it follows that academics are free to rewrite history, for example, to rectify the bias injected by the powers that wrote the textbooks.

This explains, for example the so-called multiculturalists' preoccupation with "correcting" the record to give "truth" its proper balance toward all ethnicities. In an article for *Frontpagemagazine.com*, Bridgewater State University student J. D. Cassidy described his experience with this in a history course titled *Social and Cultural History of Early Modern Europe*. The professor told the students that he had excised from the course title the words *intellectual history* because they were "not in step with contemporary scholarship," in that "intellectual history" deals primarily with "dead white males."[70]

Such political indoctrination in place of real education is too common to shock anymore, but the same student's experience in another class reveals just how far afield certain professors are in misdirecting their often unsuspecting students. Cassidy related a story about a course titled *North American Women's and Gender History*. In this class, the professor "was a flaming leftist" who ran the class "like a cult." She used two cartoon illustrations she had cut out of newspapers as the primary material for one lecture.

One illustration showed the Statue of Liberty bent over and weeping. Cassidy said that, since the sketch was made shortly after the September 11 terrorist attacks, it was obvious to him that the artist was expressing the nation's grief. The professor instead examined the drawing through the subjective prism of feminism. She asserted that the artist chose the statue because American culture allows women to cry, but not men. The artist, constrained by cultural forces (presumably, live white guys), had surrendered his artistic freedom. To the professor, this constituted proof that society has established "gender roles" that men and women must follow. She said the purpose of her history course was to locate these gender roles and reject them.[71]

After describing other courses and course materials, Cassidy concluded that many leftist professors are doing more than just indoctrinating students with their zany ideas—which is certainly troubling enough. "By substituting radical tracts for real history, leftist professors completely insulate students not only from conservative ideas, but from history itself."[72] The same could be said for any core subject where political indoctrination masquerades as teaching.

Postmodern theory holds not only that truth is defined by power, but that speech is as well. It is through such convoluted gyrations that many campus liberals rationalize selective limits on the expression of ideas. Some of the foundational reasons behind the free and open exchange of ideas are that such a process will more likely lead to the discovery of truth and serve as a watchdog against those in power. But when the reality of truth itself is rejected, the nobility of the avenues toward it, such as free expression, loses its appeal. If speech is dictated by power, then what can be wrong with regulating it? In fact, such speech management can be seen as more important than freedom of speech itself because regulation of the powerful, not the free flow of ideas, serves as the watchdog against political oppressors. In this way, the slippery slope of postmodern relativism leads us to the tyranny of political correctness against Christianity we witness on campus today.

We have been examining the war against Christianity taking place in our education institutions. Now we continue to Part II, the War for the Public Square, where we'll see the same secular forces actively seeking to scrub Christianity, by force, from American culture. Just as with the education system, the hypocrisy of the secularists is on full display everywhere you look in society. While working to sanitize the public square of all things Christian, they are anxiously promoting non-Christian values in these same venues. In Chapter Six we'll examine their efforts to cleanse the government and government property of Christianity.

part II

The War for the Public Square

People have varying views on the extent to which religious expression and symbols, particularly those related to Christianity, should enter the public square. While few would advocate government endorsement of religion, many apparently believe the public square should be a religion-free zone. In modern America, public officials tend to resolve such differences in favor of those wishing to effect a complete religious ban. Most of the time, concerns over the separation of church and state drive the scrubbing of the public square, but sometimes there is no government link at all. Because of the reputed intolerance of Christianity, societal forces often seek to purge it from public view, just to avoid the possibility that non-Christians may be offended by this "exclusive" religion.

While at the founding of this nation there was largely a Christian cultural consensus among the citizens, today in some circles the label "Christian" is considered a badge of dishonor. This is because it is perceived as incompatible with the diversity in our modern culture. Those who claim to be merely trying to remove all traces of intolerance from the public arena give little thought to acts of discrimination toward Christians, who often surrender without a fight. It could be that they either wish to avoid controversy or they anticipate that courts will be sympathetic to the "purging" view—removing Christian symbols or muzzling Christian expression.

The war for the public square has continued to unfold in a number of areas, as we'll see in Chapters Six through Ten. This chapter examines the battle to exclude Christian influence and presence from the seats of government and government property. Chapter Seven chronicles the battle against public officials, employees, and appointees. Chapter Eight focuses on the battle against the church and lay people seeking to promote their Christian beliefs and also on the attacks against Christianity in the private sector. Chapter Nine documents the state's endorsement of non-Christian values and the popular culture's insensitivity toward Christians and their beliefs. Chapter Ten examines attacks on Christians by Hollywood and the mainstream media.

chapter six

Purging Christianity from the Government and Government Property

OUR CONCERN IN THIS CHAPTER is to examine the fight to exclude Christianity from government. As we shall see, this attack on the founding principles of our nation is comprehensive in scope, occurring at every level of government, local, state, and federal, and is directed at the heart of Christian thought and practice.

Local Level

We begin at the local level, with events surrounding a public housing development in New York City in the wake of September 11. Following the terrorist attacks, the American people forged a stronger bond than any in recent memory. In seeking to help the people in New York City deal with their shock and grief, many religious leaders came forward to offer spiritual guidance, counseling, and assistance. Pastor Joan Daily, a longtime resident of a public housing development in Woodside in Queens, New York, sought permission from the New York City Housing Authority to rent a room at the Woodside Community Center to conduct a Bible study and prayer meeting for aggrieved city residents. Several Woodside residents died in the terrorist attacks. Though the facility is routinely used by various groups for a wide range of purposes, from exercise classes to adult education, the Authority denied the pastor's request. Officials cited a city policy prohibiting "religious services, unless the religious services are directly connected to the principal reason for a family-oriented event, such as weddings." The American Center for Law and Justice (ACLJ) filed a federal lawsuit against the Authority on behalf of Pastor Daily for denying her access to the facility on the basis of religious speech. The Authority would have been on firmer legal grounds had it denied access to other groups, but to deny groups to meet on public property merely because their meeting is religious in nature is a denial of their religious freedom.[1]

The separation principle reached new heights of absurdity when Johnie Heard, a resident of a government-subsidized apartment in the Detroit area, placed a sign in her window proclaiming "24-Hr. Prayer Station." Heard said the Lord directed her to display the sign to make people aware of her apartment, where she plays sermons continuously on a tape-recorded loop to welcome all lost souls. Upon learning of the prayer invitation sign, officials from the city of Taylor, which owned the apartment, sent Heard an eviction notice, ostensibly for violating the apartment complex's ban on signs. "We're not anti-religious at all," said Albert Berriz, the head of McKinley Properties, which manages the complex. "But the things you put in the windows may be offensive to others. There could be Jewish families, African-American families, atheists, or Kiwanis who have different views. We need rules of consistency so we don't have three hundred signs advertising three hundred different things." McKinley finally backed down on its eviction efforts when Liberty Counsel intervened on behalf of Heard. Following the incident, Heard said, "At times, I said, 'Lord, did I hear you right? You sure you want me to put up this sign?' But one thing about the Lord is that if you stand up for Him, He'll stand up for you against your enemies."[2]

Discrimination by Public Facilities

In Kern County, California, the County Parks and Recreation Department charged religious groups—mainly Christian church groups—an hourly fee to use a county-owned facility, while allowing other community groups to use the structure for free. The New Life Assembly, a Christian congregation located in Delano, California, filed a suit seeking equal access to the county facilities and to stop discrimination against religious groups. "No organization should be penalized because it has a religious message," said Stuart Roth of the ACLJ, the congregation's attorney. The suit was settled before trial, with Kern County agreeing to modify or repeal the ordinance and policies discriminating against religious organizations in the use of county facilities.[3]

The town of Babylon, New York, owns a building known as the Town Hall Annex, which has a gymnasium and fifteen small meeting rooms. Most of the rooms are used for city business, but a handful are available for public use. In November 1998, a small church group called Romans Chapter Ten Ministries, Inc. applied to use the facilities for Bible study every Thursday evening and worship services each Sunday morning. The town initially approved the application for 1999, and the twelve-member group met there three times in January. Pastor John Amandola then placed an ad in the newspaper announcing his church and inviting the public to attend the Thursday and Sunday meetings. Seeing the ad, an irate resident called the town commissioner, James Namely, and objected to the use of the facility for church services, whereupon Namely revoked the church's permit to meet on the city property. The church filed a federal suit alleging that the town's policy violated its free speech and free exercise rights. The United States Court of Appeals for the Second Circuit reversed the order of the district court, which had denied relief, and found that Babylon's policy was "constitutionally invalid on its face and as applied to plaintiffs." The court stated, "Because we are confident that the City will conform its conduct accordingly, we need not direct the entry of a permanent injunction. If the need for injunctive relief should arise after remand, the district court will be able to fashion an appropriate remedy."[4]

It appears the court's confidence in the city was misplaced. Following the ruling, Babylon amended its policy, but instead of tailoring it to allow access to the facility, it banned religious speech altogether. Under the new policy, non-religious groups are still permitted to use the facilities, but religious groups or churches are not. The policy states, "No organization or group may be allowed to conduct religious services or religious instruction within Town buildings or facilities." According to church attorney Vincent P. McCarthy of the ACLJ, the new policy was unconstitutionally targeted specifically at the church. "In essence, the town rejected the findings of the appeals court and has implemented an amended policy that continues to discriminate against religious organizations and people of faith," he said. "Sadly, the town continues to use taxpayer dollars to wage a legal battle that clearly places them on the wrong side of the law."[5]

Prayer and Bible study meetings are one thing, some might say, but what about meetings discussing America's Christian heritage? The Dunedin Public Library in Tampa, Florida, denied the right of Liberty Counsel to use the library's community meeting room, which is generally accessible to the public on a "first come, first served" basis. When Liberty Counsel submitted an application to use the room in late August 2002, the official in charge of scheduling meetings denied the request. In her letter, Dorothy Noggle said, "The meeting room policy strictly forbids the use of community meeting rooms for meetings/programs of a political, religious, or formal social nature."

A few months later the group submitted a second request to use the room, again to discuss America's Christian heritage, including the influence of the Ten Commandments in American law and government. For the second time, the library denied Liberty Counsel permission. The presentation was to be historical, not religious in focus—though the presenters were obviously Christian in their perspective. In a news release, Liberty Counsel's Mathew Staver stated, "One of the clearest issues in constitutional law is the concept of equal access to public facilities. Government officials may not forbid the use of common meeting rooms, otherwise open to the general public, to persons or groups desiring to address a subject from a religious or Christian viewpoint. Of all places, a public library should welcome diverse views."[6] In 2003, a similar case arose in Van, Texas, where Charles and Michelle Moore filed a federal suit against the city for refusing to allow them to use the Van Community Center for a prayer meeting, though it had permitted all sorts of other meetings and community events there. In his twenty-seven-page decision in favor of the Moores, U.S. District Judge Leonard Davis said the city's "resistance to allowing religious groups to use the center carries an implication of hostility toward religion and is inherently discriminatory."[7]

Mother Teresa: An Insult to Women's Rights?

Diversity is the mantra of the politically correct, and should be applied across the board, right? This brings us to an example of purging so extreme and so absurd that it can be rationally explained only as an act of utter paranoia about Christianity. In this case, the Freedom From Religion Foundation (FFRF) was displeased with the decision of the Madison, Wisconsin, Metro system to place Mother Teresa's picture on its April bus pass. Mother Teresa had been chosen, among other reasons, because she was part of *Time* magazine's top 100 Most Important People of the twentieth century. But FFRF president Annie Laurie Gaylor said the picture was "an insult to Madisonians who value women's rights, and the separation of church and state." Metro spokeswoman Julie Maryott-Walsh denied the charge, saying, "We just believed she was notable." Maryott-Walsh added that the May bus pass would feature another notable person: the Rev. Martin Luther King, Jr. "Some people may consider him a religious figure. We don't." In addition, plans call for the October 2003 pass to feature Mohandas Gandhi, "a religious figure to some," she said. "It is not Metro's intent to promote religion with the passes." Other celebrity figures to be featured on passes throughout the year were Philo Farnsworth, Elvis Presley, Albert Einstein, Helen Keller, Frank Lloyd Wright, and Tim Berners-Lee (founder of the World Wide Web).[8]

Such assurances did not satisfy Gaylor. "Religious figures," she said, "do not belong on monthly passes of publicly owned transportation facilities." So this remarkably strong woman, Mother Teresa—world-renowned for her selfless lifetime of charity works in poverty-stricken nations, whose Missionaries of Charity Order was sanctioned by the pope, and who won a Nobel Peace Prize in 1979 for her astonishingly good works—is an "insult" to "women's rights?" Absolutely, according to Gaylor, because Mother Teresa didn't march in lockstep with the preaching of the feminist movement. "Mother Teresa," said Gaylor, "lived in parts of the world where she saw first-hand the overwhelming poverty and tragedy resulting from women's lack of access to birth control. Yet she campaigned stridently throughout her life at every opportunity against access to contraception, sterilization and abortion for anyone."[9]

State Level

From the Halls of Government

If prayer and Bible studies in public housing authorities and government-owned recreational centers in towns and cities agitate secularists, such meetings in the halls of state government really make them nervous. In February 2003, Alabama Governor Bob Riley, his cabinet members, and senior staff began voluntary Bible studies each Tuesday morning in the governor's office in the capitol building. Riley said he got the idea while serving in the United States Congress, where many congressmen participated in Bible meetings at the U.S. Capitol. "It's voluntary," said Riley. "Anyone who wants to come is more than welcome." The governor's office said that absolutely no state business would be discussed during the meetings, and the governor was careful to have plenty of other meetings with the staff so that none of them felt pressured to attend the Bible meetings just to gain access to him. Although only eleven of his fifty-five staff members chose to attend any of the meetings, Larry Darby, Alabama director for American Atheists, said there is no way the sessions could be truly voluntary when the governor convenes them. "It's a form of Christian terrorism," said Darby.[10]

Alabama and Moore—the Ten Commandments

The separationists' angst over Christian symbols in the halls of state government is perhaps nowhere more apparent than in the notorious controversy over the display of the Ten Commandments in courthouses and seats of government all over America. In the controversy over the Ten Commandments no one has captured more attention than Alabama Supreme Court Chief Justice Roy S. Moore. On August 1, 2001, he unveiled a two-and-one-half-ton granite monument featuring the Ten Commandments, along with quotes from America's founding fathers, in the Alabama State Judicial Building's rotunda. The monument was not paid for with taxpayer funds. The ACLU, Americans United for Separation of Church and State (AU), and the Southern Poverty Law Center (SPLC) filed two separate federal lawsuits against Moore, claiming the display of the monument was unconstitutional. Before he was sworn in, however, Justice Moore had promised to display the Ten Commandments at the court and, if the ACLU sued, to "fight them with everything and every ounce of strength I have, because what they're coming against is not me, but it's against truth." Moore said the monument is a depiction of the "moral foundation of the law" that would serve to remind those who see it "that in order to establish justice, we must invoke 'the favor and guidance of Almighty God.'"[11]

The two cases were consolidated, and after a weeklong trial, District Judge Myron H. Thompson ordered Justice Moore to remove the monument within thirty days. Moore had testified at trial that, while he believed the Ten Commandments were the moral foundation of American law and that the monument certainly acknowledged God, the display of those commandments did not force anyone to follow his Christian beliefs. Judge Thompson disagreed, finding that similar displays on government property had been found permissible only when they also had a secular purpose and did not foster "excessive government entanglement with religion." The Ten Commandments monument, he said, failed that test. Thompson also found the monument to be more than a mere display. "The Court is impressed," he wrote, "that the monument and its immediate surroundings are, in essence, a consecrated place, a religious sanctuary, within the walls of the courthouse." He added, "No other Ten Commandments display presents such an extreme case of religious acknowledgement, endorsement, and even proselytization."[12] The judge, however, stayed his own order pending the outcome of an appeal to the Eleventh Circuit Court of Appeals, which affirmed the district court's ruling on July 1, 2003. The court stated, "If we adopted his position, the chief justice would be free to adorn the walls of the Alabama Supreme Court's courtroom with sectarian religious murals and have decidedly religious quotations painted above the bench."

Scholar and author Michael Novak disagreed with the ruling, pointing out that "on the outside wall of the federal courthouse in Montgomery is a much larger statue of Artemis, described in the Court's brochure as the Greek goddess of justice. No one asserts that the statue represents an establishment of religion."[13] Novak also observed that the text on the display is from the Old or Jewish Testament, not the New Testament, making it much less sectarian and much broader. Also, said Novak, the statue is at least ninety feet from the front entrance to the courthouse and impossible to read from that distance. Perhaps Novak's most convincing argument, however, was that merely calling the public's attention to the truth that America had historically treated its liberties, including its religious liberties, as endowments from God, was not necessarily the same thing as establishing a religion.[14]

Not all Ten Commandment suits have unhappy endings. Federal Judge Harry Lee Hudspeth held that a forty-two-year-old Ten Commandments display on state Capitol grounds in Austin, Texas, was not an unconstitutional establishment of religion. The judge found that the memorial was an appropriate tool "to promote youth morality and to stop the alarming increase in delinquency," thereby serving a secular purpose. He stated that no "reasonable observer" would conclude that the state sought to endorse religion with the monument.

He further noted that "each of the Ten Commandments has played a significant role in the foundation of our system of law and government" and has "both a secular and religious aspect."

Liberty Counsel's Mathew Staver agreed. "To ignore the influence of the Ten Commandments in the founding and shaping of American law and government," said Staver, "would require significant historical revisionism." Texas Governor Rick Perry issued a statement in support of the ruling, saying, "Today's court ruling is a victory for those who believe, as I do, that the Ten Commandments are time-tested and appropriate guidelines for living a full and moral life. The Ten Commandments provide a historical foundation for our laws and principles as a free and strong nation, under God, and should be displayed at the Texas Capitol."

Novak, Staver, and the governor are echoing a similar theme. Displaying the Ten Commandments in recognition of our framers' conviction that our religious liberties derive from God—and even affirming their importance in society's moral foundation—does not constitute the establishment of religion. To diminish their role in the history of this nation based on an extreme reading of the Establishment Clause is a gross overreaction and is utterly incompatible with the intent of the framers. There is a major difference between public acknowledgments of the founders' belief in the foundational importance of the Ten Commandments (and other Judeo-Christian principles) to our liberties and the government's endorsement of the Ten Commandments. While the latter should also not run afoul of the Establishment Clause, the former clearly should not.

Federal Level

Rotunda Prayer

The separationists grow even queasier when religious meetings or events take place in the halls of the federal government. When both houses of Congress passed a resolution allowing the Capitol Rotunda to be used for prayer sessions by members of Congress, Americans United for Separation of Church and State (AU) were none too pleased. "If members of Congress want a religious service, they can go to their houses of worship," said AU president Barry Lynn. "The U.S. Capitol is not a revival tent." Apparently Lynn is unaware that murals around the Rotunda wall depict a pilgrim's prayer, the baptism of Pocahontas, De Soto planting a cross on the banks of the Mississippi, and George Washington passing into Heaven. Gabe Neville, spokesman for Congressman Joseph R. Pitts, one of the sponsors of the resolution, denied they were breaking new ground. "This is not unprecedented at all," said Neville. "The House of Representatives was used as a church from when it was built until after the Civil War. The first Continental Congress opened their first session on October 14, 1774, with two hours of prayer. The original session of the U.S. Supreme Court established September 24, 1789, began with a four-hour communion service."[15] Such historical facts, sadly, make little impression on those who want to eradicate religion from government property.

John Ashcroft

That Attorney General John Ashcroft has been a thorn in the side of anti-Christian groups became obvious during his controversial Senate confirmation hearings, and criticism of him only intensified after he took office. The outspoken Christian beliefs of Ashcroft, son of a Pentecostal preacher, have rankled his detractors, so when he began conducting Bible study and prayer sessions at his office in the Justice Department (though not during work hours) his opponents fell on him anew. The *Washington Post* made a federal case out of these meetings in a story titled "Ashcroft's Faith Plays Visible Role at Justice," though the meetings were held behind closed doors. No matter. The *Post* emphasized that of the department's 135,000 employees worldwide, "some who do not share Ashcroft's Pentecostal Christian beliefs are discomfited by the daily prayer sessions—particularly because they are conducted by the nation's chief law enforcement officer, entrusted with enforcing a Constitution that calls for the separation of church and state."

"The purpose of the Department of Justice is to do the business of the government, not to establish a religion," said one Justice attorney unwilling to be named. "It strikes me and a lot of others as offensive, disrespectful, and unconstitutional." In fact, Ashcroft was not acting on behalf of the government in conducting the meetings—so there is no legitimate claim of an Establishment Clause violation. Moreover, he and his subordinates are as entitled to the free exercise of their religion as any other American citizens. He was not conducting these meetings in his official capacity and attendance was completely voluntary. He neither rewarded those who attended nor punished those who did not. The meetings were even open to non-Christians, as confirmed by Jewish employee Shimon Stein, a program analyst who regularly attended the meetings. Stein said of Ashcroft, "He's made every effort to make everyone and everything comfortable." David Israelite, Ashcroft's deputy chief of staff, agreed: "He has never in any way insinuated that I should be going to these meetings, and I never felt I've been hindered by not attending." In addition, said Israelite, "I've known John Ashcroft for fifteen years and there is no more tolerant person that I've been around in my life." Indeed, Ashcroft doesn't believe in spreading his Christian beliefs by force. "It is against my religion to impose my religion on people," he recently said in a speech. Ashcroft was merely continuing a practice he had engaged in for years, including his time serving as a U.S. Senator.[16]

Excluding Christian Influence

We have seen how every level of government in this nation founded on Christian principles is now showing Christians the door, if not barring them from entering the house of government in the first place. But more than this, radical secularists intend to remove from government property virtually every tincture of Christian content and influence. As we shall we, the scope of the attack on Christian faith and practice is breathtaking.

No Christmas–Banning the "Holiday"

One of the truly hot-button issues involving a Christian presence on government property concerns Christmas celebrations and displays. Ditsy Carmen Suarez, a resident of Miami-Dade County, Florida, noticed during the 2002 Christmas season a prominent holiday display at the Miami-Dade County Permit and Inspection Center when she entered the building. She was surprised to discover that, while a Jewish symbol and one celebrating Kwanzaa were on display, Christian symbols were conspicuously absent. This omission concerned Suarez, so she asked the employee at the information desk why a nativity scene was excluded. He demurred, saying he'd been asked that same question a number of times, but didn't know the answer.

Suarez called the county communications department, where an employee informed her that the nativity scene was disallowed because it was religious in nature and only non-religious seasonal symbols were permitted. The director of the Permit and Inspection Center confirmed the policy and added that private individuals had donated the Jewish and Kwanzaa symbols. Suarez then offered to provide a nativity display at her own expense, but her offer was rejected. According to the director, the county attorney said that a Christmas display would violate the "separation of church and state."

Suarez was understandably perplexed at the singling out of Christian symbols for exclusion on church/state grounds, especially since at least one of the other symbols permitted was religious in nature. [17] When the American Family Association (AFA) Center for Law and Policy threatened to seek a federal temporary restraining order, the Inspection Center permitted Suarez to place her display alongside the existing ones. "This is yet another case in which ignorance of the law created irrational fear of violation of the separation of church and state," said Mike DePrimo, AFA's senior litigation counsel. "If government officials were even remotely as solicitous of the rights of Christians as they are of other groups," said AFA chief counsel Stephen M. Crampton, "we would all enjoy greater freedom."

In Wildwood, Florida, the city council voted to place two angel decorations on the front lawn of City Hall over the objections (and legal threats) of the American Atheists, who had written a complaining letter to Mayor Ed Wolf about the display. In his letter, American Atheists Florida director Greg McDowell said, "Last year, while driving through Wildwood, I noticed that along with other ornamental displays, your beautiful, new City Hall had angels outside on the lawn. Angels are without question a religious symbol, and must be omitted this year and in the future.... What we want is absolute separation of religion and government." Mayor Wolf expressed dismay that the scene caused such uproar, because "there was no intent to make [the decorations] religious." Moreover, "it is not a manger scene, but little wire frames of angels and deer with clear Christmas lights probably purchased from Wal-Mart." Ron Barrier, spokesman for American Atheists, disagreed, saying, "Angels are a concept of Christianity," and besides, "churches and temples own plenty of land to display all the decorations they want."[18]

It just gets crazier. A New Jersey public school banned the classic Charles Dickens play *A Christmas Carol* because of its spiritual overtones and redemptive message. The city council of Kensington, Maryland, removed Santa Claus from its traditional tree-lighting ceremony simply because a few families said the jolly fellow would make them uncomfortable. After complaints, the council changed Santa's status from "disinvited" to "uninvited."[19] And ever watchful officials of St. Paul, Minnesota, ordered that a few red poinsettias be removed from the decorative holiday display at the Ramsey County Courthouse, which houses the city hall, because the particular flowers could be associated with Christmas and might offend certain people. Vehement complaints led to a fallback position: The city agreed to allow white poinsettias, but not red ones. City fathers of Pittsburgh coined "Sparkle Season" to enable city residents to skirt the controversy that would surely ensue if they used the word "Christmas." Ron Sims, county executive of King County, Washington, directed his employees not to say "Merry Christmas" or "Happy Hanukkah" at work.[20] The Wisconsin Department of Administration invited people to place handmade ornaments on the state's "holiday tree"—yes, "holiday tree"—and left the ornament guidelines in the hands of state bureaucrats. Lo and behold, the bureaucrats decreed that the ornaments should not be religious in nature.[21]

In Covington, Georgia, the ACLU filed suit against a public school district because its calendar designated December 25 as Christmas, which is unconstitutionally "advancing religion," as opposed to just recognizing the commonly known fact. The ACLU also filed an action against a Pittsburgh public parking lot that set aside a number of parking spaces near a Roman Catholic Church that was housing a nativity scene, to allow travelers to view the display. The ACLU's opposition to this courtesy prompted criticism from Rabbi Aryeh Spero, president of Caucus for America. "The ACLU's insistence here that common courtesy and accommodation be forbidden," wrote Spero, "bespeaks a civic mean-spiritedness, a narrow and small-minded approach to law, and reflects the insecurity and stinginess of certain ACLU-niks choosing not to share a majority-held celebration, i.e., If I don't have Christmas, neither can you. Obviously, the ACLU is animated by hostility to Christianity in the context of American public life."[22]

The City Council of Little Rock, Arkansas, changed the name of its annual December parade from the "Christmas Parade" to the "Holiday Parade," in order not to offend non-religious people or those of other faiths. As one writer quipped, "I can't wait until they find out the word 'holiday' actually means 'holy day.' What to do then?"[23] The Freedom from Religion Foundation placed an atheistic message in the Wisconsin Capitol Rotunda alongside holiday displays. After the sign was vandalized, the group re-erected it. The sign read, "At this season of the winter solstice may reason prevail. There are no gods, no devils, no angels, no heaven or hell. There is only our natural world. Religion is but myth and superstition that hardens hearts and enslaves minds."[24] Note that the high priests of tolerance and diversity did not come out in force condemning that message or its inarguably offensive content.

The state of Oregon has gotten a taste for this growing aversion to Christmas. The city of Eugene, in December 2000, banned Christmas trees from public places. Why? Well, according to the five-page single-spaced memo from City Manager Jim Johnson to all city employees, the fact that Christmas trees are in some cases "associated with a religious holiday or tradition" is sufficient reason to purge them. Adding insult to injury, Johnson said he was issuing the order in the name of diversity. There you have it: Diversity means tolerance for every religion except Christianity. After some firemen objected, Johnson agreed to allow the trees on Christmas Eve and Christmas Day on the explicit condition that he not receive a single complaint about it.[25]

City officials of the coastal community of Tillamook, Oregon—a city famous in the Northwest for its cheese and ice cream—required a private business, High Tide Espresso Drive-Thru, to remove a lighted nativity scene from the drive-through coffee kiosk it rents from the city. Cheryl Hall, the proprietor, installed the scene to honor her infant grandson, who had died earlier in the year. "It appeared to be a conflict between church and state," said City Manager Mark Gervasi. Some conflict! Only one citizen reportedly complained, but that's all it took for the city to remove the display the very next day.[26]

No Easter–Good Friday Dust-Up

Governmental deference to the Easter tradition causes separationists similar anxiety. In Monona, Wisconsin, for example, city officials made the audacious decision to close the public library and City Hall offices on Good Friday afternoon—partly because the library staff has a half-day off under their union contract. The library was only closed from noon to 3 P.M.—some Christians traditionally observe Jesus' crucifixion during this period—and City Hall was closed the entire afternoon. Monona Public Library Director John DeBacher said the library had been closed every Good Friday since he took the position in 1994 and that it was also closed on Easter Sunday in 2003 because of low patronage on previous Easters. FFRF threatened to file a formal protest with city officials to object to these closings.

FFRF's Annie Laurie Gaylor described the closings as "very disturbing" insofar as the foundation had prevailed in a 1996 court action to prevent public facilities from closing on Good Friday. "It's disturbing that a [teachers] union would allow this kind of thing to continue and circumvent the courts,"[27] said Gaylor, referring to the federal lawsuit the foundation brought against Wisconsin, challenging its Good Friday law, which stated: "On Good Friday the period from 11 A.M. to 3 P.M. shall uniformly be observed for the purpose of worship." In that case, *Freedom From Religion Foundation v. Tommy G. Thompson (Governor of Wisconsin)*,[28] the court held "Wisconsin's designation of Good Friday as a holiday... [is] in violation of the Establishment Clause of the First Amendment to the United States Constitution... because the statutes have as their express purpose the promotion of Christian worship." Not all courts have ruled that way. In *Bridenbaugh v. O'Bannon*, (1999) the Seventh Circuit Court of Appeals held that an Indiana statute recognizing Good Friday as a legal holiday for state employees did not violate the Establishment Clause. The court found that the state had shown the holiday also had a secular purpose. "It is logical for the State to choose that day as its spring holiday, as an accommodation to those state employees whose children are out of school and/or spouses are off work,"[29] the court said.

But a state law allegedly mandating observances statewide—if indeed it did—is quite different from a decision by local facilities, not even city-wide, to close on Easter. Indeed, in a case that may be more on point, *Granzeier v. Middleton*, decided on April 19, 1999, the Sixth Circuit Court of Appeals held that reasonable observers would not view the closing of county offices in Kenton County, Kentucky, on Good Friday as an unconstitutional endorsement of Christianity. In its decision the court noted that "many of the details of our commonly observed calendar have religious roots. . . . The names of our days (in English) advert to deities of the Romans. . . . Yet no one has seriously, and certainly not successfully, contended that the Establishment Clause is offended by the use of those names, nor by the practice of closing public offices almost universally on Sunday (the day observed as holy by most Christians) and frequently on Saturday (the day observed by Jews and some Christians) to the exclusion of other days that may have similar significance for some religions. Nor is the Establishment Clause offended by the dating of government documents using a system computed from events based on the Christian religion, and apparently not even by the use in official proclamations of language reflecting the religious origins of that dating system."[30] The court was precisely correct. Despite extreme separationist interpretations of the Establishment Clause, our society has always condoned—since the inception of this nation—a significant intermixture of church and state in the sense of official government deference to religious events, holidays, and even principles.

In any case, following the federal court's decision outlawing Good Friday as an official state holiday, one Wisconsin County, La Crosse, considered circumventing the court ruling simply by reinstating Good Friday as a paid holiday, but changing its name to "Spring Holiday" or "Friday before Easter." This concession was insufficient for the separationist FFRF. It didn't seem to matter that the people wanted to have a vacation during that period. As long as a hoped-for vacation happened to coincide with a religious holiday, it had to be opposed—even if the county was willing to dissociate the holiday, by name, from its religious connection.

FFRF's Gaylor admitted that the foundation has an ongoing battle with the Madison teachers union because its contract calls for the schools' spring break to occur during the Christian Holy Week—the week that includes Good Friday, Easter Sunday, and the following Monday.[31] It apparently doesn't matter to Gaylor's group that this is a convenient week for vacationers to travel, especially with the Monday for driving. The overarching agenda, however strained, seems to be to divorce the state from any recognition of religion.

Indeed, a radio and television personality in Phoenix, Arizona, David Leibowitz—a self-styled strict separationist—in an op-ed for the *Arizona Republic*, told of being put off by Gaylor's "shrillness." "Funny," wrote Leibowitz, "how believing in a cause can work: You go merrily along, so certain, until you meet someone who agrees with you so completely. Then, his or her ridiculousness changes your mind. Consider yourself warned if you fancy yourself a strict separationist when it comes to matters of church and state, as well as a patriotic American made uncomfortable by 'under God' in the Pledge of Allegiance. I was, too, until a few days ago, when I spoke to Annie Laurie Gaylor, co-founder of the Freedom From Religion Foundation."[32]

Official Good Friday observances have been attacked in other contexts as well. In Illinois, a public school teacher brought a civil rights lawsuit against the state superintendent of education, challenging the practice of making Good Friday a paid holiday.[33] And Hawaii has faced strong opposition for its tradition of observing Good Friday as a paid legal holiday for all county and state employees.[34]

No Cross–Getting Cross over the Cross

Crosses on public property have been common in America throughout history, and only recently have they been characterized as offensive as part of the cleansing of all things Christian from the public square. In the early 1930s, San Francisco erected a 103-foot-high by 39-foot-wide cross on city land atop Mt. Davidson, the area's highest point. The monument was dedicated in an Easter Sunday ceremony in which President Franklin Roosevelt participated by way of a telegram. The cross became a focal point for Easter Sunday sunrise services for years to come and was also illuminated during the Christmas season. In 1990 a federal district court denied a petition by atheists to remove the cross, but in 1996 the infamous Ninth Circuit Court of Appeals, in *Carpenter v. San Francisco,* reversed the decision, holding that the sectarian religious monument could not be maintained on city property. Margaret Crosby, staff attorney for the ACLU of Northern California, was elated. "The Court's order is a victory for religious freedom," she said in a press release. "The Court has once again told government that it has no business promoting the symbols of favored religions. In San Francisco, this means that children and adults of all faiths will be able to enjoy Mt. Davidson Park without feeling like second-class citizens."[35]

Resourceful city and county officials sought to comply with the court's ruling by selling the cross and the one-third-acre tract surrounding it to a private entity at auction. This move, clearly dissociating any government from the ongoing display of the cross, didn't satisfy certain anti-Christian groups, whose persistent objections demonstrated concerns far beyond church and state. For example, the state director for the California American Atheists said, "If a religious group wants to purchase the cross and put it on their own land, fine. But it makes no sense to have a sliver of phony 'private' land surrounded by a public park in order to keep a religious monument which is clearly unconstitutional." City voters nevertheless approved the auction sale and gave the $26,000 proceeds to the city's Recreation and Parks Department to be used for other parks. Two atheists filed suit shortly thereafter, complaining that the sale was "fixed" to ensure that a religious group would acquire title to the cross and property so that the display could be preserved. In 2002, the Ninth Circuit Court refused to invalidate the sale, so the cross remains.[36]

Another cross has also caused major controversy. This one is six feet tall and is on a rock that sits thirty feet above the Mojave National Preserve in California. A group of World War I veterans built the cross as a memorial in 1934, where it has stood since. The memorial is about twenty feet off a two-lane highway where an estimated twenty cars pass every day. According to local resident Wanda Sandoz, "You don't even see it unless you are looking up at the right place." But that was apparently immaterial to the ACLU, which filed a suit against the National Park Service in March 2001, citing the First Amendment

Establishment Clause. The federal district judge concurred and ordered that the cross be covered with a brown canvas, to the dismay of local veterans who consider the cross a historic monument. The veterans acknowledge that it is a Christian symbol, but say its primary thrust is not religious, but to honor the American war dead. Local U.S. Congressman Jerry Lewis proposed a land swap between the federal government and private landowners, hoping to eliminate the church/state issue by converting the half-acre surrounding the cross to private land. A number of groups oppose the bill, which could suggest that their opposition to the presence of the cross is motivated more by hostility to the Christian symbol than by fidelity to Establishment Clause concerns.[37]

Not all government officials are as resolute in preserving their rights to display the cross, as shown by an incident involving the State Fair Park in Oklahoma City, Oklahoma. A thirty-foot-high cross that had been on display at the state fairgrounds for almost forty years without incident all of a sudden discomfited certain people. Jim Worrell of Oklahoma City sent City Manager Jim Couch a letter on December 19, 2002, complaining that the cross violated the U.S. Constitution's prohibition against "state-sponsored religion" and threatening to file suit if it wasn't removed. Without so much as a whimper of protest, the city took the cross down and put it into storage. Eventually, said Couch, the cross would be declared surplus material and given away to a church or local organization.[38]

No Ten Commandments

The struggle of Alabama Supreme Court Chief Justice Roy Moore for the free exercise of religion in respect to the Ten Commandments is part of a national campaign to resist separationists trying to restrict the influence of these universal norms on American life. The American Civil Liberties Union (ACLU) and other separationist groups have been waging a vigorous campaign against such displays. In November 2001, the ACLU of Kentucky simultaneously sued four

Kentucky counties—Garrard, Grayson, Mercer, and Rowan—for their alleged unconstitutional displays of the Ten Commandments in public buildings, from county courthouses to hospitals. The ACLU had filed similar suits in 1999 against a number of county school districts for their Ten Commandments displays.[39]

Meanwhile, more than half of Tennessee's ninety-five counties have the Ten Commandments posted on government property, and in at least thirty of these, the displays have been posted for decades. One county, Washington, has had its display for over eighty years. But neither the prevalence of the displays nor the manifest absence of harm they have caused through the years has deterred modern separationists from targeting them for extinction.

On April 19, 2002, officials of Rutherford County, near Nashville, placed a copy of the Ten Commandments in the county courthouse alongside other historical documents such as the Magna Carta, the Mayflower Compact, and the Declaration of Independence.

The Tennessee ACLU filed suit, requesting a federal judge to issue a preliminary injunction ordering the county to remove the Ten Commandments. Attorneys representing the county argued that the Ten Commandments were historical as well as religious, and that their historical role should not be suppressed because of their religious overtones. George Barrett, the attorney arguing on behalf of the ACLU's position, said, "History is replete with the disaster of government supporting one religion over another. There is nothing more divisive than this. The founders were clearly mindful of that history."[40] U.S. District Judge Robert Echols granted the injunction and ordered that the display be removed.

No Ministering to Prisoners

The Christian-purging mentality has also manifested itself in objections to faith-based Christian charities. It doesn't matter if the state doesn't favor faith-based charities over secular ones; a complete ban is demanded.

Faith Works is a faith-based organization that ministers to prison inmates, providing treatment and rehabilitation for those addicted to alcohol and illegal drugs. The Wisconsin Department of Correction's parole conditions sometime include attending treatment programs for drug or alcohol abuse. Faith Works is one of six organizations (the other five are secular) that the department of corrections may recommend for an inmate, but an inmate is free to choose whichever one he wants. Standing against Faith Works is FFRF, which strongly objected to the use of state funds to pay for the treatment programs of those prisoners who chose Faith Works—which, incidentally, has established a successful track record. In filing suit in federal court to prevent Faith Works' alleged violation of the Establishment Clause, FFRF was challenging two funding streams to Faith Works—a grant from the Department of Workforce Development and a contract with the Department of Corrections. On January 7, 2002, Federal Judge Barbara Crabb ruled in favor of the FFRF on the claim pertaining to the Department of Workforce Development's grant to Faith Works.[41] FFRF applauded the court for invalidating what the group called a "wrongful and unconstitutional" expenditure of government funds "to make possible a ministry devoted to bringing 'homeless addicts to Christ.'"[42]

It turns out that FFRF's jubilation was premature. In a later order, on July 26, 2002, Judge Crabb ruled in favor of Faith Works on the claim pertaining to the funding stream from the Department of Corrections. Judge Crabb found that "offenders participate in the program as a result of their genuinely independent, private choice," and "thus, any appearance that the government is endorsing Faith Works is overcome by the fact that offenders must consent to the program's religious content before participating in it."[43]

On appeal, the Seventh Circuit Court of Appeals affirmed in favor of Faith Works, holding that the state's use of its program does not violate the Establishment Clause. The court's decision seemed to turn on the fact that the prisoners have a choice among programs, including secular ones. [43] The court noted that "parole officers have recommended Faith Works to some parolees, but have been careful to explain that it is a non-binding recommendation and that Faith Works is a Christian institution and its program of rehabilitation has a significant Christian element. Parole officers who recommend Faith Works are required to offer the offender a secular halfway house as an alternative. And although Faith Works will enroll an offender even if he is not a Christian, a parole officer will not recommend Faith Works to an offender who has no Christian identity and religious interest and will not advise anyone to convert to Christianity in order to get the most out of Faith Works." The state, said the court, may not require offenders to enroll. "The choice must be private, to provide insulating material between government and religion. It *is* private; it is the offender's choice."[45]

No Prayer—National Days of Prayer on City Property?

Lately, local observances of the National Day of Prayer have been coming under fire. From 1993 through 1995, residents of Oak Park, Illinois, met at the community-owned Village Hall to observe the annual National Day of Prayer. When the ACLU complained that the meetings on city property violated the Establishment Clause, the city adopted a new policy, which provided that any events in the Village Hall must benefit the public as a whole and must not be based on, promote, or espouse the philosophy, ideas, or beliefs of any particular group, entity, or organization. In February 1996, when Martin DeBoer applied to use the meeting space for a National Day of Prayer Meeting, the city invoked the new policy to deny the request, saying the activity would not benefit the public as a whole and was impermissibly "based on . . . the philosophy, ideas, or beliefs" of a particular group. Again in 1997 the city denied the group access. Interestingly, during this period the city allowed the NAACP and the League of Women Voters to use the facility.

DeBoer filed a federal lawsuit against the village of Oak Park on April 20, 1998, alleging that its policy and denials of access violated his free speech rights by conferring on the city the authority to determine whether particular events would "benefit the public as a whole." In 1999 the district court granted DeBoer summary judgment, holding that the city could not prevent groups from using the facility to pray about civic matters and could require neither that events benefit the whole public nor that meetings not be based on the ideas of a particular group. The city appealed but was shot down in September 2001 by the Seventh Circuit Court, which held that the city violated DeBoer's free speech rights by denying him equal access and engaging in unconstitutional viewpoint discrimination.[46]

No Christ—Banning Jesus from City Council Meetings and State Government

Prayers "in the name of Jesus" before city council meetings are now being challenged throughout the land. And it doesn't seem to matter to separationists whether or not the prayer is initiated by the city. Just the utterance of Christian blessings at meetings is objectionable. At a November 1999 city council meeting in Burbank, California, the minister ended his invocation prayer with "in the name of Jesus Christ." Someone in attendance was offended and filed a suit in the Superior Court of Los Angeles to ban the practice, the court complied, and the appellate court affirmed the ban in September 2002. As Burbank mayor David Laurell noted, this didn't involve the utterance of the prayer by the city council itself. The mayor also said the issue wasn't as much about separation of church and state as about freedom of expression. Laurell reportedly "cringes at the thought" of city councils being forced to censor what people are allowed and not allowed to say during prayers. "I'm all for invocations that are all-inclusive," said Laurell, "but I don't want me or anybody else to tell people that it has to be that way."

Following the ruling, city councils throughout Orange County, which has thirty-four cities, most of which have invocations at their meetings, began to reevaluate their practice. In Buena Park and La

Palma, city officials asked clergy not to mention a particular deity in their prayers—as if there were any chance of Lord Krishna being invoked. In Fullerton, the city attorney directed that invocations could begin with "Our Heavenly Father," but could not end with references to "Jesus." Debbie Borden, a resident of Huntington Beach, devised an innovative solution—to use the three minutes she was allotted as a member of the public to give the invocation. She described it as "the perfect solution" because a private individual, not the city, was initiating the prayer.[47] But Borden shouldn't be so sure her solution will fly. The California courts deemed there was sufficient "state" involvement to bar such a practice when the city called for the invocation by pastors, even though the city did not tell the pastors what to say. The courts very well might find that the three minutes allotted to each member of the public, during which time a citizen *could* choose to give a "Jesus" invocation, constitute an official endorsement of the practice. These days it takes increasingly less direct action by public officials to trigger Establishment Clause violations.

Here again, the free exercise and free expression rights of those seeking to utter the prayers in the name of Jesus are entirely suppressed, and there's evidence that the court's ruling is having a chilling effect on religious expression in the area. Pastor Ron Sukut of Cornerstone Community Church in San Clemente decided not to give the invocation at a council meeting when he was told he could not mention Jesus. "I think we have a constitutional right to choose which God we're praying to," said Sukut. "Taking that right away is what's unconstitutional." Mission Viejo mayor John Paul Ledesma said the court's ruling seems to contradict freedom of expression and is "ridiculous."[48]

The "Jesus prayer" controversy has arisen at the state level as well. A member of the Maryland senate recently objected to three such pre-meeting prayers. Senator Sharon M. Grosfeld said, "There are numerous faiths represented in the General Assembly, and in recognition of that . . . the prayers that are said . . . should be as neutral in terms of their reference to a particular god as they can be." And the Colorado State Board of Education, after an objection, discontinued its practice of pre-meeting public prayers where Jesus was mentioned.[49]

But the real winner was the state of Utah, where seventy-one-year-old Tom Snyder, a man whom some have described as an atheist,[50] sued the city council of Murray, a suburb of Salt Lake City, for denying him permission to "pray" at their meetings. In his "prayer" to "Our Mother, who art in heaven," Snyder asked for deliverance "from the evil of forced religious worship now sought to be imposed upon the people . . . by the actions of misguided, weak, and stupid politicians, who abuse power in their own self-righteousness." The state court dismissed the suit in 1999, but Snyder appealed all the way to the Utah Supreme Court, which reversed the lower court. The Utah high court cited its 1993 decision upholding Salt Lake City's right to have prayers at official events provided that they didn't discriminate against any faiths. The court held that denying Snyder his right to pray violated his rights under the Utah constitution, including its Establishment Clause. The opportunity to pray, stated the court, must be equally accessible to all who choose to participate.

In all likelihood what Snyder was really after was not the right to pray—which he doesn't seem to believe in—but rather the suppression of voluntary Christian prayer at city council meetings. And he may get his way. Following the 1993 Utah Supreme Court decision outlawing "discriminatory" prayer at Salt Lake City's official events, the city decided to end public prayer, to avoid dealing with the problems that might arise.[51]

In the next chapter we'll see how the separationists have gone beyond trying to purge the government and its property of Christian influences. They are also determined to bar Christians and those who share their values from public office. And as for those Christians who slip through into positions of power, the secularists insist that they keep their Christian views segregated from their official duties. They not only want to enforce a strict prohibition on the state endorsing Christianity; they also want to preclude Christians from influencing the course of government. In many cases they are applying de facto litmus tests against Christians who would serve in government.

chapter seven

Muzzling Public Officials, Employees, and Appointees

THIS SUBJECT MATTER OF THIS CHAPTER overlaps to a degree with that of Chapter Six, because oftentimes the banning of Christian symbols and activities from public property also involves individuals active in some capacity with the public sector. This chapter chronicles the battle against public employees, officials, and appointees, centering on the common thread of anti-Christian prejudice that underlies most of these cases.

Public Employees

Government Employees

We begin with the ACLU, which in 2002 was again up in arms, this time about signs on the outskirts of Franklinton, Louisiana, saying, "Jesus is Lord over Franklinton." The signs were paid for and owned by local area churches, so what was the problem? Well, there were two. One was that the signs were on state roads—not endorsed by the state in any way, mind you, but merely placed on state roads. The other, more serious objection was that parish road crews helped to erect the signs at the request of church members. Of course, these were just convenient legal pegs on which the ACLU could hang its hats. The real cause of the angst had nothing to do with church/state relations, since the ACLU wasn't even aware of the road crews' assistance with the signs until after it started looking into the matter. Rather, the problem arose when a motorist from New Orleans, fifty-five miles from Franklinton, drove by and was offended by the signs. The driver asked, "Can you imagine the hostility that Jews, Muslims, members of other minority faiths and non-believers must feel when living in or passing through that community?" Mayor Earle R. Brown explained that there was little significance to the road crews' helping to put up the signs. They probably would have helped any nonprofit groups erect their signs, not just churches. He said that the signs had been up for about two years, thousands of people had passed through, and no one had previously objected to them.

Although the ACLU prevailed and the signs were removed, their action caused a backlash of sorts among community residents. Following the removal of the signs, townspeople began to place on their lawns signs proclaiming "God Is Lord Over All." A local sign-maker, Scott Blair, sold almost three thousand signs (in a town where the population is around four thousand), which residents placed in Franklinton yards and storefronts. "There was sort of an outcry from the Christian community," said Gene Richards, pastor of Hill Crest Baptist Church in Franklinton. "It seems the ACLU is trying to de-Christianize the community. These signs originally were a declaration of the faith of a large majority of people in Franklinton. They were never intended to be offensive or to discriminate against anyone." Franklinton residents, in fact, established a mini-trend, placing the signs in surrounding areas. "Now they're in every town in Washington Parish," said Scott Blair.[1]

In April 2001, the Logan County Public Library in Bowling Green, Kentucky, fired employee Kimberly Draper for wearing a necklace with a cross pendant to work, even though, Draper asserts, she was told when hired in August 1998 that she was "free to wear religious jewelry." But, forty-five days later, she received a copy of the library's dress code policy, which banned "religious, political, or potentially offensive decoration." Draper's superiors told her she had to take off her necklace, out of respect for the religious diversity of its patrons. "If someone wants to check out a book, and one of us shows that we have a different religious point of view than them, it could make [the patron] uncomfortable," explained library director Linda Kompanik.[2]

It is difficult to understand how anyone could be offended by another person, albeit an employee of a local government institution, who simply is wearing jewelry reflecting her commitment to Christianity. As it turns out, this was not an isolated occurrence, as the following case involving a Texas policeman illustrates.

In the Arlington, Texas, police department, thirteen-year-veteran Sergeant George Daniels was fired for insubordination when he refused to remove a lapel cross from his uniform while on duty. Although other officers were permitted, even encouraged, to wear other insignia on their uniforms, such as Mexican flag pins and union pins, police chief David Kunkle refused to permit the cross because it "might offend someone." Daniels, a former recipient of the "Rookie of the Year" and "Officer of the Year" awards, said he believed he would be publicly denying his faith if he removed the Christian symbol.[3] Perhaps reasonable people can disagree over whether Officer Daniels should have forfeited his free expression rights to conform to his employer's demands and whether he should have been fired for insubordination. But those issues aside, the question remains: why in modern American society is the open expression of one's Christian faith deemed offensive by some? We've come a long way when government employers officially sanction the concept that the age-old symbol of Christian sacrificial love can be interpreted as evidence of bias or prejudice.

Meanwhile, in Honolulu, Hawaii, the police department decided to change its oath for incoming police officers to remove the phrase "so help me God." The department rolled over without a struggle when the Hawaiian Citizens for Separation of Church and State (HCSCS) complained. In charging police chief Lee Donohue with misconduct, HCSCS president Mitch Kahle asserted that those words, which were codified in the police department's Standards of Conduct, constituted an unconstitutional religious test. The obsequious department issued a statement expressing its commitment to the Constitutions of the United States and Hawaii and its intention henceforth to revise its oath to exclude the offending language. In addition, Kahle asked the department to get rid of a safety guide that contained a fireman's prayer mentioning "God."[4]

Congressional, State, and Local Chaplains

Not even chaplains are safe from the chilling world the separationists are trying to create, as seen when a Sacramento atheist brought a lawsuit seeking to declare congressional chaplains unconstitutional. This man might be dismissed as a renegade crank, except for one thing. The man is Michael Newdow, the same man who single-handedly succeeded in removing God from the Pledge of Allegiance and who now objects to Congress's use of chaplains, because he sees it as governmental endorsement of religion. The framers of the Constitution, however, didn't intend to preclude all government involvement with religion. And they specifically had no problem with chaplains in Congress. We don't have to speculate about that, for chaplains have ministered to members of Congress and led the morning prayer since 1789—on the federal payroll, no less.

But Newdow filed suit to stop the practice 213 years later, in the summer of 2002, alleging it was improper for the House and Senate to pay their chaplains \$148,000 and \$130,000 per year, respectively. Newdow's objection was not limited to the money, however. He said the very presence of the chaplains in Congress was unconstitutional, irrespective of their salaries. In response to the suit, twenty-two members of Congress requested the court to dismiss the action.[5]

This was not the first instance of such a case. In 1983, the United States Supreme Court ruled in *Marsh v. Chambers* that paid congressional chaplains do not constitute a violation of the First Amendment's Establishment Clause. In his opinion for the court, Chief

Justice Warren Burger wrote: "Clearly the men who wrote the First Amendment religion clauses did not view paid legislative chaplains and opening prayers as a violation of that Amendment, for the practice of opening sessions with prayer has continued without interruption ever since that early session of Congress. Moreover," he continued, "This unique history leads us to accept the interpretation of the First Amendment draftsmen who saw no real threat to the Establishment Clause arising from a practice of prayer similar to that now challenged.... The delegates did not consider opening prayers as a proselytizing activity or symbolically placing the government's official seal of approval on one religious view.... The Establishment Clause does not always bar a state from regulating conduct simply because it harmonizes with religious canons."[6]

Chaplains for state legislatures sometimes encounter opposition as well. On January 11, 1999, the Minnesota House of Representatives voted 72-60 to order chaplains not to perform "denominational" prayers. Instead, they were required to deliver only "non-denominational" prayers out of respect for the religious diversity of the House. Obviously, the action was misnamed, because it wasn't really aimed at preventing "denominational" prayers, but Christian prayers—prayers to the generic "God"—were permitted while those referring to "Jesus" were prohibited. What set off certain lawmakers, who had been considering such a ban for several years, was the performance by a parochial school choir that included references to Jesus. Representative Peggy Leppik described the songs as "particularly discomfiting... for some people."[7]

Congress and state legislatures are not the only places chaplains run into difficulties. In Portland, Oregon, police chaplain John Elms found that just performing his job was too controversial for some to handle. The Portland Police Bureau fired Elms after six years of voluntary service with the bureau, allegedly for proselytizing to police officers who had come to him for spiritual support. Apparently, Elm's major offending act was his distribution of 1,500 *God's Word for Peace Officers Bibles*, a Bible designed for officers following the

September 11 terrorist attacks. Elms explained that he decided to pass the Bibles out following a trip to New York City, where he met many victims' families.[8]

And in Ferndale, Michigan, a volunteer chaplain, Pastor Tom Hansen, came under attack because he was an outspoken critic of the homosexual lifestyle. He argued against the city's plans for a downtown gay pride festival, and at council meetings reportedly called homosexuality "an abomination to the Lord." But Hansen denied that opposing homosexuals was the focus of his ministry. When he met with local residents belonging to Soulforce, a nationwide group that urges religious leaders to be tolerant toward homosexuals, he told them that "I believe Christ died for them just as He did for me." Hansen said his opinions on homosexuality never came up in his work with prisoners. "I don't talk to the prisoners about that," said Hansen. "I'm here if they want help.... It is immaterial to me if they are gay. If they ask me, I pray for them and give them a little Bible that the Gideons provide to us for free."[9] Nevertheless, homosexual groups demanded that the city terminate Hansen, and Soulforce charged that Hansen's views amounted to "spiritual violence" to homosexuals, bisexuals, and transgendered persons.

Ferndale police captain Tim Collins said that Hansen had not expressed "any discrimination of any type to anyone." The American Family Association said that it would sue the city in a civil rights action if it dismissed Hansen, [10] and Gary Glenn, president of the America Family Association in Michigan, said that being chaplain doesn't mean you forfeit your constitutional rights. "I can't help but marvel at the reported sight Monday night when the so-called 'tolerance' and 'non-discrimination' crowds so clearly demonstrated their intolerance for Pastor Hansen's sincerely held religious views, and demanded that he be discriminated against and fired for daring to express those views."[11]

On October 28, 2002, after a four-hour meeting filled with public comments concerning the Hansen issue from the estimated one hundred residents present, all but five of whom spoke in favor of Hansen, the Ferndale City Council passed a 622-word resolution condemning Hansen. The council repudiated Hansen's "callous, outdated and hostile statements about the lesbian and gay community" and described them as "an affront to the community." The council said it found Hansen's "statements to be offensive to the tenets of diversity and the principles of freedom, acceptance, and respect for humanity that make the United States of America the great country that it is."

In the resolution the council also recognized Ferndale's "lesbian and gay community as a legitimate, important, and beneficial part of Ferndale." In a final stroke of authoritarian grandeur, the council ended its resolution with a directive to the police department to caution all police chaplains that "their actions as a police chaplain should be consistent with the beliefs contained within this resolution."[12] What else could that last statement mean, but an order that police chaplains who don't approve of homosexuality keep their opinions to themselves? Apparently the council, which paid lip service in the resolution to the constitutional free speech rights of all city employees, did not grasp the utter inconsistency of its order with its affirmation of free speech.

Military Honor Guard

Of all the prohibitions against God in the public arena, perhaps none is as inappropriate as the one involving prayers at funeral services on government property. At no time is prayer a more comforting influence, yet bogus church/state concerns once again have swallowed the free exercise rights of participants. Patrick Cubbage, a fifty-four-year-old Vietnam combat veteran and retired Philadelphia policeman, worked as a military honor guardsman at Brigadier General William C. Doyle Veterans Memorial Cemetery in New Jersey. He had participated in some two thousand burial ceremonies. Whenever he got a chance—when the families were receptive—he said a blessing at the graveside services such as "God bless you and this family, and God bless the United States of America."

Cubbage said the families "were always grateful and sometimes very moved. People would even grip my hand and say things like 'Thank you so much.'" Such unfailing gratitude wasn't enough to save Cubbage from his fate. His superiors terminated him for "departing from the standard presentation protocol," or so they said. They insisted that Cubbage wasn't dismissed for saying the blessings, but for not following the "standard phrase for each service." But Cubbage pointed out that the cemetery's pamphlet governing Flag Presentation Protocol permitted the blessings when the families approved.

Why was Cubbage fired? There were no objections from any of the families who received the blessings. But two of his fellow guardsmen reportedly complained to their supervisors, who ordered Cubbage to stop giving the blessings. When an incredulous Cubbage pointed to language in the manual permitting the blessings, his boss told him that the blessings could offend Jews and Muslims and should only be used when relatives notified the cemeteries in advance that they wanted a blessing. But no form was provided whereby a family can make such a request, and it's not something that many would think to bring up on their own. Besides, said Cubbage, "Jews and Muslims believe in God." The superior then handed Cubbage a copy of state regulations prohibiting "harassment or hostile environments" in the workplace.[13]

But what on earth have such regulations to do with the matter at hand? The complaint was not that fellow employees were being harassed, but that families might be offended—and workplace harassment laws don't cover such situations. And the suggestion that families who expressed a preference for the blessing could be offended by it is absurd on its face. Nevertheless, the complaining employees prevailed. When they objected to blessings that families had chosen to receive—apparently because they (not the families) weren't tolerant of those blessings being administered—Cubbage was fired.

In the Military

Our culture's hypersensitivity toward non-Christians has reached such heights that it has even affected our servicemen preparing for war on foreign soil. "In an effort to appease the religious intolerance of other countries," wrote John W. Whitehead of the Rutherford Institute, "American soldiers are being forced to leave their religion at home as they depart to fight for our liberties." Whitehead was referring to an order by military leaders that soldiers not wear religious jewelry or other outward symbols of their faith. One military chaplain opposed to the directive remarked, "We have all these fine young American men and women over here. They're great Americans. They're great soldiers. Yet they're expected to surrender their religious practices when they arrive." Of all people who should be permitted free rein in exercising their faith, it is soldiers risking their lives to defend our constitutional freedoms, which do not stop at the water's edge. "It would serve our military leaders well to remember that the United States Constitution applies to American citizens in whatever part of the world they may find themselves—whether it be Kuwait, Saudi Arabia, or Afghanistan," noted Whitehead.[14]

Discrimination by the Postal Service

This politically correct wartime attitude spilled over into the post office. During Gulf War II in April 2003, Jack Moody, Jr. tried to send his son, Pfc. Daniel Moody, Scriptures and religious comic books. The postal service in Lenoir, North Carolina, refused to send the material, citing a government regulation. Jack Moody said, "He [Daniel] wrote a letter to his mom and I, saying he was reading the Bible for strength. He asked us to send this stuff, so I called the post office and told them what I wanted to do. After the postal supervisor confirmed their policy, I got upset. If this was through the Kuwait or Saudi Arabian post office, I could understand. But it was the U.S. post office." The policy to which Moody referred stated, "Any matter containing religious materials contrary to Islamic faith or depicting nude or seminude persons, pornographic or sexual items, or non-authorized political materials is prohibited."

Attorneys from Rutherford said that the postal regulation, along with the orders that soldiers not wear religious jewelry, indicates a "willingness to subjugate American freedoms for the sake of not offending those in the Middle East." Rutherford president John W. Whitehead observed that the regulation was "content-based discrimination" aimed at Christian materials and essentially endorsed the Islamic faith over all other religions. "At a time when members of our armed forces are risking their lives as part of Operation Iraqi Freedom," Whitehead said, "it is inconceivable that their own freedoms and those of their parents would be curtailed by the U.S. government in an effort to impose political correctness on our armed forces. The U.S. Constitution does not bow to the religious intolerance of other nations."[15]

Public Officials

In the current climate of intolerance toward Christian expression, there is a growing sentiment among many in our culture that religion is a private matter. This is a modern misperception. As author Steve Farrell stated, "Christianity is by nature—public. Prohibiting public religious speech under the guise of 'protecting one's private religious rights,' ignores the very public, evangelical nature of religion—especially of Christianity. It is oxymoronic to tell a Christian, 'You're free, but shut up.'"[16] Of course, Farrell is correct. Jesus commanded his disciples to "go into all the world and preach the good news to all creation,"[17] and the apostle Peter wrote, "But in your hearts set apart Christ as Lord. Always be prepared to give an answer to everyone who asks you to give the reason for the hope that you have."[18]

Nevertheless, societal forces pressure Christians, especially public officials, to keep their religious views to themselves, a practice that is utterly inconsistent with American history, the attitude of the colonists, the framers of the Constitution, and government officials into the modern era. While some strict "separationists" are surely sincere in their belief that the Constitution forbids overt religious expression by public officials, they are simply wrong. Others are doubtlessly motivated by hostility toward Christianity in the public arena. Regardless, their efforts create a chilling effect on Christian expression.

Congressman Tom DeLay has been outspoken about his Christian faith, frequently lacing his speeches with biblical references and Christian messages. DeLay came under criticism for his response to a question following his speeches at a Worldview Weekend conference in Houston, Texas. An audience member asked him what could be done about colleges in Texas that preclude the teaching of creation. DeLay answered that those concerned could call their state representatives and voice their objections. "They can change things," he said. "They can throw the PC out and bring God in." That would take some time, DeLay said, "but the immediate [remedy] is don't send your kids to Baylor—don't send your kids to A&M."

The *Houston Chronicle* editorial page was outraged. "DeLay's distaste for Baylor and Texas A&M is part and parcel of his rejection of distinguished scholarship and scientific inquiry and his fanatical desire to transform American government into a theocracy. House Republicans who value reason should reconsider their bizarre commitment to have DeLay replace retiring Rep. Dick Armey as Republican leader in the House."[19] Irrespective of the merits of DeLay's comments—for which, by the way, he later apologized—what is noteworthy about this editorial is the attitude the editors displayed toward DeLay's Christian beliefs. It is one thing to question his comments about these two universities or his views on teaching creation. It is quite another to conclude that he rejects distinguished scholarship and scientific inquiry, as if belief that the cosmos is the creation of an intelligent being is incompatible with science.

This conclusion by the editors, along with their hysterical inference that DeLay favors a theocracy, reveals a certain kind of contempt toward the Christian worldview. More than that, it shows, as we've been demonstrating, that ridiculing and impugning Christians is fair game. While many demanded apologies from Congressman DeLay for his remarks, few, if any, criticized the *Chronicle*'s editors for their outrageous and bigoted comments. Christian public officials should be permitted to proclaim their faith without fear of being falsely accused of advocating a theocracy. Nothing in the Constitution requires public officials to be silent or private about their religious beliefs.

Education Secretary Rod Paige incurred the wrath of the secularists when he expressed his admiration for Christian values in an interview with the *Baptist Press*. "All things equal," he said, "I would prefer to have a child in school that has a strong appreciation for the values of the Christian community, where a child is taught to have a strong faith. . . . In a religious environment the value system is set. That's not the case in a public school, where there are so many different kids with different kinds of values." These remarks caused the separationists and liberal editorial writers to come unglued. Barry Lynn of Americans United for Separation of Church and State demanded that Paige either apologize and repudiate his comments or resign from his position. Paige's remarks, said Lynn, showed "an astonishing disrespect for both America's religious diversity and the public schools." Sandra Feldman, president of the American Federation of Teachers, said, "It is insulting for the secretary—who should be the advocate for the over fifty million children in our public schools—to say their diversity somehow compromises those schools."[20]

Nowhere in the interview did Secretary Paige show disrespect for America's religious diversity or imply that diversity is damaging to schools, nor did he demonstrate religious bigotry. As his press secretary, Dan Lengan, noted, "Secretary Paige's deep faith has helped him to overcome adversity, to find clarity, and has sustained him throughout his life. He has dedicated his entire career to promoting diversity and making sure children from all races, ethnic groups, and faiths share access to the best possible education."[21] Paige was saying that he, personally, would rather have his child in a college—he wasn't even talking about K-12—that emphasizes Christian values. He said nothing offensive or disrespectful about other religions, nor did he recommend that public schools teach Christian values.

Richard Land of the Ethics and Religious Liberty Commission of the Southern Baptist Church suspected that Paige's comments were not what upset his critics.

Land told Brendan Miniter, assistant editor of *OpinionJournal.com*, (in Miniter's words) that Paige's critics "hate him because he's effective and because he was a Baptist minister back in Texas. They hate him because he openly acknowledges his faith. They hate him because he sees leaving even one child behind in a failing school as a sin. But mostly they hate him because they have a fanatical view that anything having to do with God belongs outside the hallowed halls of a public school."

Local Officials

No, federal officials and appointees had better not be outspoken Christians, but what about local government officials? Two Florida mayors discovered that they should be more circumspect when expressing their religious beliefs. The ACLU is watching and doing its best to keep the public halls and the mouths of officials free of Christianity. In Inglis, Florida, Mayor Carolyn Risher issued a proclamation on Halloween night for nine straight years banning Satan within the town limits, and placed a copy of the document on her office wall and at four posts located on the entrances to the little community of 1,400. The proclamation read, "Be it known from this day forward that Satan, ruler of darkness, giver of evil, destroyer of what is good and just, is not now, nor ever again will be, a part of this town of Inglis. Satan is hereby declared powerless, no longer ruling over, nor influencing, our citizens."

The ACLU sent a letter to Mayor Risher demanding that she remove the posted proclamations and that the town commission rescind the mayoral edict. The ACLU was acting on behalf of Polly Bowser, an "outraged" resident of Inglis, though Bowser said she wasn't sure she wanted the lawsuit to proceed. (She said she and her family suffered when she started a petition drive to recall the mayor over the incident.) The ACLU said it would proceed with or without Bowser. "We have constitutional protections against the establishment of religions," said ACLU attorney Gary S. Edinger. "When [they are] not followed, and in fact rubbed in the nose of the public, it becomes a little more important."[22]

Auburndale, Florida, mayor Bill Sterling didn't ban the devil from his town. He issued a proclamation declaring "Auburndale for Jesus," drawing protests from the ACLU. Sterling dismissed the notion that his act had major significance, calling the proclamation a piece of paper with no authority. "We don't feel like we've violated anybody's civil rights," said Sterling. John MacKay, a Tampa lawyer, disagreed, threatening to sue the city. "Obviously, this proclamation goes to a particular religion—Christianity." Sterling explained that he had signed the document at the request of community pastors at the close of a prayer week. Sterling said he was not trying to tell residents what they should believe. "People have a right to believe the way they want to believe. If a Jewish group or a Muslim group wanted a proclamation from the city, they would get it."[23]

Making Judges "Tolerant"

San Francisco is one city that appears to have an anti-Christian bent. To accommodate a local bar association resolution, San Francisco Superior Court judges and commissioners adopted a policy prohibiting judges within their jurisdiction from membership in any organization that "discriminates on the basis of sexual orientation by excluding members on the grounds that their sexual orientation renders them 'unclean,' 'immoral,' or 'unfit.'" Presiding Judge Ronald Quidachay said, "It has long been a tradition of the bench of this State, and in particular of the bench of the Superior Court in San Francisco, to respect the rights and dignity of all litigants and counsel who appear before it and to refrain from even the perception or appearance of any type of invidious discrimination, including discrimination based on sexual orientation... The San Francisco bench has always appreciated the diversity of its own members and of the citizens who have occasion to deal with the court system. We are pleased to have the opportunity to reconfirm that commitment."[24]

Under the Superior Court policy, judges and commissioners are forbidden from being Scoutmasters, troop leaders, or members of a governing board that is affiliated with the Boy Scouts or any other organization that excludes homosexuals. The Pacific Justice Institute weighed in on the policy, saying that it is so broad that it could arguably preclude judges from being members of a church or synagogue that preaches against homosexuality. It is no secret that the policy is primarily aimed at the Boy Scout Association, which refuses to permit homosexuals to serve as Scout leaders. Dr. D. James Kennedy, with the Center for Reclaiming America, said, "This is an unconscionable, unconstitutional power grab that blatantly takes away the First Amendment rights of Christian judges. The judicial branch of government was specifically designed to protect the freedoms of religion and association. What a hypocritical thing it would be to deny judges the very same rights they are supposed to protect."[25]

Apparently emboldened by their success, homosexual activists began pressuring the California Supreme Court to amend California's Code of Judicial Conduct to prohibit all the state's judges from associating with the Boy Scouts. Like those lobbying the San Francisco Court, the Los Angeles Bar Association and the Bar Association of San Francisco claim that if judges affiliate with the Boy Scouts, they will create a perception that they have an anti-homosexual bias. In the name of tolerance, the groups seek to deny the constitutional right of California judges to associate with groups whose policies reflect values with which they disagree. The two bar associations did say they would agree to a compromise. They would be willing to allow judges to join a scout troop as long as those judges disavowed the Boy

Scout Association's moral objection to homosexuality.[26] (In 1998, even the California Supreme Court, in two cases, ruled lawful the Boy Scouts' policy refusing membership to homosexuals and atheists. The United States Supreme Court in 2000 validated the Boy Scouts' policy as well, largely on the basis of the constitutional rights of freedom of association and freedom of speech.[27]) It is significant that judges can run afoul of these policies without exhibiting any prejudice or bias personally; mere association with a group that is perceived to be biased is sufficient. Such is the broad sweep of these measures.

Public Appointees

The framers, of course, never intended to erect an absolute wall of separation between church and state. And to the extent they did prohibit the intermixture of government and religion, the ban was intended to work only one way: The federal government was barred from *establishing* a national church. Under no interpretation of the First Amendment, however, are individuals who happen to be religious prohibited from serving in government or from engaging in politics, directly or indirectly. This basic fact of history seems to have escaped actor-activist Christopher Reeve and others.

Reeve, paralyzed by a spinal cord injury he sustained in a tragic horseriding accident, has been a strong supporter of stem cell research. Speaking to a group of Yale medical students, he said that religious groups and social organizations have no right to shape public policy on stem cell research. Reeve complained that religious conservatives "have had undue influence on the critical debate," and that it is his belief "that when matters of public policy are debated, no religions should have a seat at the table."[28] One student disputed his point, saying that it is contrary to the American system to bar religious groups from participating in public policy discussions. "I don't object to anyone's religion," Reeve responded. "I'm a Unitarian myself. We're talking about the promise of science, the ethics of science, not religion."[29] But that's not the point, Mr. Reeve. The issue is not whether you object to anyone's religion, but whether you would muzzle them and lock them out of the public debate.

Dr. W. David Hager

Of course, this is exactly what Reeve and company want to do. We see this in the frantic reaction to President Bush's announcement that he was considering Dr. W. David Hager for appointment to the Reproductive Health Drugs Advisory Committee at the Food and Drug Administration (FDA). The purpose of the committee is to study and make recommendations on the safety and effectiveness of approved and experimental drugs for obstetrics, gynecology, and related specialties. Dr. Hager, a pro-life Christian, is a professor of obstetrics and gynecology at the University of Kentucky. He helped to write a petition for the Christian Medical Association challenging RU-486, the infamous "abortion pill." Because of Dr. Hager's pro-life views and promotion of abstinence before marriage, the left-wing political machine went into overdrive, with strong support from feminist pressure groups such as the National Organization for Women (NOW) and the Planned Parenthood Federation of America. Their strategy was to discredit Dr. Hager's competency as a medical doctor and characterize him as a right-wing religious fanatic. This fed into the false stereotype that devout Christians—even those who are professional scientists—are somehow at odds with empirical science, which is decidedly not the case.

Senators Ted Kennedy and Hillary Rodham Clinton both railed against Hager, with Kennedy huffing that the White House was "stacking these committees with right-wing ideologues instead of respected scientists." Senator Clinton puffed, "We're going to be in trouble in this country if we start moving toward theology-based science." But Hager has been widely published in medical journals, and in 1994, *Modern Healthcare* gave him the "Outstanding Physician in

America Award." Robert M. Goldberg, a Manhattan Institute science scholar, remarked, "The Left wants to paint Hager as some sort of anti-science faith healer. In fact he is a respected researcher and—unlike a lot of people who sit on FDA advisory panels—a practicing doctor who sees the promise and pain of medicine up close."

The groups opposing the doctor's appointment betrayed the depth of their view that outspoken Christians should not serve in such positions when they said Hager's ideological views created a conflict of interest that should disqualify him from serving, as if his Christian convictions would taint his medical objectivity. Following this line of thinking, one wonders whether an atheist's views, conversely, would color his medical objectivity, or whether doctrinaire pro-choice scientists might be too biased, for example, to acknowledge the clinically supported connection between abortion and breast cancer. Should atheists and pro-abortionists automatically be excluded from public service?

Dr. Hager strongly asserted that his Christianity and pro-life views would not keep him "from objectively evaluating medication" and therefore properly evaluating "some safety concerns [about RU-486]." Eventually, so much pressure was exerted that President Bush withdrew Dr. Hager's name from consideration. In this battle, the left wing prevailed by establishing an unfair litmus test against Christians serving in certain government positions—at least where their views might directly bear on their appointed responsibilities. Ken Connor, president of the Family Research Council, accurately described this as the latest example of "religious profiling." "What pro-abortion advocates really believe," said Connor, "is that even if a candidate is well-qualified and a good doctor, [that person] can't be an outspoken Christian and get appointed."[30]

Jerry Thacker

Consider the case of Jerry Thacker, whom President Bush nominated on January 22, 2003, to the presidential AIDS panel. Thacker has been involved in the fight against AIDS since contracting the illness in 1986. But when the *Washington Post* and other media reported that at one point in his AIDS ministry Thacker had described the disease as a "gay plague," a firestorm of protest ensued from the homosexual community. Eventually Thacker withdrew his name from consideration.

Yet there is serious doubt as to whether Thacker used the phrase derisively. The allegation arose from a biographical section on his website. "Before 1986," the site said, "Jerry Thacker was probably a lot like you. He had a beautiful family, a good church, and a rewarding ministry. He knew vaguely about the 'gay plague' known as AIDS, but it seemed a distant threat." The reference to "gay plague" is in quotes and placed in a historical context. There is no indication that Thacker meant to use the phrase disparagingly—yet the press and others immediately seized on it and began characterizing Thacker as horribly insensitive and bigoted. Many remember, however, when not long ago media outlets such as *Newsweek,*[31] the *Los Angeles Times,*[32] the *New York Times,*[33] the *Village Voice,* and *Time Magazine*, as well as individual journalists, doctors, professors, and homosexual activists frequently used that very phrase, mostly to describe the disproportionate number of homosexuals afflicted with the disease. People generally understood that "gay plague" referred to the historical fact that early on the disease was associated with homosexuals.

Thacker's real problem was that he was out of step with the dictates of secular morality: He supports abstinence education as a means of fighting AIDS and other sexually transmitted diseases; he believes that homosexuality is a sin and suggested on his website that homosexuals could overcome their problems through reliance on Jesus Christ. Far from being hateful or bigoted toward homosexuals, Thacker encouraged fellow Christians to reach out with compassion to AIDS sufferers. Unfortunately, the White House retreated and tried to distance itself from Thacker's views, which signaled that his nomination was history. "As bad as this is for Mr. Thacker," said policy analyst Peter LaBarbera of the Culture and Family Institute, "it is not just about him. The real message is that Christians and others who defend traditional sexual morality are branded as unfit for public service. This is a warning shot: You will stay silent about homosexual activism or even support it if you aspire to any public position."

Judicial Appointees

One of the most contested battlegrounds involving Christians in public service has been the president's nomination of Christian conservative lawyers to the federal bench. The Senate has the constitutional power of advice and consent over presidential judicial appointments. In recent years, Senate Democrats on the Judiciary Committee have adamantly opposed conservative nominees and, particularly, conservative Christian ones. In many cases, opposition is so fierce that Democrats won't agree to vote the nominees "out of committee" to let the entire Senate vote on the appointments. Such refusals to confirm Christian nominees are, in effect, an unconstitutional imposition of a religious test for holding office.

When President George W. Bush nominated J. Leon Holmes to the U.S. District Court for Eastern Alabama, he selected a man whose academic credentials are impeccable. Holmes graduated first in his law school class and has a Ph.D. in political science from Duke University. He has enjoyed an impressive legal career and has been endorsed by the generally liberal American Bar Association. Beyond career and academics, he is widely admired for his charitable work. But there is one problem: He is a devout orthodox Catholic who affirms the teachings of the Roman Catholic Church, including the tenet that abortion is wrong. He has served as president of Arkansas Right to Life, has been unapologetic about his fervent pro-life convictions, and refuses to bow to that secularly imposed sacrament of *Roe v. Wade*, believing it was erroneously decided.

A man of such character simply would not do for Democratic Senators Charles Schumer, Dianne Feinstein, and Dick Durbin, who strongly opposed his nomination, saying he was unfit for the federal bench. In an amazing utterance, Schumer said, "This man is an embarrassment to be nominated," and "This guy is so far off the deep end." And finally, "I do not know why this man was nominated. What he thinks is so bad."[34] Undeniably, the litmus test is as clear as it is unconstitutional: Practicing Catholics need not apply.

Professor Michael McConnell of the University of Utah experienced this same climate of anti-Christian bigotry when President Bush nominated him to the Tenth Circuit Court of Appeals. McConnell is one of the nation's leading church/state scholars, and he has assisted the Christian Legal Society in certain religious freedom cases by authoring a number of "friend of the court" briefs. He is widely respected in his profession—three hundred law professors supported his nomination—and Harvard's Lawrence Tribe said that McConnell was "likely to display an ideal judicial temperament." Harvard's Elena Kagan said, "There is no part of Michael that is activist or extremist."[35] But this support and more wasn't enough to insulate McConnell from stringent opposition from Americans United for Separation of Church and State (AU), the Human Rights Campaign (HRC), the National Abortion and Reproductive Rights Action League (NARAL), and People for the American Way (PFAW).

Kate Michelman, president of NARAL, described McConnell as "openly hostile towards women's rights" because of his criticism of *Roe v. Wade*.[36] The Human Rights Campaign—which claims to be the largest national homosexual political organization—fiercely opposed McConnell. PFAW president Ralph Neas depicted McConnell as "dangerous," saying he was "hostile to key principles of separation of church and state and argues for extraordinary legal preferences and special rights to be granted to religious organizations."[37] Furthermore, according to Neas, "McConnell is unrelentingly hostile to a constitutional right of reproductive choice and privacy."

Unlike some of his liberal judicial counterparts, McConnell said that he would honor Supreme Court precedent, even if he personally disagreed with it, because his oath of office would require it. He would not try to overturn *Roe v. Wade* at the circuit court level since it is the precedent of the United States Supreme Court and "settled law." "I am telling you under oath," testified McConnell during his confirmation hearings, "that I will conscientiously enforce the law, including laws and precedents that I don't agree with."[38] Apparently, AU executive director Barry Lynn didn't take McConnell at his word. McConnell, said Lynn, "is an activist whose ideas are on the fringes of American political and judicial thought and an ideologue who lacks the temperament necessary for the federal bench." What seemed to bother Lynn was McConnell's transparent Christianity and his belief that Christian principles underlie America's freedom tradition—a point detailed in Chapter Eleven of this book.

Lynn was also concerned that McConnell "characterized John Aschroft's remark... that Americans 'have no king but Jesus' as 'beautiful' and continued that 'freedom flourishes' only 'when man is subordinate to God.'" Lynn said he doesn't "quarrel with his right to hold such a theological view, but it would make him a better candidate for a preaching job than a position on a federal appeals court." It's hard not to conclude that Lynn believes that those with a committed Christian worldview are unsuited for the judiciary. "McConnell may be the religious right's dream nominee, but he's a nightmare for all Americans who treasure the Constitution," said Lynn. "The president's nomination of Michael McConnell for the federal bench represents a terrible assault on American freedom."[39] Contrary to Lynn's assessment, McConnell has made a career out of championing religious freedom—but he believes the Free Exercise Clause should not be smothered by an extremist interpretation of the Establishment Clause. Despite the opposition, McConnell, unlike so many other conservative nominees, was confirmed.

President George W. Bush

Secularists have been particularly bothered by President George W. Bush's open professions of his Christian faith. Their noticeable concern first arose during one of the early presidential debates in 1999, when the moderator asked the candidates to identify their favorite political philosopher. Quite spontaneously and unflinchingly, Mr. Bush responded, "Jesus Christ, because he changed my life." Following the debate, certain members of the media were highly critical of Bush's injection of Christ into the political debate. TV pundit Chris Matthews castigated Bush for invoking Christ in a debate about "secular" politics. On his MSNBC show "Hardball," Matthews said, "Well, did you ever hear of rendering unto Caesar the things that are Caesar and to God the things that are God? It seemed to me that George W. Bush did some rendering of things that are God's to Caesar tonight. It's a political debate.... This isn't about religion. It's about who gets to be the Republican nominee for president. And one guy pulls God out as his co-pilot, and the other guy pulls out Teddy Roosevelt."[40]

Matthews' implication with the Caesar reference was that even Christ Himself would agree that politics and religion don't mix. But Christ, in his pronouncement about rendering unto Caesar, was not forbidding Christians from engaging in politics. Matthews was essentially arguing that Christianity is something that should be practiced in private and only publicly, as it were, at church. Bush's debate response revealed his contrary understanding: that Christians believe that following Christ and his teachings is mandated for all aspects of life, including political life. This is not the same as advocating the governmental establishment of a religion, but merely the affirmation, consistent with the overwhelming majority of the framers of the United States Constitution, that Christians should actively participate in government and in solving society's problems.

Christians cannot and should not build a firewall between their private lives and their public persona, between their Christianity and their governance. It's impossible for anyone, including the president, to separate his belief system, his worldview, from his public life. As Christian apologist Dr. Ravi Zacharias observed, "We know that the premise of privatization is flawed because who we are in public is determined by what we have learned and cherished in private.... But it is mindless philosophy that assumes that one's private beliefs have nothing to do with public office. Does it make sense to entrust those who are immoral in private with the power to determine the nation's moral issues, and, indeed its destiny? One of the most dangerous and terrifying trends in America today is the disregard for character as a central necessity in a leader's credentials. The duplicitous soul of a leader can only make a nation more sophisticated in evil."[41]

New York Times columnist Maureen Dowd mocked Bush for "playing the Jesus card" during the presidential debate. She ridiculed Bush for saying, "When you turn your heart and your life over to Christ, when you accept Christ as the Savior, it changes your heart. It changes your life. And that's what happened to me." Dowd couldn't abide this open profession of faith by a man in pursuit of the highest office of the land, and she chose to take a shot at "exclusive" Christianity as well. She wrote, "Translation: You're either in the Christ club or out of it, on the J.C. team or off. This is the same exclusionary attitude, so offensive to those with different beliefs, that he showed in 1993 when he said that you must believe in Jesus Christ to enter heaven." Dowd continued, knowing that making fun of Christians and Christianity was perfectly permissible in our culture, especially in the pages of the elite *New York Times*. "This is the era of niche marketing, and Jesus is a niche," said Dowd. "Why not use the son of God to help the son of Bush appeal to voters? W. is checking Jesus' numbers, and Jesus is polling well in Iowa. Christ, the new wedge issue."

Since becoming president, George W. Bush has frequently called the nation to prayer and made no secret of his Christian faith and reliance on Christ for wisdom in governance. He has been especially open with his spirituality since the September 11 terrorist attacks, often peppering his speeches with references to his religion. A reporter asked Michael Gerson, President Bush's chief speechwriter, if the president understood how offended many people were by the closing lines of his State of the Union address in January 2003. The supposedly controversial words were, "The liberty we prize is not America's gift to the world, it is God's gift to humanity."

Gerson reportedly replied that this line was merely an acknowledgement that human rights are universal, derived from God, not from America. To prove Bush's statement was not out of line with our history, Gerson cited the clause from the Declaration of Independence that man is "endowed by our Creator with certain inalienable rights." The *Weekly Standard*'s Fred Barnes wrote that, despite these criticisms, President "Bush is hardly the first president to invoke God in his speeches." Barnes cited several presidents, including John F. Kennedy, who said (which may surprise Maureen Dowd), "The rights of man come not from the generosity of the state but from the Hand of God." "No one was offended by Kennedy's comment," noted Barnes. "And no one should be offended now."[42]

Barnes is correct. The infusion of religious values into political life is not, contrary to Maureen Dowd and other critics, new for American presidents. What is new is the aversion shown by our modern culture in response to it. Indeed, our founding fathers not only believed it was proper for Christian faith to guide our leaders, but they also thought it was necessary to preserve our liberties. George Washington proclaimed, "It is impossible to rightly govern the world without God and the Bible." Thomas Jefferson asked, "And can the liberties of a nation be thought secure when we have removed their only firm basis, a conviction in the minds of the people that these liberties are a gift of God?" John Quincy Adams, on July 4, 1821, said, "The highest glory of the American Revolution was this; it connected in one indissoluble bond the principles of civil government with the principles of Christianity." John Adams said, "Religion and virtue are the only foundations, not only of republicanism and of all free government, but of social felicity under all governments and in all the combinations of human society."[43]

It wasn't just the founders and early presidents who depended on their Christian faith; later presidents, including Abraham Lincoln, also heavily relied on God for strength in times of crisis and difficulty. Columnist Dave Kopel, in *National Review Online*, wrote of two of America's greatest Democratic presidents doing just that. The founder of the Democratic Party, Andrew Jackson, explained Kopel, was a Presbyterian who read his Bible daily and "applied its principles directly" in handling his most difficult struggle as president, involving the Second Bank of the United States. In announcing his decision to veto a bill to recharter the bank in 1832, Jackson used biblical imagery, as he did later on in the crisis when he said, "I will not bow down to the golden calf." And just when he was about to cave in to pressure from opponents, he heard church bells ringing, went to church, and recovered his determination to fight. Similarly, Kopel detailed the role President Harry Truman's Southern Baptist faith played in his Israel policy. Kopel concluded, "While the Jackson and Truman presidencies were not perfect, they were at their best when Jackson and Truman were inspired to follow eternal standards of morality rather than political expediency."[44]

Another manifestation of this criticism of the president for mixing religion with his governance has been the media criticism of his frequent references to "good and evil" in characterizing America's enemies in our War on Terror. This "simplistic" language of absolutes makes some in the elite media nervous, because they see it as emanating from Bush's pedestrian and intolerant Christian worldview. And they regard it as a potentially destructive influence in world relations. David Talbot, in *Salon.com*, complained that "Bush's black-and-white rhetoric fails to grasp the complexity of the world. It doesn't even reveal the truth about the darkness of Iraq." "Bush," wrote Talbot, "sees the world in the black-and-white terms of the born-again fundamentalist that he is. He has vowed to root out evil wherever it is in the world (why not original sin too while he's at it?), and each day the press is filled with the names of new countries that the U.S. is targeting."[45]

New York Times columnist Thomas Friedman joined the fray in a column entitled "The Real War" on November 27, 2001. In it he argued that the real enemy in the War on Terror was not terrorism. "Terrorism is just a tool," said Friedman. "We're fighting to defeat an ideology: religious totalitarianism." He said we fought World War II and the Cold War to defeat secular totalitarianism, but that this new war was aimed at defeating religious totalitarianism. If, by that, Friedman meant merely that we are not at war with Islam or all Muslims, he had a legitimate point. Instead, Friedman used "religious totalitarianism" generically. It's "a view of the world," he said, "that my faith must reign supreme and can be affirmed and held passionately only if all others are negated. That's bin Ladenism."

Had Friedman stopped there, his point would still have been defensible. Any group of believers, such as Muslim extremists, who are so radical about their faith that they want to destroy all other faiths (and the people holding them) are clearly religious totalitarians and dangerous. But Friedman went on to cast a much wider net. He quoted approvingly Rabbi David Hartman, from the Shalom Hartman Institute in Jerusalem, asserting that religious totalitarians were members of any faith who regarded their own religion as embodying exclusive truth—presumably, even if they didn't advocate the suppression of other faiths, whether by violent or nonviolent means. Friedman asked Rabbi Hartman how we should battle religious totalitarianism. Hartman responded, "All faiths that come out of the biblical tradition of Judaism, Christianity, and Islam have the tendency to believe that they have the exclusive truth. When the Taliban wiped out the Buddhist statues, that's what they were saying. But others have said it too. The opposite of religious totalitarianism is an ideology of pluralism—an ideology that embraces religious diversity and the idea that my faith can be nurtured without claiming exclusive truth. America is the Mecca of that ideology, and that is what bin Laden hates and that is why America had to be destroyed."

So, according to Hartman (and Friedman), the real enemy is any belief system that claims exclusive truth, even if it is wholly nonviolent toward other faiths. They seemed to be arguing that there is moral equivalence between murderous terrorists and any group claiming their religion is the one true religion. Here again we see the postmodernist mindset that indicts those, such as Christians, who assert that they have a corner on the truth. Its underlying premise is not merely that we must show those of other faiths, or of no faith at all, kindness and respect. We must also accept their belief systems as equally valid. Regardless of your faith, then, you are a religious totalitarian unless you are willing to dilute the fundamental principles of your faith to the point that it can accommodate all other faiths as equally true. "The future of the world," said Friedman, "may well be decided by how we fight this war. Can Islam, Christianity, and Judaism know that God speaks Arabic on Fridays, Hebrew on Saturdays, and Latin on Sundays, and that he welcomes different human beings approaching him through their own history, out of their language and cultural heritage?"

As we've seen, secular liberals grow nervous about Christians occupying positions of power in all branches and levels of our government. But in the next chapter we focus on their attacks against Christian pastors and lay people mostly with no connection to the government whatsoever. Again, their aim is to muzzle Christian speech when it seeks to influence society and the political system. They don't just want to prevent the government from sponsoring religion. They want to ban Christian members of the body politic from a seat at the table of our constitutional republic. Chapter Eight also shows how anti-Christian sentiment has made its way into the private sector in some of our major corporations. Again, the common thread underlying these subjects is an aversion to Christianity, not an affinity for church/state separation.

chapter Eight

Public Attacks on Churches and Christians and Purging the Private Sphere

IN THIS CHAPTER WE FOCUS ON THE WAR against churches and individuals as separationists try to prevent Christians from conscientiously practicing their faith and spreading the Gospel. As we shall see, both the public and private sectors are ongoing arenas of struggle as Christians are systematically attacked merely for exercising their constitutional rights of religious freedom.

Public Sector Attacks

Targeting Churches—Voting, Zoning, and Other Issues

One weapon used with increasing frequency by opponents of religious liberty is zoning law. The government wields enormous power in its decisions concerning how communities shall be organized and in determining whether to allow certain activities and to criminalize forbidden conduct. The power to enact zoning laws includes the power to license activities. Through a concerted effort of groups such as the American Planning Association, the National League of Cities, and the International Lawyers Association, municipalities across America are using local zoning ordinances to restrict and exclude churches in various areas. Churches used to be seen as an automatic enhancement to local neighborhoods, and cities routinely granted them special exemptions from their zoning rules, but in today's climate of growing hostility toward religion, houses of worship are seen as less desirable.

Often, the application of these laws requires subjective judgments by the zoning authorities. The less sympathetic these bodies are to encroachments on civil liberties, the more churches are at risk, and to the extent that churches are viewed in an unfavorable light, which they sometimes are, they will be afforded even less protection. The small city of Castle Hills, Texas, for example, actually compared Castle Hills Baptist Church to cancer, saying in a lawsuit against the church that it "seems to grow like a cancer, feeding on homes in much the same way as a cancerous tumor feeds on healthy cells."[1]

Local governments are discriminating against churches in a number of ways. Some authorities are excluding them from commercial districts, often because they are tax-exempt. Others are disallowing them in areas where non-religious groups are welcomed and are restricting how they may use their property. Fairly recently, three separate communities in Rhode Island denied churches permits to build in commercially zoned districts. A Michigan community refused to allow a church to meet at a shopping center despite granting access to non-religious groups. A county in Washington State has tried to enact laws regulating—mostly limiting—the size of churches and private schools.[2]

The issue of what constitutes a church arose when the town of St. Petersburg, Florida, ordered the Refuge, an inner-city church, to vacate an area zoned to permit churches. The church's ministry includes worship services, Bible studies, Bible-based counseling, outreach ministries, and evangelism. But because the Refuge ministers to the poor and needy, zoning officials arbitrarily concluded it was a social service agency rather than a church, and thereby required the church to vacate since social service agencies are not permitted in the district where Refuge's facility is located.[3] Making matters worse, there wasn't a single district in the city where social service agencies had an automatic right to locate. The city, in its brief to the court, haughtily argued that a church doesn't become a church simply by labeling itself as one. "What's in a name?" it asked. "A rose still smells like a rose regardless of the name by which it is called. [But] if the rose begins to smell like a stinkweed, it can still call itself a rose and may look like one, but it is no longer functioning as one, and so it is eventually going to have a negative impact on the rose garden and be weeded out."[4] So the church that specializes in serving the poor is not a church, but a stinkweed that must be weeded out. A three-judge panel for the Pinellas-Pasco Circuit Court ruled, however, that the Refuge was a church, and the church was permitted to stay.

While the Refuge ultimately prevailed, churches are facing opposition all over the country. The argument is not that churches should be immune from fire, safety, traffic, and other reasonable zoning regulations. But as the Refuge's Reverend Barbara Richards asked, "How can anybody come in and tell a church what they can or can't do? The size the congregation needs to be? It's ludicrous. It's an attack on people's freedom of religion."[5] But telling a church what it could or could not do was exactly what happened in Portland, Oregon, where the zoning authority told the Sunnyside Centenary United Methodist Church that it would have to curtail its meals program for low-income families and the homeless. It also ordered that its attendance at events, including Sunday worship, should be limited to seventy people and, even further, restricted Wednesday night Bible classes and other uses of the church facility.[6]

In 2000, Congress reacted to the increasingly negative trend against churches by enacting the Religious Land Use and Institutionalized Persons Act of 2000 (RLUIPA), forbidding discrimination against churches by local zoning authorities. Requiring government to treat churches on "not less than equal terms" with other assembly groups, the law established a standard of strict scrutiny—the highest standard—by which zoning laws burdening the free exercise of religion would be reviewed by the courts. Under the law, cities must now show a compelling governmental interest to prevail, and churches are using the act to defend themselves against unfair treatment throughout the country. Cassadaga, Florida, for example, was filled with "spiritualists" who believed they communicated with the dead, and there were no Protestant, Catholic, or Jewish congregations in the area. A Christian congregation with plans to begin a church purchased an acre of land outside the city, but when it applied for zoning approval, the county summarily denied it, yielding to pressure from the spiritualists who said they didn't want to be evangelized. The Alliance Defense Fund filed suit on behalf of the church, citing the Constitution and RLUIPA, and the county relented and agreed to let the church locate on the grounds.[7]

In 1997, the Vineyard Christian Fellowship, a Chicago-area church, purchased an office building for $1.2 million with plans to convert it to a church. Two days before the transaction was scheduled to close, the city council denied the church's request for an amended zoning ordinance and special-use permit. The church proceeded to closing, convinced it had the legal right—and could persuade the council accordingly—to use the building for church purposes. But the city did not change its position, and the church was forced to use the building for office purposes only and had to rent other space for church services for a number of years, to the tune of nearly half a million dollars. Although the city denied the church permission to hold worship services in the building, it allowed the Masons and other organizations to hold their events there. The church sued the city in federal court for violating its constitutional rights of free speech, assembly, and religious exercise. The church also charged that the city was in violation of the Religious Land Use and Institutionalized Persons Act. The court ruled in favor of the church.[8]

Zoning officials of Brighton Township, Pennsylvania, refused to permit the Beaver Assembly of God to build a church on its property because it was only 3.2 acres and the city requires that churches be on tracts with a minimum of five acres. The church had outgrown its small facility, located on the property before the enactment of the five-acre requirement. The city places no such burden on non-religious assembly groups. Under the code, schools are subject to a two-acre minimum, and other organizations, including strip clubs and porn shops, face no minimums at all. It is difficult to imagine how a small church with limited resources could comply with the requirement.[9]

Local Zoning Laws Against Individuals

Local zoning laws are also used against private individuals seeking to conduct Bible studies and prayer meetings within the confines of their homes, even though zoning authorities normally exercise no such restrictions on non-religious meetings. Art and Norma Ellison of Marietta, Georgia, regularly hosted prayer meetings at their home on Friday evenings for six to eight people. Most of the attendees parked in the Ellisons' driveway and the meetings were neither noisy nor disruptive. The City and Planning Department sent a letter to the couple informing them they were violating the zoning code by operating a church in a residential neighborhood and gave them ten days to discontinue their meetings.

A nearly identical situation arose in Onalaska, Wisconsin, when the city zoning authority threatened to shut down a Bible study for five college students in the home of Richard and Audrey Gilmore. Similarly, the zoning board of Denver, Colorado, told David and Diane Reiter that they would have to cut back their weekly Bible study to a monthly meeting.[10] Attorney Jay Sekulow, representing the Reiters, said city officials made it clear to the Reiters that if they were holding a weekly book club meeting, instead of Bible studies, there would be no problem, which revealed an overt hostility to the faith-based activity.[11] The city finally agreed to reverse itself, recognizing that its order was in violation of the couple's constitutional rights.[12]

As a final example, I personally received an e-mail from a pastor of a small Baptist church in a rural lake community in northeastern Arkansas, who told me his church had decided to locate there, because there were no churches within the city limits. The e-mail began, "Persecution of the Christian church is alive and well even within smaller communities in our great nation." The pastor related that the church was excited about the prospects of reaching many people in the community with the Gospel. They had difficulty finding available land to purchase, so they looked for rental property. They found a building within the city limits and asked the city council for permission to renovate it for church purposes, and the council agreed.

They continued their search for property to purchase and eventually located "the perfect spot." They applied for a zoning variance, and the council approved it on the condition that the church submit detailed construction plans for approval. Based on that assurance, the church made arrangements to close on the property. But a petition began to circulate urging the council to reject the church's authority to build and to forbid it from holding church services within the city limits on its rental property. As this book was going to press, the pastor informed me that the city is still resisting the church's efforts. But, he added, "We plan on standing firm since we feel our constitutional rights to free assembly, freedom of speech, and freedom of religion are under assault. Just thought you might be interested in another example of how Christians are being persecuted in the land of the not so free."

Muzzling Freedom of Religious Expression

Vacation Bible School

In 2001, the city of El Cajon, California, ordered the Foothills Christian Fellowship to take down its banner advertising summer Vacation Bible School because it didn't have a special permit, yet allowed the display of other temporary banners throughout the city without requiring any special permits. The only three citations given for violations of the ordinance were against Vacation Bible School banners. "The City of El Cajon is quickly deserving a reputation of outright hostile discrimination towards local ministries," said Brad Dacus, president of the Pacific Justice Institute, which undertook the legal case for the school.[13]

Discrimination in the Workplace

A social worker wanted to use part of his lunchtime break to hold prayer meetings in an empty conference room at his office at the Tehema County Department of Social Services in Red Bluff, California. His superiors not only denied him permission, they also instructed him verbally and in writing not to have his Bible and other items of faith in public view at his cubicle. Further, he was asked not to discuss his religion in the workplace. It's important to note that the department imposed no similar restrictions for non-religious activities or expressions, and it repeatedly permitted other employees to hold non-work-related meetings and events at its offices. The Pacific Justice Institute (PJI) argued that the county social services had violated the worker's rights under the Civil Rights Act of 1964, which provides that employers may not discriminate against employees on the basis of their religion.[14] "When the County allows other employees to hold birthday parties, baby showers, card games, and other non-work-related meetings to take place in the workplace," said PJI in a press release, "it must allow employees wishing to pray together a place to meet as well. Forbidding the latter amounts to religious discrimination that cannot be tolerated."[15]

State Attacks on Freedom of Religious Expression

Discriminatory Bans against Christian Leaflets

The city of Milwaukee adopted an ordinance based on a Wisconsin statute that prohibited the placement of pamphlets on vehicles, with violators to be fined from between $20 and $400. But the law was discriminatory, banning the distributing of religious leaflets while permitting others, such as those seeking to raise awareness of handicap parking rules. The city cited Rosemary Deida under the ordinance for distributing Christian literature on car windshields near City Hall.[16] When Deida challenged the law, the federal district court ruled in her favor, holding that the First Amendment does not permit the dissemination of some ideas and not others. If anything, the First Amendment affords greater protection to religious expression, which, stated the court, "holds a place at the core of the type of speech that the First Amendment was designed to protect." The court rejected the city's contention that the ordinance should be subject to less scrutiny because its purpose was not to restrict the content of the speech itself, but to reduce litter and protect private property.[17]

Do Churches Have the Rights of Free Association and Religious Expression?

In April 2002, a California Superior Court judge refused for the second time to bar an allegedly disruptive woman named Lady Cage-Barile from the Church of Christ in Hollywood. After she repeatedly disrupted church services, the church notified Cage-Barile in February of that year that her membership in the church was terminated and she could no longer enter church property. She ignored the requests and continued to appear and disrupt, calling church officials "Satan's agents." When the church had originally requested an injunction against Cage-Barile, the court denied it, saying her actions were "pure speech." The Becket Fund for Religious Liberty then joined the case with local counsel. The attorneys submitted a brief contending that "a church has a fundamental right to determine who is and who is not a member" and citing *Boy Scouts v. Dale* in support of the church's constitutionally guaranteed freedom of association.[18] Cage-Barile, according to the church, became even more disruptive, spending "part of her Sundays ripping religious literature and notices off the Church walls," shouting at congregation members, and "obstructing or impeding ingress into or egress from the church."

The church alleged that Cage-Barile's actions caused it to lose members, cancel ministries, and even occasionally resort to secret meetings. But again the court denied the church's request for an injunction. The church appealed the decision to the California Second District Court of Appeals in May, and finally, on July 2, 2002, the court ruled in favor of the church. The order of the three-judge panel stated, "The church, like any nonsectarian property owner, may decide whom to allow on its premises" and that Cage-Barile's "right of free speech does not trump the church's right to prohibit her disruptive conduct on its property."[19]

Federal Attacks

Muzzling Christian Pastors and other IRS Suppression of Christian Expression

It's no surprise that extreme separationists would object to the public expression of religious views by Christian public officials. But how about the reverse situation: pastors offering their political opinions from the pulpit? Does the so-called separation of church and state require pastors not to engage in the political arena? Is it improper for them to touch on subjects involving politics? Of course not—the U.S. Supreme Court held in *McDaniel v. Paty* (1978)[20] that ministers may serve in state legislatures and hold public office—but that doesn't keep zealots from fighting for that result through other means.

Since our moral views are so intertwined with our political views, it is difficult to imagine how pastors or priests could be expected to be silent on such matters. It is their business to lead on moral issues, and if we limit their ability to speak on political issues, we necessarily restrict them from influencing society on certain moral issues, not to mention their freedom of speech and religion. Should they keep their opinions to themselves, for example, on such issues as the life of the unborn because these questions are also political matters? Shouldn't they have a right to speak out against same-sex marriages, homosexual adoption, or polygamy if they choose to? You can see the absurdity of going down this road, and yet the Internal Revenue Service (IRS), through manipulation of Congress's tax exemption for religious organizations, has sometimes exerted a chilling effect upon the political speech and religious expression of pastors from the pulpit.

IRS Targets Free Expression Rights of Clergy

In the years following an amendment offered to a revenue bill by then-Senator Lyndon B. Johnson in 1954, the IRS has selectively used Section 501(c)(3) of the United States Code as a weapon against pastors, priests, and rabbis to inhibit them from speaking out on political matters, even when these matters are highly relevant to their faith messages. That the free speech and free exercise rights of the clergy can be so casually disregarded is a bad portent for religious freedom in this nation. It's especially troublesome if, as some have charged, the IRS applies these rules selectively against certain churches and not others. Former IRS commissioner Don Alexander made that very charge in an interview with *Insight Magazine*. "I think," said Alexander, "there was selective enforcement during the Clinton years, when a church against Clinton was audited and its exemption revoked, but Clinton and Gore making speeches from the pulpits . . . has been ignored."[21]

The accusation of selective enforcement came up again with the 2002 federal congressional elections. Catholic League president William Donohue charged that many churches (mostly African-American) in numerous states permitted political candidates to campaign in their churches. One pastor, according to Donohue, actually instructed the congregation to vote for a named Democratic candidate for office. "Not all those who stumped in the churches were candidates," said Donohue. "Bill Clinton and Al Gore campaigned for Democratic candidates in several churches. And Donna Brazile of the Democratic National Committee went so far as to admit that 'we have our literature for our churches.' This kind of rank electioneering in black churches would never be tolerated in Catholic churches. That the zealots who worship at the altar of separation of church and state have gone mute only proves how utterly unprincipled they are."[22] If, indeed, we have deliberate selective enforcement, then it is the IRS, more than those it is selectively investigating, that is engaging in partisan politics rather than trying objectively to enforce the law with respect to 501(c)(3) organizations.

Section 501(c)(3) prohibits churches and other section 501(c)(3) organizations from taking part in partisan political activity. While churches may, along with other 501(c)(3) organizations, engage in lobbying activities, churches may not endorse or oppose candidates for political office. Some experts say that churches should think twice before distributing partisan voter guides, and that churches that try to influence the outcome of elections are in jeopardy of losing their tax-exempt status along with the ability to receive tax-deductible contributions.

For example, the IRS revoked the exemption status of the Church at Pierce Creek in Binghamton, New York, for publishing newspaper ads attacking Bill Clinton in 1992.[23] But, as Mathew Staver of Liberty Counsel noted, this action was somewhat misleading. While the Church at Pierce Creek did have its tax-exempt letter ruling revoked, that revocation was largely symbolic, in that a federal court of appeals ruled that churches don't need a tax-exempt letter to be tax-exempt. Staver pointed out that, although churches may not endorse or oppose political candidates, they may "educate their members and the public regarding their core values and beliefs." Churches are also free to distribute non-partisan voter guides that "objectively" compare the candidates' respective positions on issues.[24]

While Staver is correct, not all churches are aware of their rights, and separationist groups, such as Americans United for Separation of Church and State (AU) and the ACLU, are always waiting in the wings to pounce at any opportunity. For example, in December 1998, AU boasted that it had reported eight churches to the IRS for distributing Christian Coalition Voter Guides during the November elections. Even if these reports didn't ultimately result in the loss of tax-exempt status for the churches, they probably did cast a chill upon the churches' expression. It's simply not a healthy thing to have the IRS, with all its awesome power, investigating churches in this manner.[25] In addition, AU went after the Christian Coalition itself and eventually succeeded in convincing the IRS to revoke the coalition's tax-exempt status for electioneering activities.[26]

Kevin J. Hasson, president of the Becket Fund for Religious Liberty, claimed that, just before the November 2002 elections, AU asked the IRS to investigate three cases of what AU called "improper partisan political activity by a church." Hasson contended that the fear of such investigations caused a chilling effect on free speech and free exercise rights. Hasson cited the Becket Fund's efforts on behalf of military chaplains in *Rigdon v. Perry* (1997), in which a federal court in Washington, D.C., said that the government could not bar chaplains from discussing in their sermons President Clinton's veto of the partial-birth abortion bill. Hasson admitted that, while all legal issues in this area are not settled, it is "certainly clear . . . that, when it comes to regulating political speech from the pulpit," (quoting the *Rigdon* court) "'any attempt to impinge on the [chaplains'] constitutional and legal rights is not acceptable.'"[27]

Some groups, including the Concerned Women for America (CWA), indeed view the IRS's application of the law as potentially chilling on religious expression. CWA's Michael Schwartz rightly noted, "If a church could be put out of business by the adverse decision of an IRS official, then the state has the power to suppress a church. This is something that should be of grave concern to all citizens, especially those who are church members. Even worse, the event that might trigger the suppression of a church by the government is an otherwise legal exercise of free speech, and that speech becomes punishable because it is deemed politically undesirable by officials of government. Governments should never have this much power, and churches must never be this much at the mercy of state officials."

That the IRS claims only to enforce this provision of the law when it receives a complaint from third parties is little comfort to its opponents. They envision a situation where the clergy, for fear of losing their tax-exempt status, might hold back on spiritual issues that arguably have political overtones. As a result of the law, pastors have precluded pro-life groups from holding meetings on church property, prohibited pro-family political candidates from circulating campaign fliers in their parking lots, and sometimes recalibrated their sermons to avoid forbidden subjects. As Michael Schwartz concluded, "A free people, whose nation was dedicated to religious liberty at its foundation, should never tolerate such a subordination of church to state."[28]

Concerned about this trend, in 2002 some members of Congress proposed a measure called the Houses of Worship Political Speech Act, which was aimed at removing the authority of the IRS to revoke a church's tax-exempt status for engaging in "partisan" political activity. The bill failed resoundingly, but its proponents were not discouraged. Beyond targeting the free expression rights of the clergy, the IRS has also challenged the housing tax exemption it has enjoyed since 1921.[29]

IRS v. Christian Publishers

The IRS has also been known to set its sights on Christian publishers. It challenged Christian Service Charities' (CSC) deduction of Sunday school materials for overseas use, saying they are religious and have no real value. CSC's Joel MacCollam said the IRS "claims that faith-based material (in this case, Sunday School and Vacation Bible School publications) has no intrinsic impact on human lives or development programs to warrant a corporate donor claiming tax deductions because the material is religious in content." The IRS's position, essentially is that gifts-in-kind of religious items are not deductible. Reverend Louis P. Sheldon, chairman of the Traditional Values Coalition, denounced this as "religious bigotry," saying the challenge against allowing "tax deductions for charitable Christian materials is a direct attack on faith-based charities and the work of spreading the Gospel of Jesus Christ. It is a First Amendment violation."[30]

FCC Targets Religious TV

In 2000, the Federal Communications Commission (FCC), in a decision to approve a transfer of licenses between certain TV stations, established new, very strict standards for "educational" programming that non-commercial educational stations are required to air in order to retain their licenses. Religious broadcasters and station owners were concerned that the new rules targeted Christian programs because they were not generally "educational" and that the FCC decision could force stations to drop all faith-based programming. In its written opinion, the FCC stated that "not all programming, including programming about religious matters, qualifies as 'general educational' programming." And then the FCC took direct aim at religious programs. "For example," said the commission, "programming primarily devoted to religious exhortation, proselytizing, or statements of personally held religious views and beliefs generally would not qualify as 'general educational' programming.... Thus, church services generally will not qualify as 'general education' programming under our rules."

Brandt Gustavson, president of the National Religious Broadcasters (NRB), said the FCC was trying to draw a difficult line between programs teaching *about* religion (which are acceptable to the FCC) and those involving religious exhortation or statements of personal religious belief, which are forbidden. "The order," said Gustavson, "contains a disquieting implication that the government may restrict certain strains of religious speech—disfavoring more passionate and emotional expressions of faith—while not constraining others that are more 'intellectual' and drained of human emotion."[31]

Although paragraph 44 of the order said the FCC would not "disqualify any program simply because the subject matter of the teaching or instruction is religious in nature," it added language that made religious broadcasters wonder. "We reiterate that the reserved television channels are intended 'to serve the educational and cultural broadcast needs of the entire community to which they are assigned,' and to be 'responsive to the overall public as opposed to the sway of particular political, economic, social, or religious interests.'" Two commissioners, Harold Furchtgott-Roth and Michael Powell, strongly dissented, criticizing the ruling as approaching "unacceptable content regulation." They specifically addressed the majority's assertion that church services would not qualify as general educational programming. "We ask, however, why such programming might not qualify as 'cultural' programming, just as a presentation of an opera might?"[32]

Following the ruling, a number of commentators strenuously objected. The *Wall Street Journal* editorial page described the decision as establishing "a new litmus test for speech that targets religious expression." Christian evangelist Chuck Colson wrote, "The long-term implications of the ruling are grave, not only for Christians but for anyone who values free speech. The ruling puts the FCC in the position of determining which religious expression is acceptable and which is not.... Think about it. Does this mean, for example, that the Pope's Christmas Mass would be prohibited? And how about discussion of abortion or homosexuality? Where does the censorship end?... Have no fear, this will not mean that PBS would have to reconsider airing Bill Moyers' attack on evangelicals in politics, programs celebrating alternative lifestyles, or New Age spirituality. That's 'education.' But an interview with me presenting a biblical worldview would be forbidden."[33] Congressman Michael G. Oxley, a member of the House Commerce Subcommittee on Telecommunications, protested the ruling in a letter to FCC Chairman William E. Kennard. Oxley said he would introduce legislation to nullify the objectionable portion of the ruling.[34]

Perhaps in response to the public outcry or to Congressman Oxley's threatened legislation, or both, the FCC reversed itself less than a month after its original controversial decision by voting 4-1 to rescind the "additional guidelines" concerning religious programming. In its press release explaining its reversal of the earlier ruling, the FCC said that "widespread public confusion" over the ruling was "causing considerable misunderstanding." The commission said it would return to handling broadcast programming judgments on a case-by-case basis. The lone dissenter, Commissioner Gloria Tristani, accused the majority of surrendering to "an organized campaign of distortion and demagoguery."[35]

Private Sector Attacks–Purging the Private Sector

It's not always constitutional concerns over government involvement with religion that lead to slights against Christian references and symbols. The anti-Christian virus has leaped from the government to the private sector, infecting much in its path. From our politically correct culture to the offices of corporate America, the private sector is well on its way to adopting a hostile attitude toward Christianity, having bought into the conventional wisdom that a religion of such "intolerance" is itself not worthy of tolerance. To an increasing number, Christianity is something to be ashamed of rather than celebrated.

Samaritan's Purse to Baghdad?

The Reverend Franklin Graham, son of the Reverend Billy Graham, sparked controversy following the September 11 terrorist attacks by characterizing Islam as "a very evil and wicked religion" during an interview with NBC. In a later *Wall Street Journal* column Graham sought to clarify his comments, saying he was not contending that Muslims "are evil people because of their faith. But I decry the evil that has been done in the name of Islam, or any other faith—including Christianity." He added that "the persecution or elimination of non-Muslims has been a cornerstone of Islam conquests and rule for centuries."[36] In an interview with Paula Zahn on CNN, Graham said he does not believe Muslims are evil people, despite his disagreements with them. He said, "I'm not a Muslim. I don't believe in Islam. And I have a lot of concerns and a lot of questions about their faith.... We're not fighting Islam. There are many wonderful Muslim people. I know them, I work with them, and I respect them. I just disagree."

Graham heads a Christian relief agency called Samaritan's Purse.

On March 25, 2003, Samaritan's Purse and the Southern Baptist Convention said they had workers in Jordan near the Iraqi border who were prepared to enter Iraq to provide food, shelter, and other needs to Iraqis following the second Iraqi war. Samaritan's Purse said it could provide drinking water for 20,000 people, household packages for 5,000 families, general medical kits to serve 100,000 people for three months, and materials to build temporary shelters for 4,000 families. Graham said, "As Christians, we love the Iraqi people, and we are poised and ready to help meet their needs. Our prayers are with the innocent families of Iraq, just as they are with our brave soldiers and leaders."

When asked whether they would do any evangelizing while performing their relief work, Ken Isaacs of Samaritan's said, "We do not deny the name of Christ. We believe in sharing Him in deed and in word. We'll be who we are." Isaacs added, "Compassion and service is a vital expression of Christianity. We don't have an evangelism strategy. We don't have a strategy to share our faith.... We don't have Bibles waiting in the wings, or Christian literature waiting in the wings."[37]

Mark Kelly, of the Southern Baptists' International Mission Board, also refused to deny there might be a spiritual component accompanying the aid, but indicated the primary focus would be relief. "Conversations about spiritual things will come about as people ask about our faith," said Kelly. "It's not going to be like what you might see in other countries where there's a preaching service outside clinics and things like that."[38] Graham reinforced this idea, saying, "We will offer relief to those who need it, with no strings attached. Sometimes, the best preaching we can do is simply being there with a cup of cold water, exhibiting Christ's spirit of serving others."[39]

Voices in the mainstream media condemned the proposed relief effort, and one journalist even suggested it was "immoral." The *Washington Post* called for the Pentagon to rescind its approval for Samaritan's Purse to operate in Iraq.[40] Steven Waldman, writing in *Slate.com*, urged the Bush administration to use its influence to discourage Graham, apparently having no problem here with the intermingling of church and state. "I'm not sure any of this means that America's foreign policy objectives are served by having a Bush-loving, Islam-bashing, Muslim-converting Christian icon on the ground in Iraq tending to the bodies and souls of the grateful but deeply suspicious Muslim population. Or, to put it more simply, the idea is absolutely *loopy.* The idea that the U.S. government is powerless to do anything about Samaritan's Purse seems odd. We can obliterate another nation's army in a few weeks, but when it comes to reining in a disruptive charity, well, our hands are tied?" Waldman dismissed the argument that the government shouldn't tell private relief agencies what to do. "In fact," said Waldman, "religious liberty does not trump *all* concerns. Among the concerns it does not trump is the . . . desire not to have the entire Muslim world wanting to wage war against America. And make no mistake: Franklin Graham's mission to Iraq will help convince the Arab world that America is out to convert Muslims to Christianity. What Graham is doing probably isn't illegal; it's merely immoral."[41]

There is a legitimate concern that relations between America and the Iraqi people and the Muslim world could be strained by the strong presence of Franklin Graham's organization in the relief effort. But in our culture today, it is all too easy to assume the worst of well-meaning Christians and to attack their motives with impunity. No one would dare attack the motives of those of other faiths without incurring the wrath of the guardians of political correctness. And few dare to criticize those of other religions when they attack Christians. When Mas'ood Cajee, of the National Council of Fellowship of Reconciliation, called Graham "a spiritual carpetbagger and war profiteer who trades in souls," nary a word of criticism was to be heard. No one challenged Cajee's commitment to diversity, sensitivity, and tolerance when he wrote, "Like the despised Carpetbaggers of yore, Graham plans to exploit the humanitarian crisis for his own calculating gain, by subjecting vulnerable Iraqis to his Faustian Christ-for-food program."[42]

Press Attacks and the Great Commission

Sometimes the press just doesn't understand the commitment some Christians have to their perceived duty to honor Christ's Great Commission, set forth in Matthew 28:19–20, sending them to preach the Gospel the world over. This could be seen in the incredulity of certain critics that Dayna Curry and Heather Mercer, the two Christian missionaries who were rescued from an Afghan prison for evangelizing, would dare consider doing it all over again. Brad Buchholz, writing in the *Austin American Statesman*, was clearly put off by their persistence. "How dare these Americans endanger their own lives—and those of innocents—by tempting fate yet again, carrying Christianity to cultures that forbid it. After all: Isn't the ethos of American liberty grounded in respect for all creeds, all colors, all faiths?"[43] Sadly, in Buchholz's worldview, Christian proselytizers in the service of Christ by spreading the Gospel are showing disrespect for those of other creeds, colors, and faiths.

PC Attack on American History–Anti-Christian PC Culture

Once a symbol of America's faith heritage, Plymouth Rock, Massachusetts, is now saturated with political correctness. No longer are vacationing families treated to stories of the Pilgrims who were on a mission to gain religious freedom. Instead of being touted as "the cradle of American democracy" as it was once, the site has been "transformed into a city ashamed of its past." On the grounds is a new monument plaque that documents "the devastating effect of Christianity" on America, the Pilgrims' genocide of Native Americans, and "the importance of treating Thanksgiving as a 'National Day of Mourning.'"[44] In addition, the tour guide on the site offers a revised version of history.

The town of Plymouth's decision to place the "National Day of Mourning/Genocide" plaque on the site can be traced back to an altercation between the United American Indians of New England (UAINE) and the participants in the historical Pilgrims' Progress march. The march had been a custom since the 1920s, and usually drew thousands of spectators. After the marchers paraded through town, they would wind up at Burial Hill, where they would perform an authentic Pilgrim worship service, featuring prayers and Psalm singing. Since 1970, UAINE had staged a competing event in Plymouth, called the National Day of Mourning, to commemorate the struggles of Native Americans. As stated in the December 12, 1996, issue of *Workers World*, (a publication of the Workers World Party, a self-identified socialist organization) the National Day of Mourning "targets the mythology perpetuated in Plymouth and throughout the U.S. that the Pilgrims were wonderful people who came to Massachusetts only in search of religious freedom and that Native people lived happily ever after."[45] This event included a protest of the Pilgrims' Progress march.

In 1996, some protestors, according to an approving article in *Workers World*, invited their children to "take a swing at racism" by striking a Pilgrim piñata. When the piñata was broken, children found symbols of Pilgrim "oppression" inside: "money, police badges, toy soldiers, handcuffs, and chains representing the enslavement of African-Americans and the oppression of women, and alcohol ads representing the government's use of alcohol and drugs such as crack to destroy the oppressed communities." Then, according to the article, these items "were thrown down on Plymouth Rock, and a number of protestors spat on the rock to show their hatred for that symbol."[46]

In 1997, the protestors were determined to create a media spectacle against the Pilgrims' Progress march. The protestors, in Indian dress, many of them recruited by UAINE from out of state, surrounded, blocked, and threatened the marchers, assaulting at least one of them. Some twenty-three protestors were arrested. The protest achieved the desired result, with national newspapers announcing renewed tensions between Pilgrims and Indians. Protest organizers complained of the city's excessive use of force in dealing with them, and to avoid further threatened riots, Plymouth agreed to require its local police department to apologize for its treatment of the protestors. Plymouth also agreed to donate $100,000 to the Metacom Education Fund, to allow the fund and its supporters to have a regular Thanksgiving Day event near Plymouth Rock, and to erect the new monuments containing the revised "genocide" version of history.[47]

"The pilgrims came to these shores to establish a capitalist venture and settlement here," UAINE co-leader Moonanum James, of the Wampanaog nation, declared in 1996 after that year's protest. "They stole land from Native people, were completely intolerant of Native culture and spirituality, and participated in numerous forays where they murdered indigenous peoples." So the protestors finally prevailed. A historic site celebrating America's Christian heritage has been declared politically incorrect and unacceptable, and Christian Pilgrims have been branded as plunderers and murderers.

Separation of Church and Wall Street

Like their public sector counterparts, private sector employers are also guilty of anti-Christian discrimination. Moreover, many private corporations choose to police themselves by cleansing from their products and corporate culture anything that speaks of God.

Federal law requires that employers reasonably accommodate the sincerely held religious beliefs of their employees, unless they can demonstrate such accomodations will cause them undue hardship. But in Lodi, California, a company fired a Christian from his computer job over his refusal to work on the Sabbath. People may reasonably disagree with this law on the grounds that an employer should be free to control his employees' work schedule and that employees forced against their will to work on the Sabbath can seek employment elsewhere. But this particular case went beyond clashing freedom claims between employer and employee. The employer reportedly not only refused to accommodate the employee's faith; it allegedly told him that his beliefs were "stupid and ridiculous." Also, other employees were willing to work on Sunday, which would have negated any claim by the employer that it was suffering an undue hardship by accommodating the employee. But the employer refused to budge, prompting Brad Dacus of the Pacific Justice Institute to say, "This case is distinctive in that the employer could show no justification except for insensitivity and intolerance, for not accommodating [a] Christian worker's beliefs."[48]

Dr Pepper, Seven-Up

In 2002, the Dr Pepper/Seven-Up Company (DPSU) introduced its "patriot can" for soft drinks, featuring a portion of the Pledge of Allegiance. The can included a drawing of the Statue of Liberty and the phrase, "One Nation . . . Indivisible," but conspicuously omitted the words "under God." When a twelve-year-old girl wrote to complain about the omission, the company responded that there simply wasn't enough room on the can to include the words. A glimpse of the can, however, according to critics, belies that claim. It may have been a submission to political correctness or a desire not to offend a certain segment of the population that led to the omission. But the result was to offend another segment of people—those who understand that God has been and should continue to be a part of American culture. Regardless of its motives, the company erred on the side of excluding, rather than including, God, which is happening with increasing frequency in our society.[49]

Disney

In December 2002, Disney World in Orlando, Florida, ended its twenty-eight-year tradition of making on-site religious services available to Christian guests. Though it had provided such services since 1975, Disney World officials said that the 35,000-acre site could not continue to accommodate Sunday services for Catholics and Protestants, and suggested to guests that they go off campus to attend church. This decision represented a radical departure from the beliefs and practices of the park's founder, Walt Disney, who said in an insert to a 1978 record "Magical Music of Walt Disney," "Whatever success I have had in bringing clean, informative entertainment to people of all ages, I attribute in part to my Congregational upbringing and lifelong habit of prayer." Tellingly, while eliminating Christian services, Disney has gone out of its way to solicit the homosexual community, even having an annual "Gay Day" event every year.

Pro-family and religious groups were troubled by Disney's action. Wendy Wright of Concerned Women for America criticized Disney's movement away from traditional values. "Disney," said Wright, "ought to be looking at how they can promote a healthy, family-friendly moral tone that would be good for the employees and customers alike. Kicking churches off of the property is exactly the opposite of what Disney needs to be doing... [Disney] is showing that religious families don't need to be accommodated. Disney's decision is very short-sighted because religious communities and activities help set a moral tone." Other critics pointed to the anomaly of Disney's "accommodation" policies in light of research showing that over 75 percent of Americans identify themselves as Christian and as little as two percent as homosexual.[50]

Kodak

Despite their low percentage of the population, homosexuals sometimes appear to have the power of an unchecked majority. Rolf Szabo, an employee for twenty-three years with the Eastman Kodak Company, lost his job when he stood up for his Christian principles at work. Szabo's boss at the company's headquarters in Rochester, New York, sent Szabo e-mails promoting a "Coming Out Day" for homosexuals, as part of Kodak's "Winning & Inclusive Culture" movement designed to promote diversity in the workplace. The memo included suggestions for helping homosexual employees to "come out" at work. Workers were urged to be supportive of the people coming out and acknowledge their "courage" in disclosing their homosexuality.

They were told to "be sensitive to the employee's language in defining their personal orientation" and to "acknowledge your level of awareness of this topic, and share your personal willingness to understand." The message also told employees to act quickly and responsibly if they became aware of anti-gay comments or humor at work. A footnote to one of the points cautioned employees to "keep in mind that such behaviors violate Kodak's Values as well as Kodak's Equal Opportunity Employment Policy, which all supervisors are responsible for maintaining in their areas.... Reported violations of this policy are to be thoroughly investigated. If verified, disciplinary action is to be taken."

Upon receiving the note, Szabo sent his supervisor an e-mail, with a copy to all the recipients of his supervisor's original e-mail, requesting that he not send him this type of information as he found it disgusting and offensive. The supervisor then sent another e-mail to the original employee recipients, apologizing for Szabo's remarks. Its contents are instructive regarding "tolerance:" They demand that everyone adopt the corporation's values. "As you all know," read the supervisor's response, "our strategic thrust to build a Winning & Inclusive Culture drives us to behave in ways that value everyone regardless of differences. While I understand that we are all free to have our own personal beliefs, when we come to the Kodak workplace, our behaviors must align with the Kodak Values. I apologize for the e-mail sent to all of you from Rolf Szabo this morning. Rolf's comments are hurtful to our employees, friends, and family members who are gay, lesbian, bisexual, or transgendered. This behavior is not aligned with the Kodak Values and, therefore, is not acceptable."[51]

Thereafter, the company asked Szabo to sign an employee commitment plan, acknowledging he was sorry for his e-mail calling the supervisor's e-mail "offensive" and agreeing to take steps to ensure that this type of thing would not happen again. He was told that his refusal to sign the document would result in his termination. When he refused, Kodak fired him.[52] Kodak touts itself as promoting tolerance and diversity—its website contains a "list of accolades" it has received for "equal opportunity and inclusion." Many of the honors include praise for Kodak's attitude toward the alternative sexual preferences of its employees. But while Kodak brags about its tolerance and diversity, it was obviously intolerant of Szabo's Christian beliefs. By insisting that he act contrary to his deeply held beliefs and in conformity with company values, Kodak demonstrated intolerance of his beliefs and its own hard-line exclusiveness—not to mention its encroachment on Szabo's right to religious freedom.

Motorola

Motorola is another big corporation that actively promotes a homosexual agenda through mandatory "homophobia" workshops, homosexual sex-education courses, and e-mail recruitment for gay pride parades. According to an engineer with the company, this push is causing a great deal of tension among employees and the "quiet anger" of some who disapprove of the homosexual lifestyle and homosexual activism. On a website bearing the company logo called "Motopride," Bob Williams and Audrey Lin, co-leaders of Motorola's Gay and Lesbian Business Council, wrote, "We are proud of Motorola's growing history with the gay, lesbian, bisexual, and transgendered (GLBT) community, including its support of our internal GLBT employee group and organizations that are important to us."[53] One employee of the company expressed his concern that Motorola's vision of "tolerance" was more like thought control. "I think the main issue lies in a corporate organization trying to force people to believe certain things with mandatory-type seminars and workshops," he said. "I think that's obviously a violation of numerous principles upon which this nation was founded."

Jordan Lorence, an attorney with the Alliance Defense Fund, which promotes religious freedom issues in the judicial system, sees this type of corporate policy as part of a larger trend. "Diversity training," said Lorence, "is becoming mandatory catechism class for the church of the politically correct." Lorence, addressing the modern concept of tolerance, said that Americans, traditionally, have drawn a distinction between cordial behavior and personal beliefs. "But what is happening now is that we're seeing a subtle but radical transformation of that traditional norm, and the vehicle in which this change is coming is diversity training by employers, either public or private." Lorence said there was a big difference between "being respectful of people's differences," and "compelling a uniformity of thought."

Lorence may be correct that a nationwide trend is underway. American companies are increasingly marketing specifically to homosexual consumers. And, according to the Human Rights Campaign, a national homosexual advocacy group, at least three hundred of the Fortune 500 companies make sexual orientation a part of their nondiscrimination policies. Other pro-family oriented groups are also concerned that many corporations are going beyond merely prohibiting discrimination against homosexuals and actively promoting a homosexual agenda. This puts pressure on employees who are loyal to their employers, but want to be true to their moral beliefs as well.[54]

Sandia

Sandia National Laboratories in New Mexico also allegedly discriminates against Christians and in favor of homosexual employees. In its equal employment opportunity (EEO) policy, the corporation formally recognized the Gay/Lesbian/Bisexual Networking Group and gave it access to company "funding, administrative assistance, and use of company facilities and communication channels." But when Christians in the Workplace Networking Group applied for official recognition, they were denied because the Christian workers had "not established the existence of workplace barriers based on religion." The Christian workers strongly disagreed with this assessment and documented in a letter to Margaret Harvey, the company's "diversity, EEO and affirmative action department manager," examples of the company's discrimination against Christians. For instance, the company did not allow references to religious events to be placed on its bulletin boards. Employers could collect donations for any group, provided it was nondenominational. The company's EEO networking group's policy expressly excluded religious groups, and the company required employees to remove posters, books, pictures, and screen savers with religious content. Engineers were forbidden to use biblical references in connection with projects—a reconnaissance robot named Caleb (after the biblical spy) had to be renamed.

In the letter, the Christian group said, "Because of these and similar incidents, many Christian workers are not comfortable with expressing who they are openly for fear of ridicule or reprimand from management or fellow employees." Despite the documentation, the company denied the request as well as similar follow-up requests. The group filed a lawsuit against the company for violation of its constitutional rights.[55]

During this controversy in the early part of 2000, Sandia, despite the soberingly serious nature of its business—it is one of three Department of Energy laboratories that develop top-secret weaponry for the United States government—was so preoccupied with the homosexual gay rights issue that it shut down its plant for two days in April to give employees time to take "diversity training." Attorney Stephen Crampton of the American Family Association (AFA), which represented the Christian employee group, placed the company's priorities in perspective when he said, "Apparently the DOE is more concerned with furthering diversity than it is with national security." Crampton observed that, while Sandia's policy purports to forbid religious discrimination, it "is discriminatory against religion on its face. It is an insult not only to believers in God, but to believers in freedom everywhere." It is hard to deny Crampton's point. After all, the company has subjected its employees to annual "Coming Out Day" celebrations, where they are pressured, just as in the diversity training sessions, to accept, even respect the homosexual lifestyle. Even more amazingly, the company reportedly asked some employees to remove photos of their wives and children to avoid offending homosexuals, who are not legally allowed to marry and supposedly feel uncomfortable publicizing their intimate relationships. When a reporter asked Sandia to explain these policies and alleged discriminatory acts, the company issued a written statement in which it said its policy is "to provide an employee-friendly environment free of prejudice to anyone on the basis of race, age, religion, sex, sexual orientation, or any other basic characteristic."[56]

Christian-Friendliness Frowned Upon

When corporations, on the other hand, express a friendlier attitude toward Christianity, they are often subjected to severe criticism from "tolerant" forces in society. One television producer in Boca Raton, Florida, sued her employer, asserting that the company's stuffing of Scripture into pay envelopes and holding Bible study sessions in the office created a religiously hostile workplace.[57] An openly lesbian city employee of Oakland, California, sued her personnel director for announcing at his first departmental staff meeting that he was a "Christian and he would run the organization on Christian values."[58] A bank in the Rochester, New York, area was so intent on not being associated with Christianity that it deleted a fifth-grade student's depiction of a steeple and a cross from the drawing he presented as part of a Christmas card designing contest in 2002, saying the inclusion of religious imagery was not allowed.[59]

And when Chevrolet made a decision to sponsor a Christian music tour—though it had sponsored innumerable non-religious concerts and tours in the past—it was roundly criticized as being "divisive." The month-long, sixteen-city "Come Together and Worship Tour" offered two acts featuring contemporary Christian music, Michael W. Smith and Third Day, and pastor and author Max Lucado. Phyllis Tickle, contributing religious editor for *Publishers Weekly*, said, "This is surprising—a real blurring of the lines between the commercial and the sacred. And it's unfortunate, because it compromises both sides. We know that church and state are never supposed to meet, and I think it's also a bad idea for church and Wall

Street to be meeting like this."[60] Chevrolet refused to cancel the concert, and its spokesman, Tom Wilkinson, denied that Christianity was being singularly promoted, noting that the company had sponsored a variety of concerts, from country and jazz to gospel.[61] Chevrolet insisted it wasn't sending a message of exclusion, merely targeting the Christian consumer with this particular tour. Chevrolet spokesmen Steve Betz pointed out that research reveals that in twenty-six of the forty-four markets in the Southeast—where the tour was primarily focused—Bible study and devotional reading were the main leisure activities. "This is the Bible Belt," said Betz.[62]

Anti-Religion Dress Codes

The anti-religious bias in the private sector even extends to dress codes. Western Newspapers, Inc., of Prescott Valley, Arizona, prohibited one of its employees from wearing "offensive" clothing. What was offensive? Two polo shirts with small embroidered religious symbols, one a fish reading "Jesus" and the other an American Bald Eagle reading, "Isaiah 40:31."[63]

In another such example, Cindy Dunn of Springville, Alabama, filed a lawsuit for religious discrimination against a Target store in Trussville, Alabama, alleging she was fired for refusing to remove or conceal a cross necklace to make it invisible to customers. Target denied the claim, saying that, "at Target, we respect and value the individuality of all team members and guests." But Dunn said that after she had been employed three months, store managers ordered her to tuck the necklace under her clothing because it was offensive to some. Dunn alleged that when she refused, her supervisor and a human resources manager tried to persuade her to comply. Thereafter, she said, managers began to harass and intimidate her with disciplinary actions. She said a store security employee revealed to her that he had been instructed to watch her more closely—apparently to catch her in mistakes—because the store "wanted her gone."[64]

In the next chapter we will see that the separationists are actively promoting secular values in the public square, just as they are in the education system. While celebrating "tolerance" and "diversity" as the highest virtues, the secular left displays rank intolerance toward Christians, their beliefs and values. The mounting evidence leads to the inescapable conclusion that secular forces are engaged in a war not to preserve a wall of separation, but rather to radically secularize our society.

chapter Nine

State Endorsement of Non-Christian Values and Hypocrisy in Our Culture

As we've seen, separationists object to the slightest scintilla of Christianity in the public sector (and the private sector). But they either overlook or actively encourage the state's endorsement of certain secular values they deem worthy, from the homosexual rights agenda to the precepts of radical feminism—including a woman's unfettered right to terminate her pregnancy—on to the promotion of anti-Christian obscenity masquerading as art. When the smoke from the often cacophonous debate that surrounds these assaults on culture dissipates, what remains is the bald conclusion that the object of the separationists' desire is not to preserve religious liberty by limiting government's involvement in "religion." Rather, it is to remove, piece by piece, every vestige of Christianity in our culture and replace it with values they deem preferable. Often, lofty allusions to "separation of church and state" are merely camouflage to mask their real agenda. Under their worldview and legal philosophy, there is no such thing as values neutrality. Their endgame is the wholesale substitution of secular values in the place of Christian norms, and their march toward that end is very much in progress.

Homosexual Agenda

Government-Sponsored Diversity Training

It is not just private corporations that send their employees to diversity training, as we saw in the last chapter. State governments have begun this practice as well, and it is just a tiny part of what state authorities are doing across the nation to promote a rather extreme homosexual agenda. The Minnesota Department of Corrections required its employees to attend training sessions called "Gays and Lesbians in the Workplace." Employees objecting to the program considered it little more than state-sponsored indoctrination designed to change their beliefs—mostly religious beliefs—about homosexuality. While private corporations are generally not subject to the constitutional prohibition against infringing on individuals' religious freedoms—though they are subject to other legal constraints in this area[1]—government offices and agencies are. In the Minnesota case, certain employees took their Bibles to the required sensitivity sessions and from time to time read silently from them, without interrupting the sessions in any way. Though they were never told to put the Bibles away, they were later reprimanded "for inappropriate and unprofessional conduct."

The employees, Thomas Altman and Ken Yackly, filed suit against the department for denying their free exercise, free speech, and equal protection rights. The federal trial judge held in 1999 that Altman and Yackly had stated a claim and could go to trial on the free exercise claim, but not on the others. The U.S. Court of Appeals reversed, holding that the matter could go to trial on all counts, rejecting the state's contention that the employees were guilty of insubordination. In the subsequent trial, the jury unanimously found in favor of Altman and Yackly and awarded them damages exceeding $78,000, $60,000 of which was in punitive damages. "Our clients never had an issue with the desire of the employer to ensure that co-workers treat each other with respect and dignity," said Francis J. Manion of the American Center for Law and Justice. "But when the state of Minnesota tried to force these employees to change their beliefs about homosexuality, the government crossed the line and violated their constitutional rights. The employees did nothing more than bring their Bibles to a training session with which they disagreed, and they were punished for it."[2]

The Health Departments of a number of states have permitted the distribution of a Christian-based pamphlet along with many other materials on the subject of AIDS and HIV, thereby sending the ACLU into a tizzy. The Florida Department of Health printed its logo on the cover of the pamphlet "A Christian Response to AIDS" and provided it to community organizations, together with other AIDS education materials approved by the state. The brochure contained biblically oriented content, asking such questions as: "How would Jesus respond to a person with HIV or AIDS?" In some cases, state money was used to purchase the pamphlets. Florida ACLU Director Howard Simon sent a letter to the Health Department, asking that it stop buying and circulating the pamphlets. "While the state must respond to this public health crisis and find ways to stop the spread of the AIDS virus," wrote Simon, "the state must base its message on ... medical and scientific information, rather than advocate a particular Christian set of beliefs. Sectarian messages are inappropriate for agencies of the state."

Simon's use of the word *advocate* is interesting. While some state funds were used to purchase the pamphlets, this was just "one of hundreds" the Florida Health Department approved for community groups and local health departments, according to Tom Liberti, the head of the Health Department's HIV/AIDS Bureau. This raises the question of whether there must be, as the separationists seem to "advocate," a complete cleansing of religious influences from the public sector. What if empirical evidence could be adduced to show that the Christian approach works better than some of the secular ones? Does the state have such a compelling interest in sanitizing Christian influences from its materials that it must conceal beneficial information from the public?[3]

Thought Control over Foster Parents

Under the kind of bill that one would hope could pop up only in California, state legislators approved a measure in August 2002, AB 2651, that would have allowed a teenage boy to report his foster parents for a civil-rights violation if they refused to let him dress like a girl. It is true that the legislation was ultimately vetoed by Governor Gray Davis after intense pressure from lobbying groups,[4] but the fact that such a proposal could get so close to becoming law shows the vast power of the homosexual activists. Indeed, the bill's opponents believe the only reason it didn't pass this time was that Governor Davis was in a very tight race for governor and didn't want to risk his re-election. Under the bill, California counties would be encouraged to provide sensitivity training for foster parents on "sexual orientation, gender identity, and the challenges faced by gay, lesbian, bisexual, or transgender youth, or youth with gender issues." Though the bill didn't strictly require foster parents to participate in the training program, the Campaign for California Families was convinced the law would have pressured foster parents into the training because those who declined would have been less likely to receive foster children in their homes. It is no secret that openly Christian foster parents in California have already been complaining about being blacklisted for their support of spanking and their moral opposition to homosexuality.

In addition, the bill would have required the California Department of Social Services to target for recruitment "gay, lesbian, bisexual, or transgender foster parents" and would have prohibited the state from denying placement to foster parents based on their HIV or AIDS status. The bill also would have established a toll-free telephone number that social workers would provide to foster children, encouraging them to report physical, sexual, or emotional abuse, "regardless of whether the abuse is specifically related to his or her sexual orientation or gender identity."

Absent from the discussion leading up to the California Assembly's passage of the bill were objections from such First Amendment watchdog groups as the ACLU or Americans United for Separation of Church and State. This bill undeniably would have forcibly imposed "religious" or anti-religious values on the California foster system and on foster parents. Parents seeking to raise children in accordance with a biblical model could clearly have been precluded from doing so under this bill. The bill "was a bold-faced attack on religious freedom," said Verne Teyler, executive director of Hosanna Homes, a private foster care agency.[5]

Proponents of homosexual rights often assert they do not seek special rights and don't want to infringe on the rights of others. But this bill would have infringed on the rights of people with Judeo-Christian standards and would have amounted to the state's sanctioning lifestyles it has historically considered taboo. The bill's own author, Assemblywoman Judy Chu, virtually conceded that the measure was values-oriented when she said, "Foster youth should not be . . . told that they are wrong for being who they are."[6]

Chu was not to be denied in her efforts to impose her extremism on California foster parents. In 2003, she sponsored a somewhat different version of the bill, AB 458, and it passed the assembly on May 12, 2003. Like the earlier bill, AB 458 would require foster parents to support homosexual, bisexual, and transsexual behavior and expression among foster children. It would go further than AB 2651, in that it would require mandatory training of foster parents to indoctrinate them to support homosexual behavior of foster children.[7] It would also require foster parent agencies to support homosexuals, bisexuals, and transsexuals as foster parents. And it would bar foster parents from discriminating against children under their care on the basis of sexual orientation or gender identity. This could mean that foster parents could not teach their foster children that homosexual behavior was wrong, even if their religious beliefs compelled them to do so, without violating the law against discrimination.

California is unfortunately not the only state that has dealt with the issue of the homosexuality of foster parents, as gay-inspired aggression against Larry Phillips of Missouri demonstrates. Phillips, who was a social worker at the Kansas City office of the Missouri Division of Family Services, said that his supervisor—who described himself as an "in–your-face queer who gets angrier every day"[8]—told him that he "was being intolerant" and that his religious beliefs "were affecting his ability to perform his job effectively." Why? One reason was that Phillips questioned the placement of a child with a lesbian foster parent, another was that he took a stand opposing a sexually explicit brochure that his supervisor required all his subordinates to carry and distribute to foster children. The brochure was called "What They Won't Teach You in School" and contained this sentence: "Sex can be a lot of things, women with women, men have sex with men, women have sex with men—and sometimes the best sex is with yourself."[9] "This was one sick piece of literature they were passing out, with sick drawings and language, including [profanity], that would get a radio station's license revoked if read over the air," said Phillips. He also said he was verbally assaulted, harassed, mocked, and then fired.[10] Phillips sued the state of Missouri for wrongful termination and a jury awarded him $86,000 in damages and attorney fees, finding that the Missouri Department of Social Services discriminated against him.

Codifying Transsexuality as a Protected Behavior

The political march of the homosexual lobby to legitimize formally homosexual behaviors continues unabated. On January 27, 2003, California assemblyman Mark Leno (D-San Francisco) introduced a bill, AB 196, to broaden the scope of sex discrimination under California's Fair Employment and Housing Act (FEHA). The current anti-discrimination law prohibits housing and workplace discrimination based on race, religious creed, color, national origin, ancestry, physical disability, mental disability, medical condition, marital status, sex, or sexual orientation. Since "sexual orientation" is defined as heterosexuality, homosexuality, and bisexuality, the law already prevents discrimination based on those behaviors—as it reportedly does in twelve other states. But the proposed bill is designed to widen the protective net to include transsexuality and cross-dressing by adding "gender" as a protected class. (Webster's defines "transsexual" as a person with a psychological urge to belong to the opposite sex, a desire that may be carried to the point of undergoing surgery to modify the sex organs to mimic those of the opposite sex.) Under the proposed bill, "gender" is defined as "the employee's actual sex or the employer's perception of the employee's identity, appearance, or behavior, even if these characteristics differ from those traditionally associated with the employee's sex at birth."

The bill would require employers to allow employees to dress or appear consistently with the employee's gender—as newly defined.[11] In other words, it would force employers to permit males to dress like women and vice versa and preclude business owners from enforcing their own moral standards if they disapprove of such behavior. Assemblyman John Campbell of Irvine noted several problems that attend this floating definition of gender. "This [bill] talks about 'gender,'" said Campbell, "but in the concept of the individual's perception of their gender, thereby making that protected class something that can change, can come in and out, can go back and forth, and is not identifiable through any physical attribute. This bill will cause untold lawsuits, untold new problems in the workplace, and further denies the right of businesses to earn your patronage."[12] The bill mandates fines of up to $150,000 against business owners, including nonprofits such as the Boy Scouts and Bible bookstores, for refusing to hire cross-dressing and transsexual job applicants. The law, according to Geoffrey Kors, executive director of the California Alliance for Pride and Equality, "will provide critical protections for those who are fired, evicted, or experience serious harassment because they are perceived as gender nonconforming."[13]

Assemblyman Dennis Mountjoy, in speaking out against the bill, said, "If I have a Christian bookstore, how could I possibly follow this law? How could I possibly have an employee that's here today in a dress, tomorrow may come in a suit, and then stay in a dress? How can I possibly employ this employee and still have the Christian bookstore and live by my faith?" Temecula Assemblyman Ray Haynes put it in starker terms. "You are messing with people's perception of their souls and their afterlife," he said. "You are telling people who sincerely and strongly believe in a faith that they cannot exercise that faith without being forced into bankruptcy or not owning property or not starting a business! You are imposing your belief on what you think their faith ought to say." On April 21, 2003, the California Assembly passed AB 196 by a vote of 41-34, which was the exact minimum vote required to advance the bill to the state Senate. No Republicans voted for the measure and all but seven Democrats voted yes, with three voting no and four abstaining.[14] While the state of California may be ahead of the curve in measures that contradict traditional values, the city of San Francisco will not be outdone in the race for the bottom. In 2001, the city adopted a policy allowing city employees to obtain sex-change operations at taxpayers' expense.[15]

"Tremendous Violence"

One morning in November 2002, three homosexual Catholic activists refused to leave the Hyatt Regency in Washington, D.C., despite repeated requests from hotel management and the metropolitan police, until a bishop served them the Eucharist. The D.C. police arrested them. The night before, a priest denied the three—Karen Speltz, Ken Einhaus, and Mike Perez—Communion during the Washington meeting of the U.S. Catholic bishops at a Mass at Washington's National Shrine of the Immaculate Conception. The next morning the three stationed themselves by escalators they knew a number of bishops would use, and the two men knelt with their hands outstretched. The activists said they had been emotionally shattered and had gone to the hotel to "find healing among the people who caused [us] so much suffering."[16] Later, Susan Gibbs, a Washington archdiocesan spokeswoman, said the refusal of Communion was a result of mistaken identity. Shrine officials thought the three were members of "Rainbow Sash," a pro-homosexual group committed to politicizing the Eucharist ritual. As it turns out, they were members of a different homosexual group, "Soulforce," which is an ecumenical organization that works to change church policies and doctrine concerning the treatment of homosexual, bisexual, and transgendered Christians (so-called). The priest, Michael Bugarin, said he wouldn't have denied them Communion had he known they were with Soulforce, but had an obligation to refuse them when he thought they were part of Rainbow Sash in order to "hold up the dignity and belief that we have in the Eucharist." "I regret that there was a misunderstanding on my part, and I regret the whole situation," said Bugarin.[17]

The most interesting part of this saga occurred in court on January 30, 2003, where Judge Mildred M. Edwards, after a two-day trial, found the three activists guilty of unlawful entry for refusing to leave the hotel. She told the defendants that, with her, they had one-twelfth of the perfect jury, since thirty years earlier she had assisted in the defense of Catholic anti-war activists Philip Berrigan and Elizabeth McAllister while she was a Georgetown University law student. She proved her "perfection" by suspending the imposition of their sentences—the first time in her fifteen years on the bench—and apologized on behalf of the Roman Catholic Church over the Communion incident. The judge then said, "Tremendous violence was done to you, who are the body of Christ, and the body of Christ was denied to you." She added, "As a member of your church, I ask you to forgive the church." Then, at the conclusion of her sentencing, Judge Edwards, adopting priestly vernacular, told the defendants to "Go in peace."

This story is significant for at least two reasons. First, the judge's outspoken affirmation of support for the homosexual activists from the bench shows that politically correct thinking has infiltrated our judicial institutions. Second, the judge clearly and openly intermixed her personal faith with her administration of justice. In the words of separationists, she crossed the line of mixing church and state. But as far as I could tell, there have been no cries of protest from the ACLU or from Americans United for Separation of Church and State. Perhaps to some separationists the mixture of church and state is permissible, even desirable, in furtherance of certain politically correct causes.

Diversity Sticker

In some cases, local governments affirmatively endorse the homosexual lifestyle and try to impose acceptance of it forcibly on their employees. Traverse City, Michigan, inaugurated a "diversity" sticker campaign in which it placed on city vehicles stickers that were modeled after the rainbow flag homosexuals use to celebrate their lifestyle. Over the rainbow stripes was the message, "We are Traverse City." The campaign was ostensibly in reaction to a number of race- and sexual orientation-motivated crimes and was aimed at unifying the city. It did the opposite, as citizens bombarded the city with complaints over the campaign. American Family Association president Gary Glenn said, "Homosexual activists' allies on the city commission have quickly moved from preaching tolerance of homosexual activity to forcing city police officers to display the official flag of 'gay pride' militants." One Traverse City policeman, David Leach, a thirty-year veteran, registered his strenuous objection to the campaign during an interview with a local Christian radio station. He said he found it "offensive driving a vehicle proclaiming [the homosexual] lifestyle." He later told the Associated Press, "It is a sign of the homosexual, and it's on my patrol car."

When Leach helped organize local opposition to the stickers, the Traverse City Human Rights Commission initiated an investigation against him. Apparently no one told the city fathers, the police department, or the human rights commission that the city had no business subsidizing this campaign with taxpayer money or that it was improper to investigate an officer for exercising his freedoms of speech and religion. No one, that is, until the Thomas More Center for Law and Justice sent a letter to the city manager threatening a suit unless the city stopped the investigation "today." "Clearly, this is an effort to harass and intimidate Mr. Leach on account of his religious beliefs," said Thomas More's chief counsel, Richard Thompson. The city shortly thereafter discontinued the campaign and its investigation of Officer Leach. Certain citizens were so exercised about the incident that they formed a group called "Traverse City Citizens Voting Yes for Equal Rights Not Special Rights." Its goal was to circulate a petition aimed at placing a proposed charter amendment on the city's November 2001 ballot prohibiting the city "from adopting laws or policies that grant special 'minority' or 'protected class' status, hiring quotas, or other preferential treatment to individuals who engage in homosexual behavior." The group said such policies necessarily result in discrimination against citizens who oppose the homosexual lifestyle.[18]

The Clash of Homosexual Rights with Religious Freedom

It is a mistake to view some of these changes in the law expanding homosexual rights in a vacuum, because they often come at the expense of religious freedom. A case involving a Christian doctor and a lesbian makes the point. Guadalupe Benitez of San Diego wanted to have a baby, but faced two immediate obstacles. She is a lesbian and had fertility problems. Her health care provider referred her to the North Coast Women's Care Medical Group (NCWMG), reportedly the only OB-GYN provider under her health plan. Her assigned physician, Dr. Christine Brody, told Benitez she would be willing to treat her in the early phases, but would not artificially inseminate her because of the doctor's religious convictions. Brody allegedly assured Benitez that other doctors in the group could assist her.

After treating her for eleven months, Dr. Brody and her colleague Dr. Douglas Fenton both refused to inseminate Benitez, which she claims forced her to seek treatment outside the plan. Benitez filed a lawsuit against NCWMG under the California civil rights statute that forbids businesses to discriminate on the basis of sexual orientation. She sought to recover her out-of-pocket medical expenses and compensation for the trauma she experienced as a result of being "dumped" by the doctors because of her homosexuality. NCWMG responded that the doctors' constitutional right to free exercise of religion under the First and Fourteenth Amendments trumped Benitez's statutory right and thus barred the suit.[19] The stage was set for a classic confrontation of these conflicting rights, but the trial court didn't address the issue, dismissing the action for other reasons. The California Court of Appeals, however, reversed the trial court and ordered that the matter could proceed to trial.

It is yet to be seen whether the Benitez case will go to trial and whether the defendants will assert their free exercise rights as a defense. But eventually courts are going to be called on to determine whether a state government has a compelling interest in preventing discrimination on the basis of sexual orientation sufficient to overcome the free exercise rights of the person being accused of discriminating. Are we approaching the point where Christian doctors will be forced to act against their religious convictions? What about tolerance for the beliefs of Christian doctors—or is tolerance, in such cases, only a one-way street? The question for the gay rights movement is whether it is tolerance they *seek* or conformity to their worldview they *demand*.

Truth in Love

Christians who express the view that homosexual behavior is sinful often find their religious freedom under assault. In 1998, a group of pro-family ministries printed a series of full-page ads called "Truth in Love" in newspapers throughout the United States. The ads referred to scriptural admonitions against homosexuality and included overtures to homosexuals to seek forgiveness and freedom through Jesus Christ. The ads also contained information regarding the adverse health consequences that could result from the homosexual lifestyle. The San Francisco Board of Supervisors was outraged at the ad and sent a letter to its sponsors condemning it as "hateful rhetoric." The supervisors argued that "there is a direct correlation" between hate crimes against homosexuals and the religious message communicated in the ad. The board also passed resolutions linking hate crimes and the murder of homosexuals to the "anti-gay" ads. When the board went further and lobbied local television stations not to broadcast ad campaigns centered on "converting" homosexuals, the American Family Association's Center for Law and Policy filed a federal lawsuit on behalf of the ad's sponsors. In the suit, the plaintiffs alleged that by officially opposing the religious message, the city and county were violating their First Amendment rights under the Establishment Clause and the free exercise clause.

A three-judge panel for the Ninth Circuit Court of Appeals held that the authorities had not violated the plaintiffs' free exercise rights, because they passed no laws inhibiting religious expression; they merely lobbied against the plaintiffs. As to the Establishment Clause claim, the court conceded that "official disapproval or hostility toward religion" can amount to an unconstitutional endorsement of religion. Nonetheless, it ruled against the plaintiffs in this particular case, saying the board also had a secular purpose in opposing the plaintiffs' religious views, namely, to protect homosexuals from violence. The court found the city's opposition to the plaintiffs' religious views was "only incidental and ancillary." But this was disingenuous at best, as dissenting Judge John T. Noonan made clear when he wrote that it is "difficult to think of a more direct attack" on a group's religious views than occurred in this case. The plaintiffs' chief attorney Stephen Crampton also noted that the decision "would mean that as long as a city threw in a plausible secular purpose for its actions, it could trample the free exercise of religious rights of Christians."[20]

Hate Crime Legislation–Federal and State

The federal government and many states have hate crime legislation on the books, which ramps up criminal penalties in crimes of violence when hatred of a protected group is part of the perpetrator's motive. While hate crime legislation is arguably well meaning, it has the effect of criminalizing thought, because the person is punished differently depending on whether his intended violence results from prejudice against a certain group. The laws are also suspect because they make arbitrary distinctions that lead to inequitable results. Why should a person who assaults a homosexual, for example, be subject to greater punishment than one who attacks a defenseless grandmother? Are grandmothers not entitled to equal protection of the laws?

Federal hate crimes legislation has been on the books since 1968, covering attacks based on race, religion, or national origin. Homosexual activists have been frantically lobbying the federal government to add homosexuals to the list of victims protected by the law. In 2003, Democratic Senator Tom Daschle introduced the Equal Dignity for Americans Act of 2003 (S 16) in the Senate, which would add sexual orientation, disability, and gender as protected categories under the hate crimes law. The bill would also impose "sexual orientation" provisions on workplace discrimination law, to the effect that federal employers with fifteen or more employees could not discriminate on the basis of sexual orientation.[21]

The state of Pennsylvania added a new twist to the hate-crime concept when Governor Mark Schweiker, on December 3, 2002, signed into law a bill that provided homosexuals legal protection from verbal harassment as well as hate crimes. Christian leaders expressed concern that the bill could be interpreted and enforced so broadly as to suppress the speech of pastors and preachers who may quote biblical passages condemning homosexuality.[22] Some may think such a scenario is far-fetched, but is it? The problem is that one of the underlying crimes in the statute that would trigger more severe criminal penalties is "harassment by communication." Traditionally, this "crime" has dealt with crank phone calls or threatening mail, but Christian opponents of the measure fear that this "crime" could be stretched to include the mere expression of opinions disapproving of homosexuality. While this may be a long shot, it remains a possibility, as even the *Pittsburgh Post-Gazette* acknowledged in an editorial on the subject.[23]

The Bible: Bigoted and Mean-Spirited

Biblical principles are clashing more and more with politically correct doctrine, which often judges them unacceptably offensive and intolerant. New York City's Administrative Code prohibits "bias-related violence or harassment" against homosexuals and other groups, and goes further by creating a city agency to "eliminate and prevent discrimination from playing any role in actions relating to employment, public accommodations, and housing and other real estate, and to take other actions against prejudice, intolerance, bigotry, discrimination, and bias-related violence or harassment." One feisty local pastor decided to challenge this assault on religious freedom and freedom of speech. Reverend Kristopher Okwedy of Keyword Ministries purchased advertising space for two eight-by sixteen-foot billboards in Staten Island Borough to display four separate versions of Leviticus 18:22, a Bible verse prohibiting homosexual practices. The top of the billboard begins with "Word on the street; 4 ways to say Leviticus 18:22," and the four versions are under it. One of the versions, the New International Version, reads: "Do not lie with a man as one lies with a woman; that is detestable." At the bottom it says "I AM YOUR CREATOR." The minister placed the billboards near communities inhabited by many homosexuals. The city agency ordered the removal of the billboards under the anti-harassment ordinance.

Reverend Okwedy contested the ordinance and sued Staten Island Borough and borough president Guy Molinari. Molinari, representing the borough, wrote a letter to PNE Media, the owner of the billboards, urging it to contact the city attorney and chairman of the Anti-Bias Task Force, Daniel Master, concerning the billboard. In the letter, Molinari referred to the quoted verse as one "commonly invoked as a biblical prohibition against homosexuality. Many members of the Staten Island community," wrote Molinari, "myself included, find this message unnecessarily confrontational and offensive. As borough president of Staten Island, I want to inform you that this message conveys an atmosphere of intolerance which is not welcome in our borough." Molinari also reportedly publicly condemned the language in the displayed verse as "mean-spirited" and "hate speech."[24]

In a motion to dismiss Okwedy's lawsuit before a federal judge in Brooklyn, the attorney for the city, Dana Biberman, actually argued (and thus admitted) that New York City's anti-bias policy prohibits any public expressions of intolerance toward homosexuality. "Plaintiff's billboard," said Biberman, "through using biblical quotes, expressed open hostility and intolerance of homosexuality... Whether these were quotes from the Bible or not, they were nonetheless... unnecessarily confrontational and offensive, [and] didn't belong in Staten Island."[25] The trial court granted the defendants' motion to dismiss. Pastor Okwedy appealed the ruling to the Second Circuit Court of Appeals.

A Double Standard

As we can see, in modern America it is taboo to disparage or ridicule any group or to do anything that the most hypersensitive might find offensive. Yet that prohibition does not seem to apply to protect Christians or Christianity. It just depends on whose ox (or pig) is being gored. A billboard in Pensacola, Florida, depicting Jesus Christ with an orange slice above his head instead of a halo, paired with the caption "Jesus was the prince of peas," is a good example. The billboard, ostensibly promoting vegetarianism, was rented by People for the Ethical Treatment of Animals (PETA) and was erected to coincide with Passover and Easter. Bruce Friedrich, of PETA, admitted the sign was intended to convey the message that people who eat meat are engaging in cruelty to animals.[26]

PETA placed a similar sign—this one thirty-six feet wide—on

Interstate 40 near Wilmington, North Carolina. The sign says, "He died for your sins. Go vegetarian." The words of the sign are right next to a twelve-foot-tall picture of a squinty-eyed pig, which many Christians found particularly offensive. Many also objected to the erroneous implication that Jesus was a vegetarian, saying that he was a meat eater. Few complaints were heard from those who are generally so quick to cry foul at such displays of insensitivity toward sacred figures or symbols of other religions or belief systems.[27]

Indeed, while separationists strongly object to any utterance or symbol that could remotely offend non-Christians, they fail to show a similar sensitivity to Christians. Shortly after Congress passed a resolution urging the president to issue a proclamation "designating a day for humility, prayer, and fasting for all people of the United States," opponents were upset. The Freedom from Religion Foundation opposed the resolution, for example, and in its press release made no effort to temper its remarks toward Christians, referring to their belief system as "primitive." According to the statement, "The resolution is full of references to 'God,' as if belief in one is unanimous. It is insufferable ego to imagine that, if there were a god, it would respond to these demeaning supplications. It is primitive to imagine that the natural laws of the universe could be suspended or altered by group wishful thinking. Ironically, as Congress entertains these meaningless motions, the Iraqi peoples and their supporters are praying to their god for the opposite results!"[28]

Radical Feminism Yes, Christianity No

Mandatory Contraceptives Coverage

The District of Columbia passed an ordinance in July 2000 that required all health insurance plans covering the cost of prescription drugs to include coverage for the cost of contraceptives. Contraceptives would include intrauterine devices and morning-after pills, which effectively abort embryos. Unlike similar legislation in several states, the D.C. bill did not include a "conscience clause" exempting religious employers, such as Catholic and Georgetown Universities, the Archdiocese of Washington, Providence Hospital, and the U.S. Catholic Conference. During the debates, Councilman Vincent B. Orange, who was advocating the inclusion of a conscience clause, urged the council "not to belittle established church doctrine." "This is an issue of the Bill of Rights, an issue of freedom of religion," he said. "We are trying to tell an organization to violate its own convictions." Jesuit Father Leo J. O'Donovan, president of Georgetown University, said that the measure "would require Georgetown and many other Catholic organizations to violate the consistent teachings of the Catholic Church. I believe it would be profoundly wrong, and quite likely unconstitutional, to ask Georgetown and other Catholic institutions to do this." But a homosexual councilman in support of the bill without a conscience clause stated, "I am very concerned about having religious principles impact public health policy. Are we going to say we are going to defer to Rome in terms of our views?"[29]

More recently, in January 2003, the state of New York passed a similar law, the Women's Health and Wellness Act, requiring schools and other institutions to include coverage for the cost of contraceptives in their employee health insurance policies. Certain Catholic and Baptist groups filed a lawsuit challenging the measure and strongly urged that at the very least a full religious exemption be added to the law. "The state is putting itself in the position of determining what is Catholic and what is not Catholic, and we think that's a clear entanglement of government into religious affairs," said Dennis Poust, spokesman for the New York State Catholic Conference.

While the law does include a limited religious exemption that covers churches themselves, Poust said the measure "was very clearly drawn to eliminate Catholic hospitals and nursing homes and Catholic charitable agencies—social service agencies—and to eliminate schools and universities.... All of the ministries of the Church, in effect, have been excluded and deemed to be not Catholic by the state of New York." Poust added that he anticipated that in the future the same political groups may push through a bill establishing mandatory coverage for elective abortions. "[Pro-abortion forces are] trying to get it to the point where the Church cannot remain in the business of providing health and human services. Get us out of the way because we're bad for business for Planned Parenthood," said Poust.

Planned Parenthood fired back, saying they were "troubled that Catholic social service groups, which are staffed by committed women of many faiths and serve diverse communities, would rather impose their own religious doctrine than defend equitable healthcare insurance.... Even if the lawsuit ultimately fails, this action creates a cloud of anxiety for the thousands of people employed by Catholic-affiliated services—not to mention the publics that are dependent on these services."[30] There you have it: The religious beliefs of Catholic employers are to be accorded no weight in this age of unlimited tolerance.

The Pro-Life Taboo

While Christian expression is in disfavor in certain circles, so are views grounded in Christian principles, such as pro-life advocacy. And this manifests itself in contexts other than opposition to judicial and executive branch nominees who are pro-life. Donald J. Grant, a medical ultrasound technician in Minnesota, has sued his employer, Fairview Health Services of Minneapolis, for failing to accommodate his religious beliefs as required by the 1964 Civil Rights Act. The action is based on Grant's termination after he allegedly encouraged a patient not to seek an abortion and offered to have a pastor contact her. This was the first time in his fourteen years as an ultrasound technician that Grant had ever counseled a patient on abortion. He agreed not to counsel patients on the subject in the future if the hospital would refrain from disclosing the patient's intent to have an abortion on the intake forms. Presumably, his conscience wouldn't permit him to remain silent if he were aware of the impending procedure. But instead of accommodating him, said his attorney Mathew D. Staver of Liberty Counsel, the company terminated him just two days after the incident.[31]

For four years running, pro-life activists Mark Gabriel and Michael O'Hare peacefully demonstrated on the public sidewalk outside an abortion clinic owned by Planned Parenthood in Grand Chute, Wisconsin. The signs they carried neither blocked the sidewalk nor obstructed traffic, and they have been an important part of carrying their message to the public. The city cited Gabriel for violating a city ordinance prohibiting signs from public rights of way, and he was jailed for refusing in protest to pay the fine. After repeated threats of further tickets and fines, the men decided to file a suit against the city for using an unconstitutional ordinance to encroach on their liberties. As their attorney, Liberty Counsel's Mathew D. Staver, put it, "From the time of the founding of this country, the parks, streets, and sidewalks have been places where free speech has been allowed to thrive and survive. Clearly this ordinance is unconstitutional.[32]... Our clients were lawfully and peacefully picketing and they should have the right to continue to do so without harassment and interference. The Constitution protects their right to peacefully picket."[33]

City ordinances are not the only weapons used by pro-abortion forces to suppress pro-life dissenters. In certain cases they have also invoked the federal Racketeer Influenced and Corrupt Organizations Act (RICO), aimed at organized crime and drug dealers. In October 2001, the United States Seventh Circuit Court of Appeals held that the law could be used against pro-life protestors. The Supreme Court, in *Scheidler v. National Organization for Women, Inc.,* reversed the Seventh Circuit, saying that for RICO to apply, the defendants must have been shown to have committed extortion against the abortion clinics as a "predicate act." But the protestors could not have been guilty of extortion when they extracted no property from the clinics. As Justice Rehnquist stated in his majority opinion, "But even when their acts of interference and disruption achieved their ultimate goal of 'shutting down' a clinic that performed abortions, such acts did not constitute extortion because petitioners did not 'obtain' respondents' property. Petitioners may have deprived or sought to deprive respondents of their alleged property right of exclusive control of their business assets, but they did not acquire any such property. Petitioners neither pursued nor received 'something of value from' respondents that they could exercise, transfer, or sell."[34]

"The real story here," said Catholic League president William Donohue, "is the extraordinary disrespect that the so-called champions of liberty have for free speech. The National Organization for Women . . . has proven beyond a doubt that it would use any law available as a weapon to beat down pro-life protestors."[35]

Silencing Abstinence

Christians also are criticized and sometimes pressured to keep silent when they advocate abstinence before marriage. The 2002 Miss America, Erika Harold, a devout Christian, made her views supporting abstinence well known when she promoted the cause to teenage girls in her home state of Illinois. Indeed, she won the Miss Illinois contest in June 2002 on a platform of "Teenage Sexual Abstinence: Respect Yourself, Protect Yourself." But Miss America pageant officials pressured her not to talk publicly about her views.[36] At a press conference at the National Press Club in Washington, D.C., when officials tried to keep reporters from asking Miss Harold about her abstinence message, she said, "I will not be bullied. I've gone through enough adversity in my life to stand up for what I believe in." Officials had instructed her to talk only about youth violence prevention. "They laid it on her coming over here" not to promote teen chastity, said one of her friends. "She's furious about it."[37]

Sandy Rios, the president of Concerned Women for America, said the efforts to muzzle Harold constituted "blatant censorship that betrays religious bigotry among pageant officials. . . . In an age when beauty queens are regularly disqualified for inappropriate behavior, who would have thought that a virtuous one would be silenced for virtue?" A day later, Harold announced that she had won her battle with pageant officials and would be permitted to talk about abstinence. "I don't think the pageant officials really understood how much I am identified with the abstinence message," said Harold. "If I don't speak about it now as Miss America, I will be disappointing the thousands of young people throughout Illinois who need assurance that waiting until marriage for sex is the right thing to do."[38]

Anti-Christian Art

"Choice on Earth"

While our politically correct culture is quick to denounce anyone who shows the slightest insensitivity to homosexuals and most other groups, Christians again receive no such respect. In fact, the culture revels in anti-Christian art and theater, and in various other ways disrespects Christianity and the things it holds sacred. For eight years, during the Christmas season, Planned Parenthood has been promoting "Choice on Earth" Christmas cards, adapted from the biblical text "Peace on Earth." The phrase is derived from Luke 2:13–14, "And suddenly there was with the angel a multitude of the heavenly host praising God and saying, Glory to God in the highest, and on earth peace, good will toward men." Pro-life advocates argue that the Christmas message was being degraded into "Abortion on Earth."

Jim Sedlak, of STOPP International, a project of American Life League, said, "What 'choice on Earth' really means is 'abortion on Earth.' In the season that celebrates the birth of Jesus, it is absolutely outrageous to have cards celebrating the death of babies."[39] For the 2002 Christmas season, Planned Parenthood decided to expand the use of the logo by affixing it to T-shirts as well. Sedlak denounced the move. "Instead of apologizing to Christians for distorting a scripture verse referring to the Prince of Peace, Jesus Christ, Planned Parenthood president Gloria Feldt has decided to use this offensive message to sell merchandise."[40]

Jesus: Pro-Choice?

In this vein, Reverend Mark Bigelow, a clergy advisor for Planned Parenthood, wrote a letter on November 22, 2002, to Bill O'Reilly, host of Fox News Network's "The O'Reilly Factor." "Even as a minister," said Bigelow, " I am careful what I presume Jesus would do if he were alive today, but one thing I know from the Bible is that Jesus was not against women having a choice in continuing a pregnancy. Jesus was for peace on earth, justice on earth, compassion on earth, mercy on earth, and choice on earth."

Ed Szymkowiak, national director of STOPP International, called Bigelow's comments "blasphemous." He said, "I defy either Planned Parenthood president Gloria Feldt or her clergy advisory board member, Reverend Mark Bigelow, to cite chapter and verse to support Rev. Bigelow's perverse claim that the Bible indicates 'that Jesus was not against women having a choice in continuing a pregnancy.' Planned Parenthood has publicly indicated its religion is 'choice' and its sacrament is abortion."[41] Amazingly, Planned Parenthood receives millions of dollars in government funding, having taken from taxpayers some thirty percent of its $202.7 million income in 2001.[42]

"Christianity Can Be Dangerous"

So, while some say Christianity is pro-choice, others, such as the magic-comedy team of Penn & Teller, say it is something to fear. Such was the message the act delivered during their offering of an X-rated parody of Christ's crucifixion, to the horror of many of the spectators at the World Magic Seminar, a magician's convention in Las Vegas. In the skit Teller was in costume as Christ and was on a full-sized cross that was wheeled into the room on a cart. A midget in an angel costume simulated an obscene sexual act on Teller, who was almost nude. Then Penn, dressed as a Roman gladiator, pulled away what was supposed to be the "Shroud of Turin" covering the cross. Some attendees were so shocked they walked out of the performance. Rick Neiswonger, a veteran magician turned market executive, said the stunt offended "the majority" of the four hundred people present. He told the *Las Vegas Review*, "They [the organizers] warned everybody that something offensive was going to happen, but my God, where do you draw the line. . . . This was beyond bad taste." A magician called the Amazing Jonathan disagreed, explaining, "This was performance art. I know that Penn is a practicing atheist, and I agree with him that Christianity can be dangerous. Look at the Trade Center. That was done in the name of religion."[43] Despite the controversy, ABC invited Penn & Teller to perform on its Super Bowl show.[44]

"Yo Mama's Last Supper"

Our popular culture is often anti-Christian, and the government itself (at all levels) sometimes gets in the act—with total disregard for the usual hypersensitivity to church/state involvement. The Brooklyn Museum, for example, is no stranger to controversy involving anti-Christian expression. In 2001, it placed on display a "work of art" known as "Yo Mama's Last Supper," a color photograph by Renee Cox, a Jamaican-born Roman Catholic, depicting twelve black men and a nude woman at Christ's Last Supper. Cox posed as the woman, who was intended to represent Jesus Christ, and explained that her photo "highlights legitimate criticisms of the church, including its refusal to ordain women as priests." New York Mayor Rudolph Giuliani found the work repugnant: "If you want to display viciousness, hatred, ignorance, and you want to display anti-Catholicism, racism, or anti-Semitism, then you go find a private museum that wants to pay for this or a private sponsor."[45] Giuliani also told reporters that "if it were done against another group there would be an outcry in this city that would demand that they take the photograph down, but anti-Catholicism is just accepted prejudice, it is allowed in the city and in our society."[46]

"A World that Was Very Much Accepting"

In 1999, New York's Whitney Museum of American Art, supported by the National Endowment for the Arts (NEA), was displaying the notorious "Piss Christ" by Andres Serrano, a close-up photograph of a crucifix submerged in a vat of Serrano's urine. This gem had been around since around 1989. Liberals had no objection to Serrano earning a federal grant with this vulgar work, and, of course, Serrano, ever the professional, was incredulous that people deemed "Piss Christ" offensive. "I didn't think it would be a controversial or outrageous thing to do. Since I'd been working along these lines for years without incident, I felt I was living in a world that was very much accepting what I was trying to do."[47] Serrano's enablers among the cultural elite saw nothing wrong or unduly offensive with his work either. They reserved their outrage for those, like Senator Jesse Helms, who campaigned to end federal funding for such nonsense. The elite culture had demonstrated similar insensitivity by refusing to register outrage at the late photographer Robert Mapplethorpe's federally funded exhibition celebrating homosexuality with depictions of a man urinating into the mouth of another and an artist posing with a bullwhip dangling from his posterior.

National Endowment for the Arts

Such disgusting displays and productions are hardly unusual for the NEA. The NEA gave a $31,500 grant to *The Watermelon Woman*, a "black history" film described by one reviewer as "the hottest dyke sex scene ever recorded on celluloid." It gave $36,500 to "The Dinner Party," a 140-foot triangle portraying the "imagined genitalia of thirty-nine historically important women, including Susan B. Anthony and Georgia O'Keefe." The NEA also made a handsome grant to "Highways," a Santa Monica performance center, "where genitalia and homoerotic exhibitionism are mainstays." This fine institution presented *Boys R Us*, which it promoted as "our continuing series of hot summer nights with hot fags," and *Not for Republicans*, which featured as one of its topics, "sex with Newt Gingrich's mom."[48]

Why is the NEA given a pass by the tolerance and diversity police? "No agency of the government has done more to insult the values of traditional Americans than has the NEA," observed Martin Mawyer, president of the Christian Action Network. Over the years, said Mawyer, "Christian Action Network has identified numerous NEA-supported works of art which mock religious values, highlight nudity and sexual perversion, glorify profanity, feature human mutilation, and celebrate sadomasochism and torture, to name only a few outrageous examples."[49] Why do the high priests of political correctness not intervene on behalf of Christians, whose faith is denigrated by these vulgar displays of insensitivity and intolerance? And why are these government-supported expressions of hostility to Christianity not challenged by the strict separationists? Perhaps it's not government sponsorship that they object to, but rather the sponsorship of Christian expression; the ugly truth is that government endorsement of anti-Christian norms and activities is wholeheartedly accepted.

Defiling the Virgin Mary

Even women cannot escape the wrath of the God-haters. In 1999, the Brooklyn Museum of Art was sponsoring the "Sensation" exhibition. Among the objectionable exhibits was one by Chris Ofili, which included a collage of a black Virgin Mary incorporating elephant dung.[50] That same year, New York Performance Works, a downtown New York theater, put on twelve performances of the play *'Tis a Pity She's a Whore*, which features incest, stabbing, and poisoning, and depicts the Virgin Mary as a prostitute. Wide Sky Theatre Company, in association with the New York Performance Alliance, produced the play, and postcards advertising the production contained an illustration of the Virgin Mary with the Immaculate Heart with the inscription "'Tis a Pity She's a Whore," written across her. Catholic League's William Donohue sternly criticized the play and its highly offensive advertisement, saying, "What the New York Performance Works has now done adds to the legacy of anti-Catholicism that marks this community.... The postcard illustration is worth noting: there is something about Our Blessed Mother that the depraved can't stomach."[51]

Corpus Christi

Many of the attacks on Christianity in art and theater are sponsored by homosexual forces, prompting one theater critic to ask, "Why is it that almost all the contemporary American plays that wrestle with religious issues are by and about gay folks?"[52] One logical explanation would be that homosexuals are determined to undermine the foundations of Christianity in order to legitimize their lifestyle. College campuses, in addition to offering classes and speech codes biased against Christianity, nourish this anti-Christian message by producing or sponsoring plays that are overtly disrespectful and even blasphemous.

The Gay and Lesbian Alliance Against Defamation (GLAAD), at its tenth annual awards ceremony in 1999, honored Paul Rudnick's anti-Christian play, *The Most Fabulous Story Ever Told* as the best Off-Off Broadway production. In the play, described as "Paul Rudnick's homosexual retelling of the Bible," God created Adam and Steve, a homosexual couple in the Garden of Eden, and Jane and Mabel, a lesbian couple. Not to be left out was the Virgin Mary, depicted as a lesbian. The Catholic League for Religious and Civil Rights described the play as a "routine homosexual play" that featured "full-frontal male nudity, filthy language, discussions of body parts, butch lesbians, effeminate gay men, ranting against nature, damning God for AIDS, etc." Said Catholic League president William Donohue, "I can only guess that the reason why this play captured the Off-Off Broadway award and *Corpus Christi* didn't win the Broadway and Off-Broadway award is because the boys managed to keep their pants on in the Terrence McNally play."[53]

Speaking of Terrence McNally's play, *Corpus Christi*, in 2001, three Indiana residents tried unsuccessfully to obtain an injunction to ban its performance at the Fort Wayne campus of Indiana University. Even one of the judges who refused to ban it described it as "notorious" and "blasphemous." It's no wonder. The play portrays Christ as a homosexual who engages in sexual behavior with his disciples. The residents challenging the play attempted to turn the separationists' argument back on them, contending the state, by publicly endorsing anti-Christian beliefs, was endorsing religion in violation of the First Amendment Establishment Clause. Though one of the Seventh Circuit Court of Appeals judges, in denying the claim, described it as "absurd," a dissenting judge thought it had merit.[54] Regardless of the legal issues, the fact remains that the play occurred and was condoned by the elite culture without a second thought given to the sensitivities of Christians. Indeed, to illustrate how out of touch our mainstream media is with Christian sensitivities, *Time* magazine, when *Corpus Christi* debuted, referred to it as a "serious, even reverent retelling of the Christ story in a modern idiom—quite close, in its way, to the original."[55]

Other anti-Christian, anti-Catholic plays recently produced by the homosexual community were *Burning Habits*, known as "an eight-part gay play" that attacks the Church, and *Jesus Christ, It's Your Birthday*, called "a gay play that promised to put the X back in Christmas."[56]

Seeking to Repress the Opposition

The example of *Corpus Christi* brings into focus the virulent bigotry, hostility, and hypocrisy of the anti-Christian forces in modern life. The homosexual lobby, for example, while demonstrating no sensitivity toward Christians, in stark contrast demands that its own tenets and lifestyle be treated as sacrosanct by society. At a 1998 conference sponsored by the Claremont Institute and the National Association for Research and Therapy of Homosexuality, experts considered the question of whether there is a genetic basis for homosexuality. The Los Angeles City Council passed a resolution condemning the meeting—just because the moral and medical arguments surrounding homosexuality were being considered. The council condemned the exercise as "defamation and demonization." In addition, the hotel where the meeting was scheduled to take place received harassing calls and death threats for the organizers of the conference. The hotel cancelled, and the group had to find another location.

The threats continued at the new hotel. A group of protestors pounded on cars entering the hotel garage parking facility, and three activists stood outside the meeting room screaming that the conferees were "murderers of gays," that they were responsible for Matthew Shepard's death, and they were as bad as the Ku Klux Klan. One writer commented on the striking difference between this kind of virulent reaction to criticism by the militant homosexual lobby and that of Christians in defending themselves against attack. Columnist Hadley Arkes wrote, "In truth, the campaigns of aggression and calumny are launched persistently from the other side. But when Catholics gather civilly across the street from Terrence McNally's *Corpus Christi* in New York—when they say the rosary and carry signs protesting against blasphemy—*they* are labeled as aggressors and tagged for the dark crime of censorship. This want of evenhandedness makes little impression on the media, and there is no outrage over the facts revealed again in Los Angeles: that the gay activists are seeking, overtly, to repress their opposition—to silence anyone who would call into question the homosexual life."[57]

Speaking of the media, in the next chapter we'll examine the role the mainstream media and Hollywood are playing in the war against Christianity. Their combined influence on our culture is profound and must not be overlooked by those who believe that Judeo-Christian values are vital foundations to our political liberties.

chapter ten

The Media and Hollywood Wars Against Christianity

IN THE DOCUMENTED BIAS AGAINST Christians and Christianity in our modern culture, Hollywood and Big Media play very major roles. Political correctness tells us that it is unthinkable to ridicule (almost any) group, but both of these major cultural power centers routinely disparage Christians and present them in a negative light. This anti-Christian bias manifests itself in unflattering portrayals of Christians in Hollywood films and entertainment television and also in the demonization of Christian conservatives in the media. Sometimes the Catholic Church is singled out for special ridicule, and the news media often bury stories concerning violence against Christians throughout the world. The media seem eager to portray Christians as unreasonable and violent, and to accentuate those exceptional cases in which they cross the line, such as when fanatics commit violent acts against abortionists, abortion clinics, or homosexuals. These extremists are depicted as prototypical Christians, while simultaneously, Hollywood and the media downplay the injustices and violent acts committed against Christians. In keeping with the requirements of political correctness, the media also cover up anti-Christian violence committed by militant Muslims.

Media Bias

We begin by documenting the record of anti-Christian bias in the news media, noting that, while the media are usually very careful not to offend or slight other religions, Christianity receives far less deference. In a *Washington Post* article published December 7, 1997, entitled, "A Convergence of Fixed and Shifting Holidays," reporter Bill Broadway presented a paragraph summary of the fundamental beliefs of the various religions celebrating holy days in December, from Buddhism to Shinto. A cursory review of the text reveals that the descriptions of all the religions except Christianity were mostly positive or, at worst, neutral. But Broadway described Christianity as having a "tortured early history," and the years following Jesus' crucifixion as a "time of power struggles and confused theology." He was also quick to emphasize that "such confusion persists today in Christianity's different branches." Yet nary a word is mentioned, for example, about the different sects of Islam, which are presented as having a uniform theology. Nor is there any discussion about Reformed or Observant Jews, or the splintered branches of other religions.[1]

To make matters worse, this article was reprinted in the Kidsbeat section of the *Providence Journal*, for all the children to read. This prompted one doctoral candidate in religious studies to submit a letter to the editor criticizing the shameless anti-Christian bias of the piece. Focusing on the article's depiction of Christianity as lacking consensus among its members, she said, "One must ask why nearly twenty percent of the world's population would believe something that rests on such flimsy grounds. I expect that this page will appear on bulletin boards in classrooms across America.... Today, the *Journal* has done much to contribute to religious intolerance in America."[2]

The media are also wont to disparage Christian conservatives, often using the pejorative "Religious Right" to taint them as intolerant, backwoods fanatics, and yet never labeling religious liberals, like Jesse Jackson, as the "religious left" or other leftists as "the anti-religious left." One of the most infamous examples of this is Michael Weisskopf's comment in the *Washington Post* concerning grass-roots

Christian activists. The "gospel lobby," said Weisskop, "does not lavish campaign funds on candidates for Congress, nor does it entertain them. The strength of fundamentalist leaders lies in their flocks. Corporations pay public relations firms millions of dollars to contrive the kind of grass-roots response that Falwell or Pat Robertson can galvanize in a televised sermon. Their followers are largely poor, uneducated, and easy to command."[3]

A "Staggering Double Standard"

Media elites may not be poor, but they often act in uneducated ways. On CBS's "Early Show" in June 2000, anchor Bryant Gumbel interviewed Robert Knight of the Family Research Council on the United States Supreme Court decision affirming the Boy Scout Association's constitutional right of association in denying the position of scout leadership to homosexuals. Gumbel, thinking the camera was off, was caught mouthing what appeared to be his judgment that Knight is a "f__ing idiot." CBS refused to apologize or admit any wrongdoing.[4] Its official response was: "A brief camera shot with no audio of Bryant getting up from his chair accidentally appeared on air. He was making a casual remark of some sort, but it is unclear what the comment was and in any case, it bears no relevance to the content of *The Early Show*." In an open letter to CBS demanding an apology, Brent Bozell of the Media Research Center chastised the network for its "staggering" double standard in "unequivocally" condemning racial bigotry but meeting religious bigotry with a "disinterested yawn."[5]

But the disinterested media seem to perk up when they see opportunities to depict Christians as exclusive, intolerant, and unloving. MSNBC talk show host Phil Donahue routinely expresses his opinion that Christianity is exclusive and intolerant. In interviewing clergy members about social issues, he was often sidetracked by this seeming fixation of his, berating them incredulously for their adherence to the Christian proposition—articulated by Christ himself, mind you—that salvation is through faith in Jesus Christ. On December 17,

2002, Donahue titled his program "Do You Have to Be a Christian to Get into Heaven?" Throughout the program, Donahue focused on this Christian tenet and continually encouraged the characterization of Christians as hateful, intolerant, ignorant, and bigoted. On his show two weeks earlier, he had put that very question about heaven to Reverend Jerry Falwell. In response, Falwell quoted Jesus from John 14:6, "I am the Way, the Truth, and the Life. No man cometh unto the Father but by Me." After many in the audience applauded, Donahue reportedly expressed disdain and sometime later decided to pursue the question in a full program. On the December 17, 2002, program Donahue had five panelists, three of whom expressed the view that faith in Christ was necessary for salvation.

When one of the three, Reverend Albert Mohler, president of Southern Baptist Theological Seminary, expressed that position in response to Donahue's question, Donahue showed displeasure. "I just think that has the potential, and already has caused," said Donahue, "an awful lot of havoc here among the Lord's people. If you tell me that I'm not going to Heaven, then why should you respect me? If the Lord doesn't respect me, why should you?" Reverend Mohler replied, "Well, the Lord respects you enough to have sent Jesus Christ, His Son, to assume human flesh, to die for your sins." One of the other panelists, Rabbi Shmuley Boteach, an author and national radio talk show host, responded, "Well, Phil, sadly, Reverend Mohler is a spiritual racist... who wants nothing less than a spiritual lynching." Boteach went on to accuse Mohler of converting Jesus from "one of the greatest teachers the world has ever known" to a KKK member and the "chief enforcer of anti-Semitism the world has ever known." Donahue implicitly concurred with the rabbi's rantings about Christianity, saying, "And he the Christian Klansman goes to Heaven. The guy in the sheet goes to Heaven, I think is what he's saying."[6]

ABC Television apparently has a problem airing expressions of gratitude to Jesus. In its morning talk show "The View," panelist Joy Behar said she was ending her diet when she slipped in, "Thank you, thank you, Jesus, is all I have to say! Goodbye to that damn scale and this whole diet. I'm sick of it." The Media Research Center reported that the West Coast feed of the show bleeped "Jesus" but aired "damn." On a later show Behar complained about this. She said, "The other day... I used the phrase 'Thank you, Jesus' because my diet was over.... For the West Coast, they took it out. They would not allow me to say 'Thank you, Jesus.' I think that's wrong." She said the program had received about a hundred complaint letters. Behar said she was a Roman Catholic. "Jesus and I are pals, OK? Get with the program."[7]

Jesus Freaks, Bozos, and Losers

Broadcast media mogul Ted Turner has become notorious for his anti-Christian comments. Although he is the founder of the CNN cable television network, Turner apparently feels no obligation to temper his derisive remarks. And despite the continual contempt he has shown for Christianity, we've not heard a word of protest from the tolerance police for his flagrant intolerance and insensitivity. In a speech at a United Nations peace summit on August 29, 2000, Turner openly denigrated his Christian upbringing. To a highly approving audience, he said he rejected Christianity when he discovered "it was intolerant because it taught we were the only ones going to Heaven. That confused the devil out of me, since that would have left Heaven a very empty place." Darren Logan, a foreign policy analyst with the Family Research Council, said the speech was "the most blasphemous thing I have ever heard in my life."[8] Waxing eloquent, Turner continued:

> Instead of all these different gods, maybe there's one God who manifests himself and reveals himself in different ways to different people. How about that?... Basically, the major religions which have survived today don't have blood sacrifice and they don't have hatred behind them. Those which have done the best are the ones that are built on love... It's time to get rid of hatred. It's time to get rid of prejudice. It's time to have love and respect and tolerance for each other.

This was nothing new for Turner. At a retirement party for CNN anchor Bernard Shaw, Turner expressed his amazement that a number of his employees present had attended Ash Wednesday religious services—as signified by the ceremonial ashes they were wearing on their foreheads. "I was looking at this woman, and I was trying to figure out what was on her forehead. At first I thought you were in the [Seattle earthquake]. What are you, a bunch of Jesus freaks?" asked Turner. "You ought to be working for Fox." While Christians roundly criticized Turner for his remarks, the media, as usual, gave him a pass. Indeed, our culture rewards such behavior. Shortly after the incident, Harvard University's John F. Kennedy School of Government bestowed on Turner the prestigious Goldsmith Career Award for Excellence in Journalism.[9] Just imagine what would have ensued had Turner instead maligned blacks, women, or homosexuals. Would Harvard have honored him then?

Turner has also shared his insights that Christianity is a "religion for losers," and pro-life advocates are "Bozos."[10] And at a February 1999 meeting of the National Family Planning and Reproductive Health Association, he employed Polish ethnic humor to make fun of the Pope, telling him to get with the twentieth century.[11] CNN "Moneyline News Hour" co-anchor Stuart Varney, a devout Christian, reportedly resigned because of Turner's repeated Christian-bashing.[12] Turner's bitterness toward Christianity might be explained by his revelation that as a young man he accepted Jesus Christ at a Billy Graham Crusade, but later rejected Him following his sister's death and his father's suicide.[13]

A Church at Odds with Its Motto?

When it comes to Christianity, some reporters seem unable simply to report the news. In a *Washington Post* news story—not an editorial—reporter Craig Whitlock wrote about the controversy surrounding sectarian prayer in the Maryland State Senate Chambers. He quoted one pastor as praying, "Father, it is an abomination to you for leaders to commit wickedness. We pray you will guard their minds from Satan's evil thoughts. We pray that you will keep our leaders from doing evil. We pray that our leaders recognize that we are all accountable to you for our actions." Not content to let the words speak for themselves, the reporter added, "The pastor's stern words seemed at odds with the motto of his church listed at the bottom of its letterhead: 'A warm-hearted church with a heartwarming message.'"[14]

This reportorial undercutting of Christianity has been going on for years. Bernard Goldberg, in his book *Bias*, which documents the liberal bias of the media, related that producer Roxanne Russell referred to Christian activist and Republican presidential candidate Gary Bauer as "the little nut from the Christian group." And have you ever noticed the prevalence of stories discrediting biblical Christianity in the nation's leading magazines during the Christmas or Easter seasons? Columnist Don Feder observed that during Holy Week in 1996, *Newsweek* and *U.S. News & World Report* both had cover stories debunking Christianity. *Newsweek*'s headline was "Rethinking the Resurrection," and *U.S. News*'s was "In Search of Jesus: Who was he?" Both, said Feder, amounted not to coverage of a scholarly debate, but "slick skepticism." He went on: "Would any of these publications have the chutzpah to run a cover story questioning the authenticity of Moses' message ('Moses, Man or Myth') or dissing Islam's founder ('Muhammad—Charlatan or What?')."[15]

New Republic magazine, in its January 21, 2002, issue, ran a cover story entitled, "What Would Jesus Have Done? Pope Pius XII, the Vatican, and the Holocaust." Observers were outraged at the article's overt attack against Christianity. In a Newsmax.com article, author Harry Crocker charged that the *New Republic* article characterized the New Testament, the symbol of the Cross, and the Catholic Church itself as "inherently anti-Semitic." Crocker noted that the "article is especially important because it shows that anti-Catholic hate is being mainstreamed."[16]

The American Taliban

Anti-Christian slander grew significantly during the early days in the War on Terror following the September 11 attacks. The media often described Christians as "the American Taliban," or as a fundamentalist group similar to Islamic fundamentalists. In other words, Bible-believing Christians are morally equivalent to violent Islamic radicals. Sometimes the connection is made directly, as we saw in one of Bob Norman's columns in the *New Times Broward-Palm Beach.* In "De Regier, Plumbing the Depths of the Christian Taliban," Norman wrote, "The underbelly of the Christian Right is as scary as anything that ever dwelled in a Tora Bora cave. If September 11 taught us anything, it should have been to distrust religious fundamentalists of any kind, to leave them stranded on the banks of the political mainstream where they belong... Jeb [Bush] has been catering to evangelical loonies ever since he took office; he routinely appoints way-out-there Christian wackos to key posts and backs the Religious Right on issues like abortion, the death penalty, and education. As for President Bush, I need utter only one word: 'Ashcroft.'"

Specifically, Norman attacked Governor Jeb Bush's nomination of Jerry Regier to head the Florida Department of Children and Families. "Regier's oft-stated goal in life," said Norman, "is to take over our secular, Godless government and help create a Christian nation. He's a key agent in a radical movement that to me sounds a lot like the Taliban, only with a Bible instead of a Qu'ran."[17] Singing from the same anti-Christian hymnbook, columnist Robyn E. Blumner commented in the *St. Petersburg Times*, "The religious right has spent more than twenty years chipping away at the wall of separation between church and state, trying in Taliban-like ways to inject religion into public schools and the operations of government."[18]

Similarly, promoters of *Why the Religious Right Is Wrong About Separation of Church and State*, by Robert Boston, sharply attacked the "radical religious right" in an almost full-page advertisement in the *Los Angeles Times.* "The radical religious right has declared war on America," warned the ad. "It's a religious war."[19] Even politicians sometines get into the act. Outgoing Democratic Senate Majority Leader Tom Daschle complained to the media that domestic religious fundamentalism was causing a climate of hate in the United States. He too seemed to be comparing Christian conservatives to the Taliban when he said, "You know, we see it in foreign countries, and we think, 'Well, my God, how can this religious fundamentalism become so violent?' Well, it's that same shrill rhetoric, it's that same shrill power.... And that's happening in this country. And I worry about where, over the course of the next decade, this is all going to go."[20]

A Grand Democratic Strategy

Readers of the *Houston Chronicle* may think they know where "this is all going to go"—especially after the *Chronicle* covered a group called the Texas Faith Network (TFN), an organization "opposed to fundamentalist theology and activism in the education and political arenas." At a TFN conference in Houston, participants concluded that the true enemy in the "war on terrorism" is, as you might have guessed, "religious fundamentalism."[21]

Newsweek's Howard Fineman caused quite a stir in some circles when he reported that the Democratic Party had concocted a strategy to marginalize its Republican opponents by likening them to Muslim extremists. "The theory goes like this," Fineman wrote. "Our enemy in Afghanistan is religious extremism and intolerance. It's therefore more important than ever to honor the ideals of tolerance—religious, sexual, racial, reproductive—at home. The GOP is out of the mainstream, some Democrats will argue [this] year, because it's too dependent upon an intolerant religious right."[22] This theme, of course, was by no means new, as elements in the press have been pushing it for some time. In 2001, *New York Times* foreign correspondent Douglas Jehl, for example, in an article describing the Saudi government's challenge in dealing with radical Muslims, subtly—or perhaps not so subtly—referred to Islamic extremists simply as "the religious right."[23]

Christians as Persecutors

The media sometimes take indirect potshots at Christianity and Christians as well. In an unsigned editorial discussing the discovery of the possible burial box of James, the brother of Jesus, the *Boston Globe* gratuitously referred to Christianity as a persecutor of Judaism. "The artifact," said the *Globe*, "publicized earlier this month in an archeology review, recalls a time when Christianity was a sect of Judaism, not its persecutor.... Scholars have rediscovered James and are placing him at the forefront of early Christianity. Their work cannot undo the centuries of anti-Semitism that have disfigured Christianity."[24] This column is as inaccurate as it is incendiary, if it was intending to suggest that the Holocaust should be blamed on Christians. As the *Massachusetts News* staff wrote in a counter-editorial, "Are we to believe that the *Globe* is blaming the Holocaust on Christians? No one believes that. William Shirer reported that Hitler hated Christians and many were put to death.... Many Christians ... died as heroes and heroines because they had the courage to fight Hitler."[25]

Media Distortions

Another manner by which the media demonstrate their anti-Christian bias is in the selection of news stories and the relative emphasis placed on them. The Media Research Center (MRC) reported that the media rather downplayed the massive March for Life in Washington, D.C., on the thirtieth anniversary of the United States Supreme Court's decision *Roe v. Wade*. An anti-war march just four days before was scarcely attended, yet the broadcast networks' morning and evening news shows ran a total of twenty-six segments on the event, fourteen before the march began. By contrast, the March for Life, in which tens of thousands participated, received a mere nine segments. In fact, the networks often merged the segments on the pro-life march with those on counter-demonstrations by pro-abortion groups with around one hundred in attendance, fostering the false impression that neither side of the debate was better attended than the other. And even though a Planned Parenthood rally drew an estimated 150 people, CBS's Dan Rather said, "Tens of thousands of demonstrators on both sides of the issue filled the streets of Washington today," implying that they were equally attended. During the anti-war protests, all the networks ran sound bites from likable marchers, according to MRC. Yet the network stories covering the pro-life march "did not include a syllable from any participant, on stage or in the crowd," concluded MRC's Tim Graham.[26]

Hands off Radical Islam

Journalistic distortion is also apparent in the decision to suppress reporting when Christians are subjected to brutalities, especially when the perpetrators are Muslim. "The murder, torture, and persecution of Christians in the Third World, and even prosperous countries, is one of the worst, and least-reported, of global human rights abuses," noted former *Time* magazine senior correspondent and Beijing Bureau Chief David Aikman. The radical Islamic regime in Khartoum in Sudan has killed more than two million non-Muslims—mostly Christians—who have refused to convert to Islam. Nevertheless, "mainstream press coverage [of this persecution] is tepid and understated as a rule," according to some media watchers.[27] Similarly, when three Southern Baptist missionaries were killed in a Muslim terrorist attack in Yemen on December 31, 2002, the major media reacted, characteristically, with relative disinterest.

Likewise, much of the press was silent over the Muslim identity of attackers who brutalized and killed Christians in Nigeria after becoming outraged over a newspaper story. The Muslim mayhem was reduced to a two-sided, blameless dispute by CNN correspondent Nancy Curnow, who casually referred to the story as "religious violence between Muslims and Christians." And when a Muslim murdered a Christian medical missionary in Lebanon, the *New York Times* headlined the story, "Killing Underscores Enmity of Evangelists and Muslims." This wasn't a duel between two consenting combatants, but a murder. But speaking of enmity, the widower of the victim, Bonnie Witherall, announced his forgiveness for the murderer. "It's not easy," said Garry Witherall. "It took everything I have, but I can forgive these people because God has forgiven me."[28]

At home in America, the D.C. sniper case had the American public riveted for months, and many in the D.C. area lived in terror. When suspects John Muhammad and John Malvo were captured, very little emphasis was placed on Muhammad's ties to radical Islam, and his religious beliefs were dismissed as a possible motive for the killings. According to military analyst Christian M. Weber, "Muhammad fits the pattern of the disaffected outcast who becomes increasingly radicalized under the influence of Islamism." Weber said Muhammad "seems to follow the model of John Walker Lindh, Richard Reid, and Jose Padilla—men exposed to Islam who become disenchanted with the movement's pace and progress and who take the road to jihad."[29] Yet, the mainstream media not only did not address Muhammad's connection to Islam forthrightly; they arguably suppressed it.

Another Double Standard

The major media often exhibit a double standard in their portrayal of murders and other acts of violence, depending upon the identity and motive of the perpetrators and the victims. Murders committed against homosexuals by those presumed prejudiced against them receive top billing and endless replay. Those committed by homosexuals and anti-Christian bigots are swept far under the rug. In videotapes made by Eric Harris and Dylan Klebold before massacring their fellow students at Columbine High School in April 1999, the two revealed a deep antipathy toward Christianity. "What would Jesus do?" Klebold yells while making faces at the camera. "What would I do?" Then he points an imaginary gun at the camera and says, "Boosh!" Harris says, "Yeah, I love Jesus. I love Jesus. Shut the f—up.... Go Romans. Thank God they crucified that a—hole." Then both kids chant, "Go Romans! Go Romans! Yeah! Whoo!" Klebold also referred to Christian student Rachel Scott as a "godly whore" and a "stuck-up little b—." Yet in its twenty-page cover story report of the tragedy, *Time* magazine mentioned nothing about these comments.[30]

We saw this same deliberate omission of the anti-Christian aspect in the reporting of some networks on a shooting inside a Fort Worth church in 1999. While NBC reported that the shooter was "ranting anti-religious curses," and ABC revealed that a witness said, "The gunman appeared to be taunting Christians," both CBS and CNN kept quiet on and perhaps even suppressed any speculation on the shooter's motive. The Media Research Center reported that CBS began its news report on the story with "If forty-seven-year-old Larry Ashbrook had a motive to his madness, it apparently died with him.... Police say the shooter had no criminal record, no hate-group ties."[31] (According to the media, hate is a possible motive only if it comes from Christians, not against them.)

Pro-Life Victims and Victims of Homosexual Violence Don't Count

We read and hear a great deal about the violence of pro-life fanatics—so much that if we didn't know better we might conclude this is normal behavior for Christians. Of course, that's absurd. Almost all Christians condemn such behavior. But what about when pro-life activists are the victims of violence? Can you even remember reading about an instance of that? Two men, Fred Hart and Jim Dawson, were peacefully protesting the Family Health Care Clinic in Little Rock, Arkansas, in May 2001. Two women drove by shouting obscenities from their vehicle. One emerged from the truck, grabbed Hart's sign and began running. When she tripped and fell, Hart reached down to retrieve the sign and she allegedly stabbed him in the side with a knife. The lady's story was that during a discussion over abortion Hart "threw her to the ground" and somehow got cut in the process. Fortunately for Hart, his fellow protestor Jim Dawson videotaped the event. But weeks after Dawson turned the video over to police, the investigation was still open. Some believe that if this had involved a pro-lifer stabbing a pro-abortionist, the media would have spread it all over the front page. Laura Echevarria of the National Right to Life Committee says the media's lack of interest in the story is indicative of their bias against abortion foes. "It's not surprising," she said. "There have been many instances where our affiliates and other individual pro-lifers have had death threats and bomb threats, and the media don't cover that."[32]

And where was the media outrage when middle-aged Chicago churchgoer Mary Stachowicz was allegedly killed by her nineteen-year-old homosexual coworker, Nicholas Gutierrez? Chicago police said Gutierrez confessed to killing Stachowicz in his apartment after she questioned him about his lifestyle. She asked, "Why do you have sex with boys instead of girls?" This allegedly prompted Gutierrez—according to a state's attorney—to punch, kick, and stab her until he got tired, at which point he put a plastic garbage bag over her head and strangled her. Next he crammed her body into a crawlspace under his apartment floor. As columnist Rod Dreher aptly noted, there was no moral difference between this act and the murder of homosexual Matthew Shepard by three rednecks.

Yet the media went wild over the Shepard murder and virtually ignored that of Stachowicz, just as they did that of Jesse Dirkhising, the thirteen-year-old boy who was raped and murdered by homosexuals in Benton County, Arkansas, in 1999.[33] Dirkhising's attackers drugged him, strapped him to a bed, gagged him with his own underwear, repeatedly sodomized him, and then tortured and strangled him. Following the mayhem, one of the murderers left the bedroom to eat a sandwich, and by the time he returned, Dirkhising had died. The murderers were living together in an apartment that "reeked of excrement and was littered with drug paraphernalia and residue." But this murder didn't fit the politically correct formula and was virtually ignored—only forty-six stories in all. But when Shepard was murdered in 1998, the media shamelessly exploited the tragedy, using it to advance their agenda. The media published more than three thousand stories, including forty-five in the *New York Times* and twenty-eight in the *Washington Post*. The case became a driving force for homosexual rights, hate crime legislation, and anti-Christian feelings.[34]

Journalist Andrew Sullivan, a self-professed homosexual, analyzed the media's contrasting treatments of the Shepard and Dirkhising cases in an article for the *New Republic*. I quote at length:

> Difficult as it may be to admit, some of the gay-baiting right's argument about media bias holds up.... You might argue that the Shepard murder was a trend story, highlighting the prevalence of anti-gay hate crimes. But murders like Shepard's are extremely rare... the murders of Shepard and Dirkhising are both extremely rare, and neither says much that can be generalized to the wider world. So why the obsession with Shepard and the indifference with regard to Dirkhising? The answer is politics. The Shepard case was hyped for political reasons: to build support for inclusion of homosexuals in a federal hate crimes law. The Dirkhising case was ignored for political reasons: squeamishness about reporting a story that could feed anti-gay prejudice, and the lack of any pending interest-group legislation to hang a story on.[35]

The media also didn't draw lasting attention to the 1997 murder of ten-year-old Jeffrey Curley in Cambridge, Massachusetts. One of the two men convicted of the murder and now serving life sentences testified that he was incited to molest and kill the boy based on literature put out by the North American Man-Boy Love Association (NAMBLA) that he accessed on his computer. Jeffrey Curley's father sued NAMBLA in federal court for $200 million.[36]

National Public Radio and Public Broadcast Service

National Public Radio (NPR), the taxpayer-funded radio organization, is notorious for its reputed liberal bias. On December 19, 1995,

Andrei Codrescu uttered inflammatory anti-Christian remarks in his "All Things Considered" commentary on NPR. Referring to Christ's rapture of His church, Codrescu said, "The evaporation of four million [people] who believe in this [Christian] crap would leave this world a better place." Later, when pressed for an apology, Codrescu unrepentantly said he apologized "for the language but not for what I said." Donald E. Wildmon, president of the American Family Association, urged NPR to fire Codrescu, pointing out that had he similarly disparaged Jews, blacks, women, or homosexuals, he would have been terminated. NPR reportedly did later apologize for the comments.[37]

KSUT-FM, an NPR station in Pagosa Springs, Colorado, recently refused to run a paid ad by a local dentist. Dr. Glenn Rutherford uses the phrase "Gently Restoring the Health God Created" as a theme for his dental practice. Rutherford, a devout Christian, said that his motto is not so much a statement of faith as "an acknowledgment that we don't create health. We merely restore health which was imparted to us by our Creator."[38] When he tried to air that theme in his ads with KSUT, a station representative told him, "Well, we had a staff meeting and there was universal agreement that that couldn't go on." The station staff agreed that the spot could not contain the word, "God." Dr. Rutherford said, "I was a little incensed the station could run gay and lesbian coalition sponsorship spots—but I couldn't mention God in mine?"[39] Rutherford requested an apology from station officials.

Notably, KSUT often uses its own slogan, "Diverse programming for a multi-cultural world."[40] Donald E. Wildmon, founder of American Family Radio network, said that because NPR is tax-supported, stations like KSUT that refuse such advertisements "are practically engaging in a form of government-sponsored censorship."[41] David Barton, president of Wallbuilders, in an interview with Joe Scarborough on MSNBC described a television report he had seen in which NPR station managers across the country were interviewed about KSUT's decision. One of them, said Barton, accused American Family Radio of hypocrisy because it would never permit satanic or Islamic or anti-abortion groups on its airwaves. Barton drew a telling conclusion from this comparison. "NPR sees this, the mention of God," said Barton, "in the same way that a Christian group would see a satanic group. I thought that says a whole lot about NPR."[42]

In another regrettable incident, NPR reporter David Kestenbaum, on January 22, 2002, seemed to imply that the Traditional Values Coalition (TVC), a Christian pro-family ministry, was involved in the terrorist anthrax attacks on our nation's capital. Kestenbaum's exact words from the transcript are:

> Two of the anthrax letters were sent to Senators Tom Daschle and Patrick Leahy, both Democrats. One group who had a gripe with Daschle and Leahy is the Traditional Values Coalition, which, before the attacks, had issued a press release criticizing the senators for trying to remove the phrase 'so help me God' from the oath. The Traditional Values Coalition, however, told me the FBI had not contacted them and then issued a press release saying NPR was in the pocket of the Democrats and trying to frame them.[43]

If Kestenbaum was not trying to taint TVC, it's difficult to understand why he gratuitously mentioned it in that context. TVC chairman Reverend Lou Sheldon had no doubt. He said, "When we realized we were being accused of murder—because several people died [postal workers who delivered the letters to the Senate building]—when we realized that is what NPR was saying, [that] we were potential murderers, I was outraged."[44] House Majority Whip Tom DeLay lambasted NPR over the incident, and a congressional subcommittee confronted NPR executives about continued congressional funding of an organization with an overtly anti-Christian bias. House Labor and Health and Human Services Appropriations Subcommittee Chairman Ralph Regula accused NPR of "irresponsible journalism" and said the smear "erodes NPR's credibility." California Representative Ken Calvert said he had "become jaded to the fact that the news media use the airwaves to promote their liberal agenda," but

NPR had "crossed the line from simple bias to outright libel."[45] A year after its show aired, NPR issued an apology and retraction, saying its "report violated NPR editorial principles. No one had told our reporter that the Traditional Values Coalition was a suspect in the anthrax mailing. No facts were available then or since then to suggest that the group had any role in the anthrax mailing. NPR deeply regrets this mistake and apologizes for any false impression that the coalition was in any way involved in this investigation."[46]

Public Broadcast Service (PBS), the tax-supported national television broadcast company, gets no better marks from conservatives than NPR. It funded, for example, a documentary attacking the Boy Scouts Associations' ban on homosexuals, presenting only one side with no rebuttal.[47] It also ran a heralded seven-part series on "Evolution," which many argued was a one-sided perspective. Michael J. Behe, professor of biological sciences at Lehigh University in Pennsylvania, whose research has involved delineation of design and natural selection in discrete subsystems of DNA replication, was particularly critical of the series. He wrote that the essential feature of an unbiased presentation is "whether it addresses opposing views accurately, in their strongest forms," while propaganda, "ignores or caricatures its opponents or gives weak, watered-down renditions of their arguments." He went on to say that the series trumpeted not just evolution in general, but Darwinism (random mutation and natural selection) in particular. "Yet the show," he said, didn't bother to disclose that "some scientists and academics—plus the vast majority of the public—are profoundly skeptical of natural selection as the driver of evolution."[48] Other scientists, such as Dr. Jonathan Sarfati, a physical chemist and spectroscopist, criticized the production as a "propaganda effort" that gave the impression that only the religious criticize evolution.[49]

One of PBS's main commentators, Bill Moyers, is particularly suspect in the bias department. He couldn't mask his disappointment following the decisive Republican victory in the 2002 election. In his commentary posted on the PBS website, he unloaded on the predicament the nation had just placed itself in with the election. "For the first time in the memory of anyone alive," wrote Moyers, "the entire federal government—the Congress, the Executive, the Judiciary—is united behind a right-wing agenda for which George W. Bush believes he now has a mandate. That mandate includes the power of the state to force pregnant women to give up control over their own lives." But the real zinger came when he turned his sights on what he considered the real source of the problem. "And if you like God in government, get ready for the Rapture. These folks don't even mind you referring to the GOP as the party of God. Why else would the new House Majority Leader [Tom DeLay] say that the Almighty is using him to promote 'a Biblical worldview' in American politics?"[50] Moyer's view, aired at the behest of the public trough, seems to be that Bible-believing Christians have no business in government. And if one happens to get elected or appointed—let alone to a position of considerable influence, Heaven forbid—he should have the decency to keep his trap shut about his religious beliefs.

Not content merely to hammer Christianity, PBS also happily promotes alternatives—Islam, for example. In 2002, the network ran a two-hour special documentary, one week before Christmas, no less, on the prophet Muhammad to "counter negative images" of Muslims. Alex Kronemer, the producer of "Muhammad: Legacy of a Prophet," is an American convert to Islam. His purpose was to demonstrate that "every Muslim is not Osama bin Laden." According to Kronemer, "Americans get most of their images about Islam and Muslims from the headlines. Demonstrations and shouting in the streets make the news, and those images are repeated." PBS presented Islam as the "latest revelation of the one true God." In the movie a woman said, "Muhammad told his followers to not do to him what the Christians did to Jesus—make him holy," perhaps implying, and this during Christians' Holy Week, that Christ's deity was a fabrication.

According to some reviewers, the movie treated the events and claims of Islam uncritically and as truth. The academic commentators for the show were all believing Muslims,[51] and nary a church/state separationist could be seen protesting this taxpayer-funded propaganda apologetic for another religion. It would be unheard of for PBS to produce and air a documentary featuring, say, the objective evidence for the Resurrection or the virtues of Christianity for Western thought and culture. Daniel Pipes, director of the Middle East Forum and author of *Militant Islam Reaches America*, said, "All of this suggests that the American taxpayer is subsidizing an attempt to proselytize Islam in America." PBS insisted that its viewers sent no negative responses about the documentary or its choice to run it during the week of Christmas. But it is difficult to counter the charge that this was a pro-Muslim production inasmuch as Kronemer essentially admitted it. If there were any doubt that an agenda was behind this, the doubt was removed when PBS followed up the next night with "Muslims," a two-hour "Frontline" special. While PBS can try to refute the charge by citing documentaries it has produced on Christianity, a closer look belies the claim, as when it aired "Jesus to Christ," a documentary tracing the "transformation" of the "real" Jesus from a Jewish carpenter to Christ of Christian "mythology."[52]

Major Media to Christians: "Stay Out of Politics!"

PBS's Bill Moyers is not the only journalist with a dim view of Christians holding positions of political power. Consider the words of former *USA Today* Supreme Court reporter Tony Mauro in a *USA Today* op-ed discussing President Bush's nomination of John Ashcroft for U.S. attorney general. Mauro wrote, "In John Ashcroft's America, he said in 1999, 'We have no king but Jesus.'" But, said Mauro, "In the Justice Department . . . it is the Constitution that is king . . . Ashcroft will need to assure the nation that he can enforce the Constitution and the laws of Congress when they run contrary to the laws of Jesus, as they surely will. A larger question . . . will be: Can a deeply religious person be Attorney General?"

Echoing the same theme, MSNBC's Brian Williams asked *Newsweek*'s Howard Fineman, following a debate among Republican presidential candidates, whether the candidates' positions weren't "rather strident . . . anti-gay, pro-Jesus, and anti-abortion and no gray matter in between?" And a 2002 *U.S. News & World Report* article entitled "God's candidate," profiling Arkansas Senate candidate Jim Duggar, said, "For some, there can be no higher calling than public service, but when God himself taps you to take the mound, well."[53] To these journalists a deep Christian faith is a liability for public service. Senator Charles Grassley lamented this reality in an interview during Ashcroft's Senate confirmation hearings, saying, "It's a sad commentary that John Ashcroft's Christian religious beliefs can't be considered an asset in the same vein that Joseph Lieberman's religious faith was considered an asset during the last election."[54]

Perhaps the journalists' view is a result of their own beliefs and practices. A number of studies have shown that the members of the national media are much less religiously observant than the average American. A 1995 study by the Center for Media and Public Affairs showed that some seventy percent of major media journalists seldom or never attend religious services, while almost half of all Americans attend services more than once a month.[55]

Hollywood Bias

Sanitizing and Excusing Violence by Islamic Extremists

The mean-spiritedness that characterizes so much of the news media's treatment of Christianity is also on display in Hollywood, where, among other things, we again see a sanitized treatment of radical Islamic violence. Author and movie critic Michael Medved pointed out that Hollywood's latest crop of terrorist movies depicted terrorists as anything but Islamic fanatics bent on killing Americans and destroying the United States. In the movie *Bad Company*, the terrorists are Yugoslav extremists planning to detonate a stolen nuclear bomb under Grand Central Station. In *The Sum of All Fears*, neo-Nazi European industrialists are the terrorists of choice who—adding insult to injury—buy a lost Israeli bomb intending to unleash it at the

Super Bowl, hoping to start a full-blown nuclear war between America and Russia.

What's worse, the Tom Clancy novel upon which this movie is based had Muslims as the terrorist group, but Arab-American lobbyists pressured Paramount Pictures to change their identity. By way of contrast, said Medved, Hollywood made no effort to change the identity of our enemies from previous world wars. Medved also noted the "unique Islamic imperative to impose theocracy. From Pakistan to Saudi Arabia, from Iran to Nigeria (or at least that part of the country controlled by Islam), theocratic regimes impose a brutal, medieval version of Koranic law."[56] Medved has a valid point. While the media and other liberal forces constantly portray efforts of Christian groups to restore religious freedom in America as attempts to impose theocracy, liberals rarely report on real-life theocracies in Muslim countries.

The UK-based Institute for the Study of Islam and Christianity (ISIC) says there is a "disturbing trend" among politicians and the media to make excuses for Muslim violence by blaming those who create the conditions that presumably give rise to the violence rather than focusing on the perpetrators of the violence. As an example, the institute cited an instance in which Western journalists blamed Christian missionaries in Afghanistan for the death threats the Taliban issued against them because the missionaries were "not being . . . sensitive to the local culture." Likewise, according to the ISIC, when Muslims killed eight people during riots in India, many in the media implied that it was the fault of Reverend Jerry Falwell because he had made disparaging comments about Islam.[57]

Hollywood's Negative Slant

But it's not just what Hollywood does for Islam that concerns many observers. It's also how Tinseltown negatively portrays Christians, many of whom were offended by the controversial movie *The Last Temptation of Christ* because of its irreverent and heretical presentation of Christ as sinful and lustful, of the apostle Paul as a liar, and of Judas Iscariot as a hero. But since the release of that film in the late 1980s, Hollywood has arguably become even more militant and disrespectful toward Christianity. Christians are regularly depicted as freaks, serial killers, and sexual perverts. Many films have caricatured televangelists as amoral hucksters. Hollywood is quick to show the pathetically warped "Christian" extremism of neo-Nazi paramilitary groups, not bothering to note fascism's real roots in atheism, paganism, and secularism. Instead, disrespecting sacred Christian beliefs and Christ Himself has become commonplace.

In *Where the Heart Is* (2000), Natalie Portman plays a pregnant young lady, who, after being abandoned by her boyfriend in Sequoia, Oklahoma, begins living secretly in a Wal-Mart. When she gives birth inside the store with the help of the town's substitute librarian, she gains national media attention. A Bible-thumping fanatical religious couple from Midnight, Mississippi, learns of the child born out of wedlock and travels to Oklahoma to lecture Portman. The crazy couple ultimately kidnaps the infant and then leaves her in the crib of a local nativity scene.

In the 2002 movie *Frailty*, Matthew McConaughey plays a crazed religious fanatic who tells his two sons that he is on a mission from God to kill demon-possessed people. He then proceeds to go on a murder spree. One reviewer commented, "Some will find it downright blasphemous because *Frailty* isn't satisfied with just saying 'Christians can be disturbing.' It pushes further to say, at its heart, Christianity can be disturbing."[58] Ed Vitagliano of the American Family Association said the movie sends the message that "those who believe in God and are religious can turn into axe-wielding, murderous maniacs." He said, "Hollywood seems to only portray Christians in a negative light." "Very rarely is there a movie which shows the Christian faith in a positive light."[59]

Sometimes, according to Vitagliano, Hollywood is even more concerned with making an anti-Christian point than in making money.[60] Film critic Michael Medved framed it differently, but agreed that Hollywood is not always driven solely by the dollar. "The Hollywood community wants respect even more than it wants riches," said Medved in his best-selling book, *Hollywood vs. America*. "Above all, its members crave acceptance and recognition as serious artists. Money is not the main motivation for their current madness."[61]

Actress Amanda Donahoe gleefully described a scene she played in *The Lair of the White Worm*. "I'm an atheist," said Donahoe, "so it actually was a joy. Spitting on Christ was a great deal of fun."[62] In the movie *Misery* the lunatic nurse wore a cross, in *Eye for an Eye* the rapist wore one as well. In *Copycat*, the serial killer played by Harry Connick, Jr. constantly invoked "Jesus."[63] Even Disney movies are sometimes overtly anti-Christian. The recently released *Bubble Boy*, for example, was described by Ted Baehr, president of the Christian Film and Television Commission and publisher of *Movieguide*, as "the most virulently, explicitly anti-Christian film I've ever seen."[64] In this movie the Christian parents of a boy with a deficient immune system are portrayed as absolute idiots with a portrait of President Ronald Reagan prominently displayed in their home. The mother makes cross-shaped cookies for her son and tells him he's fortunate to be trapped in the bubble because the world outside is "so evil." When the boy becomes upset, the mother tells him to repeat the Pledge of Allegiance "over and over." All of this was in just the first five minutes of the movie.

The flipside of this anti-Christian-Hollywood coin is that pro-Christian movies are so panned by the Hollywood sycophants that they often have difficulty getting off the ground. Examples are *Evelyn,* starring Pierce Brosnan, and the Civil War epic *Gods and Generals*. The average moviegoer might be perplexed, if not discouraged, by the critics' rejection of these movies, if unaware that an anti-Christian bias could be coloring their opinions. Roger Ebert, for example, sneeringly opened his review of *Gods and Generals* saying, "Here is a Civil War movie that Trent Lott might enjoy." The movie tells the story of the very serious and brilliant Christian general Stonewall Jackson. According to one reviewer, "It is chock-full of prayers to Jesus

Christ."[65] The movie's producer, Ron Maxwell, believes his "unorthodox" portrayal of the South and his unapologetic Christianity clearly turned off many critics who couldn't see beyond their prejudice. "Look, I've had thirty years in the business," said Maxwell. "I've read a lot of reviews, and some of them are funny and dismissive. But I've never seen an effort [like this] to actually suppress a movie, to scare people away from it." Despite the movie's dismal reviews by liberal critics, Michael Medved gave it four out of four stars and said he believed the movie would be one of the best films of 2003. Medved contends that most critics have an ideological agenda.[66]

Actor-director Mel Gibson said he feels an effort was undertaken to suppress *The Passion*, his film about the last twelve hours in the earthly life of Jesus Christ, centering on His suffering and death. In a news conference announcing the film in September 2002, Gibson admitted he had experienced difficulty in finding a United States studio or distributor for the movie.[67] Gibson has denied that the movie's approach is potentially disparaging to Jews. "This is not a Christian versus Jewish thing. '[Jesus] came into the world and it knew him not.' Looking at Christ's crucifixion, I look first at my own culpability in that."

Jesuit Father William J. Fulco, National Endowment for the Humanities professor of ancient Mediterranean studies at Loyola Marymount University in Los Angeles, who translated the movie script into Aramaic and Latin, said he saw no hint of anti-Semitism in the film. Fulco added, "I would be aghast at any suggestion that Mel is anti-Semitic."[68] Nevertheless, certain political and religious groups and some in the mainstream press have been very critical of Gibson's *Passion*. Boston Globe columnist James Carroll denounced Gibson's literal reading of the biblical accounts. "Even a faithful repetition of the Gospel stories of the death of Jesus can do damage exactly because those sacred texts themselves carry the virus of Jew hatred," wrote Carroll.[69] A group of Jewish and Christian academics has issued an eighteen-page report slamming all aspects of the film, including its undue emphasis on Christ's passion rather than "a broader vision."

The report disapproves of the movie's treatment of Christ's passion as historical fact. But to ensure the accuracy of the work, Gibson enlisted the counsel of pastors and theologians, who affirmed the accuracy of the script. Don Hodel, president of Focus on the Family, said, "I was very impressed. The movie is historically and theologically accurate." Ted Haggard, pastor of New Life Church in Colorado Springs, Colo., and president of the National Evangelical Association glowed, "It conveys, more accurately than any other film, who Jesus was."[70]

The moral is that if you want the popular culture to laud your work on Christ, make sure it either depicts Him as a homosexual or as an everyday sinner with no particular redeeming value (literally). In our anti-Christian culture, blasphemous works like *Corpus Christi* and *The Last Temptation of Christ* are celebrated, while *The Passion* is condemned.

Anti-Life TV

Network television also gets its digs in against Christians and their values, such as the high regard they place on human life and protection of the unborn. In *Absolute Strangers*, a 1991 TV movie, Henry Winkler's character seeks a court order to abort his comatose wife's baby to save her life. Then the "absolute strangers" show up, two fire-breathing pro-life intermeddlers, and fight for legal guardianship over the child so that the pregnancy can proceed to term.[71] Though the movie was based on real-life events, pro-life advocates say it was extremely one-sided. Reverend Donald E. Wildmon of the American Family Association said, "It's a pro-abortion movie." Henry Herx, director of the U.S. Catholic Conference Office for Film and Broadcasting, complained about the movie's casual treatment of the abortion question. "It seems to me the decision for the abortion was made rather quickly and without deep consideration," said Herx. "One would think they would want to build up the moral dilemma and feel the pain of the husband."[72]

The 1996 star-studded HBO movie *If These Walls Could Talk* hit abortion opponents from a number of angles. First set in 1952, Demi Moore's character, a widow, pregnant after a one-night stand, dies in a failed illegal abortion. Fast forward twenty years, and a married woman (Sissy Spacek) with four children, living in the same home that Moore's character occupied, discovers she's again pregnant. While deciding whether to terminate her pregnancy, she is harangued by her hippie daughter. Another twenty years later, still in the same location, a third woman (Ann Heche), is impregnated by her married college professor. Pro-life activists surround the abortion clinic where the woman is planning to obtain an abortion. In an ensuing altercation, an anti-abortion fanatic murders the pregnant woman's loving physician, played by Cher. One synopsis of the movie glowingly described it as "a poignant examination of the evolution of the abortion debate, beginning with the tragedy of illegal back-alley abortions and ending with the violence so prevalent at women's clinics today."

An episode of "Law and Order" on NBC took its shot in January 2003, featuring an insane pro-life introvert stalking and murdering an abortion doctor. Although incidents like this have occurred in real life, they are extraordinarily rare occurrences involving lunatics and are completely unrepresentative of the pro-life movement, which is entirely peaceful and respectful, in stark contrast to the lucrative but grisly violence and disrespect meted out hourly on unborn human beings in abortion clinics across America.

Catholic-Bashing TV

While evangelical Christians are often singled out for ridicule by Hollywood, a strong case could be made that Catholics are targeted every bit as much, even more, some would argue. To their credit, a number of Catholics and Catholic organizations, such as the Catholic League for Religious and Civil Rights, led by William Donohue, have done a thorough job monitoring anti-Catholic discrimination. Each year the league compiles a report on anti-Catholicism, which documents the ongoing saga. Liberal media watchdog and columnist Brent Bozell also has his finger on the pulse of anti-Catholic and anti-Christian discrimination. His Media Research Center compiles evidence of bias against Christians in the media and entertainment industry. In his syndicated column of March 21, 2003, with Creators Syndicate, [73] Bozell listed a number of examples:

- On an episode of CBS's "Family Law," a priest had sired a child prior to taking his vows. Tony Danza's character, addressing the question of whether the priest should raise his child, said, "Maybe the kid would be better off without all that superstitious crap screwing her up."

- In ABC's "The Job," a stripper dressed as a nun disrobed during a police interrogation and placed her foot in her questioners'—male and female—crotches. In a separate scene a monsignor placed his personal reputation above the sanctity of the confessional.

- In HBO's "Sex in the City" a single mother's boyfriend pressures her to baptize their child to placate his drunken, bigoted Irish-Catholic mother. The single mother, Miranda, agrees on the condition that "Christianity" not be mentioned in the sacrament.The show's narrator, commenting on the priest's willingness to perform the ceremony under such circumstances, says, "The truth is, in these troubled times, the Catholic Church is like a desperate thirty-six-year-old single woman, willing to settle for anything it can get."

- CBS's David Letterman joked, "The Gambino crime family will probably fall apart. That will make the largest crime organization in the city... the Catholic Church!"

- NBC's Jay Leno quipped in commenting on Notre Dame's football victory, "I guess going to a Catholic school as a young boy, you really learn how to run fast."

- Bill Maher on ABC's "Politically Incorrect" said, "I have hated the

Church way before anyone else. I have been pounding religion for nine years on this show." In another show Maher said that the Church should "drop the pretense and just go gay.... It's high time you gay Catholics stood up and announced to the world, "We're here, we're queer, get Eucharist."

Now, granted, anti-Catholic prejudice isn't new, and, as we've seen, the long march against Christianity in the public schools and elsewhere has been going on for decades, but what we can't ignore is that America wasn't always hostile to Christianity. In fact, Christianity used to be welcome in the public square, and was considered an absolutely essential part of America's public life.

America's Christian heritage is rarely taught in our schools these days—but it is a vital historical fact, and we will look into it in the next chapter.

part III

The War in Perspective

This section examines the broader picture of Christian influence in America. Chapter Eleven traces America's Christian beginnings. Because our schools are no longer emphasizing America's Christian origins—indeed, our culture has taken pains to rewrite our history free of factual references to the strong Christian influence that dominated this nation in its formative years—many Americans are doubtlessly unaware of this history. The purpose of this chapter is to set the historical record straight.

Chapter Twelve contains a series of interviews with some of America's Christian leaders, offering their perspectives on the existence and extent of anti-Christian discrimination in this nation, the relationship between faith and freedom, and what the future holds.

chapter eleven

America's Christian Roots

AMERICA IS THE GREATEST, FREEST NATION in the history of the world. Is our freedom an accident or the result of specific influences that preceded and accompanied the founding of the republic? If it's the result of specific influences, what were they? There are two major schools of thought on these questions: one is that the American tradition of freedom is the product of secular Enlightenment ideals, and the other that American freedom is a direct outgrowth of the Christian religion. Resolving this fundamental question is important, even beyond our interest in setting straight the historical record of the origin of American liberty. For how can we ultimately preserve our freedom if we don't understand its primary sources?

Right now, competing forces driven by opposing worldviews are locked in a struggle over the direction of American society, the role of government, and the freedom of the individual. Each claims to champion the principles of America's founders as authority for their respective positions, which is why it is imperative that we get to the bottom of this. If, as secularists argue, America was founded on secular principles, and America is thereby the freest nation in history, it stands to reason that liberty lovers would want to preserve that secular tradition. On the other hand, if our freedom is a byproduct of a largely Christian consensus and Christian principles, it would behoove us to be mindful of those realities.

Some may blanch at the mere suggestion that our freedom could have originated from Christian-based principles, because they view Christianity as an authoritarian, inflexible religion antithetical to liberty. They think of Christianity as synonymous with intolerance and rigidity and incompatible with freedom of choice. Some harbor the irrational fear that Christians want to establish a theocratic Christian state. That could be one reason they are afraid to allow the facts of history to speak for themselves. Ironically, if secularists would open themselves up to America's historical record, their fears would be allayed, as they would come to understand that Christianity undergirds, rather than undermines our freedoms. Indeed, Christian precepts formed the intellectual underpinnings of American constitutional government.

The conventional wisdom in America today, cultivated by decades of historical revisionism, is that secularism dominated the thinking of the signers of the Declaration of Independence and the framers of the Constitution. Secularists are fond of pointing to high-profile American heroes, such as Thomas Jefferson and Thomas Paine—both of whom are famously associated with fierce advocacy of individual liberties—and Ben Franklin, saying they were not Christians, but Deists. Deism, essentially, is the belief in a Deity who, after creating the universe according to certain natural and moral laws, abandoned it to run on its own according to those laws and without his intervention. While these few men may not have been orthodox Christians, they certainly weren't by any means atheists. Moreover, this undue emphasis on influential colonial Americans whose Christian credentials are in doubt distorts the true picture of the movers and shakers who brought our constitutional government into existence. The overwhelming majority of them were Christians, and not casual ones at that, but devout, practicing, Bible-believing Christians.

In this chapter, I'll explain America's Christian roots and attempt to correct some of the rampant secular revisionism in our culture and educational system today. One of the first things to remember is that this nation was begun by Christians whose ancestors came to America for the very purpose of escaping religious persecution and seeking religious liberty.

The Church of England, the Separatists, and the Puritans

By the early seventeenth century, England, under James I, had developed into a land of acute religious intolerance. The church governing body became increasingly concerned over two "fanatical" movements, the Separatists and the Puritans. The Puritans were the much larger group, but were perceived as a lesser threat to church authority because they merely wanted to purify the church from within. The Separatists were a smaller group that began as a congregation under Pastor James Robinson in Scrooby, England. This church, established in 1602, was not originally seeking to break away from the Church of England or to formally rebel against it. Robinson and his members considered themselves good Anglicans and believed that the church was separating itself from them by abandoning Biblical principles, not the other way around. "It is not we which refuse them, but they us," said Robinson.[1]

When intolerance intensified into persecution—non-Anglican Christian ministers were routinely silenced, jailed, or banished under the licentious James I—Robinson's congregation left for the Netherlands in search of religious freedom, settling in Leyden, Holland, and forming the English Separatist Church.[2] While the Separatists did acquire significantly greater freedom there, they still lacked the degree of religious autonomy they sought. In addition, they were concerned that they were being absorbed into the Dutch culture. They decided to set out for the New World to establish a biblically based society as Englishmen.

The English Virginia Company financially underwrote the venture, authorizing the Separatists (today known as the Pilgrims) to settle just north of Jamestown, Virginia. The Pilgrims set sail from Plymouth, England, in September 1620 aboard the *Mayflower* and reached America over two months later. Due to strong winds that blew their ship off course, they landed much farther north than they had anticipated. As they realized they were outside the Virginia Company's jurisdiction and thus free of any sovereign authority, the Pilgrims resolved to enter into an agreement providing for their self-governance, which came to be known as the Mayflower Compact. They executed the document on November 11, 1620, aboard the ship in Provincetown Harbor, Massachusetts, but eventually settled the next month in Plymouth.[3]

This was the first time in recorded history that a free community of equal men created a new civil government by means of a social contract.[4] Thus the colonists, united in this contract, formed a government whose authority was derived from the consent of the governed and which established the principle that all men were entitled to equal treatment under the law.[5] These principles were later incorporated into the United States Constitution, giving lie to the widely held belief that the Constitution's idea of social contract was a secular construct borrowed from John Locke, as espoused in his *Second Treatise of Civil Government* in 1690. As author M. Stanton Evans notes, "The Compact was executed on November 11, 1620—predating Locke's *Second Treatise* by seven decades."[6] "In the American context—one might say, especially in the American context—all the ideas and institutions of free government, including contract theory, far predated Locke, and did so in the most explicit terms imaginable."[7]

The Mayflower Compact acknowledged the Pilgrims' purpose in the voyage —"for the Glory of God and the advancement of the Christian Faith"—and it expressly purported to be a covenant between them and their sovereign God. As historian Paul Johnson wrote, "What was remarkable about this particular contract was that it was not between a servant and a master, or a people and a king, but between a group of like-minded individuals and each other, with God as a witness and symbolic co-signatory."[8]

The Puritans were quite different from the Separatists, as they believed the church should be reformed from within. But the more they tried to initiate reform, the greater resistance they encountered under Charles I. They eventually concluded that the only way to reform the church was to leave England and establish a purer version of the church in America, which would provide an example for the homeland church to follow. By thus removing themselves from the corruptive influences of the church, they could live in humble obedience to God. They truly believed, according to author Peter Marshall, "that the Kingdom of God really *could* be built on earth, in their lifetimes.... They knew that they were sinners. But like the Pilgrims, they were dedicated to actually living together in obedience to God's laws, under the Lordship of Jesus Christ."[9]

The Puritans left for America in droves in the 1630s, convinced God had chosen them specifically to carry His light to America. They believed that their faith could germinate and prosper in a new land, free from the oppression of the crown and the Church of England. The New England historian, clergyman, and author Cotton Mather said, "Thus was the settlement of New England brought about... to express and pursue the Protestant Reformation." John Winthrop, captain of the Puritan ship *Arbella*, wrote "A Model of Christian Charity," which was an eloquent statement of the Puritans' Christian mission and a declaration of their obedience to God. He expressed their intention of glorifying God: "that we shall be as a City upon a Hill, the eyes of all people are upon us."[10]

Beyond the Pilgrims and the Puritans in New England, all early American settlements, from Massachusetts to Georgia, were comprised of Christians of all denominations,[11] and indeed, all of the early American colonies were established on Christian principles.[12] But it was the Puritans, with their biblically based governments modeled on their church covenants, who laid the primary foundation for our constitutional government.[13] For the Puritans, the concept of self-government was a distinctly Christian ideal, as historian Perry Miller makes clear. "The Puritans," wrote Miller, "maintained that government originated in the consent of the people . . . because they did not believe that any society, civil or ecclesiastical, into which men did not enter of themselves was worthy of the name. Consequently, the social theory of Puritanism, based upon the law of God, was posited also upon the voluntary submission of the citizens."[14]

The Great Awakening

Skeptics may concede that America had Christian beginnings, but argue that the faith of its early settlers dissipated through the generations so that, by the time of the Revolution, America was as much, if not more, under the influence of French Enlightenment thinking as Christianity. This view conveniently ignores the dramatic spiritual impact of America's Great Awakening, which began around 1734. This was a nationwide Christian revival that not only re-stoked America's spiritual flames, but provided a unity and cohesiveness to the colonies that was lacking in the first century and a half of their history.[15] America truly found itself spiritually during this period, honing its unique cultural identity centered on Christian principles.

Paul Johnson went so far as to say that the Great Awakening "sounded the death-knell of British Colonialism."[16] Johnson wrote, "It could be argued that it was in the eighteenth century that the specifically American form of Christianity—undogmatic, moralistic rather than credal, tolerant but strong, and all-pervasive of society—was born, and that the Great Awakening was its midwife."[17] The Great Awakening, said Johnson, "proved to be of vast significance, both in religion and politics."[18] The biblical message cut across denominational lines and was spearheaded by spiritual and oratorical giants such as Jonathan Edwards and George Whitefield (whose voice was so strong, according to Benjamin Franklin, that thirty thousand people could hear him at once).[19] Edwards' wife, in a letter to her sister, marveled at Whitefield's ability to captivate and influence his audiences. "It is wonderful to see what a spell he casts over an audience by proclaiming the simplest truths of the Bible. . . . Our mechanics shut up their shops, and the day laborers throw down their tools to go and hear him preach, and few return unaffected."[20]

Benjamin Franklin, in his *Autobiography*, made the point even more colorfully, as he related an occasion when he attended a Whitefield sermon determined to contribute nothing to the offering plate. Franklin wrote:

> I perceived he intended to finish with a collection, and I silently resolved he should get nothing from me. I had in my pocket a handful of copper money, three or four silver dollars, and five pistoles of gold. As he proceeded, I began to soften and concluded to give him the coppers. Another stroke of his oratory made me ashamed of that and determined me to give the silver; and he finished so admirably that I emptied my pocket wholly into the collector's dish, gold and all.[21]

The core theme of these preachers' sermons was man's sinfulness and his need for salvation through faith in Jesus Christ, which would also lead to changed hearts and Christian good works.[22]

It wasn't just the well-known evangelists who led the charge for a respiritualization of America. Pastors throughout the land, especially in New England, were extremely important in framing the colonial mindset. The Black Regiment, as the clergy came to be called, was a fierce opponent of British tyranny and a driving force in the decision of the colonies to seek independence.[23] The clergy also mentored America's minutemen, who persistently stood guard against British attack. As John Wingate Thornton observed, "To the Pulpit, the Puritan Pulpit, we owe the moral force which won our independence."[24]

State Constitutions

At the time of the Revolution, all but a fraction of the American colonial population was Christian, and largely Protestant. At least seventy-five percent of the colonists had grown up in Puritan families. More than half of the remaining twenty-five percent were followers of Calvinism, in one form or another.[25] Some argue the Calvinist influence was much greater. Indeed, according to scholar John Eidsmoe, "many, if not the vast majority of colonial Americans came from Calvinistic backgrounds. The colonists lived in the shadow of the Reformation." Eidsmoe quotes Dr. Loraine Boettner as saying "that about two-thirds of the colonial population had been trained in the school of Calvin."[26]

The state constitutions also based their authority on the Christian religion, though perhaps not to the extent that the colonial charters did. Writing in the mid-1860s, B. F. Morris observed in his *Christian Life and Character of the Civil Institutions of the United States*, "The men who have founded states on written constitutions have always resorted to religious sanctions to give practical power to their constitutions and to enforce the laws of the government."[27] State constitutions were filled with religious references permitting varying amounts of religious freedom. Contrary to current understanding, at least eight of the American colonies in 1775 had established churches—those preferred, sanctioned, and supported by the state. Even Supreme Court Justice Hugo Black acknowledged this fact in, of all places, his majority opinion banning voluntary public school prayer. Black wrote, "Indeed as late as the time of the Revolutionary War, there were established churches in at least eight of the thirteen former colonies and established religions in at least four of the other five."[28] Other scholars have said that at least nine of the thirteen colonies had established churches at the time.[29]

The American Revolution

By the early 1760s the Americans had attained de facto independence from Britain.[30] But the British were facing financial difficulties, having amassed an enormous debt fighting the French and Indian War. Consequently, England increased taxes on the colonists, seeking to make up the shortfall.[31] Contrary to the conventional teaching, the colonists were not radicals seeking a revolution. They were British loyalists—they prided themselves in being English[32]—whom the British had backed into a corner through ever-increasing taxes and infringements on their rights as Englishmen. M. Stanton Evans has pointed out that the British infringements on the colonists' rights were radical in terms of the "colonists' long-accustomed, and highly cherished, way of doing things." Evans wrote, "The new imperial program included three major tax bills, draconian restraints on trade," and the suspension of jury trials and colonial legislative powers. "The British also moved to close off the Western spaces to immigration from coastal regions and install an Anglican bishopric in New England—the very thing the Puritans had fled the homeland to avoid."[33]

As for the increased taxes, the new British measures were a departure from their previous practice, which was to use taxes primarily as a tool to regulate trade. The new duties were for the express purpose of raising revenue. The British even admitted they were adopting a new structure of taxation. British statesman Edmund Burke, defending the American position, said, "Leave the Americans as they anciently stood.... Do not burthen them with taxes; you were not used to do so from the beginning. Let this be your reason for not taxing."[34] It was thus the British who were implementing radical, "revolutionary" changes. They claimed absolute authority over the colonists, who rejected the notion that any earthly authority could acquire unlimited sovereignty.[35] The colonists didn't seek to overthrow the British government but rather to attain independence for themselves in America, after having exhausted all other options with the British. They were adherents to the rule of law and strikingly more traditionalist than the British.[36]

The Declaration of Independence

The conventional wisdom reinforced by our public schools and universities is that Thomas Jefferson and the founders of this Republic were Deists and Enlightenment humanists whose philosophy was secular and rationalist. According to modern thinking, these ideas, traced further into the past, originated with the Greeks and Romans; and when the founders used religious terms or referred to a deity, their terms were generic at best, and at worst, were cynical attempts to dupe and win over the common Christian colonist. It is not Christianity, say the skeptics, but Enlightenment humanism that generated the ideas articulated in the Declaration of Independence.[37]

It is hardly surprising that many people accept this secularist view of our founding, since it has been aggressively trumpeted at least as far back as 1922, when the intellectual Carl Becker released his work on the Declaration. Becker was an admirer of Hegel and Marx and theorized that the American Revolution and French Revolutions were mere links in an evolutionary chain of history that would culminate in Communism as its purest expression. This was the worldview through which Becker perceived history and which influenced his seminal work on the Declaration, which planted the seeds of the belief that our system of government is secularly based. Becker's view has been dominant more or less since the 1920s and remains so today.[38]

But modern scholarship has exposed it as a fallacy. The French scholar Michel Villey, himself a humanist, and other scholars, such as Richard Tuck of England, have shown that Greek and Roman ideas concerning "rights" did not form the philosophical underpinnings of the American (or English) system as secularists insist. Author Gary Amos explained that the concept of inalienable rights couldn't have come from the Greeks or Romans, but is traceable to the Scriptures. The Greeks, said Amos, were polytheists who would never have subscribed to the notion that "all men are created equal and are endowed by their Creator (singular) with certain unalienable rights."[39] Moreover, according to Amos, the Greeks believed the universe originated from an impersonal divine force, not a personal God as revealed in the Bible. Human beings were an extension of that divine force; there was virtually no distinction between humans and the divine, so the Declaration's concept of men being endowed by their creator would never have occurred to the Greeks. Only in the Bible are the components of the Declaration's phrase, "all men are created equal and are endowed by their Creator (singular) with certain unalienable rights" present. It is a biblical concept (Genesis) that God created man in His image and likeness. Only because of this are all men entitled to equal treatment and inalienable rights. The Greeks, apparently, did not subscribe to a doctrine of equality or equal rights, and neither did the Romans.[40] Had Thomas Jefferson chosen to do so, he could have endorsed secularism in his draft of the Declaration, but instead chose language compatible with a biblical worldview.[41] Even had he chosen secularist language, it likely would have been cut from the edited document, as we'll see.

Indeed, many who cling to the theory of the secularist origin of our founding rely heavily on the supposed Deism and even Enlightenment skepticism of Thomas Jefferson, Benjamin Franklin, and others. Aside from Jefferson and Franklin and perhaps a few others, this is demonstrably untrue. The late scholar M. E. Bradford of the University of Dallas, who studied the religious backgrounds of the signers of the Declaration and the Constitution, concluded that the overwhelming majority of them were strong, practicing Christians.[42] Bradford found that fifty-two of the fifty-six signers of the Declaration were Trinitarian Christians. Similarly, of the fifty-five signers of the Constitution, fifty to fifty-two were orthodox Christians.[43] As for the denominational affiliations of the signers of the Constitution, "twenty-nine were Anglicans, sixteen to eighteen were Calvinists, two were Methodists, two were Lutherans, two were Roman Catholic, one lapsed Quaker and sometimes Anglican, and one was open Deist. The Deist was Benjamin Franklin, who attended every kind of Christian worship, called for public prayer, and contributed to all denominations."[44] These affiliations are not surprising, given the Christian upbringing and education of these men.[45] M. Stanton Evans observed that colonial Americans "generally were raised on Scripture, accustomed to institutions that embodied Christian precept, and instructed by pastors attentive to the political meaning of religious doctrine."[46] British parliamentarian Edmund Burke said of the American colonists in 1770, "The people are Protestants; and of that kind which is the most adverse to all implicit submission of mind and opinion.... This is a persuasion not only favorable to Liberty, but built upon it."[47]

It would be a mistake to conclude that, because the founders were not Enlightenment skeptics, they were therefore somehow enemies of science or reason. In fact, quite the opposite is the case, as Michael Novak observed:

> The most important thing is this: the founders saw themselves laboring within a long community of inquiry, at home simultaneously in the world of biblical and classical examples and in the practical world of the eighteenth century. For most of them, the Bible and plain reason went hand in hand, moral example for moral example.[48] ... Far from being contrary to reason, faith strengthens reason. To employ a poor analogy, faith is a little like a telescope that magnifies what the naked eye of reason sees unaided. For the founders, it was evident that faith in the God of Abraham, Isaac, and Jacob magnifies human reason, encourages virtue, and sharpens a zest for liberty.... Moreover, a free society demands a higher level of virtue than a tyranny, which no other moral energy has heretofore proven capable of inspiring except Judaism and Christianity.[49]

But what about Jefferson? The consensus seems to be that he was a Deist, but as M. Stanton Evans noted, Jefferson clearly "believed in the creative, sovereign, and superintending God of Scripture" but also thought that Platonic doctrine had corrupted the original monotheism of the Bible. He was probably a Unitarian rather than a Deist.[50] David Barton points out that Jefferson called himself a Christian: "I am a real Christian, that is to say, a disciple of the doctrines of Jesus."[51] But even if we assume that Jefferson was not a believing Christian, the question remains what kind of influence he exerted on the Declaration as its original drafter (he was not a signer of the Constitution).

Despite Jefferson's absence from Congress during the period (February–May 1776) when most of the debate over independence occurred, John Adams believed that Jefferson's "peculiar felicity of expression" made him the right candidate to pen the original draft of the Declaration. But as M. Stanton Evans explained, it is incorrect to assume that because Jefferson wrote the first draft, the document is a product of his individual beliefs. Jefferson himself dispelled this notion. "Neither aiming at originality of principles or sentiments, nor yet copied from any particular and previous writing, it was an intended to be an expression of the American mind."[52]

Jefferson's draft, said Evans, was vetted by a congressional committee led by the devout John Adams, and Congress itself took an active role in editing and rewriting it, including two references to a providential God. Congress made over eighty changes and deleted nearly five hundred words. The Declaration was thus a "corporate statement" of Congress.[53] Evans rejects the claim that the ideas incorporated into the Declaration were the same as those expressed in the French Declaration of the Rights of Man. The differences in their themes come precisely in their attitude toward religion. The French "rights" did not originate from God, but were "simply asserted as self-justifying concepts." The Declaration's "inalienable rights" were a product of "biblical theism."[54]

Admittedly, the founders didn't rely solely on the Bible. They didn't create their ideas in a political science vacuum. They were scholars of government and history who borrowed from the ideas of great thinkers after conducting enormous research. At the Constitutional Convention, Benjamin Franklin made this very point, saying, "We have gone back to ancient history for models of government, and examined the different forms of those Republics.... And we have viewed modern states all round Europe."[55]

Just what were the sources the founders tapped? A group of contemporary political scientists engaged in a ten-year study, examining over fifteen thousand political writings of the Founding Era (1760–1805), to answer that question. The research revealed that the most frequently cited authorities of the 180 names examined (listed in the order of declining frequency, with the corresponding percentages representing the frequency of citations from that author in relation to the total number of citations examined) were: Montesquieu 8.3%, Blackstone 7.9%, Locke 2.9%, Hume 2.7%, Plutarch 1.5%, Beccaria 1.5%, Cato 1.4%, De Lolme 1.4%, and Puffendorf 1.3%.[56] Although these writers profoundly influenced the founders' thinking and writings, the researchers concluded that the founders cited the Bible vastly more often than any other source. They cited scripture four times more than Montesquieu or Blackstone and twelve times more than Locke. Indeed, thirty-four percent of the direct source quotations were from the Bible.[57]

David Barton amply demonstrated[58] the strong Christian credentials of all these men upon whom the founders relied, except for Hume. Even Locke, who many have argued was a Deist, was in fact a Christian, according to Barton. Barton noted that the same charge was made against Locke during the Founding Era, and refuted by James Wilson, one of the original U.S. Supreme Court justices and a signer of the Declaration. "I am equally far from believing Mr. Locke was a friend to infidelity [a disbelief in the Bible and Christianity]," said Wilson. "The consequence has been that the writings of Mr. Locke, one of the most able, most sincere, and most amiable assertors of Christianity and true philosophy, have been perverted to purposes which he would have deprecated and prevented had he discovered or foreseen them."[59] In addition, though the founders had access to the works of the great secular thinkers, like Voltaire and Rousseau, they cited them much less frequently and often critically.[60]

The two most highly quoted secular writers were the Frenchman Montesquieu and the Englishman Blackstone. They were both strong Christians. Montesquieu's signature work in political science was *The Spirit of Laws*. He believed that God is the source of all law: "Men make their own laws, but these laws must conform to the eternal laws of God." Interestingly, he compared Christianity with Islam and concluded that Judeo-Christian theism was better suited to good government. "A moderate government is most agreeable to the Christian religion," he said, "and a despotic government to the Mahommedan." He wrote that Christianity, which directs people to love one another, would bless every nation with the best political laws. Christianity, he said, "is a stranger to mere despotic power."[61] Blackstone's voluminous *Commentaries on the Laws of England* was the primary legal sourcebook for American lawyers during the early days of the republic. Blackstone also believed that all law is derived from God—the God of the Bible. "The doctrines thus delivered we call the revealed or divine law, and they are to be found only in the Holy Scriptures.... Upon these two foundations, the law of nature and law of [biblical] revelation, depend all human laws; that is to say, no human law should be suffered to contradict these."[62]

George Washington

Secularists have frequently leveled the charge that George Washington was a Deist. If the father of this nation wasn't a Christian, they reason, we would be hard-pressed to demonstrate that America itself has Christian roots. Again, the facts resoundingly refute the revisionists on this point. The skeptics refer to Washington's generic references to "Providence" rather than to Christ as proof of his non-Christianity. But that is selective reporting at its most egregious. Washington was a dedicated vestryman in the Episcopal Church. His mother, a strong Christian, trained him in the habit of prayer to the God of the Bible.

The secularists will have a hard time explaining Washington's twenty-four-page personal daily prayer book, "The Daily Sacrifice," in which appear his favorite prayers in his own handwriting. A perusal of the pages of the little book conclusively shows that he was not a Deist. His Sunday morning prayer, for example, ends with, "pardon, I beseech Thee, my sins, remove them from Thy presence, as far as the east is from the west, and accept of me for the merits of Thy son Jesus Christ... Bless my family, kindred, friends and country, be our God and guide this day and forever for His sake, who lay down in the grave and rose again for us, Jesus Christ our Lord. Amen." His Sunday evening prayer closes with, "These weak petitions, I humbly implore Thee to hear, accept and answer for the sake of Thy Dear Son, Jesus Christ our Lord, Amen." And in Monday morning's prayer, he asked, "Daily frame me more and more into the likeness of Thy Son, Jesus Christ, that living in Thy fear, and dying in Thy favor, I may in Thy appointed time attain the resurrection of the just unto eternal life."[63]

Other Washington quotes unmistakably affirm his Christianity. In a speech to the Delaware Indian Chiefs, he said, "You do well to wish to learn our arts and ways of life, and above all, the religion of Jesus Christ... Congress will do everything they can to assist you in this wise intention."[64] Washington urged the troops under his command "to live and act as becomes a Christian soldier."[65]

D. James Kennedy and Jerry Newcombe speculate that "the quiet dignity of his faith may have in some way helped create the misunderstandings about what [Washington] believed." They may find support for their theory in the very words of Washington's mother herself, who issued him this admonition as he was leaving her for a life of service, "Remember that God is our only sure trust. To Him, I commend you.... My son, neglect not the duty of secret prayer."[66] Kennedy and Newcombe relate that Martha Washington's granddaughter, Nelly Custis, was very upset that people questioned Washington's Christian faith. In a letter to historian Jared Sparks, she wrote, "His life, his writings, prove that he was a Christian. He was not one of those who act or pray, 'that they may be seen of men.' He communed with his God in secret."[67] John Marshall, chief justice of the United States Supreme Court from 1801 to 1835, made a similar observation about Washington. "Without making ostentatious professions of religion, he was a sincere believer in the Christian faith, and a truly devout man."

David Barton agrees that Washington was a strong Christian. But he goes farther and suggests that Washington "was an open promoter of Christianity. For example, in his speech on May 12, 1779, he claimed that what children needed to learn 'above all' was the 'religion of Jesus Christ,' and that to learn this would make them 'greater and happier than they already are.'"[68]

Hamilton, Madison, Jay

How about the three authors of the *Federalist Papers*: Alexander Hamilton, James Madison, and John Jay? These three men did as much as any others to ensure ratification of the Constitution through their profound and learned defense of its principles, contained in those writings now known as *The Federalist Papers*. Listen to Alexander Hamilton: "I have carefully examined the evidences of the Christian religion, and if I was sitting as a juror upon its authenticity I would unhesitatingly give my verdict in its favor. I can prove its truth as clearly as any proposition ever submitted to the mind of man." Hamilton, along with the Reverend James Bayard, helped to form the Christian Constitutional Society. The society's first two objectives, said Hamilton were, "the support of the Christian religion" and "the support of the United States."[69] Hamilton was convinced that "natural liberty is a gift of the beneficent Creator, to the whole human race; and that civil liberty is founded in that; and cannot be wrested away from any people, without the most manifest violation of justice."[70]

James Madison, the "Father of the Constitution" and fourth president of the United States, who spoke 161 times at the Constitutional Convention, second only to Gouverneur Morris, was also a committed Christian. He studied at Princeton under one of the nation's foremost theologians, the Reverend John Witherspoon, who famously charged, "Cursed be all that learning that is contrary to the cross of Christ."[71] Madison said that "Religion [is] the basis and foundation of Government."[72] He wrote in the margins of his personal Bible, "Believers who are in a State of Grace, have need of the word of God for their Edification and Building up therefore implies a possibility of falling."[73] His other notes make clear that he firmly believed in the divinity of Jesus Christ.

John Jay was the first chief justice of the United States Supreme Court. On October 12, 1816, he said, "Providence has given to our people the choice of their rulers, and it is the duty, as well as the privilege and interest of our Christian nation to select and prefer Christians for their rulers."[74]

The Constitution

As we have seen, biblical principles, more than any other influence, inform the United States Constitution. "As much as I love, esteem and admire the Greeks, I believe the Hebrews have done more to enlighten and civilize the world. Moses did more than all of their legislators and philosophers," said John Adams.[75] Between the time of the signing of the Mayflower Compact in 1620 and the drafting of the United States Constitution in 1787, New England Christians wrote some one hundred different governmental charters of various forms that laid the foundation for the Constitution.[76]

The framers formulated the Constitution based on their Christian worldview, or, as some would say, their Judeo-Christian worldview.[77] They believed that man was created in God's image and likeness, as stated in Genesis 1:26–27. This is extraordinarily significant. The concept that man was created in the image and likeness of God means that man has intrinsic worth and dignity. As such, man is endowed with inalienable rights that no other men can rightfully take away; he is entitled to freedom. So the Biblical affirmation of man's inherent worth is fundamental, indeed indispensable, to political liberty. Today's conventional wisdom, as we've observed, says otherwise. It preaches that Christian doctrine is inimical to freedom because it is intolerant, inflexible, and authoritarian. Freedom, it says, derives from tolerance of all ideas—that is, acceptance of the notion that all ideas are equally valid.

Some say today that moral relativism, not biblical absolutes, is the ticket to freedom. But this is manifestly untrue, both in theory and historically. As M. Stanton Evans wrote, "No system of political liberty has ever been created from such notions [moral relativism], nor is it theoretically conceivable that one could. On the other hand, the most brutal forms of despotism, from the age of Renaissance to our own, have been developed exactly on this basis."[78] This is because, explained Evans, only if we subscribe to absolutes is there any basis upon which to affirm man's dignity. If morality is relative, there is no basis upon which to protect human rights against the tyranny of the majority or the arbitrariness of government.[79] Ultimately, relativism necessarily devalues humanity in general and the individual in particular.[80] Just look at Nazi Germany and the Soviet Union as two twentieth-century examples of despotism and brutality that sprang from a rejection of Christian moral principles.

But the framers understood that man's entitlement to freedom and his realization of it are dramatically different things. Why? Because of another equally valid biblical principle that they embraced as much as they affirmed the notion of man's inherent dignity as a special creature of God: Man's intrinsically sinful nature because of the Fall.

The framers did not believe, as did the French *philosophes* who gave birth to the French Revolution, that man is basically good and that human nature is perfectible. Regardless of their differences over the specifics of the mechanics of government, they essentially agreed that post-Fall man, although still bearing great dignity, is nevertheless sinful in nature. They fervently believed in Old Testament Scripture such as Jeremiah 17:9, "The heart is deceitful above all things, and desperately wicked: who can know it?" The same moral critique, of course, permeates the New Testament. Paul, in Romans 7:18, said, "In my flesh dwelleth no good thing."

Alexander Hamilton said, "Take mankind in general, they are vicious."[81] Jay said, "The depravity which mankind inherited from their first parents, introduced wickedness into the world. That wickedness rendered human government necessary to restrain the violence and injustice resulting from it."[82] Patrick Henry said, "Show me that age and country where the rights and liberties were placed on the sole chance of their rulers being good men, without a consequent loss of liberty."[83]

But if a consensus existed that man is sinful, wouldn't that lead to the adoption of authoritarian rule by the best and brightest in a society? That is, if man is so unruly, is there any way other than some form of dictatorship to ensure order? The fallacy of this conclusion is that it considers only the sinfulness of the people being ruled. As M. Stanton Evans pointed out, the ruling class is also afflicted with original sin. And rulers are subject also to the further corrupting influence of power.[84] So unless the rulers are properly restrained, they will subjugate their subjects. Such as been the rule, rather than the exception, in world history. Indeed, from their understanding that all men, including rulers, are sinful, and their awareness that all men are equal before God, the framers concluded that no man is above the law. That's why they formed a government based on the rule of law, that is, a government of laws, not of men.

While we tend to think of the Greeks as authors of democratic principles, neither they nor any of the other ancient peoples enjoyed political freedom on the scale that Americans do. And it is precisely because they had no concept of restraints on government. They permitted popular participation in government, but they did not impose constitutional limitations on their rulers. They specifically did not believe that all men were equal in the eyes of God, or in their case, the gods. To them, as well as to most ancient peoples, the ruling class was above the common man. Reinforcing this belief, said Evans, was their view that the rulers were the conduits to the gods. A man who has unmediated and unchecked access to a deity is one to be feared and in whom authoritarian rule could naturally reside.[85] Moreover, the state's interest was wholly superior to that of the individual, as can be seen in the writings of Plato and Aristotle.[86]

Thus the framers understood that to ensure liberty government had to be invested with sufficient authority to establish order and enforce the rule of law. But unless restraints were also imposed upon the government, it would tend toward absolutism and deprive people of liberty. Their challenge was to find that proper balance. James Madison described it this way in Federalist 51: "If angels were to govern men, neither external nor internal controls on government would be necessary. In framing a government which is to be administered by men over men, the great difficulty lies in this: you must first enable the government to control the governed; and in the next place oblige it to control itself."

The framers proceeded to design a Constitution that would both empower and limit government. The limitations on government are the key to understanding our freedom. As we've seen, the very notion of limitations on governmental power is uniquely based on biblical principles.[87] Without a firm belief in God—Who is more powerful than all the earthly rulers combined—there is no adequate basis upon which to limit the authority of rulers.[88] The framers limited government in a number of ways. They instituted a system of federalism, which divided governmental power vertically between the federal, state, and local governments. They further divided the federal government horizontally into three branches—the separation of powers doctrine—with an elaborate scheme of checks and balances among the branches to prevent any branch from becoming too powerful at the expense of the others and of the people's individual liberties. They created a bicameral legislature to further retard rapid government action at the congressional level. They established enumerated powers and reserved the balance to the states and the people. As a further safeguard on the tendency of government toward absolutism, they established the Bill of Rights. And to ensure that these constitutional limitations could not be easily eroded, they established a very difficult amendment process.

It was specifically because the framers subscribed to the twin biblical principles of 1) man's inherent dignity by virtue of creation and 2) man's present sinful nature as a result of the Fall that they drafted a Constitution based on the principle of limited government. But they also understood one other pivotal truth. No matter how profound an organizing document they devised in the Constitution, and regardless of its built-in safeguards against excessive governmental power, there was one other extra-constitutional factor that would be essential to preserving American liberties: the underlying faith and morality of the people.

Constitution Undergirded by Christianity

The men who established our constitutional system of government firmly believed that the Christian convictions of the body politic were foundational to American freedom. John Adams said, "We have no government armed with power capable of contending with human passions unbridled by morality and religion.... Our Constitution was made only for a moral and religious people. It is wholly inadequate for the government of any other." By this, of course, Adams was not suggesting that Christians aren't sinners. He knew better. He meant that people needed religious and moral standards to maintain a free society.[89] Adams also said this nation was founded on "the general principles of Christianity." A free government "is only to be supported by pure religion or austere morals. Public virtue cannot last in a nation without private, and public virtue is the only foundation of republics."[90] And Washington said, "True religion affords to government its surest support."[91] Even the secularists' darling Thomas Jefferson said while he was president, "No nation has ever yet existed or been governed without religion. Nor can be. The Christian religion is the best religion that has ever been given to man and I as chief Magistrate of this nation am bound to give it the sanction of my example."[92]

In fact, so widely accepted was the proposition among the founders that Christianity was necessary for freedom that it is difficult to find anyone influential who disagreed with it, quite unlike the situation in revolutionary France, where anti-Christian secularism was predominant.[93] The Americans' acceptance of the interdependence of faith and freedom was so pronounced that French historian Alexis de Tocqueville observed it some fifty years into the new republic. "There is no country in the world in which the boldest political theories of the eighteenth-century philosophers are put so effectively into practice as in America," said Tocqueville. "Only their anti-religious doctrines have never made any way in that country.[94]... For Americans the ideas of Christianity and liberty are so completely mingled that it is almost impossible to get them to conceive of the one without the other."[95] And again, "There is no country in the world where the Christian religion retains a greater influence over the souls of men than in America.... Religion in America takes no direct part in the government of society, but it must be regarded as the first of their political institutions; for if it does not impart a taste for freedom, it facilitates the use of it.... I do not know whether all Americans have a sincere faith in their religion—for who can search the human heart?—but I am certain that they hold it indispensable to the maintenance of republican institutions."[96]

Biblical Law as Foundational to American Law

In addition to the Constitution being established on Christian principles, it is also true that much of our law is based on Christian law and morality. "The Ten Commandments are the moral and legal foundations of Western civilization," said Professor Israel Drapkin.[97] America's common law tradition can also be traced through English common law back to its roots in biblical revelation. "While the Roman law was a deathbed convert to Christianity," wrote law professor John C.H. Wu, "the common law was a cradle Christian."[98]

In *Church of Jesus Christ of Latter Day Saints v. United States*,[99] a case in 1890 in which Mormons asserted that polygamy laws were an encroachment on their religious liberties, the U.S. Supreme Court held that Christian beliefs would be the standard by which the practice would be judged. The Court stated, "The organization of a community for the spread and practice of polygamy is, in a measure, a return to barbarism. It is contrary to the spirit of Christianity and the civilization which Christianity has produced in the Western world." In another case that same year, *Davis v. Beason*,[100] the Court held that "bigamy and polygamy are crimes by the laws of all civilized and Christian countries.... Probably never before in the history of this country has it been seriously contended that the whole punitive power of the government, for acts recognized by the general consent of the Christian world in modern times as proper matters for prohibitory legislation, must be suspended in order that the tenets of a religious sect encouraging crime may be carried out without hindrance."

The Establishment Clause and the Free Exercise Clause

The two "religion clauses" of the First Amendment appear at the beginning of the Amendment. "Congress shall make no law respecting an establishment of religion" (the Establishment Clause) "or prohibiting the free exercise thereof" (the Free Exercise Clause). As constitutional scholar George Goldberg stated, "It was equally agreed that, just as the federal government should be prohibited from telling people how to worship, it should be prohibited from telling them how not to worship."[101]

The framers had a clear understanding of the phrase "establishment of religion," given their experiences with the "established" Church of England and the established religions of the various states. The Establishment Clause was to serve two functions. It would forbid the federal government from setting up a national church, and it would prohibit the federal government from interfering with the church/state relations of the individual states.[102] That's why the framers worded the clauses so carefully. As Evans observed, "The agency prohibited from acting is the national legislature; what it is prevented from doing is passing any law '*respecting*' an establishment of religion. In other words, Congress was forbidden to legislate at all concerning church establishments—either for or against. It was prevented from setting up a national established church; equally to the point, *it was prevented from interfering with the established churches in the states*."[103]

Supreme Court Justice Joseph Story, in his *Commentary on the Constitution of the United States* (1779–1845), affirmed this point and also explained that it was proper for government to encourage the Christian religion. "Thus, the whole power over the subject of religion was left exclusively to State governments, to be acted on according to their own sense of justice and the State Constitutions." Story also wrote, "Probably, at the time of the adoption of the Constitution, and of the . . . [First Amendment], the general, if not the universal, sentiment in America was, that Christianity ought to receive encouragement from the State, so far as such encouragement was not incompatible with the private rights of conscience, and the freedom of religious worship. An attempt to level all religions, and to make it a matter of state policy to hold all in utter indifference, would have created universal disapprobation, if not universal indignation."[104]

Though increasing religious diversity eventually led to disestablishment in the states, "in 1775, no fewer than nine colonies had such arrangements."[105] From the time of the Constitutional Convention to when the Bill of Rights was adopted, "six of the original thirteen states—Connecticut, Georgia, Maryland, Massachusetts, New Hampshire and South Carolina—had officially supported churches."[106] Other states made Christian belief a prerequisite to holding office.[107] Moreover, it was clear that these six states were unwilling to enter the Union unless the federal Constitution contained a provision prohibiting the federal government from interfering with their established churches.[108]

While the Establishment Clause seems to get most of the attention today, often ignored is the equally important Free Exercise Clause. Theoretically, there should be no tension between the two religion clauses because they were both designed, essentially, to promote religious freedom by prohibiting federal interference in the matter. Indeed, originally, according to George Goldberg, there was no tension between the clauses.[109] But today the clauses are often in conflict in court cases, as we have seen. In bending over backwards to prevent the "establishment of religion," the courts often suppress individuals' free exercise rights. Such a result would rarely occur if the Supreme Court had not, through unbridled judicial activism, stretched the scope of the Establishment Clause far beyond its intended and clearly stated parameters.

That the Establishment Clause was never intended to permit federal interference with the religious decisions of the several states is manifest in the words of Chief Justice John Marshall, considered by some to be the greatest jurist in American history. "Had the people of the several states, or any of them, required changes in their constitutions, had they required additional safeguards to liberty from the apprehended encroachments of their particular governments, the remedy was in their own hands, and would have been applied by themselves," wrote Marshall.[110] In other words, the Establishment Clause operated to forbid the *federal* government from establishing a national religion or prohibiting the free exercise of religion; it did not so forbid the states. But in 1940 in *Cantwell v. Connecticut*, the Supreme Court held that these prohibitions apply to the state governments as well, through a legal fiction called "incorporation." In a massive, unconstitutional shift of power, the federal Establishment Clause and Free Exercise Clause were made applicable to the states through incorporation into the Due Process Clause of the Fourteenth Amendment. This meant that the federal government could now prevent the states from "establishing" religion or interfering with its free exercise. Through time, with the declining Christian consensus in America and the advance of secularism,[111] the scope of the Establishment Clause was extended further.

Today, as we've shown, the federal courts prevent all kinds of religious activities that are only remotely connected with state action or supported with state funds. That is how the First Amendment Establishment Clause, which was originally intended to apply solely to the federal government, prevents not just the state, but also state-funded institutions, such as our schools, from involvement in religion. But it is not just the state's affirmative endorsement of religion that the courts forbid, but sometimes the mere presence of religion in the public arena. Through convoluted reasoning, federal courts, for example, have, as we've observed, forbidden voluntary prayer in public schools and student-sponsored prayer at athletic events—even though the state isn't endorsing a particular religion or requiring students to participate. The long arm of the federal government, in its zeal to prevent an establishment of religion, now often interferes with the free exercise rights of individuals. Thus the Establishment and Free Exercise Clauses are often in full conflict. In the name of preventing the establishment of religion (erroneously referred to as upholding the separation of church and state), which was intended to promote, not restrict religious freedom, the courts suppress the free exercise rights of individuals, students and adults alike. This is precisely the kind of authoritarian tyranny the founders sought to avoid.

In addition to applying the Establishment Clause to the states, the courts have also extended its scope to absurd proportions. The federal government was never intended to be hostile to religion.[112] While it was "forbidden to interfere with the people's religious life," "it was not required to abandon its own."[113] The Continental Congress frequently engaged in religious observance, from days of fasting and prayer to appeals for divine assistance. One of its first acts in 1774 was to appoint a chaplain. In 1780, because English Bibles were in short supply, Congress passed a resolution encouraging states to print an American Bible. As noted earlier, Congress passed the Northwest Ordinance to promote religion and morality, and it funded a project to provide Indians with a Christian education.[114]

Congress continued to promote Christian religious interests after the Constitution was ratified through appointment of official chaplains, recitation of prayers, recognition of days of thanksgiving, and continued appropriations for the Christian education of Indians. So, before, during, and after the adoption of the First Amendment, Congress had its hands all over religion. Which, as Stan Evans stated, presents a radically different picture from the revisionist version that this country was founded by secularists and Deists intent on creating a "wall of separation" between church and state.[115]

Indeed, Justice Story made clear that the religion clauses of the First Amendment were not designed to force the state into impartiality between the Christian religion and other religions. Story wrote:

> The real object of the [First Amendment] was, not to countenance, much less to advance Mahometanism, or Judaism, or infidelity, by prostrating Christianity; but to exclude all rivalry among Christian sects, and to prevent any national ecclesiastical establishment, which should give to an hierarchy the exclusive patronage of the national government.[116]

There is no doubt about the answer to our question at the beginning of this chapter. American freedom is not an accident, nor is it a child of the Enlightenment. The historical record is clear; America's unique experience in freedom is a direct outgrowth of the Christian religion. If Christian faith is thus foundational to our liberties, how can we sustain our freedom if our Christian consensus is declining? How will this constitutional republic withstand the assault of rampant cultural relativism? In the next and final chapter, some of America's leading Christian figures answer these questions and more.

chapter twelve

America's Liberty at the Crossroads

THE GREAT AMERICAN STATESMAN Patrick Henry said in his later years, "Oh, how wretched should I be at this moment, if I had not made my peace with God."[1] On his deathbed he affirmed his Christian faith to his doctor with even greater conviction, poignantly recognizing that Christianity had been under constant attack but always emerged victorious. "Doctor," said Henry, "I wish you to observe how real and beneficial the religion of Christ is to a man about to die . . . I am, however, much consoled by reflecting that the religion of Christ has, from its first appearance in the world, been attacked in vain by all the wits, philosophers, and wise ones, aided by every power of man, and its triumphs have been complete."[2]

As Henry observed, Christianity has withstood the onslaught of attacks throughout history, but will America itself survive as the world's torchbearer of liberty against the incessant assaults on its Christian foundations? For this concluding chapter I interviewed six of the nation's foremost Christian thinkers for their learned opinions on the underlying reasons behind the anti-Christian sentiment in America today and what the current trend, unabated, would mean for the future of American freedom.

Dr. James Dobson is the founder and chairman of Focus on the Family, a communications, counseling and resource ministry dedicated to the preservation of the home. Dr. Dobson is heard daily by more than 200 million people on over 4,200 radio stations throughout the world. He is a licensed psychologist with a Ph.D. in Child Development from the University of Southern California School of Medicine.

Dr. Michael Novak is the director of Political and Social Studies and holds the George Frederick Jewett Chair in Religion, Philosophy, and Public Policy at the American Enterprise Institute in Washington, D.C. He is the author of more than twenty-five influential books on the philosophy and theology of culture, including *On Two Wings: Humble Faith and Common Sense at the American Founding.* In 1994, Novak received the prestigious Templeton Prize for Progress in Religion.

Dr. Marvin Olasky is editor-in-chief of *World*, a professor at the University of Texas at Austin, and the author of fourteen books, including *Compassionate Conservatism*. He is also a syndicated columnist, a senior fellow at the Acton Institute, a church elder, and the chairman of the board of City School, which brings together rich and poor children in Austin.

Dr. D. James Kennedy is the senior minister at Coral Ridge Presbyterian Church in Fort Lauderdale, Florida. He is the founder and president of Evangelism Explosion International, the first ministry to be established in every nation on earth, and the chancellor of Knox Theological Seminary and founder of the Center for Christian Statesmanship in Washington, D.C. He also founded the Center for Reclaiming America, which seeks to equip men and women to work in their communities to transform our culture.

Nancy Pearcey is the Francis A. Schaeffer Scholar at World Journalism Institute, visiting professor at the Torrey Honor's Institute of Biola University, and senior fellow at the Discovery Institute. Pearcey has been writing on science and worldview since the late 1970s. Her most recent book is the forthcoming *Set the Gospel Free: The Transforming Power of Christian Worldview.*

Author, speaker, and Christian apologist Dr. Ravi Zacharias has spoken in over fifty countries, including in the Middle East, Vietnam and Cambodia and in numerous universities worldwide, notably Harvard, Princeton, and Oxford University. His weekly radio program, "Let My People Think," is broadcast on more than one thousand stations worldwide, and he has appeared on CNN and other international broadcasts.

I asked each of the participants to answer two questions, the first having to do with adversity Christians currently face in America and the second concerning the relationship of faith and freedom and the prospects for America's future as a free nation, given the relentless assaults on our Christian traditions.

1. Why do you suppose that Christians have been singled out for discrimination in American society, generally by those who insist that tolerance is the highest virtue? That is, why does our culture deem it permissible to denigrate deeply held Christian beliefs while insisting on the greatest deference for most other faiths and even secular worldviews? Could it have anything to do with Christianity's perceived judgmentalism, its exclusive truth claims, or its adherence to moral absolutes? If so, how do other religions, which also have exclusive truth claims and strong moral standards, get a pass?

Dr. James Dobson

Conservative Christians are subjected to such virulent hostility primarily because we pose a threat to the leftist, immoral agenda of the media and entertainment industries. When believers conform to the dictates of scripture, they have the temerity to stand against abortion, euthanasia, "population control," condom distribution, pornography, sexual license, and the tax-and-spend policies of liberal government. Above all else, religious conservatives are hated because some of them—very few, unfortunately—are willing to oppose the gay and lesbian agenda in all its excesses, from the push to legalize same-sex "marriage" and adoption to the lowering of the age of consent, the advancement of pro-homosexual school curriculum, and the construction of "bath house" establishments.

In contrast to those who promote immorality, committed Christians invoke the name of God in advocating purity and charity and advocating the sanctity of human life, the permanence of marriage, abstinence, brotherhood, and bringing up children in the fear and admonition of the Lord. Those who take the scriptures literally stand by the side of the highway to perdition, warning travelers that dangers lie ahead and urging them to take a higher road. For this, we are despised. Jesus Himself told us we would be hated for what has been called "the offense of the cross." Ultimately, this is what elicits such hostility from those who are opposed to our system of values.

Liberal activists discriminate against conservative Christians for political reasons as well. Evangelical Christians and conservative Catholics are a potent and growing force in the public square, with some estimates suggesting that they number as many as forty million strong. A group that size dwarfs other voting blocs! Those on the leftist end of the spectrum realize that Christians pose this threat to their goals; therefore, Christians are met with an even greater degree of animosity. It is true that some other religious groups, such as Muslims, promote traditional values here in the United States. However, these groups are not typically as politically active as Christians, and are not as well-organized or well-represented in terms of sheer numbers.

As for Christianity's perceived judgmentalism, it would be difficult to argue that *anyone* could be more judgmental than those who preach "tolerance" as the highest of virtues. For example, the gay rights movement has said, in effect: "We don't merely want your tolerance, we demand your *acceptance* and *affirmation*—forcibly, if necessary. We will change the laws in order to thrust our lifestyle upon you. But we will not tolerate the views of those who oppose us. We will label anyone who disagrees with our agenda as hateful, bigoted, and homophobic, and on that basis we will endeavor to eradicate all opposing viewpoints from the public square." This can already been seen in the push within several states to legalize gay marriage. And most ominously, it is evidenced in the introduction of "hate" crime laws prohibiting language that might "incite" people to discriminate against others. This dangerous legislation provides no exceptions for pastors and other people of faith who might take exception to homosexual behavior on purely biblical grounds.

Dr. Michael Novak

A small minority of Americans, about six or seven percent, mostly from the highly educated elite, have their reasons for despising Christianity, and they make their hostility to Christianity quite evident. They do not represent American culture, but they do represent a small, articulate, and potent voice in that culture. This elite seems to dominate the national voices of the legal profession (although not, I think, the local voices among most lawyers), a large segment of movie stars, and a significant number of opinion leaders in the media. Of course, feminists, gays, and the fanatical secularists who gather around People for the American Way and the American Civil Liberties Union (although there are many good people in these organizations too) are also directly opposed to traditional Christian belief and practice, and therefore to orthodox Catholics and faithful evangelicals.

Curiously, even many mainstream Christians of the mainline, who tend to be rather more liberal in a number of areas, exhibit a strong emotional reaction when the subject of "the Christian Right" comes up. They seem to abhor being held to account regarding their own Christian values, at least from *those* people. Coming from those people, after all, is a point of view about Christian belief which liberals no longer share (although of course they once did).

Traditional Christian beliefs have always been counter-cultural; it was so in the days of ancient Rome, through the Middle Ages, in the early period of the Enlightenment, and it is so today. As the great sociologist Robert Nisbet once wryly noted, built into the name "Enlightenment" itself is a powerful form of bigotry, distinguishing the people of light from the people of darkness. Belief in Christianity is darkness; the rejection of it is light. Similarly, Elliott Abrams in his book on American Judaism points out that some high percentage of American Jews who do not consider themselves religious have a particular abhorrence of orthodox Jews, and are made uncomfortable by visible signs of Jewish devotion and traditional belief. They usually manage to keep this revulsion concealed from the public, but every so often it bursts through quite vividly. Perhaps some dislike "the religious right" for analogous reasons.

Many Americans may have a bad conscience about their rejection of the traditional views of Judaism and Christianity. They know deep down that something vital and true springs from those roots, and still moves them. On the other hand, they have "modernized" in certain parts of their mind, and they do not know how to put this modernization together with their traditional longings. They hate those who exacerbate this tension in their own souls.

You will note, for instance, the difference between American atheists and European atheists. The Americans who reject religion do so with a kind of emotional violence, and at the same time are quick to boast about their own moral superiority, honesty, compassion, idealism. In other words, they have to protect their own self-image by insisting that they are even more deeply religious than those who might seem to be so just by going to church or synagogue. "Anything believers can do/I can do better."

By contrast, the European atheist is much more self-assured in his atheism, and often manifests the sly smile of the complete cynic and nihilist, who happily believes in nothing at all.

Dr. Marvin Olasky

I don't see Christians as singled out for discrimination in American society generally—after all, big chunks of American society are heavily populated by Christians—but the bias is clear in two sectors of society (academia and media) that in turn influence others. I see five reasons for such academic and media scorn: two arising from dominant values within those sectors, two from weaknesses within Christianity, and one connected to God's mysterious will.

First, since Christianity has the most adherents of any religion in America, and in the past has had cultural leadership, academic and media secularists see it as a threat in a way that domestic Islam or other religions with exclusive truth claims are not. Elite secularists might even see adherents to non-Christian faiths as helpful, since "the enemy of my enemy is my friend."

Second, societies—and particularly societal elites—typically need opponents to denigrate, so they can define themselves by what they are not. In the past Jews and blacks filled the position of the designated denigrated; it's great that anti-Semitism and racism have declined substantially, but prejudice abhors a vacuum. Biblical Christians, poorly represented among the academic and media elite, were easy targets for the hatred that would otherwise have been aimed at others.

Third, many biblical Christians, beginning in the late nineteenth century, developed a separatist mentality based on the idea that the world would grow worse and Christians could retain personal purity by staying clear of university and media dens of iniquity. The message of many fundamentalist pastors became, "Mama, don't let your babies grow up to be journalists." As Christians abandoned the fight for key societal sectors anti-Christians became more aggressive and eventually dominant.

Fourth, some separatists alienated their children by setting up "don't touch" and "don't taste" rules so narrow as to provoke rebellion. Those children often equated liberty with license and became virulently opposed to biblical moral values.

Fifth, some of the harassment of Christians is inevitable. After all, Christ himself warned that many will hate and persecute those who trust in Him. Christians should oppose harassment and pray that it will not turn into persecution, but we should not be shocked when the going gets tough.

Dr. D. James Kennedy

Well, I think that there's probably pretty general consensus among most knowledgeable people that the one thing that the "tolerant" cannot tolerate is Christianity, which they would like to brand as being intolerant. It has also been said that tolerance is the last virtue of a degenerate society. I think that many times people don't realize it, but when you begin to allow every kind of immorality and degeneracy and perversion imaginable, the one thing you will not allow is to have anybody criticize you for doing these things. Extraordinarily successful people can admit to any kind of immorality, depravity, perversion of any sort on any talk show on television and nobody will so much as lift an eyebrow and certainly would not find fault or criticize them for what they say. So yes, tolerance is the last virtue of a degenerating society. I think the fact that Christianity is the majority religion in America has to be a big part of the reason it is singled out for intolerance. I don't think that anyone is overly concerned about the view of Zoroastrians.

In addition, when you don't want to obey the Commandments of God, you find it very difficult to acknowledge that these are absolute truths presented by an absolute God that demands absolute obedience when you have determined you are not going to obey and so you must get rid of absolutes to begin with.

Consider Allan Bloom's *The Closing of the American Mind*. The very first sentence of the book says the one thing you can be sure that every graduate of an American public high school has learned: that there is no such thing as absolute truth and everything is relative. Of course if you ask these students why that is so, many of them would probably respond, "Well haven't you ever heard of Einstein and his theory of relativity? Einstein taught that all things were relative." Well, the fact is Einstein said nothing of the sort. In fact, when he found that the theory of relativity was being smeared over into all kinds of other disciplines besides physics, he said, "Relativity applies to physics, not ethics." So relativists basically have a desire to live according to their own rules and do their own thing and not be obedient to

God. Because when you say there are no absolutes, you are professing atheism, because God is the ultimate absolute and His word is the next ultimate absolute and that's what they want to reject because of their own sin.

I think a good example of this was an interview I heard a number of years ago when Sir Julian Huxley was being interviewed on public television shortly before he died. Now Sir Julian was the director of UNESCO, the United Nations Educational, Scientific, and Cultural Organization, and he was a leading evolutionist. He was also the grandson or nephew of Thomas Huxley, who was Darwin's bulldog and who popularized evolution in Darwin's day. He was asked why scientists jumped at *The Origin of Species*. Most people would say that they had been taught that Darwin presented such a massive amount of evidence that their scientific integrity required that they accept it as truth. Well, the leading evolutionist in the world said, and I quote, "I suppose that the reason we leapt at the *Origin* was that the idea of God interfered with our sexual mores." Now that has nothing to do with philosophy or absolute truth or anything. It has to do with our emotions, our genes, and our passions and I think that applies to a lot of this rejection of absolute truth.

Concerning your question about Christianity's perceived judgmentalism, it reminds me of when I was down on skid row in Tampa, shortly after I became a Christian. I had been invited down there to preach the gospel to the people on the streets. The streets were mostly made up of alcoholics who were staggering around and one thing I heard from virtually every one of them that I tried to talk to was this: "The Bible says take a little wine for your stomach." They all knew that verse. It's the same thing with the people who believe in relativity. The one verse they know is "Judge not lest ye be judged." You might ask them, "Well, what do you think of Christ's statement when he says, 'Judge righteous judgments.' What do you think about that?" Well, they never even have heard of it. But the Bible does say that. The fact of the matter is, there is a whole book in the Bible titled *Judges*. So the Bible does call upon us to make judgments and God has appointed that there should even be people in the office of judging other people and the church is given the responsibility of passing judgment upon those that are living either in heresy or in scandalous sin. So again they are showing that a little bit of knowledge is a dangerous thing. Jesus is talking there about the fact that in our daily conversation, we shouldn't always be finding fault with people but again He says there are times when we must make righteous judgments.

Nancy Pearcey

Christians are called to be missionaries to their world, and that means learning the language and thought forms of the people we want to reach. In America, we don't need to learn a new language, but we do have to understand the thought forms of our culture in order to communicate effectively.

The most significant change in modern times is a divided view of truth—which means that challenges to Christianity come in two different forms. On one side, there's postmodern relativism, where nothing is true or false, right or wrong. In the typical public school classroom today, English teachers have tossed out their red pencils, as though correct spelling or grammar were nothing but social constructs imposed by those in power. Postmodern categories are applied especially to areas like morality and religion, reducing them to nothing but subjective personal experience or quaint ethnic customs.

Paradoxically, however, if you go down the hallway to the science classroom, you'll find that the ideal of objective truth still reigns supreme. Darwinian evolution is not open to question, and students are not invited to judge for themselves whether it is true or not. Evolution is treated as public knowledge that all are expected to accept, regardless of their private beliefs. The reason for this sharp contrast is a split in the concept of truth itself. The influential apologist Francis Schaeffer used the imagery of two stories in a building: Truth has been divided into a "lower story," where concepts are rational and verifiable, over an "upper story" of noncognitive experience, which is the locus of personal meaning. Sociologists describe it as the fact/value split. The "fact" realm includes whatever qualifies as public knowledge—scientific, objective, and rational. The "value" realm includes religion, morality, the arts, and humanities, which have been reduced to merely private, subjective experience.

To communicate effectively in the public arena, Christians need to realize that nonbelievers are constantly filtering what we say through the fact/value grid. When we state a position on an issue like abortion or homosexuality, *we* intend to state an objective moral standard—but *they* think we're merely expressing a subjective emotional response. *We* talk about a moral truth important to the health of society—but *they* say we're just making a political power grab.

The "tolerance" of which you speak in your question applies only to the value realm (the upper story), where there is no objective truth that could possibly function as a standard for judging ideas right or wrong. Thus "tolerance" has become a cover-up term for postmodern relativism. If you question Darwinian evolution, however, you quickly discover that there is no tolerance for dissent in the fact realm (the lower story), because there we are talking about what really happened and not just people's private beliefs.

The reason postmodernists find Christians so irritating is that we keep violating the rules by speaking of our beliefs in terms of real, objective truth. This is regarded as a category mistake. That's why our message won't even make sense to people unless we first challenge the split view of truth itself. Biblical Christianity makes cognitive claims about the entire scope of reality, not only the spiritual realm but also the physical cosmos, historical events, and human nature. It is not merely our subjective experience.

A primary reason secularists are gentler in their treatment of other religions is that most seem odd and foreign, so that Americans are prone to regard them as merely ethnic and cultural customs. As a result, they pose no threat to the secularist agenda. The reason Christianity is dangerous is that a good number of Americans actually believe it, and offer its teachings on human nature, the family, the state, and so on, as a basis for civil society. Clearly, their views must be debunked as irrational superstition.

The reason all religions are treated as equivalent is that, in the fact/value dichotomy, none of them is about truth anyway. Their actual content does not matter. The postmodernist "knows" they are merely private, upper-story experiences or noncognitive cultural rituals. Christians need to argue that genuine pluralism does not mean reducing all views to relativistic equivalence. It means respecting those who make genuine truth claims, and giving them a voice in the public debate. Once someone has accepted the fact/value split, then all values are relative. With no objective standard, all that's left is one person imposing his or her private prejudices on others, which is by definition oppressive.

What's more, if values are nothing but *what I personally value*, then to attack my values is to attack me. Thus when Christians make public moral statements, they are interpreted as making a personal attack. It's like saying I dislike the shape of your nose.

In this intellectual climate, Christians can no longer simply assert specific rules of biblical morality. We have to defend the very concept of moral truth (an oxymoron today). We have to engage in apologetics to show people that they themselves cannot really live according to the relativism they embrace. Like everyone else, they irresistibly and unavoidably make moral judgments that they believe are grounded in reality in some way. That's part of what it means to be human. And if a person's philosophy gives no basis for human nature, then there's something wrong with his philosophy.

Dr. Ravi Zacharias

Our culture does preach tolerance as among the highest virtues. And yet it is intolerant of Christianity just as it lashes out at hypocrisy as the worst vice, and can be hypocritical in its own deductions based on the worldview that it assumes. But to be tolerant of something is not the same thing as believing something that is tolerated to be true. Rightly understood, the willingness to coexist with counter-perspectives is the best use of the term. Yet a person generally uses tolerance to condemn any absolute strain in a person's belief system, and while they condemn that, they obviously borrow some hierarchy of ethics of their own in order to criticize that which runs afoul of their own thinking.

The anomaly is it is logically impossible to live by the entailments of relativism. Even Bertrand Russell concluded this. He said, "Even though I don't believe in God, I have to live as though a God actually exists." Though they tell you that rationally you cannot come to an absolute, they try to smuggle in empirical data or existential data because rationally it is indefensible. So the fact is that they are living beyond their logical means, and their own logic would actually drive their philosophy into silence. For example, consider the logical consequences of Eastern mysticism's argument that reality is an illusion. There is very clearly an inability to live by the logical outworking of their own presuppositions. The Christian faith has the built-in reality that it can be constantly attacked and cannot come back with the same type of vociferous reaction. It's the same kind of principle in democracy. Democracy gives you the privilege of freedom and that freedom is sacred. As God has fashioned us, He gave us the freedoms, reminding us that if we violated the law, there would be some necessary consequences. So they take advantage of the familiarity of the situation, knowing that there will not be a counter-response as other religions are culturally protected. There is another very important thing here, and that is the 1960s decade and the writings of certain philosophers and academicians. Professor Jay Parini, a professor of English from Middlebury College, said after the Vietnam War, a lot of students didn't just crawl back into their library cubicles, but stepped into academic positions. Now they have tenure and the work of reshaping the universities has begun in earnest. Anytime someone affirms morality, it doesn't matter whether they are religiously minded or politically minded, this culture will attack them. Because if you can take away those who deny your right to interpret morality anyway you want, you are then utterly free in any sense.

What we need to realize here is that these are different religions. They are not saying the same thing. Consider the woman at the well and the woman with the alabaster ointment who came to Jesus washing His feet with her hair. I don't know if we realize what a cultural crossing of a line that was, especially since she was in the home of a Pharisee. It is interesting to me that Jesus commended her and then said wherever the gospel is preached, there shall also be told what this woman has done to me. It's a fascinating testimony to what Jesus meant by the notion of forgiveness and the acceptance of every human being as of intrinsic worth, not in any way to be vitiated by gender. So the truth of the Christian claim and the teachings of Jesus Christ are so different. Gautama Buddha left his wife on the day that his son was born, enraging his father-in-law. You see a completely different value placed on things like marriage. Marital responsibility, fidelity, commitment, the place of the individual human being regardless of gender and appearance—to think that all of these religions teach the same thing is really to be dishonest with these religions.

There is no way a Buddhist will say that his or her faith is the same thing as that of the Muslim. There is no way a Muslim will say that his or her faith is the same as that of a follower of Jesus Christ, who believes that Jesus died on the cross and rose again from the dead. Muslims deny the resurrection of Jesus. They deny the crucifixion of Jesus—that He actually died on the cross. So they are not saying the same thing, no more than conflicting political theories are saying the same thing at their core. The foundational vision that they have is at points of tension and some of them are points of contradictions. Religions are mutually exclusive in their core fundamental beliefs. So the question of truth reemerges. How do you measure it? It should be done with academic integrity. It should be done with the gentleness of spirit and the recognition that there are mutually exclusive truth claims here. My approach is often that each religion or worldview must consider the four questions of life on origin, meaning, morality, and destiny. The answers to these questions frame a person's worldview, and the worldview that is most coherent and consistent is one in which every assertion on these four questions correspond with reality and when those assertions are systematized, there is a coherent worldview. I believe the greatest search in the human heart today is for meaning and coherence, and the reason we are mangled in our day-to-day living is because we are mangled in belief at the core. As Chesterton said, we have become a culture with its feet firmly planted in midair. There is no grounding to the belief.

When people make such statements as, "All believers believe the same thing," it is the ultimate disrespect of a religious worldview to say we are all saying the same thing. What if we turned to such a person and said, "Actually, you are saying the same thing that Hitler has said. There's really no difference between you, Hitler, and Nietzsche; you are all really saying the same thing." Why is it that people who hold that all-encompassing worldview do not like to be lumped in with contrary positions, but they want religions to be so watered down to say the same thing? It is a complete disrespect for the religions of the world and in the name of tolerance is intolerant of them.

Regarding the charge that Christians are judgmental, I frequently encounter that accusation in open forums. I invariably counter by saying, where does Jesus say, "Judge not lest ye be judged?" and almost no one has been able to pinpoint where he said it. What Jesus says prior is "When you abide in my word, you are my disciples, then ye shall know the truth and the truth shall set you free." "Judge not lest ye be judged," of course, comes from the Sermon on the Mount, in the context of praying, fasting, and then He talks about judging. He says don't pray out in public in order to show off. Do not fast in order that you get the approval of men. What He is really saying is not whether you pray or whether you fast or whether you judge, but how you pray, fast, and judge. Then Jesus tells us in the Gospel of John to judge rightly and not to just stop judging, but to stop judging *by appearances*. God tells us in the Old Testament so clearly to walk not on the counsel of the ungodly. How do you know that unless you make your judgments? Thus Jesus is saying to remember that the same measurement by which you measure others, you also will be measured. He is warning against duplicitous judgment that holds up one standard for another and not for yourself. In fact, after that verse, He went on to say, "Why are you worried about the speck in your brother's eye when you've not dealt with the beam in your own?" So first, it is a reminder to us that we have a standard by which we are to live and that we must judge ourselves by too. Second, I've often said to students, "So you believe the New Testament when Jesus said 'Judge not lest ye be judged.' Do you then believe that Jesus is who He claimed to be and He was right in what He said?" So to use a text while denying the very context of the person and authority is again defying logic. They misread the context and ironically deny the very text that they are using to attack Christians. It is impossible to live without making judgments. What God is telling us is to judge rightly and not duplicitously.

Related to this subject is your question about how Christians can be more effective in persuading a relativist culture that their affirmation of certain biblical prescriptions, such as those against homosexual behavior, are compatible with a loving religion. How does one hate the sin and love the sinner? Well, it is a very critical issue in our times and I think it was George Will years ago who made the comment, "Any stigma can lick a good dogma." and what has happened is they stigmatize the Christian religion as intolerant and on the basis of that, they can lash out. The answer is not as elusive as the skeptic often makes it out to be. Anybody who has been a father or a mother knows the distinction between the two. You see your son or your daughter go in a path that you utterly despise. It is the wrong way. But you never ever stop loving that son or daughter. You are always there to reach out when they need you and when they come, you do not heap it upon their heads. You are there to celebrate with the fatted calf, as it were, and the robe, the return of the prodigal son. I think it is critical that we understand that the liberal who castigates the conservative and decries the possibility of loving the sinner and hating the sin is the same liberal who gets into ad hominem arguments all the time and attacks the person. I've seen it on many a debate floor. They go for the person. They attack the person when what they should be doing is attacking the idea. You see, there is such a thing as egalitarianism and elitism. In God's economy, egalitarianism is about people. We are all equal before Him. Elitism is an idea. Some ideas are wrong and need to be dealt with. What happens in the counter-cultural worldview is they make people elitist and all ideas egalitarian, making them equal, and that's where the problem lies. I think we need to recognize that we dare not celebrate certain lifestyles. We must look at certain ideas and lifestyles we cannot accept; we condemn the lifestyle or at least do not celebrate that lifestyle with people. We can accept the person as a fellow human being without celebrating their belief. I've said everyone has a right to believe but not everything believed is right. It needs to be done and it can be done. Our Lord Himself showed the way.

2. Do you believe, as many of America's founding fathers did, that faith (Judeo-Christian values and principles) and freedom are inseparable? That is, if we fully abandon our faith tradition, which is foundational to our liberties, will our liberties diminish and eventually evaporate? If so, how can we return to our faith tradition with such a pluralistic cultural mix in America today? Is a full-blown revival necessary?

Dr. James Dobson

Without a doubt, faith and freedom are inseparable. They are two sides of the same coin. On one side is freedom, and on the other is responsibility, which is itself derived from an individual's internal moral standards. In the absence of these principles of responsible behavior, freedom will, over time, degenerate into anarchy and chaos. Given a choice between chaos and tyranny, people will always choose tyranny. Stated another way, the only way to combat chaos is to *limit* personal freedoms through tougher, more intrusive laws, expanded police presence, and bigger prisons. Dictators emerge from that circumstance.

Nevertheless, we support a pluralistic culture, wherein people are free to believe in very different ways. The Bill of Rights supports those and other freedoms. We can, however, certainly hope that the people will see the wisdom of embracing Judeo-Christian values. The real question is whether our moral tradition—which stems from, but is not limited to—our biblical faith, is good for the country as a whole. In America, important elements of the Judeo-Christian belief system have become foundational principles of secular law. "Thou shalt not murder" and "thou shalt not steal" were direct edicts from God long before they were embodied in our federal and state laws. But both the religious and the irreligious can agree that such principles are good for society. Similarly, our Founding Fathers instituted a system of government that is built on three separate but equal branches, because they had an understanding of man's sinfulness, which naturally leads to corruption and tyranny. But even those who don't believe in the biblical teaching of man's sinful nature will agree that our system of checks and balances is beneficial.

As for the concept of revival, I believe that it is essential—not only in terms of changing the hearts and lives of individuals, but in terms of improving our society on a broad scale. Looking back over history, it is remarkable to consider the positive changes that were brought about by the growth of Christianity. Our entire "Western" way of life, which is built upon the principles of freedom, democracy, and morality, came about because Judeo-Christian principles replaced the ideologies of the Greco-Roman world that celebrated immorality and cheapened human life. Unfortunately, the influence of Christianity is weakening in the West at the dawn of the twenty-first century, and many of the evil practices of those ancient civilizations are creeping back into our culture. If we are to effectively halt the advance of these immoral ideals, a sweeping spiritual revival *must* take place. I pray that it might happen in our lifetime.

Dr. Michael Novak

It is clear that virtually all of the top hundred founders of the United States—including the ones who signed the Declaration of Independence or the Constitution, or both—held that republican governance and respect for individual human rights are inconsistent with atheism. As Tocqueville notes, they gave a whole series of reasons why they believed that atheism undermines the beliefs and practices on which republican governance and respect for human rights rest.

We in our own day are testing that proposition, aren't we? Contrary to our founders, many of our most highly educated elites seem to hold, as Freud did, that being religious indicates a neurosis, a need for a crutch. Our cultural elites talk as if unbelief represents an emotional advance beyond belief. Secure in this belief, they feel free to abandon every outward sign of religion. They entrust the future of the republic, if not to atheism, then at least to official indifference with respect to religion. We will discover the outcome of this new experiment in another two or three generations.

For it is usually the case that the first generation to reject religion continues to live from the internal capital they have inherited from belief and its inward practices. However, they have now made themselves incapable of passing on the inner beliefs and practices of their own life to their children. Thus their children grow up in an entirely different situation, and even more so do the children of their children. In this way, the loss of belief is not generally felt throughout society for at least three or possibly four generations.

Dr. Marvin Olasky

The University of Texas school song (to the tune of "I've been working on the railroad") begins, "The eyes of Texas are upon you, all the livelong day. The eyes of Texas are upon you, you cannot get away." A highly mobile mass society like ours encourages anonymity that enables people without an internal gyroscope to twist and turn in all directions. We think we can get away from God's observation, and so we engage in many acts that are harmful to ourselves and others.

Biblical faith and freedom have been inseparable in American history, in large part because of our ancestors' understanding of *coram deo*—"in the sight of God." It's theoretically possible that a sense of someone other than God watching—perhaps the eyes of Texas—could push individuals to keep liberty from turning into license. A general emphasis on virtue could possibly fill the bill, but people who believe No One's watching will normally allow specific temptations to trump moralistic statements.

I suspect, therefore, that if biblical belief evaporates so will our liberties. "Freedom's just another word for nothing left to lose," Janis Joplin sang before she drugged and drank herself to death. She could not have been more wrong. Anyone with nothing to lose is a leaf blown around by cultural and ideological winds, and leaves are not free. Previous generations of Americans understood the "bondage of the will" that is our natural lot without God's grace. Unless God shines his grace on us we are enslaved, and when individuals are enslaved bondage for an entire society is not far behind. And that's one reason it's good to sing, "God shine His grace on thee."

American society has always been a mix of worldviews, but we've always had a critical mass devoted to biblical principles: the Bible describes believers as salt, both preserving a culture and giving it taste. We still have that critical mass; will the next generation? Without revival and reformation, I suspect not. But I'm not about to predict the future: only God knows.

Dr. D. James Kennedy

First, there is no question that Christianity is foundational to our liberties. This country was founded by a society that was overwhelmingly Christian. In 1776, 98 percent of the people in American professed to be Protestant Christians, 1.8 percent professed to be Roman Catholic Christians, and 0.2 percent professed to be Jewish. That means that 99.8 percent of the people in America in 1776 professed to be Christians. In 1620, they were all Christians, in 1630 when the Pilgrims came, they were still all Christians, but as late as 1776 it was 99.8 percent. So this country was founded by an overwhelming percentage of Christian people and of course all you hear about are the few that weren't. These are the only people that the public media and the schools ever talk about. Jefferson, Franklin, and so on were the tiny minority that weren't Evangelical Christians. So when those Christians founded this country, it wasn't a theocracy. There was more liberty here than had ever existed in the world anywhere else. Patrick Henry said, "America was not founded by religionists but by Christians. It was not founded upon religions but upon the gospel of Jesus Christ." And for that reason people of every religion came here and found complete freedom to exercise their religion as they saw fit. The fact of the matter is that a Christian nation, overwhelmingly Christian, grants more freedom to everybody else than any other nation in the world. And the people that cry theocracy, if you go to whatever nation it is that holds the view that they hold, you will find a tiny fraction of the freedom and liberty that Christians gave to everybody in this country. The atheists: go to Russia and see what kind of freedom the Soviet Union gave people. If they are Muslims, go to Saudi Arabia or Iran or Afghanistan and see what kind of freedom those people have there. No matter where you go, Christians provide more liberty for more people.

Indeed, Washington talked about morality and religion being the twin pillars of our society and of our Constitution and therefore that those who labor to subvert those pillars need not claim the mantle of patriotism because they are not patriotic. They are opposed to the very foundations upon which this nation was built. Andrew Jackson said, "the Bible, sir, is the rock upon which this Republic stands." Of course, today, this is a view that is totally alien to many Americans.

But I have a very optimistic outlook in spite of everything that we've said and this astonishes many people. I believe that not only are we going to win, I believe we are in fact winning the battle for cultural moral value. Nothing on the surface would give that impression. What do I base that upon? Well, if you look at the Gallup organization figures, they show that about eighty-five or eighty-six percent of the American people have professed to be Christians over the last thirty years or so. That doesn't change very much. But then they ask a collection of questions such as, "Have you had a personal experience with Jesus Christ that has transformed your life?"; "Have you been born again?"; which is basically the same thing, and "Do you have the assurance of eternal life?" The nominal Christian would simply not answer affirmatively because he wouldn't even know what you're talking about. By the way, let me point out to you that it's only in Christianity that you have nominal and real believers.

A nominal Christian may have joined a church, been baptized, and confirmed, but he has never been born again or regenerated and therefore no other religion has regeneration because no other religion has the Holy Spirit who regenerates people. And therefore, only Christianity has nominal and real members. But the real Christians in this country that would answer positively the questions that I gave you—and no such polls are perfect—have gone up from in the last thirty or forty years from about twenty-three percent to between forty-five and fifty percent. Now I think that is extraordinarily encouraging and I believe that in the next ten to fifteen years, those figures are going to go up to fifty, fifty-five, fifty-seven, or fifty-eight percent. And we're going to see a huge sea change in this country when that happens and many of the ungodly, immoral, unethical things that are called by all kinds of other names rather than what they really are, various kinds of sin, these things are going to melt like the frost before the rising sun as this nation becomes more and more Christianized. And you are going to see changes everywhere. Fifteen years from now this country, I believe, and I'm not a prophet, but I believe that what we have seen is going to show that that is actually what is happening and we are very close to that crux when it's going to shift from a majority of non-Christians to a majority of Christians and that is going to be a very interesting time. I have said that Springtime is coming to America. Not much on the surface shows it right now, but it's happening.

Nancy Pearcey

Christians have two tasks: First, we are called to preach the gospel in language people will understand. And our message will not be taken seriously unless we also exhibit the character of God in our practical mode of life. In the days of the early church, the thing that most impressed outsiders was the community of love among believers. "Behold how they love one another." In every age, the credibility of the biblical message depends on authentic communities exhibiting God's love and grace.

Second, we are called to be channels of grace to the wider culture in which we live. Because of the fact/value dichotomy, the great towering ideals that once guided our civilization have crumbled into a morass of subjective relativism. We need to challenge the postmodernism that has marginalized religion and morality as private experience, reassert their status as objective knowledge, and reclaim a place at the table of public discourse.

Dr. Ravi Zacharias

America is living in what I consider one of the hinges of history that will determine the country's future. The more I read the documents of the founding fathers, the more I am fascinated by the insight, the brilliance of the founding documents. The late Russell Kirk, who wrote the book *The Roots of American Order,* examined those roots; the founders believed in the seminal connection of life's sacredness and freedom. The only way it can be sacred is if there is transcendent moral order. In fact, I believe more and more that the only way one can condemn racism logically and morally is in a framework of theism. Naturalism severs the nerve of intrinsic worth and we become the accidental collocation of atoms. Naturalism has no philosophical basis on which to condemn racism. That's why Nazism and the philosophy of Nietzsche took hold of the naturalistic worldview, because they had no rational basis for an equal intrinsic worth and they started to obliterate and deny the right of individuals. My belief is that the founding fathers knew this. George Washington said that in his final address. That in vain would you seek to find the moral order apart from a religious worldview. And if the closing words of the Declaration of Independence are right, which says, for example, "and for the support of the declaration and the firm reliance and the protection of divine providence, we mutually pledge to each other our lives, our fortunes, and our sacred honor." I think they knew it. They understood. They said it in a kind and gentle way so that it was not an overbearing worldview but an undergirding worldview. If America's leaders do not realize that a moral basis for freedom is rooted in a transcendent moral order, then in the end, we will violate both our essential work and the practical outworking.

The founding fathers understood the ramifications of liberty and the necessity of the sacred dignity of each life. Those who deny that our framers were predominantly Christians are engaged in a falsehood. But suppose they persist. An inescapable fact is that the Constitution and the Bill of Rights could never have been framed in a Hindu, Muslim, or Buddhist worldview. It is only in the Judeo-Christian worldview that such documents make sense and reflect an order.

Now, about how can we return to our essential faith tradition with such a pluralistic mix in American society? Is a full-blown revival is necessary?

I think there are multiple strands that come in. I'm a firm believer in the fact that unless theological institutions and our seminaries start training leaders to think again and think well, and to be able to articulate their positions well, we'll be running for a long time against the wind. We'll be swimming against the tide. Secondly, we need to go back in our homes and teach our young people how to think properly, how to think critically. Our institutions and our homes are our places of great importance. Our musicians have a very key role here because this is a culture of music and the arts. We need to return to solid thinking in the lyrics of our songs, not just the floaty feeling that punctuates our worship. Our worship has to have integrity returned. There are many, many ways in which I think this needs to be done but not the least of which is we start cleaning up our own house first: our families, our institutions, our leadership. And last but not least, I guess I would say we cannot live in hibernation. We have to be on the front lines and keep moving. The best way to lose a battle is to stop moving and to sort of get behind your own fort and think you'll be safe out there. We have to be in the public arena. And I think the day will come when some of these other worldviews will find the beauty of following Christ, and it's already happening in many part of the world. But America has to be strong and we need to pray that our leadership will continue to be of the caliber and the quality that is willing to stand against the tide. We, I think, have statesmanlike material in the country, and that's what the nation will need to be strong, courageous, and humble at the same time.

A Final Word

Christianity and Judeo-Christian principles, as we've seen, are essential to the unique political liberties Americans enjoy. By this we do not mean a state-sponsored religion, but a body politic largely committed to these moral underpinnings—especially to the principle that human life, because created in God's image, is sacred. As Dr. Dobson indicated, Christians support a pluralistic culture, where people are free to believe and worship as they choose, but we can hope that more people will embrace the Judeo-Christian values that support the moral foundations upon which our freedoms are based. The task of preserving our liberties will be exceedingly more difficult to the extent that our culture and our courts suppress Christian religious expression and ostracize those who advocate Christian principles.

Christians committed to their faith and to American freedom, I believe, have an unmistakable right, if not a duty, to engage in the political arena and to seek to influence the course of this country. They must not be intimidated from participating in the political process by distorted notions of the proper role of religion in politics. If they remain silent, especially about the moral foundations behind their policy preferences, they can expect those policies to crumble under their own weight, and if not, certainly by the onslaught of secular forces opposed to such measures. But as Dr. Ravi Zacharias observed, Christians should not limit their participation to the political arena. They should also seek to influence the culture in a positive moral direction. And they can begin by endeavoring to clean their own houses, their churches. And as Nancy Pearcey affirmed, Christians must confront the postmodern assaults against our moral absolutes and fight to reclaim a society based on objective truth.

Will our light of liberty slowly extinguish through the passage of time and successive generations, as suggested by Dr. Michael Novak and Dr. Marvin Olasky, because present generations are rejecting our foundational religion? Or are we already on the road to restoration, as Dr. D. James Kennedy asserts?

None of us knows for sure what the future holds, but there appears to be a consensus that America, to remain a free nation, must rededicate itself to its foundational Judeo-Christian moral underpinnings. And for that to happen, Christians must champion unfettered religious freedom, oppose those forces that threaten it, and strengthen their own churches, without which any hope to influence the political system and our culture will be futile.

Notes

Chapter 1

1. *Everson v. Board of Education*, 330 U.S. 1 (1947).

2. Josh McDowell and Bob Hostetler, *The New Tolerance, How a cultural movement threatens to destroy you, your faith, and your children* (Wheaton, Ill: Tyndale House Publishers, Inc., 1998), 53.

3. *Doe v. Santa Fe Independent School District*, 168 F. 3d 806, 810 (5th Cir. 1999). This was the Court of Appeals case reviewing District Judge Kent's ruling.

4. Don Rowland, "Jimmy and Raymond at School," *The Christian Informer*, July, 1998.

5. Ibid.

6. Ibid.

7. Josh McDowell and Bob Hostetler, *The New Tolerance, How a cultural movement threatens to destroy you, your faith, and your children* (Wheaton, Ill: Tyndale House Publishers, Inc., 1998), 7.

8. Letter from Steven W. Fitschen, National Legal Foundation, October 1997.

9. Ibid.

10. *Roberts v. Madigan*, 921 F.2d 1047 (10th Cir. 1990).

11. "Christian-Based Fast-Food Chain Sued," Charisma News Service, October 30, 2002.

12. News Release, "Legal Action Forces Teacher Union to Respect Rights of Religious Objector," National Right to Work Legal Defense Foundation, Inc., January 16, 2003.

13. Matthew Brouillette, "The Case for Choice in Schooling: Restoring Parental Control of Education," The Mackinac Center for Public Policy, 1. Brouillette has two post-graduate degrees in education and history and served as the Director of Education

Policy for the Mackinac Center for Public Policy between 1998 and 2002.

14. Ibid.

15. Editorial, "Reding, Wrighting & Erithmatic," *The Wall Street Journal*, October 2, 1989, as cited by Matthew Brouillette, "The Case for Choice in Schooling: Restoring Parental Control of Education," The Mackinac Center for Public Policy, 1.

16. Andrew J. Coulson, "Market Education: The Unknown History (New Brunswick: Transaction Publishers, 1999), 75, as cited by Matthew Brouillette, "The Case for Choice in Schooling: Restoring Parental Control of Education," The Mackinac Center for Public Policy, 1.

17. Gary Amos and Richard Gardiner, *Never Before in History, American's Inspired Birth* (Dallas, Texas: Haughton Publishing Company, 1998), 73.

18. Ellwood P. Cubberly, *Public Education in the United States* (New York: Houghton Mifflin Company, 1919), 12.

19. Stuart G. Noble, *A History of American Education* (New York: Farrar & Rinehart, Inc., 1938), 22.

20. D. James Kennedy and Jerry Newcombe, *What if the Bible had Never Been Written* (Nashville, TN: Thomas Nelson Publishers, 1998), 88. April Shenandoah, "History of America's Education, Part III: Universities, Textbooks, & America's Founders," *The Progressive Conservative*, Volume 14, Issue # 40, April 14, 2002.

21. Gary DeMar, *America's Christian History, The Untold Story* (Atlanta, GA: American Vision Inc. 1993), 99.

22. April Shenandoah, "History of America's Education, Part III: Universities, Textbooks & America's Founders," *The Progressive Conservative*, Volume IV, Issue # 40, April 14, 2002.

23. Ellwood P. Cubberly, *Public Education in the United States* (New York: Houghton Mifflin Company, 1919), 43-44; Gary DeMar, *America's Christian History, The Untold Story* (Atlanta, GA: American Vision Inc. 1993), 100.

24. Stuart G. Noble, *A History of American Education* (New York: Farrar & Rinehart, Inc., 1938), 25-26.

25. Ibid.

26. Gary DeMar, *America's Christian History, The Untold Story* (Atlanta, GA: American Vision Inc. 1993), 99.

27. April Shenandoah, "History of America's Education, Part III: Universities, Textbooks & America's Founders," *The Progressive Conservative*, Volume IV, Issue # 40, April 14, 2002.

28. Tim LaHaye, *Faith of Our Founding Fathers* (Green Forest, AR: Master Books, 1990), 78.

29. Edward H. Erwin, "The Faith of Our Founding Fathers," *Words for the Walk*, 1998.

30. Tim LaHaye, *Faith of Our Founding Fathers* (Green Forest, AR: Master Books, Inc., 1990), 78.

31. Ellwood P. Cubberly, *Readings in Public Education* (New York: Houghton Mifflin Company, 1919), 15–16.
32. Gerald L. Gutek, *An Historical Introduction to American Education* (Prospect Heights, Ill.: Waveland Press, Inc., 1991, 1970), 4.
33. *New England's First Fruits*, a pamphlet published in London in 1643, based on a letter dated, "Boston, September 27, 1642," describing the founding of Harvard College.
34. Ellwood P. Cubberly, *Public Education in the United States* (New York: Houghton Mifflin Company, 1919), 51.
35. Ibid., 15–16.
36. D. James Kennedy and Jerry Newcombe, *What if the Bible Had Never Been Written* (Nashville, TN: Thomas Nelson Publishers, 1998, 88.
37. Ellwood P. Cubberly, *Public Education in the United States* (New York: Houghton Mifflin Company, 1919), 16.
38. Ibid., 276.
39. Gerald L. Gutek, *An Historical Introduction to American Education* (Prospect Heights, Ill.: Waveland Press, Inc., 1991, 1970), 6.
40. Ellwood P. Cubberly, *Public Education in the United States* (New York: Houghton Mifflin Company, 1919), 18-19.
41. Matthew Brouillette, "The Case for Choice in Schooling: Restoring Parental Control of Education," The Mackinac Center for Public Policy.
42. Gerald L. Gutek, *An Historical Introduction to American Education* (Prospect Heights, Ill.: Waveland Press, Inc., 1991, 1970), 11-12.
43. Ellwood P. Cubberly, *Public Education in the United States* (New York: Houghton Mifflin Company, 1919), 20.
44. Gerald L. Gutek, *An Historical Introduction to American Education* (Prospect Heights, Ill.: Waveland Press, Inc., 1991, 1970), 9.
45. Ellwood P. Cubberly, *Public Education in the United States* (New York: Houghton Mifflin Company, 1919), 41.
46. Stuart G. Noble, *A History of American Education* (New York: Farrar & Rinehart, Inc., 1938), 21-22.
47. Stephen B. Presser, *Recapturing the Constitution, Race, Religion, and Abortion Reconsidered* (Washington, D.C.: Regnery Publishing, Inc. 1994), 150-159.
48. Ellwood P. Cubberly, *Public Education in the United States* (New York: Houghton Mifflin Company, 1919), 88.
49. Matthew Brouillette, "The Case for Choice in Schooling: Restoring Parental Control of Education," The Mackinac Center for Public Policy.
50. Ellwood P. Cubberly, *Public Education in the United States* (New York: Houghton Mifflin Company, 1919), 92.
51. Ibid., 110.

52. Stuart G. Noble, *A History of American Education* (New York: Farrar & Rinehart, Inc., 1938), 149.
53. Matthew Brouillette, "The Case for Choice in Schooling: Restoring Parental Control of Education," The Mackinac Center for Public Policy. 2001.
54. Ibid.
55. Ellwood P. Cubberly, *Public Education in the United States* (New York: Houghton Mifflin Company, 1919), 164.
56. Matthew Brouillette, "The Case for Choice in Schooling: Restoring Parental Control of Education," The Mackinac Center for Public Policy. 2001.
57. Ibid.
58. Ibid.
59. Ibid.
60. Ibid.
61. Stuart G. Noble, *A History of American Education* (New York: Farrar & Rinehart, Inc., 1938), 156.
62. Ellwood P. Cubberly, *Public Education in the United States* (New York: Houghton Mifflin Company, 1919), 232.
63. Ibid., 234-235.
64. 330 U.S. 1 (1947.)
65. U.S. Supreme Court Justice William Rehnquist, in a dissenting opinion in *Wallace v. Jaffree,* 472 U. S. 38 (1985), stated, "the wall of separation between church and state is a metaphor based upon bad history, which should be frankly and explicitly abandoned," as a "mischievous diversion of judges from the actual intention of the drafters of the Bill of Rights."
66. Actually, Jefferson's language ostensibly advocating a wall of separation between church and state was introduced into our case law in the earlier Supreme Court case of *Reynolds v. U.S.* 98 U.S. 145 (1878), but the language didn't yet give rise to a revolution in church/state case law. In that case, Chief Justice Waite quoted Jefferson's famous language in an 1802 letter to the Danbury Baptist Church: "Believing with you that religion is a matter which lies solely between man and his God; that he owes account to none other for his faith or his worship; that the legislative powers of the government reach actions only, and not opinions, I contemplate with sovereign reverence that act of the whole American people which declared that their legislature should 'make no law respecting an establishment of religion or prohibiting the free exercise thereof,' thus building a wall of separation between church and State." In Chapter Seven, I discuss recent scholarship arguing that Jefferson's language was taken out of context by our courts.
67. *Everson v. Board of Education,* 330 U.S. 1, 18 (1947).
68. Ibid., 15-16.
69. Gerard V. Bradley, *Church-State Relationships in America* (Westport, Conn:

Greenwood Press, 1987), 1.
70. Paul G. Kauper, "Everson v. Board of Education: A Product of the Judicial Will," *Arizona Law Review* 15 (1973): 307.
71. Daniel L. Dreisbach, *Everson and the Command of History, Everson Revisited, Religion, Education and Law at the Crossroads* (Lanham, Maryland: Rowman & Littlefield Publishers, Inc. 1997), 23-24.
72. Ibid., 24.
73. *Engel v. Vitale*, 370 U. S. 421, (1962).
74. George Goldberg, *Church, State, and The Constitution, The Religion Clauses Upside Down* (Washington, D.C.: Regnery Gateway, 1984, 1987), 68.
75. *Engel v. Vitale*, 10 N.Y.2d 174, 218 N.Y.Supp.2d 659, 176 N.E.2d 579 (1961), as reported by George Goldberg, *Church, State, and The Constitution, The Religion Clauses Upside Down* (Washington, D.C.: Regnery Gateway, 1984, 1987), 69-70.
76. Ibid., 69.
77. Ibid.
78. The court made this clear in *Santa Fe Independent School District v. Doe*, 530 U.S. 290, 313 (2000), "Thus, nothing in the Constitution as interpreted by this Court prohibits any public school student from voluntarily praying at any time before, during, or after the schoolday. But the religious liberty protected by the Constitution is abridged when the State affirmatively sponsors the particular religious practice of prayer."
79. *Wallace v. Jaffree*, 472 U. S. 38 (1985). The court said that the Establishment Clause does not forbid voluntary silent prayer, but in this case, the Alabama legislature already had a statute in place permitting silent time for meditation. So when the legislature amended the statute to read "meditation or voluntary prayer," the court concluded that it was suggesting prayer, because there was no other reason for the additional language. As such, the statute had no secular purpose and was invalidated.
80. *United States v. Nixon*, 418 U.S. 683 (1974).
81. Don Rowland, "Jimmy and Raymond at School," *The Christian Informer*, July, 1998.
82. Joan Little, "City Schools Issue Rules About Students, Religion," *The St. Louis Post-Dispatch*, July 11, 1996.
83. Prepared Testimony by Colleen K. Pinyan, Esq. The Rutherford Institute Coordinator, Office of Public Affairs, Before the Senate Judiciary Committee "Religious Discrimination in the Classroom and Workplace," Federal News Service, September 12, 1995.
84. Joan Little, "City Schools Issue Rules About Students, Religion," *The St. Louis Post-Dispatch*, July 11, 1996.
85. *Chandler v. Siegelman*, 230 F. 3d 1313 (11th Cir. 2000).

86. Ibid.

87. "The Prayer Corner," Institute for First Amendment Studies, January/February 1999.

88. *Santa Fe Independent School District v. Doe*, 530 U.S. 290 (2000).

89. Ibid.

90. Ibid.

91. M. Stanton Evans, *The Theme is Freedom; Religion, Politics, and the American Tradition* (Washington, D.C. : Regnery Publishing, Inc. 1994), 285.

92. Scott Finn Putnam, "Poca Pre-game Prayer Protests Supreme Court Ruling," *The Charleston Gazette*, October 20, 2000.

93. Ibid.

94. Frank J. Murray, "Federal Court Hears Lawsuit Over Kindergarten Christian; New York school may relent, may let tot say grace at meals," *The Washington Times*, April 12, 2002.

95. Ellen Sorokin, "Deal Reached on Praying Child; School to Allow Kindergartner to Say Grace at Snack Time," *The Washington Times*, June 12, 2002.

96. Kenneth C. Crowe II, "Kindergartner's prayer case settled; Saratoga Springs School Board agrees to Permit 'Nondisruptive' Prayer, Admits No Wrongdoing," *The Times Union*, June 12, 2002.

97. Ibid.

98. Kenneth W. Starr, *First Among Equals, The Supreme Court in American Life* (New York, N.Y.: Warner Books , 2002), 96-97.

99. 505 U.S. 557 (1992).

100. Kevin O'Hanlon, "ACLU to Appeal Dismissal of Lawsuit Over School Prayer," The Associated Press, November 20, 2002.

101. *Adler v. Duval County School Board*, 250 F.3d 1330 (11th Cir. 2001).

102. *Cole v. Oroville Union High School Dist.*, 228 F. 3d 1092 (9th Cir. 2000); *Jones v. Clear Creek Independent School District*, 977 F. 2d 963 (5th Cir. 1992).

103. *American Civil Liberties Union of New Jersey v. Black Horse Pike Regional Board of Education*, 84 F. 3d 1471 (3rd Cir. 1996).

104. Church and State Bulletin, "Supreme Court Skips Florida Graduation Prayer Case," Americans United for Separation of Church and State, January 1, 2002.

105. Mandi Steele, "Officials Try to Censor Religious Speech, Allow Salutatorian to Give Graduation Address Only After Legal Threat," *WorldNetDaily.com*, June 11, 2002.

106. Ibid.

107. Kevin O'Hanlon, "ACLU to Appeal Dismissal of Lawsuit Over School Prayer," The Associated Press, November 20, 2002.

108. Carrie Smith, "Payout for Prayer Lawsuit Irks Board. Schools Must Pay Attorneys $23,000 for Student's Suit," *The Charleston Daily Mail*, August 16, 2002.

109. Eric Eyre, "Despite Court Order, Students Pray," *The Charleston Gazette Online*, May 31, 2002.
110. Ibid.
111. Letter from Steven W. Fitschen, *National Legal Foundation*, February 20, 2002.
112. Ibid.
113. Ibid.
114. "Celine Dion Song Banned: 'Too Christian' for School, Students' choice of music at graduation leads to legal scrap over 1st Amendment," *Worldnetdaily.com*, June 8, 2003.
115. Frank Santiago, "Lord's Prayer Plan Sparks Suit," *Des Moines Register*, April 3, 2002.
116. "Iowa Students Object to Singing Lord's Prayer at Graduation," The Associated Press, April 3, 2002.
117. "Lord's Prayer Can't Be Sung At Iowa High School Graduation," The Associated Press, May 13, 2002.
118. David Limbaugh, "Enemies, Not Guardians of Religious Freedom," *Creators Syndicate*, September 14, 2002.
119. "Poll: Should a School Choir Be Allowed to Sing at Churches?" Channel 9 *Eyewitness News* (WFTV-TV), November 19, 2002.
120. Art Moore, "Gospel Choir Now Allowed in Churches," *Worldnetdaily.com*, November 23, 2002.
121. Ibid.
122. Art Moore, "District Censures Worker for Prayer E-Mail, Forwarding President's Proclamation Broke Religious-Speech Policy," *WorldNetDaily.com*, August 2, 2002.
123. Press Release, "ACLJ Files Federal Suit Against Texas School District Over E-Mail Policy That Prohibits Religious Messages," The American Center for Law and Justice, August 1, 2002.
124. Joyce Howard Price, "School district drops religious-speech ban," *The Washington Times*, September 23, 2002.
125. Art Moore, "District Censures Worker for Prayer E-Mail, Forwarding President's Proclamation Broke Religious-Speech Policy," *WorldNetDaily.com*, August 2, 2002.

Chapter 2

1. "Court Bars Religious Tiles from Columbine," *Reuters*, June 27, 2002.
2. Ibid.
3. Robert B. Bluey, "Supreme Court Asked to Hear Columbine Religious Speech Case," *CNSNews.com*, November 15, 2002.
4. Robert Marus, "Supreme Court Declines Case Over Columbine Memorial Tiles," *ABPNews*, January 14, 2003.

5. Ibid. The courts permitting this kind of school viewpoint discrimination usually rely on a 1988 Supreme Court Case of *Hazelwood School District v. Kuhlmeier*, 484 U.S. 260 (1988), which gave school officials authority to regulate the contents of a school newspaper.

6. "Child's Religious-Poster Case Can Have Another Hearing," The Associated Press, April 1, 2001.

7. "Mother Sues School Over Son's Censored Jesus Picture," Charisma News Service, November 10, 1999.

8. "Picture of Jesus Lands Kindergartner in Court," *CNSNews.com*, April 13, 2001.

9. John W. Whitehead, "Life, death: Censored Speaker Teaches Students," *The Daily Courier*, December 2, 2002.

10. Ibid.

11. "Montana Schools Sued for Anti-Christian Bias," *Charisma News Service*, October 23, 2002.

12. Matt Pyeatt, "School Prevents Student Group from Holding 'Easter' Can Drive," *CNSNews.com*, March 12, 2002.

13. Ibid.

14. Press Release, "New York City Schools Sued in Federal Court Over Policy Discriminating Against Christians During Christmas Season," Thomas More Law Center, December 10, 2002.

15. Jeff McKay, "Suit Claims NYC Schools Discriminate Against Christians," *CNSNews.com*, December 11, 2002.

16. Tanya L. Green, J.D., "'Political Correctness Hinders Religious Expression," Concerned Women for America, December 20, 2001.

17. "Public Schools and Christmas: The Season Wrapped in Red Tape," The Associated Press, December 21, 2001.

18. Joe Kovacs, "School Bans Saying 'Christmas'; Veteran teacher dumbfounded by order precluding mention of holiday," *Worldnetdaily.com*, December 13, 2002.

19. Kelly Boggs, "A Constitutional Christmas," *Baptist Press News*, December 20, 2002.

20. Anthony Pelliccio, "Shhhh, Don't Tell the ACLU... But Merry Christmas, *Opinioneditorials.com*, December 17, 2002.

21. Bryan J. Brown, "SCASD's Christless Holiday," Center for Law & Policy Analysis Press Release, November 20, 2000.

22. News Brief, "Parents Fight School Christmas Ban," *Charisma News Service*, December 23, 2002.

23. David Montgomery, "A PC Christmas," *FrontpageMagazine.com*, December 24, 2002.

24. Amy Hetzner, "School Rejected Girl's Religious Cards, Suit Says," *The Milwaukee Journal Sentinel*, March 22, 2001.

25. Ibid.

26. Ibid.

27. Ibid.

28. "Wisconsin School Board: Girl May Hand Out Religious Cards," The Associated Press, August 29, 2001.

29. Kerby Anderson, "Bible Distribution," Kerby Anderson Commentary, *Probe.org*, August 26, 1999.

30. News Release, "School Officials Trash Truth for Youth Bibles and Ten Commandments Book Covers," Liberty Counsel, May 19, 2000.

31. Alan Sears, "Just in Time for Christmas...A Wonderful Gift from the Lord," Alliance Defense Fund Special News Alert, December 19, 2002.

32. Steve Doland, "Medford Board Settles with Family over Bible Story," *The Burlington County Times*, November 6, 2002.

33. Jessica Cantelon, "Parents of Second Grader Sue School for Religious Discrimination," *CNSNews.com*, August 1, 2002.

34. Editorial, "A Biblical Victory in Atlanta," *The Tampa Tribune*, January 30, 1996.

35. Brendan Miniter, "God-Free School Zones," *OpinionJournal.com*, April 15, 2003.

36. Robert B. Bluey, "Religious-Themed Candy Dispute Resolved in Nevada," CNSNews.com, December 13, 2002.

37. Ellen Sorokin, "Students Try Court on Christian Gifts," *The Washington Times*, January 14, 2003.

38. Mathew Staver, "Students Suspended for Distributing Candy Canes File Lawsuit," Liberty Counsel Press Release, January 13, 2003.

39. Ted LaBorde, "Students: Religious Candy May Bring Punishment," *The Union Times*, January 1, 2003.

40. Ibid.

41. Mathew Staver, "Federal Court Upholds Right of Students to Distribute Candy Canes with Religious Message to Fellow Students," Liberty Counsel News Release, March 17, 2003.

42. Associated Press, "Judges Ponder Kindergartner's Role in Free Speech Case," January 10, 2003.

43. Steven W. Fitschen Letter, *National Legal Foundation*, October 1997.

44. "Alabama School District Settles, Allows Girl to Wear Cross," *Catholic World News*, March 2, 2000.

45. Susan Jones, "'Jesus Christ' Sweatshirt in Maine Will be Allowed," *CNSNews.com*, March 6, 2001; Gordon Bonin, "School Cool to Girl's 'Jesus' Sweat Shirt," *Bangor Daily News*, February 14, 2001.

46. Diane Morey Hanson, "Students Sue Northville High School," *Credo Classic*, December 11, 2000.

47. Scott Hogenson, "Bible Club Returns to High School Campus," *CNSNews.com*, April 2, 2001.

48. Letter from Steven W. Fitschen, National Legal Foundation, October 1997.

49. Jon Dougherty, "School Sued for Barring Bible Club," *Worldnetdaily.com*, January 7, 2003.

50. *Widmar et al. v. Vincent et al.*, 454 U.S. 263 (1981).

51. 98 Stat. 1302, 20 U.S.C. §§§§ 4071-4074. You can find a very lucid and thorough discussion of the equality principle in Kenneth W. Starr, *First Among Equals, The Supreme Court in American Life* (New York, N.Y.: Warner Books , 2002).

52. *Board of Education of the Westside Community Schools v. Mergens*, 496 U.S. 226 (1990).

53. Kenneth W. Starr, *First Among Equals, The Supreme Court in American Life* (New York, N.Y.: Warner Books , 2002), 100-104.

54. *Good News Club et al. v. Milford Central School*, 533 U.S. 98 (2001).

55. Rich Jefferson, "L.A. Public Schools: No Bible Clubs Here, *Focus on the Family Citizen*, 2002.

56. Jason Pierce, "School Sued Over Religious Access Denial," *CNSNews.com*, June 25, 2001.

57. David Overstreet & Doug Clark, "See You at the Pole, September 18, 2002," National Network of Youth Ministries Press Release, September 2002.

58. Richard K. Jefferson, "Lawsuit Filed Against Public School Officials for Censoring 'Lunch Bunch' Bible Club; Another example of a lawsuit that shouldn't need to be filed," Alliance Defense Fund Press Release, January 22, 2003.

59. *Child Evangelism Fellowship of New Jersey, Inc. v. Stafford Township Sch. Dist., Civil Action No. 02-4549 (MLC)* (D.N.J. December 10, 2002), as reported by Christian Legal Society in its Press Release, "Court Stops School's Discrimination Against Religious Group," December 11, 2002.

60. Charles Osgood, "Religious Released Time," *The Osgood File*, February 4, 1999.

61. *Zorach v. Clauson*, 343 U.S. 306 (1952).

62. *Zorach v. Clauson*, 343 U.S. 306, 313-314 (1952).

63. "School District Censors Student Religious Speech," Pacific Justice Institute Press Release, June 25, 2002.

64. "School District Censors Religious Speech," Pacific Justice Institute Press Release, June 25, 2002.

65. October 2002 News, *Los Angeles Lay Catholic Mission*, October 2002.

66. Ryan McCarthy, "School Rallies to Retain Sign; The ACLU Says the Message 'God Bless America' Divides Kids by Religion and is Unconstitutional," *The Sacramento Bee*, October 6, 2001.

67. Erika Chavez and Ryan McCarthy, "Rocklin Vows to Keep 'God Bless America,'" *The Sacramento Bee*, October 13, 2001.

68. Ibid.

69. *Stone v. Graham*, 449 U.S. 39 (1980).

70. Ibid., 41.

71. Ibid., 43-45.

72. "ACLU Loses Ten Commandments Decision; judge says display can stay," The Associated Press, January 24, 2003.

73. "Kentucky Officials Ordered to Remove Ten Commandments Displays," The Associated Press, June 25, 2001.

74. "N.C. Senate Endorses Ten Commandments Displays in Schools," The Associated Press, July 19, 2001.

75. "N.C. Lawmakers OK Ten Commandments Bill," The Associated Press, July 27, 2001.

76. "Onslaught of Ten Commandments Legislation Under Consideration in State Legislatures Nationwide," Americans United for Separation of Church and State Press Release, February 3, 2000.

77. "School Board to Appeal 10 Commandments Order," The Associated Press, June 21, 2002.

78. Robert Aderholt, "Ten Commandments Defense Act," Press Release from Congressman Aderholt, March 20, 2002.

79. "Madison Schools Take Heat for Pledge Ban, Meeting to Reconsider Ban Monday," *TheMilwaukeeChannel.com*, October 9, 2001.

80. Mark Walsh, "Madison Board Oks New Pledge, Anthem Policy," *Education Week on the web*, October 24, 2001.

81. "Madison School Board Removes Pledge of Allegiance Ban in Schools," *Fox News*, October 16, 2001.

82. "Pledge of Allegiance decision reversed," *CNN.com*, October 16, 2001.

83. "Madison School Board Removes Pledge of Allegiance Ban in Schools," *Fox News*, October 16, 2001.

84. "Wisconsin School Board Slammed for Barring Pledge of Allegiance," *Fox News*, October 12, 2001.

85. 310 U.S. 586 (1940).

86. 319 U.S. 624 (1943).

87. 292 F.3d 597 (9th Cir. 2002)

88. *Newdow v. United States Congress*, 292 F.3d 597, 608 (9th Cir. 2002).

89. *Roe v. Wade*, 410 U.S. 118 (1973). *Roe* had a companion case, *Doe v. Bolton*, 410 U.S. 179 (1973).

90. "Flap After Court Rules Pledge of Allegiance Unconstitutional," *Fox News*, June 27, 2002.

91. Editorial, "One Nation Under God," *The New York Times*, June 27, 2002.

92. Editorial, "A Godforsaken Ruling," *The Los Angeles Times*, June 27, 2002.

93. Editorial, "One Nation Under Blank," *The Washington Post*, June 27, 2002.
94. "Flap After Court Rules Pledge of Allegiance Unconstitutional," *Fox News*, June 27, 2002.
95. Chris H. Sieroty, "Congress Reacts to 'Under God' Ruling," *The Washington Times*, June 26, 2002.
96. Byron York, "The Democrats' Pledge Concession, They all believe in original intent now," *Nationalreviewonline*, June 28, 2002.

Chapter 3

1. Charles Francis Potter, *Humanism: A New Religion*, cited by David A. Noebel, *Clergy in the Classroom, The Religion of Secular Humanism* (Manitou Springs, Colorado: Summit Press, 1995.), 8.
2. Robert L. Waggoner, "Organized Humanism Produces A Growing Anti-Christian Society," undated.
3. Ibid.
4. Samuel L. Blumenfeld, *N.E.A.: Trojan Horse in American Education* (Boise, Idaho: The Paradigm Company, 1984).
5. Charles W. Moore, "Banning Prayer from the Public Square Is a Postmodern Notion," *Charles W. Moore*, 1999.
6. *Torcaso v. Watkins*, 367 U.S. 488, 81 S.Ct. 1680 (1961).
7. *Torcaso v. Watkins*, 367 U.S. 488, 495, 81 S.Ct. 1680 (1961).
8. Robert L. Waggoner, "Do All Public Schools Now Teach Humanism?" (Robert L. Waggoner, 1998).
9. Humanism and Its Aspirations, Humanist Manifesto III, a successor to the Humanist Manifesto of 1933," *American Humanist Association*, 2003.
10. *Humanist Manifesto I and II* (Buffalo, N.Y.: Prometheus Books, 1977), 17, as set out in: Tim LaHaye and David Noebel, *Mind Siege* (Nashville, TN: Word Publishing, 2000), 125.
11. April Shenandoah, History of America's Education, Part II: Noah Webster and Early America, *The Progressive Conservative*, Volume IV, Issue # 34, April 3, 2002.
12. Ellen Sorokin, "No Founding Fathers? That's our new history," *The Washington Times*, January 28, 2002.
13. Ibid.
14. Paul Vitz, *Censorship: Evidence of Bias in Our Children's Textbooks* (Ann Arbor, MI: Servant Books, 1986),
15. D. James Kennedy, "Christian History Censored from Public Schools," Kentucky Gateway Christian Coalition, 2001.

16. Paul Vitz, *Censorship: Evidence of Bias in Our Children's Textbooks* (Ann Arbor, MI: Servant Books, 1986), 14.

17. Ibid., 16.

18. Ibid., 1.

19. Ibid., 80.

20. "Fact Sheet, Religion & Schools," Rocky Mountain Family Council, undated.

21. Paul Vitz, *Censorship: Evidence of Bias in Our Children's Textbooks* (Ann Arbor, MI: Servant Books, 1986),

22. Heather D. Koerner, "Documented Thanksgiving," *Focus*, 1999.

23. Abraham Lincoln, "Proclamation of Thanksgiving," Washington D.C., October 3, 1863.

24. NEA Handbook 1995-1996 (Washington, D.C.: National Education Association, 1995), 266.

25. Amy C. Sims, "New Jersey Stands Up for Founding Fathers," *Fox News*, February 12, 2002.

26. Ibid.

27. Ellen Sorokin, "No Founding Fathers? That's our new history," *The Washington Times*, January 28, 2002.

28. Kay S. Hymowitz, "Anti-Social Studies, So many ideas for improving the curriculum—all of them bad," *The Weekly Standard*, May 6, 2002.

29. Brian Kennedy, "Teaching American History in the Schools: The Claremont Institute & The Teaching Teachers Project," *The Progressive Journal*, Volume IV, Issue # 67, June 17, 2002.

30. Ibid.

31. Ibid.

32. Rob Morse, "Reading, writing and Ripken," *The San Francisco Examiner*, September 10, 1995.

33. National Standards for Social Studies Teachers, National Council for the Social Studies, April 1997.

34. Kay S. Hymowitz, "Anti-Social Studies, So many ideas for improving the curriculum—all of them bad," *The Weekly Standard*, May 6, 2002.

35. Ibid.

36. Dr. Gary W. Phillips, "The Release of the National Assessment of Educational Progress (NAEP) The Nation's Report Card: U.S. History 2001," United States Commissioner of Education Statistics Press Release, May 9, 2002.

37. Michael A. Fletcher, "Study: History Still a Mystery to Many Students, Six in 10 Seniors Lack Basic Knowledge; 4th, 8th-Graders Post Modest Gains," *The Washington Post*, May 10, 2002.

38. Ibid.

39. Eric Buehrer, "How to Evaluate Your Child's Textbooks," *Gateways to Better Education*, 2002.
40. C. Bradley Thompson, "The Historians vs. American History," *CNSNews.com*, February 26, 2003.
41. Ibid.
42. Ibid.
43. Larry Witham, "Report Charges Textbooks 'Hide' Problems with Islam," *The Washington Times Weekly Edition*, February 10-16, 2003.
44. Matthew Maddox, "Islam Should Not Be Main Religious Focus in Public Schools," *The Battalion*, January 29, 2002.
45. Ibid.
46. "U.S. Schools: God Out, Allah In," Thomas More Law Center, June 26, 2002.
47. Ibid.
48. "Teacher, Mother of 7th Grader Speaks Out about 'Forced Islam,'" The American Center for Law and Justice.
49. All the examples are taken from an article by John Haskins, "It's 1984 in Massachusetts—And Big Brother is Gay," *Insight on the News*, December 17, 2001. I was unable to determine from the context whether Haskins borrowed them from Blumenfeld.
50. Matt Pyeatt, "Mom Sues Over Ejection from School Assembly on Homosexuality," *CNSNews.com*, May 13, 2002.
51. Local Briefs, "School Settles Suit Over Mother's Exclusion," *The St. Louis Post Dispatch*, May 22, 2003.
52. Craig Branch, "Public Education or Pagan Indoctrination, A Report on New Age Influence in the Schools," *Christian Research Journal*, Fall issue 1995.
53. Ibid.
54. Craig Branch, "Public Schools, the Sorcerer's New Apprentice? Part 4," Apologetics Resource Center, undated.
55. Don Closson, "Self-Esteem Curricula," *Probe Ministries*, 1996.
56. Ibid.
57. A. James Rudin, "The Vexing Issue of Church and State," *Star-Telegram.com*, August 6, 1999.
58. "New York Trial—First Amendment Rights or Veiled Attacks on Public School System," *American Atheist*, March 3, 1999.
59. Berit Kjos, "Indian Spiritism in Public Schools," *The Watchman Expositor*, 1989.
60. Ibid.
61. "Parents Object to Human Sacrifice in School Show," The Associated Press, December 19, 2002.
62. Diane Lynne, "4th-Graders to 'Celebrate' the Dead, Kids to put together altar, bring in photos of deceased kin, pets," *Worldnetdaily.com*, October 22, 2002.

63. Michael Coit, "Petaluma School's Day of Dead Celebration Challenged," *The Press Democrat*, October 22, 2002.

64. Dale Hoyt Palfrey, "The Day of the Dead," *Mexico Connect*, 1995.

65. Diane Lynne, "4th-Graders to 'Celebrate' the Dead, Kids to put together altar, bring in photos of deceased kin, pets," *Worldnetdaily.com*, October 22, 2002.

66. Samuel L. Blumenfeld, "Death Education at Columbine High," *Worldnetdaily.com*, May 27, 1999.

67. Ibid.

68. Dr. Gerald L. Atkinson, "A Deeper Look at the Littleton Massacre, Part 2," *Dads Against the Divorce Industry*, No. 138, October 18-24, 1999.

69. Fergus M. Bordewich, "Mortal Fears: Courses in 'Death Education' Get Mixed Reviews," *The Atlantic Monthly*, February 1988.

70. Michael Chiusano, "Parents' Rights," *National Review*, September 30, 1996.

71. Fergus M. Bordewich, "Mortal Fears: Courses in 'Death Education' Get Mixed Reviews," *The Atlantic Monthly*, February 1988.

Chapter 4

1. Cheryl Wetzstein, "Study Links Teen Sex to Depression, Suicide," *The Washington Times*, June 4, 2003.

2. "Sex Education—Is it Working," *Concerned Women for America*, January 23, 1998.

3. Janice Crouse, Ph. D. "Yet Another Liberal Myth Exposed, Parents Want Character-Based Education for Their Children," Beverly LaHaye Institute, February 13, 2003.

4. Ibid.

5. Jason Pierce, "Louisiana Abstinence Program Is Target of ACLU Lawsuit," *CNSNews.com*, May 22, 2002.

6. "ACLU, Louisiana Governor's Program on Abstinence Settle Abstinence-Only-Until-Marriage Suit," Siecus Policy Update, November 2002.

7. "Sexual Abstinence Speakers Canceled; Teachers' Union Drops Workshops," *The Record*, October 17, 2002.

8. In fact, one study showed the failure rate for pregnancy for committed adult couples during the first year of use and between 36.3% and 44.5% for young, unmarried minority women. Dr. Joanna K. Mohn, "NJ Senate Must Pass Stress Abstinence Bill (S-868) to Best Protect Teens," New Jersey Family Policy Council, 2002.

9. "New Study Shows Higher Unwed Birthrates Among Sexually Experienced Teens Despite Increased Condom Use, Report finds that overall reduction in teen pregnancy is due to abstinence, not increased contraceptive use," The Consortium of State Physicians Resource Councils, February 10, 1999.

10. Eve Tushnet, "No Protection: Federal Study Highlights' Condoms' Ineffectiveness," *National Catholic Register*, 9.02.01-9.08.01.

11. Joanna K. Mohn, M.D., Lynne R. Tingle, PhD, Reginald Finger, MD, MPH, "An Analysis of the Causes of the Decline in Non-marital Birth and Pregnancy Rates for Teens from 1991 to 1995," *Adolescent & Family Health*, Volume 3, Number 1, April 2003.

12. Robert E. Rector, "The Effectiveness of Abstinence Education Programs in Reducing Sexual Activity Among Youth, *Heritage Foundation Research Backgrounder* #1533, April 8, 2002.

13. "New Study Shows Higher Unwed Birthrates Among Sexually Experienced Teens Despite Increased Condom Use, Report finds that overall reduction in teen pregnancy is due to abstinence, not increased contraceptive use," The Consortium of State Physicians Resource Councils, February 10, 1999; Robert E. Rector, "The Effectiveness of Abstinence Education Programs in Reducing Sexual Activity Among Youth, *Heritage Foundation Research Backgrounder* #1533, April 8, 2002.

14. Robert E. Rector, "The Effectiveness of Abstinence Education Programs in Reducing Sexual Activity Among Youth, *Heritage Foundation Research Backgrounder* #1533, April 8, 2002.

15. Linda P. Harvey, " 'Gay' Groups Join Planned Parenthood to Attack Abstinence Funding," *Mission America*, undated.

16. Jim Brown and Jody Brown, "The Homosexual Agenda: A Classic Marketing Strategy That's Working," Agape Press, November 15, 2002.

17. Linda P. Harvey, "Homosexual Agenda Escalates in Public Schools," *NewsWithViews.com*, July 15, 2001.

18. David Limbaugh, "NEA: Protection or Indoctrination," *Creators Syndicate*, February 27, 2002.

19. Edwin Acevedo, "They Want to Change the World; Local Gay Teens Fight Anti-Gay Harassment," *Post-Standard (Syracuse, NY)*, December 17, 2002.

20. Bryan Robinson, "Anti-Bullying Program or 'Gay Agenda?' W. Va. School Tolerance Plan Targeted for Allegedly Promoting Homosexuality," *ABCNews.com*, October 9, 2002.

21. Maria Elena Kennedy, "Family Group Counters 'Tolerance' Laws with New 'Opt-Out' Form," *CNS News*, January 18, 2001.

22. Greg Hoadley, "Back to School: Do You Know What Your Kids Are in For?" Center for Reclaiming America, August 28, 2002.

23. "How to Promote Homosexuality in School," Concerned Women for America, March 23, 2001.

24. "Pro-Homosexual Video Targets Elementary and Middle Schools," Concerned Women for America, March 2, 2000.

25. "Middle School Students Secretly Given Pro-Homosexual Instruction," Pacific Justice Institute Press Release, October 16, 2002.

26. Ellen Sorokin, "Parents Protest Gay-Themed School Plays," *Washington Times*, February 21, 2002.
27. "GLSEN Attacks Faith and Families," Concerned Women for America, October 19, 1999.
28. Dick M. Carpenter II, Ph.D., "Safe Schools, Free Speech, and the Truth," *Focus on the Family*, 2002.
29. Greg Hoadley, "The Homosexual Agenda: It's No Longer About Tolerance," Center for Reclaiming America, undated.
30. "Public School Pushes Homosexual Agenda and Discriminates Against Christian Student During 'Diversity Week'—Federal Lawsuit Filed," Thomas More Law Center Press Release, July 10, 2002.
31. John Haskins, "It's 1984 in Massachusetts—And Big Brother Is Gay," *Insight on the News*, December 17, 2001.
32. *Saxe v. State College Area School District*, 240 F. 3d. 200 (3rd Cir. 2001).
33. Robert W. Lee, "Making A Difference," *The New American*, March 11, 2002.
34. "School Retreats from Pro-Homosexual Policy After Student Christian Club Threatens Lawsuit," Thomas More Law Center Press Release, October 14, 2002.
35. "California School Forced by ACLU Suit to Stifle Free Speech," Traditional Values Coalition, August 15, 2000.
36. Shannon Darling, "VUSD Settles with Gay Student; School District to pay $130,000, train educators," *Visalia Times-Delta*, August 14, 2002.
37. Shannon Darling, "9th-Graders to Get Gay-Sensitivity Training," *Visalia Times-Delta*, October 3, 2002.
38. Press Release, "Pacific Justice Institute Pledges to Defend Objectors to Pro-Gay Training," Pacific Justice Institute, August 21, 2002.
39. David Limbaugh, "NEA: Protection or Indoctrination," *Creators Syndicate*, February 27, 2002.
40. "Just the Facts About Sexual Orientation & Youth: A Primer for Principals, Educators and School Personnel," *American Psychological Association*, 2003.
41. Charlene K. Haar, "Teachers' Unions, Roadblocks to Reform," *The American Enterprise*, September/October 1996.
42. "NEA's Guide to the 'Extreme Right,' Overview and Introduction to the Extreme Right: A State's Approach," National Education Association.
43. Briefly—and it's far more complicated than this—but Second Amendment advocates, in addition to championing freedom, are fighting for the right to defend themselves and their families, which is the essence of a pro-life position. And while this is grossly oversimplified too, pro-life proponents fight to protect the most innocent of human lives. In also favoring capital punishment, they are likewise advocating respect for life—and recommending execution for those who are adjudicated guilty of ending innocent lives.

44. "EEOC Orders NEA to Stop Discrimination Against Christian Teachers," *Charisma News Service*, October 25, 2002.

45. Marc Morano, "School Worker Wins Battle Over Union's Support of Abortion," *CNSNews.com*, November 26, 2002.

46. "Decoding the NEA Resolutions," *The Phyllis Schlafly Report*, Volume 33, No. 1, August 1999.

Chapter 5

1. D. James Kennedy and Jerry Newcombe, *What if Jesus Had Never Been Born?* (Nashville: Thomas Nelson, 1994), 52.

2. H. Wayne House, "Anti-Christian Bias in Higher Education," 19.

3. D. James Kennedy noted that 78% of Americans claimed to be Christians. D. James Kennedy with Jerry Newcombe, *The Gates of Hell Shall Not Prevail* (Nashville: Thomas Nelson, 1996), 9, quoting from Richard N. Ostling, "In So Many Gods We Trust," *Time*, January 30, 1995, 72; A more recent survey showed the percentage to have increased to eighty. The Rev. Thomas R. Swain, "Christians Need to Walk the Walk," *The Hutchinson News*, November 15, 2002. And a Barna Research Group survey found that 85% of Americans considered themselves Christians. *Barna Research Online*, January 29, 2002.

4. Phillip E. Johnson, "What (If Anything) Hath God Wrought?"*Academe*, September 1995.

5. James Tunstead Burtchaell, "The Decline and Fall of the Christian University," *First Things*, April 1991.

6. Paul Johnson, *A History of the American People* (New York: Harper Collins 1997), 968; William R. Marty, "Overcoming the Silence," *The Journal of Interdisciplinary Studies: An International Journal of Interdisciplinary and Interfaith Dialogue*, 1998-1999.

7. George M. Marsden, "Religious Professors Are the Last Taboo," *The Wall Street Journal*, December 22, 1993.

8. Charles Colson, *Against the Night: Living in the New Dark Ages* (Ann Arbor, MI: Vine Books, 1989), 85.

9. David French, "FIRE's Guide to Religious Liberty on Campus," The Foundation for Individual Rights in Education, 2002.

10. Mike S. Adams, "The Campus Crusade Against Christ," Agape Press, July 17, 2002.

11. "Biology Professor Refuses to Recommend Students Who Don't Believe in Evolution," The Associated Press, January 30, 2003.

12. Ted Olsen, "Weblog: Texas Tech Professor Drops Evolution Belief Requirement," *Christianity Today*, April 2003.

13. Naomi Schaefer, "Houses of Worship: Fear of God in Harvard Yard," *The Wall Street Journal*, January 29, 1999.
14. Ibid.
15. Ibid.
16. Ibid.
17. "Position Statement: Political Correctness in Higher Education," *Focus on the Family*, 2002.
18. Jim Brown and Ed Vitagliano, "Professor Dumped Over Evolution Beliefs," Agape Press, March 11, 2003.
19. Piper Fogg, "Science Administrator Who Questioned Evolution Is Reinstated at Mississippi U. for Women," *The Chronicle of Higher Education*, March 17, 2003.
20. Andrea Garrett, "Intolerant Tolerance: Anti-Christian Bigotry on Campus," *CBN-News.com*, July 10, 2002.
21. Matt Kaufman, "Unequal Justice," *Boundless.org*, 1999.
22. Mike S. Adams, "The Campus Crusade Against Christ," Agape Press, July 17, 2002.
23. "Double Standard at Washington University, Saint Louis," Foundation for Individual Rights in Education, October 9, 2002.
24. Joyce Howard Price, "Student Bar Group Oks Pro-Lifers," *The Washington Times*, October 17, 2002.
25. Dan Flynn, "Temple U. Sued for Hauling Christian Student to Psychiatric Ward, Lawsuit: Administrators Banned Protest of Sacrilegious Play Then Assaulted Student," *Accuracy in Academia*, February 2001.
26. Alex Lapinski, "Temple U. Faces Student's Civil Rights Lawsuit," University of Pennsylvania Wire, March 2, 2001.
27. Veronica Daehn, "Religious Beliefs Present Hurdles for Nebraska Coach's Career," *The Daily Nebraskan*, April 11, 2002.
28. Ted Olsen, "Separation of God and Gridiron, Newspaper reports assistant football coach lost his job for religious beliefs," *Christianity Today*, June 25, 2002.
29. Don Follis, "Coach's Faith Concerns Athletic Director," *Peoria Trader*, May 5, 2002.
30. Veronica Daehn, "Religious Beliefs Present Hurdles for Nebraska Coach's Career," *The Daily Nebraskan*, April 11, 2002.
31. "Student Studying Religion Sues State after Scholarship Funds Cut Off," The Associated Press, December 9, 2002.
32. "State Relents, Gives Scholarship to Student Majoring in Religious Studies," The Associated Press, January 27, 2003.
33. Ellen Sorokin, "Christian Student Group Sues Rutgers Over Access," *The Washington Times*, January 7, 2003.
34. John Leo, "Playing the Bias Card," *U.S. News & World Report*, January 13, 2003.
35. Stew Padasso, "UNC Hopes to Resolve Dispute with Christian Group," The Asso-

ciated Press, December 31, 2002.

36. John Leo, "Playing the Bias Card," *U.S. News & World Report*, January 13, 2003.

37. Jim Brown, "Educator Unearths 'Systematic Discrimination' Against Campus Christian Groups," Agape Press, February 3, 2003.

38. Joyce Howard Price, "Princeton Bioethicist Argues Christianity Hurts Animals," *The Washington Times*, July 4, 2002.

39. Benjamin Wallace-Wells, "The Theologian and the Wonk," *The Dartmouth Review*, December 15, 1998.

40. Jon Dougherty, "Students Sue U of Texas Over Free Speech, Group Says College Officials Censored Pro-Life Message," *Worldnetdaily.com*, October 3, 2002.

41. "Censorship on Campus," *Liberation Journal*, 1999-2000.

42. Ron Nissimov, "Conservatives Criticize UH Policy on Free Speech," *The Houston Chronicle*, March 17, 2003.

43. Matthew Cella, "Appeals Court Upholds Ban on VMI Prayer," *The Washington Times*, April 29, 2003.

44. Diana Lynne, "'Spiritual Warfare' Grips Univ. of Wisconsin, 2nd-year resident dismissed after questioning Islamist lecturers," *Worldnetdaily.com*, June 14, 2002.

45. Mike S. Adams, "The Campus Crusade Against Christ," Agape Press, July 17, 2002.

46. David Pearson, "Homosexual Activism Strong at UNC-Chapel Hill, Study Addresses 'Social Discrimination' of 'Sexual Minorities,'" Agape Press, July 12, 2002.

47. Ibib.

48. Rolando Garcia, "Gay Tolerance Brings Controversy to Faculty," *The Battalion Online*, March 27, 2003.

49. Jon Ward, "Lawmaker Tells Colleges to Curb Sex Education," *The Washington Times*, May 17, 2003.

50. Simon J. Dahlman, "A Revealing Look at "Academic Freedom," *Boundless.org*, 1999.

51. Ibid.

52. Charles Colson, "When 'Isms' Fail, Speech Codes Thrive," *Boundless.org*, undated.

53. Matt Kaufman, "Are Speech Codes Doomed?" *Boundless.org*, 1999.

54. "Univeristy of South Carolina Mandates Political Indoctrination and Orthodoxy," Foundation for Individual Rights in Education, May 12, 2002.

55. Ibid.

56. Philip Terzian, "It's Hardly News That College Faculties Are Dominated by Liberals," *Saint Paul Pioneer Press*, September 19, 2002.

57. Sara Russo, "Bias Revealed Among Ivy League Faculty, Professors Voted 84% for Gore, 9% for Bush," *Accuracy in Academia*, February, 2002.

58. Matt Pyeatt, "College Commencements Still Dominated by Liberals," *CNSNews.com*, May 21, 2002.

59. Melissa Sanchez, "Controversial Talk Interrupted," *The State News*, February 26, 2003.
60. Benjamin Wallace-Wells, "The Theologian and the Wonk," *The Dartmouth Review*, December 15, 1998.
61. Bruce Barron, "When Speech Codes Silence," *Boundless.org*, April 26, 1999.
62. Editorial, "Stolen Conservative Papers No Priority for Colleges," *Accuracy in Media*, December 12, 2002.
63. Patrick Poole, "Book Burning 101, Censorship replaces free speech as hallmark of colleges, universities," *Worldnetdaily.com*, July 19, 2000.
64. Andrea Billups, "Dirty Dozen Exposes Absurd College Courses," *The Washington Times*, September 7, 2000.
65. Alan Sokal, "A Physicist Experiments with Cultural Studies," *Lingua Franca*, May/June 1996.
66. Ibid.
67. J.D. Cassidy, "An Education Ain't What It Used to Be," *FrontPageMagazine.com*, February 4, 2003.
68. Jim Leffel, "Understanding Today's Postmodern University," *Xenos Christian Fellowship*, 2003.
69. Ibid.
70. J.D. Cassidy, "An Education Ain't What It Used to Be," *FrontPageMagazine.com*, February 4, 2003.
71. Ibid.
72. Ibid.

Chapter 6

1. "ACLJ Files Suit Against NYC for Prohibiting Prayers Following Sept. 11 Attacks," American Center for Law and Justice, February 28, 2002.
2. Joel Kurth, "Christians Defend Rights in Court," *The Detroit News*, June 24, 2002.
3. Randy Hall, "California County Agrees to Halt Discrimination against Christian Congregation," *CNSNews.com*, April 1, 2003.
4. *Amandola v. Town of Babylon*, 251 F.3d 339 (2nd Cir. 2001).
5. "ACLJ Files Suit Again Against Babylon, NY for Discriminating Against Christian Church," American Center for Law and Justice Press Release, October 9, 2001.
6. "Liberty Counsel Sues Public Library Over Policy that Bans Religious Viewpoints in Community Meeting Room," Liberty Counsel News Release, January 9, 2003.
7. "ACLJ: Federal Court Finds Texas City Policy Prohibiting Religious Meetings Unconstitutional," *Business Wire*, January 8, 2003.
8. Anita Weier, "Teresa on a Metro Pass? Heaven Forbid," *The Capital Times*, April 5, 2003.

9. Ibid.

10. Phillip Rawls, "Gov. Holds Bible Study at Ala. Capitol," The Associated Press, February 27, 2003.

11. John Aman, "ACLU, Allies, Bring Suit Against Chief Justice Moore," *ReclaimingAmerica.org*, January 1, 2002.

12. "Judge Ordered to Remove Ten Commandments," The Associated Press, November 18, 2002.

13. The Greek goddess of justice is actually Athena.

14. Michael Novak, "That Ten Commandments Case, What constitutes an establishment of religion?"

15. Julia Duin, "Lawmakers to Gather for Private Prayer Event," *The Washington Times*, November 30, 2001.

16. Dan Eggen, "Ashcroft's Faith Plays Visible Role at Justice, Bible Sessions with Staffers Draw Questions and Criticism," *The Washington Post*, May 14, 2001.

17. "Miami-Dade County Finds Room for Jesus on Threat of Lawsuit," AFA Center for Law and Policy Press Release, December 17, 2002.

18. Kristina Henderson, "Florida Atheists Challenge Angels on Lawn of City Hall; Mayor suggests if someone is offended, ignore display," *The Washington Times*, December 5, 2002.

19. John O'Sullivan, "Scrooge on the Prowl, the anti-Christmas movement," *Nationalreviewonline*, December 19, 2001.

20. John Leo, "Seasonal Symbols make Some People See Red," Universal Press Syndicate, December 17, 2001.

21. John Rossomando, "Residents Sue Over Religious Tree Ornaments," *CNSNews.com*, November 9, 2001.

22. Rabbi Aryeh Spero, "Seasonal Hostility Virus," *The Washington Times*, December 25, 2002.

23. Tim Wildmon, "Have a Merry ——mas?" *AFA Online*, December 19, 2000.

24. Joe Kovacs, "Christmas in America becomes battleground, As holiday traditions draw national controversy, believers, pagans grapple over Jesus' inclusion," *Worldnetdaily.com*, December 14, 2002.

25. Tim Wildmon, "Have a Merry ——mas?" *AFA Online*, December 19, 2000.

26. Joe Kovacs, "School bans Christmas, but OK with Halloween, Despite massive promotion of October holiday, district reverses approval of talk on Jesus' birth," *Worldnetdaily.com*, December 19, 2002; Kelly Boggs, "A Constitutional Christmas."

27. Bill Novak, "Good Friday Closings Spark Protest," *The Capital Times*, April 17, 2003.

28. *Freedom From Religion Foundation v. Tommy G. Thompson (Governor of Wisconsin)*, Civil No. 95-C-6634-S, U.S. District Court, Western District of Wisconsin (1996).

29. *Bridenbaugh v. O'Bannon*, 185 F.3d 796 (C.A. 7 Ind. 1999).

30. *Granzeier v. Middleton*, 173 F. 3d 568 (C.A. 6 Ky. 1999).

31. Bill Novak, "Good Friday Closings Spark Protest," *The Capital Times*, April 17, 2003.

32. David Leibowitz, Freedom from Religion? Just Give Me Freedom from Shrillness," *The Arizona Republic*, March 9, 2003.

33. *Metzl v. Leininger*, 57 F.3d 618 (C.A. 7 Ill. 1995).

34. "What's so bad about Good Friday? Four good reasons why the legislature should act to abolish the state's official recognition of the Good Friday holy day," and "Photos from the HCSSC Good Friday Protest at the State Capitol," *Lava.net*, March 28, 2002.

35. "U.S. Supreme Court Refuses to Hear San Francisco's Appeal in Mt. Davidson Cross Case," ACLU Press Release, March 17, 1997.

36. J.K. Dineen and Nick Driver, "Court Ruling Upholds Mt. Davidson Cross," *San Francisco Examiner*, December 13, 2002.

37. Daniel B. Wood, "A Large-Scale Battle Over a Small Cross," *The Christian Science Monitor*, May 6, 2003.

38. Steve Lackmeyer, "Cross Removed from State Fair Park," *The Oklahoman*, February 27, 2003.

39. Chris Kenning, "Lawsuit Targets 4 Counties, Biblical laws posted in public buildings," *The Courtier-Journal*, November 28, 2001.

40. "Federal Judge Considers Another Ten Commandments Case," The Associated Press, May 7, 2002.

41. *Freedom from Religion Foundation v. McCallum*, 179 F. Supp.2d 950 (W.D. Wis. Jan. 7, 2002).

42. "Faith-based Funding Costing Taxpayers Unparalleled Sums," Freedom From Religion Foundation News Release, January 10, 2002.

43. *Freedom From Religion Foundation, Inc. v. McCallum*, 214 F. Supp. 2d 905 (W.D. Wis., 2002).

44. Alan Sears, "Another Tremendous Win for Religious Freedom," Alliance Defense Fund Special News Alert, April 3, 2003.

45. *Freedom from Religion Foundation, Inc. v. McCallum*, _ F.3d. _, 2003 WL 1733521 7th Cir. (Wis.) Apr. 2, 2003.

46. DeBoer v. Village of Oak Park, *Christian Legal Society*, October 26, 2001.

47. Catrine Johansson, "City Councils Ban Jesus from Prayer," *The Orange County Register*, January 12, 2003.

48. Ibid.

49. Andy Butcher, "Ban on Public 'Jesus' Prayers," Charisma News Service, January 22, 2003.

50. Patty Henetz, "Court: Atheist Can Pray at City Meeting," The Associated Press, April 11, 2003

51. Ibid.

Chapter 7

1. "Townspeople Protest Challenge to 'Jesus Is Lord' Signs," The Associated Press, March 5, 2002.
2. Dylan T. Lovan, "Woman Who Said She was Fired for Wearing Cross Sues Library," The Associated Press, February 1, 2002.
3. Lawrence Morahan, "Policeman Fired for Wearing Cross Takes Case to Supremes," *CNSNews.com*, August 6, 2001.
4. "God Banned from Police Pledge," *CNSNews.com*, September 25, 2002.
5. Joyce Howard Price, "22 on Hill Oppose Lawsuit to Rid Congress of Chaplains," *The Washington Times*, December 1, 2002.
6. Marsh v. Chambers, 463 U.S. 783 (1983).
7. "State Lawmakers Ban 'Jesus' from Prayers," *Maranatha Christian Journal*, March 1999.
8. Maxine Bernstein, "Police Bureau Terminates Chaplain," *The Oregonian*, September 25, 2002.
9. Michael P. McConnell, "Police Chaplain Stands by His Beliefs," *The Daily Tribune*, October 16, 2002.
10. Bill Laitner, "Pastor's Views May Cost Job, Antigay words are issue; vote expected," *The Detroit Free Press*, October 25, 2002.
11. Allie Martin, "Police Chaplain's Stand on Homosexuality Jeopardizes His Job, Soulforce Labels Comments 'Spiritual Violence,'" Agape Press, October 21, 2002.
12. Ferndale City Council Resolution, October 28, 2002.
13. David O'Reilly, "Honor Guardsman Is Fired for Blessings," *The Philadelphia Inquirer*, January 22, 2003.
14. John W. Whitehead, "Religious Apartheid for American Troops Abroad," The Rutherford Institute, March 17, 2003.
15. Kim Gilliland, "Postal Service Faces Lawsuit, Lenoir soldier's family: Regulations violate religious freedom," *The Hickory Daily Record*, April 8, 2003.
16. Steve Farrell, "Stiff Right Jab—Public Christianity," *SierraTimes.com*, February 9, 2003.
17. Mark 16:15.
18. 1 Peter 3:15.
19. Editorial, "Fanatic DeLay Proves He's Far Outside Conservative Mainstream," *The Houston Chronicle*, April 19, 2002.
20. Alan Cooperman, "Paige's Remarks on Religion in Schools Decried; Critics Call On Education Secretary to Repudiate Published Statement or Resign," *The Washington Post*, April 9, 2003.

21. Ibid.
22. "ACLU threatens to Sue Mayor for Banning Satan," The Associated Press, January 26, 2002.
23. "Florida city's declaration for Jesus draws ire of ACLU," The Associated Press, December 29, 2001.
24. Ellen Sorokin, "San Francisco Judges Cut Ties to Scouts Over Gays," *The Washington Times*, August 7, 2002.
25. Greg Hoadley, "City of San Francisco Exhibits Anti-Christian Bias, Says Legal Group," Center for Reclaiming America, August 2002.
26. Ellen Sorokin, "San Francisco Judges Cut Ties to Scouts Over Gays," *The Washington Times*, August 7, 2002.
27. *Boy Scouts of America et al v. Dale*, 530 U.S. 640 (2000).
28. "Reeve Speaks on Stem Cell Research," *The Yale Herald*, April 4, 2003.
29. "Reeve: Keep Religious Groups Out of Public Policy," The Associated Press, April 3, 2003.
30. "FDA Candidate Irks, Abortion Pill Advocates, The Christian Medical Association says critics fear David Hager's 'well-grounded' opposition," *Christianity Today*, December 9, 2002.
31. Daniel McGinn, "Anatomy of a Plague: An Oral History," *Newsweek*, June 3, 2001.
32. Jenifer Warren and Richard C. Paddock, "Randy Shilts, Chronicler of Aids Epidemic, Dies at 42; Journalism: Author of 'And the Band Played On' is Credited with Awakening Nation to the Health Crisis," *The Los Angeles Times*, February 18, 1994.
33. Jack Begg, "Word for Word/Nameless Dread; 20 years Ago, the First Clues to the Birth of a Plague," *The New York Times*, June 3, 2001. The section from the *Times* story reads: "For more than a year the epidemic officially remained unnamed. A patient in San Francisco was given a diagnosis of F.U.O.: fever of unkown origin. Some scientists and journalists referred to K.S.O.I. (Kaposi's Sarcoma and Opportunistic Infections) or GRID (Gay-Related Immune Deficiency). A *New York* magazine feature story termed it 'The Gay Plague.' In September 1982, the C.D.C. finally put a name to it: Acquired Immune Deficiency Syndrome."
34. Ken Connor, "Schumer: Catholics Need Not Apply," Family Research Council Washington Update, April 17, 2003.
35. "Michael W. McConnell Confirmed as a judge on the U.S. Court of Appeals for the 10th Circuit," The Becket Fund Press Release, November 2002.
36. "CLS Supports Nomination of Michael McConnell to the Tenth Circuit," *Christian Legal Society*, September 17, 2002.
37. "Another Judicial Appointment Hearing Coming Up," *Talkleft.com*, September 15, 2002.
38. Edward Walsh, "Court Nominee Says His Views Won't Color Rulings, Senators Question Conservative Professor on Writings," *The Washington Post*, September 19, 2002.

39. The Rev. Barry W. Lynn, "Americans United for Separation of Church and State Statement on Michael McConnell," September 17, 2002.
40. Chris Matthews, "Assessment of Tonight's Republican Presidential Debate in Iowa," *CNBC News Transcripts*, December 13, 1999.
41. Ravi Zacharias, *Deliver Us from Evil: Restoring the Soul in a Disintegrating Culture*, (Dallas: Word Publishing, 1996), 109, 111.
42. Fred Barnes, "God and Man in the Oval Office," *The Weekly Standard*, March 17, 2003.
43. William J. Federer, *America's God and Country: Encyclopedia of Quotations* (Coppell, TX: FAME Publishing, 1994).
44. Dave Kopel, "Religious Fright, The Left is appalled by President Bush's faith," *NationalReview.com*, March 18, 2003.
45. David Talbot, "Axis of Stupidity," *Salon.com*, February 14, 2002.

Chapter 8

1. Haya El Nasser, "Giant Churches Irk Some Neighbors," *USA Today*, September 23, 2002.
2. "A Major Threat to Churches: Zoning Laws," *Christian Law Association*, 1999.
3. "The Refuge Pinellas, Inc. v. City of St. Petersburg," The Christian Legal Society News Release, October 1, 2001.
4. Testimony of Steven T. McFarland before the Committee on the Judiciary of the United States Senate, June 23, 1999.
5. Christina Headrick, "City's Rules, Religions Collide," *The St. Petersburg Times*, November 26, 2000.
6. Michelle Malkin, "Zoning Out Religious Freedom," *Creators Syndicate, Inc.*, February 24, 2000.
7. Alan Sears, "A Victory for the Gospel in the "Metaphysical Mecca," *ADA Weekly News Alert*, October 29, 2002.
8. Amy E. Nevala, "Judge Backs Evanston Church," *The Chicago Tribune*, April 3, 2003.
9. Mathew Staver, "Church Files Federal Lawsuit Against Town Over Zoning Requirements," Liberty Counsel News Release, January 15, 2003.
10. Mathew Staver, "Zoning Threatens Religious Liberty in the New Millennium," *NLJ Online*, February 2000.
11. Valerie Richardson, "Home Bible Study Makes Colorado Woman a Lawbreaker," *The Washington Times*, August 12, 1999.
12. "ACLJ Secures Victory for Denver Couple Ordered to Limit Prayer Meetings in Their Private Home by City of Denver," ACLJ Press Release, December 22, 1999.

13. "El Cajon Lashes Back Against Vacation Bible Schools," Pacific Justice Institute Press Release, July 26, 2001.

14. "Social Worker Prevented from Christian Expression," Pacific Justice Institute Press Release, August 2, 2001. The federal statute prohibiting discrimination in the workplace on the basis of religion is 42 U.S.C. 2000 (e). The law applies to any employer with at least fifteen employees.

15. "Religious Workplace Discrimination Lawsuit Filed," Pacific Justice Institute Press Release, May 2, 2002.

16. Ken Paulson, "Woman Proves You Can Fight City Hall," *The Augusta Chronicle*, December 30, 2001.

17. *Deida v. City of Milwaukee*, 176 F. Supp.2d 859 (E.D. Wis., 2001).

18. News Release, "Judge refuses again to bar disruptive woman from Hollywood church, Can a church decide who its own members are?" The Becket Fund for Religious Liberty, April 12, 2002.

19. Litigation Report, "Church of Christ in Hollywood v. Lady Cage-Barile," The Becket Fund for Religious Liberty, November 27, 2002.

20. 435 U.S. 618 (1978).

21. John Berlau, "Churches Must Follow IRS Gospel," *Insight* magazine, October 22, 2001.

22. William Donohue, "Candidates Campaign in Churches," Catholic League for Civil and Religious Rights, November 4, 2002.

23. "News Report: A Warning on Church Voter Guides," The EO Tax Bulletin, 1996.

24. Mathew Staver, "Churches May Distribute Non-Partisan Voter Guides," Liberty Counsel Press Release, October 25, 2000.

25. "Americans United Reports Eight Churches to IRS for Distributing Christian Coalition Voter Guides During November Elections," Americans United for Separation of Church and State Press Release, December 10, 1998.

26. Jeremy Leaming, "IRS Strips Christian Coalition of Tax-Exempt Status," First Amendment Center, June 11, 1999.

27. "IRS is asked to preserve clergy's right to preach about politics, Becket Fund says AU to investigate pulpit speech is 'chilling,'" The Becket Fund for Religious Liberty Press Release, December 2, 2002.

28. Michael Schwartz, "Houses of Worship Political Speech Protection Act," Concerned Women for America, March 26, 2003.

29. "Court Dismisses Clergy Housing Case," *BPNews*, August 27, 2002.

30. Frank York, "Let's End the Anti-Christian Bigotry of the IRS," September 2000.

31. Jon E. Dougherty, "FCC Targets Religious TV, New decision could threaten evangelistic programming," *Worldnetdaily.com*, January 7, 2000.

32. Ibid.

33. Charles Colson, "The FCC Targets Religious Programming: Ruling Undermines

Freedom of Expression," *Breakpoint Commentary*, January 24, 2000.

34. Jon E. Dougherty, "FCC Defends Religious Broadcasting Decision, Congressional challenge to ruling, even atheists up in arms," *Worldnetdaily.com*, January 13, 2000.

35. Jon E. Dougherty, "Religious Broadcast Ruling Gutted by FCC, Public outcry brings 4-1 decision, 'puts lid back on Pandora's Box,'" *Worldnetdaily.com*, January 29, 2000.

36. "Rev. Franklin Graham Plans Aid for Iraq," The Associated Press, April 1, 2003.

37. Alan Cooperman and Caryle Murphy, "2 Christian Groups' Aid Effort Questioned," *The Washington Post*, March 28, 2003.

38. Mark O'Keefe, "Plans Under Way for Christianizing the Enemy," Newhouse News Service, March 25, 2003.

39. James Rosen, "Evangelicals Plan Relief Missions to Iraq. They hope to deliver food and medicine, say they won't preach," *The Fresno Bee*, April 14, 2003.

40. Editorial, "Evangelize Elsewhere," *The Washington Post*, April 15, 2003.

41. Steven Waldman, "Jesus in Baghdad, Why We Should Keep Franklin Graham Out of Iraq," *Slate.com*, April 11, 2003.

42. Mas'ood Cajee, "Franklin Graham: Spiritual Carpetbagger," *Counterpunch*, April 11, 2003.

43. Brad Buchholz, "Onward, Christian Soldiers," *The Austin American Statesman*, June 30, 2002.

44. Douglas W. Phillips, "Plymouth Crock," *CitizenLink*, November 22, 2002.

45. "Day of Mourning: Native Protest Stops Pilgrim's Progress," *Workers World*, December 12, 1996.

46. Ibid.

47. Douglas W. Phillips, "Plymouth Crock," *CitizenLink*, November 22, 2002.

48. "Christian Employee Harassed and Fired," Pacific Justice Institute Press Release, April 26, 2001.

49. Jeff Johnson, "Dr Pepper Skips 'Under God' on Patriotic Cans," *CNSNews.com*, February 8, 2002.

50. David Sisler, "Not for Sunday Only, Every Knee Shall Bow—Except Mickey's," *AFAOnline*, January 2, 2003.

51. Joe Kovaks, "Kodak Fires Man Over 'Gay' Stance, 320-year veteran of global film giant objected to pro-homosexual memo," *Worldnetdaily.com*, October 24, 2002.

52. Greg Hoadley, "Anti-Christian Bigotry in the Corporate World," *Reclaiming America*, October 2002.

53. Diana Lynne, "Motorola Seen Promoting Homosexuality, 'Homophobia' workshops, other activism creating tension in the workplace," *Worldnetdaily.com*, August 2, 2002.

54. Lawrence Morahan, "Corporate Diversity Training a Cover for Homosexual Activism," *CNSNews.com*, August 2, 2002.

55. Julie Foster, "Christians Sue Lab for Discrimination, Accuse Sandia of giving special rights to 'gays,' denying believers equal treatment," *Worldnetdaily.com*, May 4, 2000.
56. Ibid.
57. Bill Douthat, "Woman Sues Ex-Employer Over Religious Hostility," *The Palm Beach Post*, January 30, 2003.
58. "Homosexuals Continue to Attack Christian Values," Charisma News Service, July 31, 2002.
59. Lauren Stanforth, "HSBC Apologizes for Altering Artwork," *Rochester Democrat and Chronicle*, January 30, 2003.
60. Ted Olsen, "Weblog: Chevrolet Sponsors Christian Music Tour—Critics Cry 'Divisive' and 'Troubling,'" *Christianity Today*, October 21, 2002.
61. Stuart Elliot, "Questions About G.M. Sponsorship," *The New York Times*, October 24, 2002.
62. David Crumm, "Chevy Has Faith in Tour, But Christianity-themed concerts spark controversy," *The Detroit Free Press*, October 23, 2002.
63. Allie Martin and Jody Brown, "Co-Worker Offended by Shirts with Christian Symbols, Complaint Causes Employer to Restrict What Christian Employee Can Wear," Agape Press, April 22, 2002.
64. Jon Dougherty, "Woman Fired for Wearing Cross? Says Target Managers 'targeted' her for discrimination," *Worldnetdaily.com*, March 16, 2002.

Chapter 9

1. Private corporations are prohibited by federal statute, however, from religious discrimination against their employees (42 U.S.C. 2000 (e).
2. "Minnesota Officials Guilty of Religious Discrimination for Punishing Employees Who Brought Bibles to Diversity Training Session," American Center for Law and Justice Press Release, August 2, 2002.
3. David Royse, "ACLU Urges Recall of Religious AIDS Pamphlet," The Associated Press, April 3, 203.
4. Daniel Guido, "California Governor Vetoes Pro-Homosexual Foster Care Bill," *CNSNews.com*, October 2, 2002.
5. Ibid.
6. David Limbaugh, "Sensitivity Training for California Foster Parents," *Creators Syndicate, Inc.*, August 27, 2002.
7. "2003 California Bills: Bill Details, AB 458 (Chu) Transsexual Indoctrination of Foster Parents," Campaign for California Families, 2003.
8. "Christian Social Worker Fired By Homosexual Boss," *Maranatha Christian Journal*, April 24, 2000.

9. Ibid.

10. "Man Objecting to Foster Parents Fired," *Christianity Today*, February 9, 1998.

11. "California Transsexual Discrimination Bill Analysis," *CNSNews.com*, March 24, 2003.

12. "Bill Would Force Hiring of Cross-Dressers, Even Boy Scouts, Bible bookstores subject of California law," *Worldnetdaily.com*, April 21, 2003.

13. "Transgender Rights Bill Passes California Committee," *tgcrossroads.org*, March 21, 2003.

14. "Bill Would Force Hiring of Cross-Dressers, Even Boy Scouts, Bible bookstores subject of California law," *Worldnetdaily.com*, April 21, 2003.

15. Julie Foster, "California's Transsexual Legislation, Governor vetoes one measure, another still pending," *Worldnetdaily.com*, August 10, 2001.

16. Arthur Santana, "Judge Declines to Sentence 3 Catholic Gay Activists," *The Washington Post*, January 31, 2003.

17. Joe Feuerherd, "Gay Catholics Denied Communion Found Guilty," *National Catholic Reporter*, February 14, 2003.

18. Julie Foster, "'Not Guilty' for Opposing 'Diversity' Sticker, Cop: 'It is a sign of the homosexual, and it's on my patrol car,'" *Worldnetdaily.com*, January 16, 2001.

19. "2 Doctors Cited Religious Beliefs," The Associated Press, February 11, 2003.

20. Ed Vitagliano, "Legal Group Appeals Court Decision Upholding Bigotry Against Christians, San Francisco Allowed to Stigmatize Religion to Protect Homosexuality," Agape Press, April 5, 2002.

21. Robert Knight, "Daschle Combines ENDA, 'Hate Crimes' Bills," Culture and Family Institute, February 12, 2003.

22. Ellen Sorokin, "Critics Fear Law for Gays will Muzzle Preachers," *The Washington Times*, December 4, 2002.

23. "Editorial: Hate, speech and the law, New legislation poses a dilemma," *The Pittsburgh Post-Gazette*, December 2, 2002.

24. Michael DePrimo, "AFA Center for Law & Policy Files Suit Against Staten Island Borough President Guy Molinari," AFA Press Release, September 11, 2000.

25. Julie Foster, "Testing the Faith, Group to Challenge N.Y. 'anti-bias' law, Staten Island rejects Bible verse as 'offensive' to homosexuals," *Worldnetdaily.com*, May 13, 2001.

26. "Clergy Say Florida Billboard of Vegetarian Jesus is Sacrilegious," The Associated Press, April 14, 2003.

27. Molly Hennessy-Fiske, "PETA Sign Equates Pig with Lamb," *Newobserver.com*, April 17, 2003.

28. "Oppose Day of 'Fasting and Prayer,' Congress Entertains More Religious Window-Dressing," Freedom from Religion Press Release, March 27, 2003.

29. "D.C. Council forces Catholics to Violate Beliefs," *The Denver Catholic Register*, July 19, 2000.

30. David Thibault, "Religious Groups Sue Over Mandatory Contraceptive," *CNSNews.com*, January 1, 2003.

31. Robert B. Bluey, "Hospital Worker Sues Over Firing For Pro-Life Counseling," *CNSNews.com*, November 15, 2002.

32. Allie Martin, "City Sued by Pro-Lifers Over Ban on Sidewalk Signs," Agape Press, January 13, 2003.

33. Mathew Staver, "Protestors File Federal Lawsuit After Town Bans All Signs From Public Sidewalks," Liberty Counsel Press Release, January 7, 2003.

34. *Scheidler v. National Organization for Women, Inc.*, 123 S.Ct. 1057 (U.S. 2003).

35. "Supreme Court Affirms Rights of Abortion Foes," Catholic League for Religious and Civil Rights, February 26, 2003.

36. "Miss America 'Bullied' Over Abstinence," Charisma News Service, October 9, 2002.

37. George Archibald, "Miss America Told to Zip it on Chastity Talk," *The Washington Times*, October 9, 2002.

38. George Archibald, "Pageant Permits Promotion of Chastity," *The Washington Times*, October 10, 2002.

39. Joe Kovacs, "Matters of Life and Death, Is 'Choice on Earth' 'Abortion on Earth?' Planned Parenthood enraging Christians by twisting Bible theme on holiday cards," *Worldnetdaily.com*, November 26, 2002.

40. Sean Loughlin, "No peace over Planned Parenthood's holiday card," *CNN.com/Inside Politics*, December 3, 2002; Joe Kovacs, "Matters of Life and Death, Is 'Choice on Earth' 'Abortion on Earth?' Planned Parenthood enraging Christians by twisting Bible theme on holiday cards," *Worldnetdaily.com*, November 26, 2002.

41. Jeff Johnson, "Planned Parenthood Clergy Advisor Says Jesus was Pro-Abortion," *CNSNews.com*, December 4, 2002.

42. "STOPP: Planned Parenthood Expands Attack on Christianity With New Line of 'Choice on Earth' T-Shirts," *U.S. Newswire*, November 26, 2002.

43. "Penn & Teller Ridicule Christ's Crucifixion, Comedy duo presents skit where angel performs sex act on 'Jesus,'" *Worldnetdaily.com*, January 20, 2003.

44. Norm Clarke, "Catholic League Leader Wants Penn & Teller Punished for Raunchy Skit," *The Las Vegas Review-Journal*, January 22, 2003.

45. Gregory J. Rummo, "Yo Mama's Last Supper," On that day, there will be a lot of, ahem, nervous throat clearing," *The Herald News*, February 25, 2001.

46. "Another Brooklyn Art Exhibit Draws Fire," *Maranatha Christian Journal*, February 16, 2001.

47. Editorial, "Andres Serrano's Precious Bodily Fluids," *The Washington Times*, August 21, 1989.

48. "National Endowment for the Arts," The Jeremiah Project, 1998.
49. Michael Kilian, "Censors in Retreat; In the War Against Art, The Momentum Seems to be Shifting," *Chicago Tribune*, May 26, 1996.
50. "Sensation Exhibition: Too Hot for Canberra: 99.4, Sensation prevails in New York: too hot for Canberra," The Arts Law Centre of Australia, 1999.
51. "Artists Identify Virgin Mary as Whore," Cathlic League for Religious and Civil Rights, February 25, 1999.
52. Lawson Taitte, "Bible Given a Redo; 'Fabulous Story' adds gay stereotypes, makes a mostly divine creation," *The Dallas Morning News*, December 8, 2001.
53. "Gay Group Rewards Bigotry Against Christians," Catholic League for Religious and Civil Rights, March 30, 1999.
54. "Recent Cases," *Entertainment Law Reporter*, January 2002.
55. Richard Zoglin, "Jesus Christ Superstar?; Terrence McNally's controversial play about a gay Messiah finally debuts. What's all the fuss?" *Time* magazine, October 5, 1998.
56. Roger Armbrust, "League Lashes 'Anti-Catholic' Theatre Annual Report Includes NY Productions; Catholic League for Religious and Civil Rights," Information Access Company, April 2, 1999.
57. Hadley Arkes, "Fear and Loathing in L.A.," The Claremont Institute, November 11, 1998.

Chapter 10

1. Bill Broadway, "A Convergence of Fixed and Shifting Holidays," *The Washington Post*, December 6, 1997.
2. Sandra T. Keating, "Letter to the Editor," *The Providence Journal-Bulletin*, December 21, 1998.
3. Michael Weisskopf, "Energized by Pulpit or Passion, the Public is Calling; 'Gospel Grapevine' Displays Strength in Controversy Over Military Gay Ban," *The Washington Post*, February 1, 1993.
4. Fred Jackson, "Media Research Center Accuses CBS of 'Religious Bigotry'," *AFR News*, July 13, 2000.
5. L. Brent Bozell III, "How Can CBS Condone Religious Bigotry on its Network?" An Open Letter to CBS News, July 13, 2000.
6. Al Dobras, "Phil Donahue Ridicules Christian Salvation Doctrine, Meanwhile, ACLU worked overtime to take Christ out of Christmas and PBS celebrated Islam," Concerned Women for America, January 9, 2003.
7. Melanie Hunter, "ABC Censors Thanks to Jesus," *CNS News*, May 31, 2002.

8. Austin Ruse, "Turner Attacks Christianity at U.N. 'Peace Summit'," *Newsmax.com*, August 30, 2000.
9. Lory Hough, "Ted Turner Receives Goldsmith Career Award," Kennedy School of Government News Stories, March 14, 2001.
10. Terry Mattingly, "The Very Rev. Ted Turner Speaks," Scripps Howard, March 14, 2001.
11. Willaim A. Donohue, "Catholic League's 1999 Report on Anti-Catholicism," Catholic League for Religious and Civil Rights, 1999.
12. Carl Limbacher, "Turner's Anti-Christian Bigotry Prompts CNN Anchor to Quit," *Newsmax.com*, March 14, 2001.
13. Dan Wooding, "Jane Fonda, Ted Turner Need Prayer, Not Gossip," *ChristianAnswers.Net*, January 8, 2000.
14. Craig Whitlock, "Prayer-Givers in the Senate Straying From the Chamber's Informal Rules," *The Washington Post*, January 19, 2003.
15. Don Feder, "Soulless Waging War on Christians," *The Boston Herald*, April 8, 1996.
16. H.W. Crocker III, "Liberal Lies and the War Against Religion," *Newsmax.com*, February 5, 2002.
17. Bob Norman, "De Regier, Plumbing the depths of the Christian Taliban," *The New Times Broward-Palm Beach*, August 29, 2002.
18. Robyn E. Blumner, "Congress is Crossing the Line with Religion," *The St. Petersburg Times*, April 7, 2002.
19. Gregory Koukl, "Church and State: The Separation Illusion," *Stand to Reason*, 1998.
20. "Tom Daschle Blasts Religious Right, Talk Radio," Traditional Values Coalition, November 22, 2002.
21. "Religious Fundamentalism is the Enemy," *Texas Eagle Forum*, November 2002, citing *The New American*, September 23, 2002.
22. Howard Fineman, "Bush's Next Challenge: Dodging No. 41's Fate," *Newsweek*, December 31, 2001.
23. Douglas Jehl, "A Nation Challenged: Saudi Arabia; Holy War Lured Saudis As Rulers Looked Away," *The New York Times*, December 27, 2001.
24. Editorial, "Brother James," *The Boston Globe*, November 3, 2002.
25. Editorial, "How Anti-Christian Will Boston Globe Get?" *The Massachusetts News*, November 4, 2002.
26. Tim Graham, "MRC Study: ABC, CBS, and NBC Aired 26 Segments on Anti-War Rallies, But Just Nine on Abortion," Media Research Center Media Reality Check, January 23, 2003.
27. "10 Most 'Spiked' Stories of 2001, WND's annual survey highlights year's major underreported events," *Worldnetdaily.com*, January 29, 2002.

28. Rod Dreher, "These Victims Are People, Too," *National Review Online*, November 26, 2002.
29. D.C. Sniper Terror, Muhammad's Other Road to Jihad, Analyst Suspects He Had Coaching in his Radicalization," *Worldnetdaily.com*, October 31, 2002.
30. Steve Rabey, "Videos of Hate, Columbine killers harbored anti-Christian prejudice," *Christianity Today*, February 7, 2000.
31. "Shooter's Anti-Christian Motive Missed & Noted; Nets Avoiding Pardons," Media Research Center CyberAlert, September 17, 1999.
32. "Abortion Foe Stabbed; Media Silent," *CNSNews.com*, April 16, 2003.
33. Rod Dreher, "These Victims Are People, Too," *National Review Online*, November 26, 2002.
34. Toby Harnden, "Liberal Media Ignores Rape-Killing of Boy, 13," *The London Telegraph*, March 30, 2001.
35. Andrew Sullivan, "Us and Them," *The New Republic*, April 2, 2001.
36. Bill O'Reilly, "Factor Follow-Up Interview with Robert Curley," *Fox News Network, The O'Reilly Factor Transcript*, September 25, 2002.
37. Sydney Cleveland, "National Public Radio Is a Source of Anti-Christian Bigotry, NPR Calls for 'Evaporation of Four Million Christians,'" *Dovenet*, 1998.
38. Don Jones, "KSUT Yanks Ad with 'God' in it," *The Durango Herald*, February 7, 2003.
39. Terry Phillips, "NPR Station Censors 'God,'" *Family News in Focus*, February 19, 2003.
40. Don Jones, "KSUT Yanks Ad with 'God' in it," *The Durango Herald*, February 7, 2003.
41. Chad Groening and Jody Brown, "Liberals Want Their Own Radio Talk-Show Network, Conservative Radio Exec Suggests They Save Taxpayer Money, Team with NPR and PBS," Agape Press, February 18, 2003.
42. Joe Scarborough, "MSNBC Reports for March 4, 2002," *MSNBC Transcript*, March 4, 2002.
43. Bob Edwards and David Kestenbaum, "Headline: Speculation on the perpetrator of the anthrax letters," *National Public Radio Transcript*, January 22, 2002.
44. Wes Vernon, "Congressional Uproar Over NPR Smear," *NewsMax.com*, May 2, 2003.
45. Wes Vernon, "Rep. DeLay Condemns NPR for Anti-Christian Smear," *NewsMax.com*, March 1, 2002.
46. Art Moore, "NPR 'regrets' smear of Christian Group, Report suggested lobbyist fit FBI profile of culprit in anthrax case," *Worldnetdaily.com*, February 11, 2003.
47. Letter to U.S. Congress and President Bush, "Defund PBS and NPR," *www.PetitionOnline.com*.
48. Michael Behe, Ph.D., "Fatuous Filmmaking," *Worldnetdaily.com*, 2001.

49. Jonathan Sarfati, "Darwin's Dangerous Idea," *AiG's Response to PBS-TV series Evolution*, September 24, 2001.

50. Greg Hoadley, "Bill Moyers: Anti-Christian Bigotry at Your Expense," Center for Reclaiming America, November 13, 2002.

51. "The Greatest Christmas Insult Possible," *Oregon Magazine*, 2002.

52. Jack Kinsella, "Special Subscriber's Report: PBS to Set Record Straight on Islam," *The Omega Letter Intelligence Digest*, Volume 15 Issue: 13, Friday, December 13, 2002.

53. Carin Larson, "Media Should Treat Christian Politicians Equally," *Campus Carrier*, August 22, 2002.

54. "The Ashcroft Hearings, Two U.S. Senators discuss the nomination of John Ashcroft for US Attorney General," *PBS Online*, January 18, 2001.

55. Carin Larson, "Media Should Treat Christian Politicians Equally," *Campus Carrier*, August 22, 2002.

56. Michael Medved, "P.C. Hollywood Distorts Terror War Realities," *Worldnetdaily.com*, June 10, 2002.

57. Patrick Goodenough, "Christian Group Questions Tendency to 'Tiptoe Around Islam,'" *CNSNews.com*, November 27, 2002.

58. Kyle DuVall, "Frailty Review" *Shotgun Reviews.com*, 2002.

59. Richard C. Brown, "AFA: Frailty Shows Hollywood's Dislike of Christians," *Christian Headline News*, April 22, 2002.

60. Bob Kellogg, "'Frailty' Paints Christians as Maniacs," *Family News in Focus*, April 26, 2002.

61. Robert Knight, "Good Flicks Beat Bad Flicks, Is Hollywood Slowly Learning that Morality Can Pay Off at the Box Office?" Culture and Family Planning Institute, July/August 2002.

62. Dr. Phil Stringer, "The Entertainment Media," *Independent American Party Viewpoints.*

63. Rabbi Yechiel Eckstein, *Christian News*, February 10, 1997, reported in "Culture, Et Cetera" in *The Washington Times*, March 3, 1997.

64. Robert Knight, "Good Flicks Beat Bad Flicks, Is Hollywood Slowly Learning that Morality Can Pay Off at the Box Office?" Culture and Family Planning Institute, July/August 2002.

65. Ted Baehr, quoted by Robert Knight, "Good Flicks Beat Bad Flicks, Is Hollywood Slowly Learning that Morality Can Pay Off at the Box Office?" *Culture and Family Planning Institute*, July/August 2002.

66. Art Moore, "Civil War Epic Shut Down by 'PC' Crowd?" *WorldNetDaily.com*, March 22, 2003.

67. "Mel Gibson Funds New Church," The Associated Press, May 1, 2003.

68. Bettijane Levine, "Scholars Express Concern Over Gibson's 'Passion,'" *The Los Angeles Times*, April 27, 2003.

69. James Carroll, "The True Horror in the Death of Jesus," *The Boston Globe*, April 15, 2003.
70. "Mel Gibson's Film Endorsed By Christian Leaders," *Charisma News*, July 7, 2003
71. "TV: Abortion Docudrama Causes Controversy," American Political Network Abortion Report National Briefing, March 15, 1991.
72. Elizabeth Wasserman, "Personal Tragedy, Public Drama; Nancy Klein's family measures progress in inches. Now they have two years worth of inches to show since doctors said Klein had only a 5% chance of over emerging from her coma," *Newsday*, 1991.
73. L. Brent Bozell III, "Anti-Catholic 'Entertainment'," *Creators Syndicate, Inc.*, March 21, 2003.

Chapter 11

1. Benjamin Hart, *Faith & Freedom, The Christian Roots of American Liberty* (Bernardino, CA: Here's Life Publishers, 1998).
2. Gary DeMar, *America's Christian History, The Untold Story* (Atlanta, GA: American Vision Inc. 1993), 53-54.
3. Ibid., 55.
4. Peter Marshall and David Manuel, *The Light and the Glory* (Grand Rapids, MI: Baker Book House Co. 1977), 120.
5. M. Stanton Evans, *The Theme is Freedom, Religion, Politics, and the American Tradition* (Washington, D.C.: Regnery Publishing, Inc. 1994) 193; Peter Marshall and David Manuel, *The Light and the Glory* (Grand Rapids, MI: Baker Book House Co. 1977), 120.
6. M. Stanton Evans, *The Theme is Freedom, Religion, Politics, and the American Tradition* (Washington, D.C.: Regnery Publishing, Inc. 1994), 194.
7. Ibid., 184.
8. Paul Johnson, *A History of the American People* (New York, NY: HarperCollins 1997), 30.
9. Peter Marshall and David Manuel, *The Light and the Glory* (Grand Rapids, MI: Baker Book House Co. 1977), 145.
10. *Winthrop Papers*, II, 292-295.
11. D. James Kennedy and Jerry Newcombe, *What if the Bible Had Never Been Written*, (Nashville, TN: Thomas Nelson Publishers, 1998), 85.
12. Gary DeMar, *America's Christian History, The Untold Story* (Atlanta, GA: American Vision Inc. 1993), 61.
13. Dr. David C. Gibbs, Jr. with Jerry Newcombe, *One Nation Under God, Ten Things Every Christian Should Know About the Founding of America* (Seminole, FA: The Christian Law Association 2003), 36.

14. Perry Miller and Thomas H. Johnson, eds., *The Puritans* (New York: Harper & Row, 1963), 188; Gary Amos and Richard Gardiner, *Never Before in History, America's Inspired Birth* (Dallas TX: Haughton Publishing Company, 1998), 40.
15. There was one exception. The New England Confederation of 1643, a mutual safety league, consisting of four Puritan colonies in Massachusetts and Connecticut. See Dr. David C. Gibbs, Jr. with Jerry Newcombe, *One Nation Under God, Ten Things Every Christian Should Know About the Founding of America* (Seminole, FA: The Christian Law Association 2003), 80.
16. Paul Johnson, *A History of the American People* (New York, NY: HarperCollins 1997), 307.
17. Ibid., 109.
18. Ibid., 110.
19. Perry Miller and Thomas H. Johnson, eds., *The Puritans* (New York: Harper & Row, 1963), 188; Gary Amos and Richard Gardiner, *Never Before in History, America's Inspired Birth* (Dallas TX: Haughton Publishing Company, 1998), 54.
20. William J. Federer, *America's God and Country: Encyclopedia of Quotations* (St. Louis, MO: Amerisearch, Inc., 1994/2000), 685-686.
21. Benjamin Franklin, *The Autobiography of Benjamin Franklin*, in Charles W. Eliot, ed., *The Harvard Classics*, vol. 1 (New York: Collier, 1909), 101-102.
22. Dr. David C. Gibbs, Jr. with Jerry Newcombe, *One Nation Under God, Ten Things Every Christian Should Know About the Founding of America* (Seminole, FA: The Christian Law Association 2003), 82.
23. Ibid., 94.
24. Ibid., 94-95, 109.
25. A. James Reichley, *Religion in American Public Life* (Washington: The Brookings Institution, 1985), 54-55.
26. Loraine Boettner, *The Reformed Doctrine of Predestination* (Philadelphia: Presbyterian and Reformed, 1972), 389, quoted in John Eidsmoe, *Christianity and the Constitution, The Faith of Our Founding Fathers* (Grand Rapids, MI: Baker Books, 1987), 19; see also Tim LaHaye, *Faith of our Founding Fathers*, (Green Forest, AR: Master Books, Inc. 1990, 68-69.
27. B.F. Morris, *Christian Life and Character of the Civil Institutions of the United States, Developed in the Official and Historical Annals of the Republic* (Philadelphia, PA: George W. Childs, 1864), 83.
28. *Engel v. Vitale*, 370 U.S. 421 (1962).
29. M. Stanton Evans, *The Theme is Freedom, Religion, Politics, and the American Tradition* (Washington, D.C.: Regnery Publishing, Inc. 1994), 275. Constitutional scholar George Goldberg says that six of these states still had established churches at the time of the Constitutional Convention. See text accompanying footnote 106.
30. Ibid., 210.

31. Ibid., 217.
32. Ibid., 207.
33. Ibid.
34. Bernard Knollenberg, *Origin of the American Revolution* (Collier, 1962), 23; M. Stanton Evans, *The Theme is Freedom, Religion, Politics, and the American Tradition* (Washington, D.C.: Regnery Publishing, Inc. 1994), 219.
35. M. Stanton Evans, *The Theme is Freedom, Religion, Politics, and the American Tradition* (Washington, D.C.: Regnery Publishing, Inc. 1994), 224.
36. Ibid., 225.
37. "The Philosophical and Biblical Perspectives That Shaped the Declaration of Independence," Gary Amos in H. Wayne House, ed. *The Christian and American Law, Christianity's Impact on America's Founding Documents and Future Direction* (Grand Rapids, MI: Kregel Publications 1998), 51.
38. Ibid., 52.
39. Ibid., 53-54.
40. Ibid.
41. Ibid., 74.
42. M.E. Bradford, *A Worthy Company* (Marlborough, NH: Plymouth Rock Foundation, 1982); M. Stanton Evans, *The Theme is Freedom, Religion, Politics, and the American Tradition* (Washington, D.C.: Regnery Publishing, Inc. 1994), 272.
43. D. James Kennedy and Jerry Newcombe, *What if the Bible Had Never Been Written*, (Nashville, TN: Thomas Nelson Publishers, 1998), 90.
44. William J. Federer, *America's God and Country: Encyclopedia of Quotations* (St. Louis, MO: Amerisearch, Inc., 1994/2000), 180. Another source, W.W. Sweet, compiled a different list of affiliations, but it still shows the predominance of the Christian influence among the signers of the Constitution. According to Sweet, there were 19 Episcopalians, 8 Congregationalists, 7 Presbyterians, 2 Roman Catholics, 2 Quakers, 1 Methodist, 1 Dutch Reformed, and 1 Deist, Edmund Randolph, who later became a Christian convert. William Warren Sweet, *Religion in the Development of American Culture*, 1765-1840 (New York: Charles Scribner's Sons, 1952), 85, quoted in Vincent Carroll & David Shiflett, *Christianity on Trial, Arguments Against Anti-Religious Bigotry* (San Francisco, CA: Encounter Books, 2002), 185.
45. D. James Kennedy and Jerry Newcombe report that "Virtually all the men who wrote the Declaration of Independence, the Articles of Confederation, the Constitution, and the Bill of Rights . . . had received a strong, well-integrated education. In the lower grades, the Bible was the chief textbook, and the church or home the classroom." D. James Kennedy and Jerry Newcombe, *What if the Bible Had Never Been Written*, (Nashville, TN: Thomas Nelson Publishers, 1998), 88.
46. M. Stanton Evans, *The Theme is Freedom, Religion, Politics, and the American Tradition* (Washington, D.C.: Regnery Publishing, Inc. 1994), 35.

47. Tim LaHaye, *Faith of our Founding Fathers*, (Green Forest, AR: Master Books, Inc. 1990), 67.
48. Michael Novak, *On Two Wings, Humble Faith and Common Sense at the American Founding* (San Francisco, CA: Encounter Books, 2002), 27.
49. Ibid., 30.
50. M. Stanton Evans, *The Theme is Freedom, Religion, Politics, and the American Tradition* (Washington, D.C.: Regnery Publishing, Inc. 1994), 240.
51. David Barton, "The Founding Fathers and Deism," *Wallbuilders*, 2002. More controversially, Barton disputes the charge that Jefferson deleted from his Bible references to Jesus' miracles. According to Barton, Jefferson made it clear that his little Bible was not intended for his own purposes, but to be used to teach the Indians. He simply brought to the Indians the "red letter" portions of the New Testament, says Barton, in order to introduce them to Jesus' moral teachings.
52. Carl Becker, *The Declaration of Independence* (Vintage, 1958), 25-26; M. Stanton Evans, *The Theme is Freedom, Religion, Politics, and the American Tradition* (Washington, D.C.: Regnery Publishing, Inc. 1994), 233.
53. M. Stanton Evans, *The Theme is Freedom, Religion, Politics, and the American Tradition* (Washington, D.C.: Regnery Publishing, Inc. 1994), 231-232.
54. Ibid., 247.
55. James Madison, *The Papers of James Madison*, Henry D. Gilpin, editor (Washington: Langree and O'Sullivan, 1840), Vol. II, 984, June 28, 1787, quoted in David Barton, *Original Intent, the Courts, the Constitution, & Religion* (Aledo, Texas: Wallbuilder Press), 1996, 213.
56. Donald S. Lutz, *The Origins of American Constitutionalism* (Baton Rouge, LA: Louisiana State University Press, 1988).
57. David Barton, *Original Intent, the Courts, the Constitution, & Religion* (Aledo, Texas: Wallbuilder Press), 1996, 225.
58. Ibid., 213-226.
59. James Wilson, *The Works of the Honourable James Wilson*, Bird Wilson, editor (Philadelphia: Lorenzo Press, 1804), Vol. I, 67-68, "Of the General Principles of Law and Obligation," quoted in David Barton, *Original Intent, The Courts, the Constitution, & Religion* (Aledo, Texas: Wallbuilder Press), 1996, 219.
60. Donald S. Lutz, "The Relative Influence of European Writers on Late Eighteenth Century American Political Thought," *American Political Science Review* 189 (1984): 189-97; Charles S. Hyneman and Donald S. Lutz, *American Political Writing During the Founding Era* 1760-1805, Vols. 1 and 2 (Indianapolis: Liberty Fund Press, 1983) quoted in "Operation Josiah: Rediscovering the Biblical Roots," John Eidsmoe in H. Wayne House, ed. *The Christian and American Law, Christianity's Impact on America's Founding Documents and Future Direction* (Grand Rapids, MI: Kregel Publications 1998), 84.

61. Montesquieu, *The Spirit of Laws*, New York: Hafner, 1949, 1962), 1:1, quoted in John Eidsmoe, *Christianity and the Constitution, The Faith of Our Founding Fathers* (Grand Rapids, MI: Baker Books, 1987), 55.

62. Sir William Blackstone, *Commentaries on the Laws of England*, quoted in John Eidsmoe, *Christianity and the Constitution, The Faith of Our Founding Fathers* (Grand Rapids, MI: Baker Books, 1987), 58.

63. William J. Federer, *America's God and Country: Encyclopedia of Quotations* (St. Louis, MO: Amerisearch, Inc., 1994/2000), 657-658.

64. George Washington, *Writings* (1932), 15:55, from his speech to the Delaware Indian Chiefs on May 12, 1799. Quoted in David Barton, *Original Intent, the Courts, the Constitution, & Religion* (Aledo, Texas: Wallbuilder Press), 1996, 168.

65. M. Stanton Evans, *The Theme is Freedom, Religion, Politics, and the American Tradition* (Washington, D.C.: Regnery Publishing, Inc. 1994), 34.

66. William J. Federer, *America's God and Country: Encyclopedia of Quotations* (St. Louis, MO: Amerisearch, Inc., 1994/2000), 635-636.

67. D. James Kennedy and Jerry Newcombe, *What if the Bible Had Never Been Written*, (Nashville, TN: Thomas Nelson Publishers, 1998), 68.

68. David Barton, "The Founding Fathers and Deism," *Wallbuilders*, 2002.

69. Sarah K. Boulton, *Famous American Statesmen*, 126, Stephen Abbot Northrop, D.D., *A Cloud of Witnesses* (Portland, OR: American Heritage Ministries, 1987, 208, quoted in William J. Federer, *America's God and Country, Encyclopedia of Quotations*, (Coppell, TX: Fame Publishing 1994), 274.

70. Keith Fournier, *In Defense of Liberty* (Virginia Beach, VA: Law & Justice, Spring 1993), Vol. 2, No. 2, 7, quoted in William J. Federer, *America's God and Country, Encyclopedia of Quotations*, (Coppell, TX: Fame Publishing 1994), 274.

71. Stephen K. McDowell and Mark A. Beliles, *America's Providential History* (Charlottesville, VA: Providence Press, 1988), 93; David Barton, *The Myth of Separation* (Aledo, TX: WallBuilder Press, 1991), 92, 93, 119.

72. June 20, 1785, Robert Rutland, ed., *The Papers of James Madison* (Chicago: University of Chicago Press, 1973), Vol. VIII, 299, 304; David Barton, *The Myth of Separation* (Aledo, TX: WallBuilder Press, 1991), 120.

73. William J. Federer, *America's God and Country, Encyclopedia of Quotations*, (Coppell, TX: Fame Publishing 1994), 412.

74. *The Correspondence and Public Papers of John Jay*, Henry P. Johnston, ed. (NY: Burt Franklin, 1970), Vol IV, 393, as quoted in William J. Federer, *America's God and Country, Encyclopedia of Quotations*, (Coppell, TX: Fame Publishing 1994), 318.

75. John Adams, handwritten comments on his copy of a book by the Marquis de Condorcet, *Outlines of an Historical View of the Progress of the Human Mind*, reprinted in Zoltan Haraszti, *John Adams and the Prophets of Progress* (Cambridge: Harvard University Press, 1952), 246. "Operation Josiah: Rediscovering the Biblical

Roots," John Eidsmoe in H. Wayne House, ed. *The Christian and American Law, Christianity's Impact on America's Founding Documents and Future Direction* (Grand Rapids, MI: Kregel Publications 1998), 87.

76. D. James Kennedy and Jerry Newcombe, *What if the Bible Had Never Been Written*, (Nashville, TN: Thomas Nelson Publishers, 1998), 92.

77. Michael Novak asserts that "all American Christians erected their main arguments about political life from materials in the Jewish Testament." He said they did so for three reasons. They loved Old Testament stories and were very familiar with them. They also did so to avoid denominational disputes, which could be largely avoided by reference to the Old Testament. Third, says, Novak, the New Testament didn't add much to the discussion of government that wasn't already covered in some way in the Old Testament. Michael Novak, *On Two Wings, Humble Faith and Common Sense at the American Founding* (San Francisco, CA: Encounter Books, 2002), 7.

78. M. Stanton Evans, *The Theme is Freedom, Religion, Politics, and the American Tradition* (Washington, D.C.: Regnery Publishing, Inc. 1994), 42.

79. Ibid., 43.

80. Ibid., 50.

81. Alexander Hamilton, "Remarks to Constitutional Convention," June 22, 1787, quoted by Padover, *The Mind of Alexander Hamilton.*

82. "Operation Josiah: Rediscovering the Biblical Roots," John Eidsmoe in H. Wayne House, ed. *The Christian and American Law, Christianity's Impact on America's Founding Documents and Future Direction* (Grand Rapids, MI: Kregel Publications 1998), 98.

83. Ibid.

84. M. Stanton Evans, *The Theme is Freedom, Religion, Politics, and the American Tradition* (Washington, D.C.: Regnery Publishing, Inc. 1994), 96-97.

85. Ibid., 136-137.

86. Ibid., 137.

87. Ibid., 30.

88. Michael Novak, *On Two Wings, Humble Faith and Common Sense at the American Founding* (San Francisco, CA: Encounter Books, 2002), 29-30.

89. Richard Vetterli and Gary Bryner, *In Search of the Republic* (Roman and Littlefield, 1987), 70, quoted in M. Stanton Evans, *The Theme is Freedom, Religion, Politics, and the American Tradition* (Washington, D.C.: Regnery Publishing, Inc. 1994), 317.

90. Commager and Morris, eds. *The Spirit of Seventy-Six* (Harper, 1967), 379.

91. David Barton, "The Importance of Morality and Religion in Government," *Wallbuilders*, 2002.

92. From Rev. Ethan Allen's handwritten history "Washington Parish, Washington City" in the Library of Congress MMC Collection, 1167, MSS, as quoted in James H.

Hutson, *Religion and the Founding of the American Republic* (Washington, D.C.: Library of Congress, 1998), 96; also quoted in Michael Novak, *On Two Wings, Humble Faith and Common Sense at the American Founding* (San Francisco, CA: Encounter Books, 2002), 31.

93. M. Stanton Evans, *The Theme is Freedom, Religion, Politics, and the American Tradition* (Washington, D.C.: Regnery Publishing, Inc. 1994), 35.

94. Alexis de Tocqueville, *The Old Regime and the French Revolution* (New York: Doubleday, 1955), 153, quoted in Michael Novak, *On Two Wings, Humble Faith and Common Sense at the American Founding* (San Francisco, CA: Encounter Books, 2002), 31.

95. Ibid.

96. Alexis de Tocqueville, *Democracy in America* (Vintage, 1955), Vol I, 316.

97. Israel Drapkin, M.D., *Crime and Punishment in the Ancient World* (Lexington: MA: Lexington Books, 1989), 50, quoted in D. James Kennedy and Jerry Newcombe, *What if the Bible Had Never Been Written*, (Nashville, TN: Thomas Nelson Publishers, 1998), 46.

98. John C. H. Wu, *Foundation of Justice: A Study in the Natural Law* 65 (1955), quoted in "God's Revelation: Foundation for the Common Law," Herbert W. Titus in H. Wayne House, ed. *The Christian and American Law, Christianity's Impact on America's Founding Documents and Future Direction* (Grand Rapids, MI: Kregel Publications 1998), 51.

99. *Church of Jesus Christ of Latter Day Saints v. United States*, 136 U.S. 1, 49 (1890)

100. *Davis v. Beason*, 133 U.S. 333 (1890).

101. George Goldberg, *Church, State and the Constitution, The Religion Clauses Upside Down* (Washington, D.C.: Regnery Gateway 1984), 11.

102. Ibid.

103. M. Stanton Evans, *The Theme is Freedom, Religion, Politics, and the American Tradition* (Washington, D.C.: Regnery Publishing, Inc. 1994), 284.

104. Joseph Story, *A Familiar Exposition of the Constitution of the United States*, (Lake Bluff, IL: Regnery Gateway, [1859] 1986), 316, quoted in Gary DeMar, *America's Christian History, The Untold Story* (Atlanta, GA: American Vision Inc. 1993), 82.

105. M. Stanton Evans, *The Theme is Freedom, Religion, Politics, and the American Tradition* (Washington, D.C.: Regnery Publishing, Inc. 1994), 275.

106. George Goldberg, *Church, State and the Constitution, The Religion Clauses Upside Down* (Washington, D.C.: Regnery Gateway 1984), 10.

107. M. Stanton Evans, *The Theme is Freedom, Religion, Politics, and the American Tradition* (Washington, D.C.: Regnery Publishing, Inc. 1994), 276.

108. George Goldberg, *Church, State and the Constitution, The Religion Clauses Upside Down* (Washington, D.C.: Regnery Gateway 1984), 10.

109. Ibid.

110. Ibid., 12.

111. Michael Novak observes that America's Christian consensus turned in a new direction sometime after World War II. Michael Novak, *On Two Wings, Humble Faith and Common Sense at the American Founding* (San Francisco, CA: Encounter Books, 2002), 113.

112. George Goldberg, *Church, State and the Constitution, The Religion Clauses Upside Down* (Washington, D.C.: Regnery Gateway 1984), 12.

113. Ibid., 13.

114. M. Stanton Evans, *The Theme is Freedom, Religion, Politics, and the American Tradition* (Washington, D.C.: Regnery Publishing, Inc. 1994), 278-279.

115. Ibid., 280-281.

116. Ronald D. Rotunda and John E. Nowak, "Introduction" to Joseph Story, *Commentaries on the Constitution of the United States* (Durham: Carolina Academic Press, 1987, originally published 1833), 701, quoted in Stephen B. Presser, *Recapturing the Constitution, Race, Religion, and Abortion Reconsidered* (Washington, D.C.: Regnery Publishing, Inc. 1994), 232.

Chapter 12

1. Norine Dickson Campbell, *Patrick Henry—Patriot and Statesman* (Old Greenwich, CT: Devin Adair, 1969/1975), 417, quoted in Dr. David C. Gibbs, Jr. with Jerry Newcombe, *One Nation Under God, Ten Things Every Christian Should Know About the Founding of America* (Seminole, FA: The Christian Law Association 2003), 124.

2. Stephen Abbottt Northrop, D.D., *A Cloud of Witnesses* (Portland, Oregon: American Heritage Ministries, 1987), 227, quoted in William J. Federer, *America's God and Country: Encyclopedia of Quotations* (St. Louis, MO: Amerisearch, Inc., 1994/2000), 290.

Index